25 BEST
NATIONAL PARKS TO FLY FISH

TERRY & WENDY GUNN

STONEFLY
PRESS

640 Clematis St. #588
West Palm Beach, FL 33402
FAX: 877-609-3814

For information about discounts on bulk purchases, or
to book the author for an engagement or demonstration,
please contact Stonefly Press at inquiries@stoneflypress.com,
or visit us at Stoneflypress.com.

stoneflypress.com

Printed in the United States

20   19   18   17   16   1   2   3   4   5

FSC

Library of Congress Control Number: 2016943605

Stonefly Press

Publisher: Robert D. Clouse
Acquiring Editor: Robert D. Clouse
Managing Director: Patrick Kelley
Managing Editor: Bennett J. Mintz
Cartographer: Nat Case and mapformation, LLC.
Copy Editor: Rick Kughen
Proofreader: Charlotte Kughen
Front Cover Photo: Andrew Maurer
Back Cover Photo: Floating the Snake River is the perfect way to
enjoy great fishing and spectacular scenery. Scott Sanchez

This book is dedicated to
Lefty Kreh,
the best-known fly fisherman in history—"the sport's Babe Ruth,
but even bigger." When the Good Lord made Lefty,
he broke the mold.

A 2003 inductee in the International Game Fish Association's
Hall of Fame, Lefty was called "the best known and most respected
fly-casting instructor and fly-fishing author in the world."
In the ensuing 13 years, his stature has only grown!

Whether by the printed word or video or at countless sports or outdoor shows,
Lefty Kreh has touched more lives and converted more people to fly fishing
than anyone ever has or ever likely will. He has truly given back unselfishly
to the fly-fishing community with his teaching skills, innovations and
humor, and adding immeasurably to the level of enjoyment and
satisfaction of the sport of fly fishing.

It is for that reason—and many more—we dedicate this book,
25 Best National Parks to Fly Fish, to an iconic American original,
Bernard "Lefty" Kreh. To us and so many others, you have been
our teacher and mentor … thanks old friend!

Terry and Wendy Gunn

Umpqua River in Southern Oregon. Marshal Moser

Contents

Acknowledgments

We want to thank each chapter author for his or her generous contribution to this epic project. They have willingly and without hesitation shared fishing secrets—fly patterns, tackle selections, locations and hot spots—that in some instances had taken them years to acquire. Their selection and verification of restaurants, motels, campgrounds and even nearby medical facilities went beyond our wildest hopes and expectations. With all that in mind, we encourage you, whenever possible, to reward these people by supporting their local businesses.

And thanks to Bennett Mintz for putting all those random and diverse words into something cohesive. Tight lines, Ben.

Both the Yellowstone and the Gardner hold excellent populations of Salmonflies. Walter Wiese.

About the Authors

TERRY GUNN has been a full-time fly-fishing guide for more than 30 years, as well as a renowned author, photographer, and public speaker. He and his wife Wendy (a fly-fishing expert in her own right) have owned and operated Lees Ferry Anglers Fly Shop and Guide Service since 1989, and Cliff Dwellers Lodge in Marble Canyon, Arizona, since 2001.

Terry and Wendy co-host *Fly Fish Television Magazine* and have produced two educational videos, *Introduction to Fly Fishing* and *Introduction to Fly Casting*. They have fly fished around the globe in both fresh and salt water, and Terry holds more than ten International Game Fish Association world records for multiple species of fresh- and saltwater fish.

Terry and Wendy and their son Troy live in Marble Canyon, Arizona.

*Who doesn't enjoy the brilliant colors of a wild
brook trout? Kaweah Marble Fork. Andrew Maurer*

Foreword

FROM A CROUCHING POSITION in tall grass, I rose up just enough to see a cutthroat resting near the bottom of the crystal clear water. One hundred yards upstream, I saw my son execute a beautiful cast, then saw the strike, and his fly rod bend. I quietly spooled out a pile of fly line and, with one long backcast, the Royal Coachman landed gently on the surface a few feet in front of my quarry. The gorgeous cutt looked up and shot to the surface in an aggressive strike. As I reeled it in, two sandhill cranes passed overhead, their bugling calls rattling against the hillsides.

On the previous morning, I had shared the riverbank with a bull bison that was kicking up a cloud of dust in his wallow. It does not get much better than this—four September days and nights in Yellowstone National Park, in the fourth meadow of Slough Creek.

I learned the fly-fishing craft, including the art of tying, from Dave Clark, park ranger and coauthor of *Silver Creek: Idaho's Fly Fishing Paradise* (Caxton Press). After a day's work at Craters of the Moon National Monument, Dave and I would drive over to this famous stream to tease the giant browns with a carefully tied midge or Callibeatis on a size 22 hook (my eyesight was better then). From Idaho, I moved to Alaska, and chased sockeye and kings, resident rainbows, and grayling in wild rivers such as the Gulkana, the Klutina, the Situk, and the brooks in Katmai, Wrangell St. Elias, and Lake Clark National Parks.

Because I am not a combat fisherman, I will hike miles and miles to have a stream to myself. Even in Alaska, if I could see another person on the river, I moved on to find my own stretch. One evening in a late Alaskan summer, I was walking the sandy bank of the Copper River, headed to a clear water tributary I had spied from the air. I was miles from my truck, alone when I came across a pile of bear scat. It was still steaming. This made me think about the fish slime all over my waders from the recent catch of a sockeye, the fact that I was in the middle of nowhere, and there was an Alaskan brown bear nearby. I stood still and listened, made some noise, and contemplated that I was sharing this wild place with another fisher. For me, it made the experience even better.

Now in Washington, D.C., when I want to escape, I grab my 2-wt. and head to Shenandoah, hike in a few miles to avoid the crowds, and work one of the many small streams for those beautiful brook trout on my version of a Mr. Rapidan (a fly developed by the legendary Harry Murray, whose chapter on the Shenandoah National Park is featured in the pages that follow).

In my four decades with the National Park Service, I have enjoyed wonderful fly-fishing experiences within our National Parks. These extraordinary landscapes have been set aside, in the words of Teddy Roosevelt, for the "benefit of the people." For those of us who seek to tease wild fish with feathers in a setting that evokes deep appreciation for nature, wilderness, and quiet contemplation, there is no better place than the National Parks.

The Honorable Jonathan B. Jarvis has served in the National Park Service since 1976 as ranger, biologist, superintendent, and regional director. He was worked in nine different national parks, and in 2009 was confirmed as the 18th Director of the National Park Service. He still ties his own flies.

Jonathan B. Jarvis

Sharon Lance fishing the Gunnison River in the depths of the Black Canyon of the Gunnison National Park. Mark Lance.

Introduction

AMERICA'S TREASURES: OUR NATIONAL PARKS.

There is no better way to explore and become intimate with our parks than from standing at the edge of the water with a fly rod in hand. These pages contain the information you will need to plan your trip and more as you fly fish the grandeur of America's national parks.

It's important to recognize that the parks generally don't begin or end at the park gate. There are miles and miles of notable surrounding waters—some just as good, some better—than the those within the park itself. We've expanded our boundaries of "park waters" to include nearby communities, forest lands and other notable fishing opportunities. Perhaps you'll use this book as a planning guide for your next vacation. We're sure that some readers will use this as a foundation for the ultimate "bucket-list" fly-fishing road trip. The parks are organized in something of a travelogue from the northeast through the Shenandoah, into the south, and eventually out west. This means you can literally turn the page and arrive at the next national park with the information you need to have an enjoyable and productive fishing trip and park visit.

It is our greatest hope that this book motivates you and gives you an excuse to pack the car, start driving east to west or west to east, and fish for lake trout or salters (sea-run brook trout) in New England if you've never done it. Ever caught a tarpon, bonefish or permit? They're waiting for you in both Biscayne Bay and Everglades National Parks. How about a long weekend catching smallmouth bass in Acadia National Park? Think about westslope cutthroat trout in Glacier National Park. How about Chinook salmon and chrome bright steelhead in Olympic National Park—and that's to say nothing about what you'll find in Denali and Katmai National Parks!

This book could not have been attempted (much less completed)without the efforts of our chapter and sidebar researchers and writers. These local experts are the fly shop owners, outfitters, volunteers, guides, conservationists, and other experts who walk the trails, fish the park's waters, and dedicate themselves to the park's preservation. Many are people who either designed the flies that are used or who developed the rigging and casting techniques to make everything so appealing.

While describing the fly fishing in Grand Teton National Park, Scott Sanchez writes, "[Lake] Taggart has a number of rock points to use as a casting platform, and there is a meadow on the far side that will give you room for a backcast. Leeches, streamers and size 12- to 16-nymphs such as scuds, midge larva, or those with peacock bodies are the best flies; this is true on most back county lakes …"

Where else can you get the kind of information that includes not only the flies to use, but the rocks and open areas to use when casting?

Many of the chapter authors spend upward of 200 days each year guiding or fishing in waters you might see only once or twice in a lifetime. Use their experience to your advantage.

Have you ever heard of Old Faithful and the Firehole River in Yellowstone? Is there an American or a flyfisher who hasn't? However, have you heard about the landlocked Atlantic salmon, brown trout, smallmouth bass, bluefish, mackerel and striped bass in Maine's Acadia National Park? Some of its more popular waters include Eagle and Echo Lakes, and Jordan and Long Ponds. Jordan Pond is the deepest lake in Acadia with depths of more than 120 feet. And don't even try to count the miles of streams that generally run to the Atlantic Ocean with sea-run brook trout.

Then, there's South Carolina's Congaree National Park. The three rivers located in its heart offer world-class fishing that have remained a secret for a long time. The Saluda River—a tailwater—flows from the bottom of Lake Murray, offering a coldwater fishery unlike any other in the country. The Broad River—flowing from the north—is a smallmouth bass angler's dream. These two rivers merge to form the Congaree River. The Congaree flows easterly and forms the southern boundary of Congaree National Park.

The Congaree River boasts large numbers of smallmouth and largemouth bass. In the spring, stripers up to 40 pounds migrate to spawn in the upper stretch of the Congaree River and then move into the Saluda River for the summer. Forty pound stripers on a fly? Oh, yes!

What about Capitol Reef National Park in Utah? Never thought about fishing it? This park is larger than both Bryce and Zion National Parks combined. Early inhabitants referred to the area as the "land of the sleeping rainbow" because of its multicolored sandstone, which contrasts with green riverbanks and arid desert vegetation, all nestled beneath deep blue skies. Another Capitol Reef–area icon is scenic Byway Highway 12 and the Hogsback.

This section of the Escalante Grand Staircase is only an hour from the park and could entertain the explorer for weeks. Stream waters that drain the Boulder Mountains Aquarius Plateau pass through here. High-quality small stream fishing is abundant with prolific hatches. The Boulder, Calf, and North Creeks, as well as the Escalante River, are regularly explored by anglers, but they require some hiking and know-how. In fact, the last river system mapped in the United States was the Escalante River.

Glacier National Park's north and middle forks of the Flathead River offer the opportunity to chase westslope cutthroat trout, a species that has been an integral part of the local watershed for 14,000 or more years. Glacier National Park offers very accessible high-mountain lakes in the park where fly fishers should come prepared with small Parachute Adams patterns, caddis, and spruce moths. A slowly stripped peacock, a brightly colored Prince Nymph, or a small Wooly Bugger will also attract fish hiding near structures.

Yosemite is within hailing distance of two of California's enormous population centers—the San Francisco Bay Area and Los Angeles. Yosemite attracts millions of visitors annually, yet the park's trout are hungry, not terribly selective, and willing to grab nearly any well-placed and well-presented fly of a reasonable pattern and size. Try any variety of standard patterns of caddis such as Elk-hair, X-caddis, EC-caddis, and many mayfly patterns, Pale Morning Duns, Blue-winged Olives, and the all-around Adams in sizes 16-18.

These are both big and relatively small parks, all with access points, maps, camping, lodging, fast food, and (in some cases) fine dining. It's all here—fabulous fly fishing in 25 of our nation's national parks.

Each chapter covers a separate national park and its surrounding areas. The exception is Yellowstone. Because it is so large, we have written it as one long chapter that's broken out into five mini-chapters—one for the introduction, and one each for the northern, southern, eastern, and western portions of the park. We've also covered both fishing and access points in Wyoming, Montana and Idaho.

Because Alaska is such a different entity, we have separated its parks from others in the West.

Time to go explore; let's go to the park. Let's go fly-fishing.

Additional National Parks to Consider

We chose not to include a few national parks for a variety of reasons, primarily lack of fly-fishing opportunities combined with their remote locations. This is in no way meant to imply that there isn't good—or even great—fly fishing. Our choices came down to a simple a matter of priorities. We felt it was better to concentrate on more easily accessible parks that are conducive to both a family vacation and a fly-fishing trip.

Here are four additional parks to consider:

Dry Tortugas

About 70 miles west of Key West is Dry Tortugas National Park. The park covers about 100 square miles and is primarily open water with seven small islands. The park is accessible only by boat or seaplane and home to Fort Jefferson, coral reefs, and extensive marine life.

This is strictly boat fishing water, and you'll need one capable of making a roundtrip of more than 140 miles without refueling since there are no services in the park. Incidentally, the name, Dry Tortugas, means there is no fresh water either.

The park waters offer a wide variety of targets for fly rodders equipped with 8- to 12-weight rods and big game fly reels. Potential quarry includes black, red and goliath grouper, mutton and yellowtail snapper, tarpon, jack crevalle, mangrove (gray) snapper, barracuda, bar jacks, and bull sharks.

You should bring plenty of 3- to 4-inch baitfish-style flies in sizes 1 to 1/0 along with a variety of saltwater poppers. The crash and take of a snapper or grouper on a topwater popper makes the long boat ride worthwhile.

For more information about Dry Tortugas National Park, including historic Fort Jefferson, camping opportunities, ferry and seaplane service, visit www.nps.gov/drto/index.htm.

Isle Royale

Isle Royale National Park is on Isle Royale and adjacent islands in Lake Superior, within Michigan. It was established on April 3, 1940, designated as a National Wilderness Area in 1976, and made an International Biosphere Reserve in 1980. The park covers 894 square miles, with 209 square miles above water.

Anglers seeking to combine some hiking, canoeing, kayaking, camping or family time with fly fishing might want to consider this park. Target species include lake and brook trout, northern pike, yellow perch and walleye.

Be aware that Lake Superior waters extend 4.5 miles out from the island and are designated catch-and-release only for all brook trout, including all bays and harbors. Also, inland waters are now designated catch-and-release only in all lakes, streams, and creeks. Only artificial lures and barbless hooks may be used in all lakes, streams and creeks.

Regulations change seasonally, so be sure to check the latest.

Isle Royale National Park has two developed areas of interest to flyfishers:

Windigo is located at the southwest end of the island and is the docking site for the ferries from Minnesota. Windigo includes a camp store, showers, campsites, and a boat dock.

Rock Harbor is located on the south side of the northeast end with a camp store, showers, restaurant, lodge, campsites, and a boat dock. Non-camping, sleeping accommodations at the park are limited to the lodge at Rock Harbor.

During the summer months, the park is accessible by ferries, floatplanes, and passenger ships from Houghton and Copper Harbor in Michigan and from Grand Portage in Minnesota. Private boats travel to the island from the coasts of Michigan, Minnesota, and Ontario. Isle Royale is quite popular with day-trippers in private boats. Day-trip ferry service is provided to and from the park via Copper Harbor and Grand Portage

Isle Royale National Park is closed for the full winter season due to the difficulty of travel and the hazards of wilderness survival during the winter months. Isle Royale is the only U.S. National Park to close for the entire winter season.

For more information about Isle Royale National Park, including camping opportunities and ferry and seaplane service, visit www.nps.gov/isro/index.htm.

Voyageurs

Voyageurs National Park was established in 1975, but evidence shows that humans have been living in the park area for 10,000 years. Signs of Native Americans, fur traders, and homesteaders, as well as evidence of logging, mining, and commercial fishing are scattered throughout the park.

Voyageurs National Park is located on the U.S./Canadian border, and it's Minnesota's only national park. It includes the waters of Rainy, Kabetogama, Namakan and Sand Point Lakes. In all, Voyageurs has 344 square miles of navigable waters for boating, canoeing, kayaking, and, of course, fly fishing.

Virtually all fishing in Voyageurs National Park is by boat in the seemingly endless string of lakes and bays. Here, the walleye is king. However, you can also fish for northern pike, crappie and smallmouth bass Even though it's a national park, a Minnesota fishing license is required. Make sure you get a copy of the Minnesota Fishing Regulations and know the slot (size) limit for the lakes. Park rangers enforce state fishing regulations.

Private lodges (camps) with rental boats and guide services dot the park and adjoining areas. Although none of these camps is fly-fishing-specific, all can point a dedicated fly-flinger in the right direction. And it's not too difficult to transfer knowledge about plugs and bait to streamer patterns and fly-rod poppers!

Lake Kabetogama, Namakan Lake, and Rainy Lake are world-class fishing lakes known for their walleye production as well as jumbo black crappies, huge smallmouth bass, and giant northern pike.

For more information about Voyageurs National Park, visit www.nps.gov/voya/index.htm.

Wrangell-St. Elias

Alaska's Wrangell-St. Elias National Park covers 13.2 million acres, and could fit the entire nation of Switzerland, along with Yellowstone and Yosemite National Parks, within its borders. Wrangell-St. Elias was established in 1980; it stretches from one of the tallest peaks in North America (Mount St. Elias at 18,008 feet) to the Gulf of Alaska.

This park swarms with five varieties of salmon, as well as rainbow trout, Dolly Varden trout, grayling, and the stuff of fly-fishers' dreams. Some of the northernmost populations of steelhead are found within the park/preserve. However, nearly all fishable waters can be accessed only by boat, float plane, or through any of the numerous private lodges and fish camps.

There are only two roads (both unpaved gravel) that actually enter the park: Nabesna and McCarthy Roads. The National Park Service does not maintain these roads, though both are usually passable to all vehicles during the summer months. Conditions can change quickly, so you should always stop by a park visitor center to check on current road conditions. You can also check with the Alaska Road Traveler Information Service for the latest conditions. Most major car rental companies in Anchorage forbid customers the usage of their vehicles on gravel roads.

For a day trip, contact charter flying services in and around Anchorage. You can also scour the ads online or in your favorite fly-fishing magazine for the lodge or camp that best meets your time frame and financial requirements.

An Alaska state fishing license is required for all anglers ages 16 and older. Bag and possession limits vary by species and by area. Fishing regulations are available at the park visitor center, or on the State of Alaska website or at www.nps.gov/wrst/index.htm.

Terry & Wendy Gunn

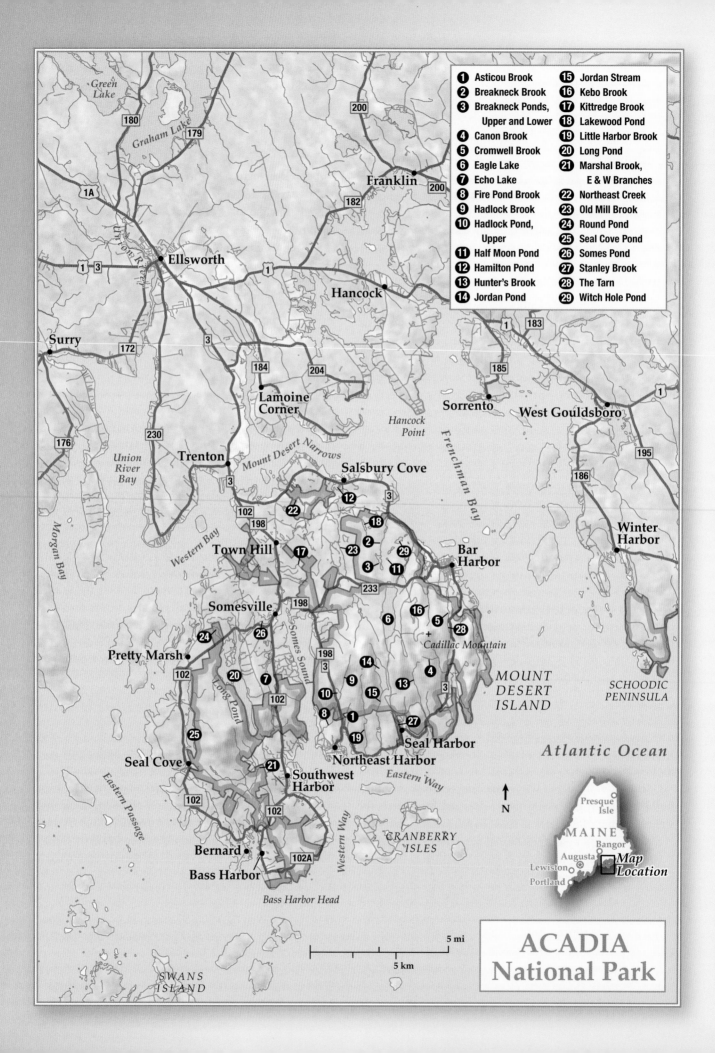

ACADIA
National Park

❶ Asticou Brook	⓯ Jordan Stream
❷ Breakneck Brook	⓰ Kebo Brook
❸ Breakneck Ponds,	⓱ Kittredge Brook
Upper and Lower	⓲ Lakewood Pond
❹ Canon Brook	⓳ Little Harbor Brook
❺ Cromwell Brook	⓴ Long Pond
❻ Eagle Lake	㉑ Marshal Brook,
❼ Echo Lake	E & W Branches
❽ Fire Pond Brook	㉒ Northeast Creek
❾ Hadlock Brook	㉓ Old Mill Brook
❿ Hadlock Pond,	㉔ Round Pond
Upper	㉕ Seal Cove Pond
⓫ Half Moon Pond	㉖ Somes Pond
⓬ Hamilton Pond	㉗ Stanley Brook
⓭ Hunter's Brook	㉘ The Tarn
⓮ Jordan Pond	㉙ Witch Hole Pond

Acadia National Park

➤ **Location:** Acadia National Park is in northern coastal Maine just more than an hour from Bangor. Travel time is three hours from Portland; four-and-a-half hours from Manchester, New Hampshire; and just under five hours from Boston. Full service airports are available in all four cities.

Acadia National Park is in what is known as Downeast Maine. In 1916, President Woodrow Wilson established Sieur de Monts National Monument on Mount Desert Island. It was designated a national park in 1919, making it the first such park east of the Mississippi River. Originally known as Lafayette National Park, it was renamed Acadia National Park in 1929. It is best known for its hiking, biking and sightseeing, though Acadia also offers a variety of fresh- and saltwater fishing—much of which is greatly underutilized.

At just more than 47,000 acres, Acadia is the twelfth smallest national park. Conversely, it has the ninth highest amount of traffic, with more than 2.5 million visitors each year. Roughly 30,000 acres of the park are on Mount Desert Island. Slightly more than 2,725 acres are located on Isle au Haut, and about 2,365 acres are located on the Schoodic Peninsula. Within the park boundaries are a number of private in-holdings that the park service is trying to acquire.

The land around Acadia National Park was once home to the Native American Wabanaki tribe. There is evidence of American Indians living in the region as early as 4,000 BCE. The first European to see the area was Samuel de Champlain, who sailed by in 1604. He noted its size, topography, and offshore hazards—one of which "made a hole in our pinnace (a small boat) close to the keel." He also noted its closeness to the mainland, along with the cliff-lined shores that gave it the appearance of "seven or eight mountains one alongside the other." Champlain originally named this land Mount Desert Island.

Landscape architect Charles Eliot is credited with coming up with the idea of establishing a national park on Mount Desert Island. His dream was made a reality by George B. Dorr, referred to as the "Father of Acadia National Park," and

his father, Charles W. Eliot (who was president of Harvard University at that time). Together, they raised the money needed to procure the land, and they lobbied the state and federal government for recognition and support.

Between 1915 and 1933, millionaire industrial magnate and philanthropist John D. Rockefeller, Jr. designed, directed and financed the construction of a network of gravel carriage trails throughout the park. He brought in landscape architect Beatrix Farrand to design the floral accompaniment to the trails. These trails cover more than 50 miles and are open

Jordan Pond. Diana Mallard

to foot and bike traffic only. In places, they are lined with granite stones known as "coping stones" (as in coping with the steep drop-offs) or as "Rockefeller's teeth." There are 17 granite bridges and two gate lodges.

Cadillac Mountain is the most prominent feature in Acadia National Park. At just higher than 1,525 feet, it is the highest point in the park. Also, Cadillac Mountain is the highest point within 25 miles of the coast from the Cape Breton Highlands in Nova Scotia to the Mexican Peaks about 180 miles south of Texas. It was named after the French explorer Antoine Laumet de La Mothe, sieur de Cadillac. It is also one of the first—if not the first—places in the United States touched by the sun each morning.

Top. Author on a small, wild brook trout stream. Diana Mallard

Above. Wild brook trout. Diana Mallard

Somes Sound. Diana Mallard

Thunder Hole is another natural popular feature with visitors to Acadia National Park. Waves crash into the shore and are forced into this small natural crevice, exploding with a thunderous boom and spray. The noise is caused by water driving against air pockets trapped in the cavern. It is best viewed between tides and during or after a storm. Caution should be used around the feature, and visitors must stay within the marked boundaries.

The Park Loop Road is one of Acadia's most popular man-made attractions. It begins at the Hulls Cove Visitor Center and runs for 27 miles through the interior and eastern edge of the Mount Desert segment of the park. The road was partially funded by John D. Rockefeller, Jr. Work began on the road in 1922 and completed in the 1950s. It connects to the equally scenic Cadillac Mountain Summit Road.

Acadia National Park is home to roughly 40 species of mammals, including beavers—reintroduced to the park in 1920 after they were eradicated through trapping—black bears, bobcats, chipmunks, coyotes, red foxes, gray squirrels, moose, muskrats, porcupines, red squirrels, and white-tailed deer. At one time, the area was home to the now locally extirpated eastern cougar and gray wolf. The park has a robust and diverse plant, insect and avian population as well.

Of most interest to those reading this book, Acadia National Park is also home to native Eastern brook trout. Also, there are introduced lake trout— known locally as a togue—landlocked (Atlantic) salmon, brown trout, and smallmouth bass. Saltwater fish species include bluefish, mackerel and striped bass.

There are purported to be 22 lakes or ponds in Acadia National Park. Most are managed as coldwater fisheries. Water quality in the park is very good. Most of the lakes and ponds are extremely clear with gravel bottoms. Eagle and Echo Lakes, along with Jordan and Long Ponds, are some of the more popular waters. Jordan Pond is the deepest lake in Acadia with depths of more than 120 feet. The Tarn is the shallowest at less than five feet. While there are formal boat launches on many ponds, some ponds require a portage of varying lengths to reach the water and are therefore best fished from a canoe or personal watertcraft.

According to the Maine Department of Inland Fisheries and Wildlife, the best lakes and ponds to catch landlocked salmon are Long and Jordan Ponds, and Eagle and Echo Lakes. As for brook trout, they recommend Witch Hole, Upper Breakneck, Lower Breakneck, Lakewood, Half Moon, and Upper Hadlock Ponds and Echo Lake. Those seeking lake trout should consider Eagle Lake and Jordan Pond. Brown trout can be found in Seal Cove Pond. If smallmouth bass are on your list, try Long, Round, Somes and Seal Cove Ponds. For largemouth, your best bet is Hamilton Pond.

Brook trout can also be found in some of the streams within Acadia National Park. Some are resident and some enter the streams from the lakes and ponds to spawn. Streams with brook trout include Asticou, Breakneck, Canon, Cromwell, Fire, Hadlock, Hunter's, Kebo, Kittredge, Little Harbor, Old Mill, and Stanley Brooks, as well as the east and west branches of Marshal Brook. Brook trout are also found in Jordan Stream and Northeast Creek.

Also, Acadia National Park is home to rare sea-run brook trout, known locally as salters. Sea-run brook trout are a form of diadromous fish, meaning they migrate between salt and fresh waters. Diadromous fish differ from anadromous fish, which live in salt water and enter fresh water only to spawn. Sea-run brook trout live and spawn in fresh water, but move into salt water to feed. These fish move back into their natal streams a month or so later than those found in Cape Cod and Long Island. This makes them some of the most saltwater-dependent brook trout in the country. Sea-run brook trout also do not have access to much estuary habitat. As a result, while they do not venture too far from the stream mouths, they do spend more time in the open ocean than many other salters. Sea-run brook trout can be found in Stanley and Hunters Brooks, and they might be present in other streams as well. By the time these fish have returned to the streams, they have spent months feeding on minnows in salt water. As such, they are best fished for using small streamers.

Bluefish, mackerel and striped bass can be caught off the beach from July through September. Places to try include Sargeant Drive on Somes Sound, and Frazer Point on Schoodic Peninsula. Look for terns feeding, which is a sign that baitfish are in the area—and game fish are nearly certain to be nearby.

Green Lake, some 20 miles to the north of the park, is home to rare Arctic char—formerly known as blueback trout. It is one of only 12 native populations in the contiguous United States. Two of these waters were recently infected with invasive smelts, forcing costly and risky reclamations. Two other lakes, including Green Lake, have what Maine Fish and Game experts refer to as a low abundance of Arctic char. With just 8-12 viable populations, these are some of the rarest salmonids in the country. Arctic char are deepwater fish making them difficult—but not impossible—to catch on fly tackle. Your best chance to do so is in the spring and fall when they enter shallow water to feed and spawn respectively. They are best targeted using small minnow patterns. Green Lake is also one of just four native landlocked salmon lakes in the state.

Services are limited within Acadia National Park. The area is, however, serviced by the quaint coastal tourist towns of Bar Harbor and Southwest Harbor. The former is one of the most bustling and beautiful seaside towns in Maine. It is visited by cruise ships as well as tourists travelling by automobile. It boasts myriad lodging, dining and retail offerings. Southwest Harbor is smaller, but none the less desirable. Ellsworth, which is approximately ten miles north of the park, is a large city with a diverse retail and dining infrastructure.

Acadia National Park is a beautiful place. While not known for its fishing, the fishing you'll find there is better and more diverse than most realize. Most importantly, the waters there are some of the most underutilized fisheries in the state. It is actually quite rare to see anglers when you drive, bike or walk through the park. However, those who do fish Acadia are often quite satisfied with what they find.

➤ **Hatches:** Hatches in Acadia National Park occur much earlier than those found in interior Maine. However, they are not what you would call robust or overly diverse. Midges, mayflies, caddis and stoneflies are all present. Most of the lakes and ponds in the park have gravely bottoms that are not conducive to burrowing mayflies such as the Hexagenia, which are found elsewhere in the state. However, these insects do hatch sporadically, and midges are always present. For the most part, moving water is limited to small freestone streams, which also are not known for their hatches, though mayflies, caddis and stoneflies do hatch sporadically.

➤ **Tackle and Gear**

Rods and Line: When fishing dry flies, we recommend a 9-foot, 5-weight and floating line rig. If you want to fish wet flies, which in many cases is your best option, a 9-foot, 6-weight with a sinking line is a good choice. The small streams can be fished with a shorter and lighter rod in the 6- to 8-foot and 2- to 4-weight range with a floating line. When fishing salt water, a 9-foot 8- or 9-weight with an intermediate or sinking line is your best bet.

Terminal Tackle and Flies: Flies for fishing the lakes and ponds should include different stages of mayflies and caddis in a variety of sizes and colors. Woolly Buggers, streamers and crayfish are good choices. Small streams are best fished with attractor dries and terrestrials in the headwaters, and small streamers are best in the lower section where you could encounter salters. Clousers and Deceivers are a good option for the salt water.

Sea-run brook trout stream. Diana Mallard

Fishing where the stream meets the ocean. Diana Mallard

CLOSEST CITY OR POINT OF ENTRANCE

Numerous towns and villages are close to Acadia, ranging from quiet little fishing villages such as Bass Harbor or Corea, to larger and more well-known resort towns such as Bar Harbor. The Mount Desert Island or Acadia map covers the main portion of the park on Mount Desert Island and the surrounding villages. The Schoodic map covers the portion of Acadia National Park that is located on the mainland and the communities surrounding it.

AIRPORTS AND CAR RENTALS

Bangor, Maine, 75 minutes
Portland, Maine, 3 hours
Manchester, New Hampshire, 4.5 hours
Boston, Massachusetts, 5 hours

OPENING AND CLOSING OR FISHING DATES

April through September

FEES

Park entrance and user fees change periodically. For up-to-date fees, free days and other exceptions, visit www.nps.gov/acad/index.htm.

CLOSEST FLY SHOPS

Van Raymond Outfitters

388 S. Main St.
Brewer, ME 04412
207-989-6001
www.vanraymond.com
info@vanraymondoutfitters.com

L.L. Bean

95 Main St.
Freeport, ME 04032
877-755-2326
www.llbean/com/freeport
(Open 24 hours, 365 days a year)

CLOSEST GUIDES & OUTFITTERS

Acadia Guide Service

14 Albert Meadow
Bar Harbor, ME 04609
207-669-8236
info@acadiaguideservice.com

Eagle Mountain Guide Service

48 Bunker Dr.
Otis, ME 04605
207-537-5282
emgsinfo@gmail.com

CLOSEST LODGING

Blackfriar Inn

10 Summer St.
Bar Harbor, ME 04609
207-288-5091
www.blackfriarinn.com
stay@blackfriarinn.com

The Moorings Inn Waterfront

133 Shore Road
Southwest Harbor, ME 04679
207-244-5523
www.mooringsinn.com
mooringsinn@roadrunner.com

Harbour Cottage Inn

9 Dirigo Road
Southwest Harbor, ME 04679
207-244-5738
www.harbourcottageinn.com
info@harbourcottageinn.com

BOB MALLARD lives in central Maine. He owned and operated Kennebec River Outfitters from 2001 to 2015. Bob is a blogger, writer, author, fly designer and sales rep. His flies have been featured in several books and articles. Bob has appeared on radio and television and has been featured in newspapers, magazines and books. Bob has written about fly fishing, fly tying, fisheries management and conservation in newspapers and magazines at the local, regional and national level. His regular column—Gearhead—appears in *Southern Trout* online magazine. Bob is also the Northeast Regional Editor for *Fly Fish America*. He contributed two chapters to Terry and Wendy Gunn's *50 Best Tailwaters to Fly Fish* (Stonefly Press, 2013). His *50 Best Places Fly Fishing the Northeast* (Stonefly Press, 2014) and *25 Best Towns Fly Fishing for Trout* (Stonefly Press, 2015) are currently available. His next book, *50 Best Places Fly Fishing for Brook Trout* (Stonefly Press), is due out in 2016.

CLOSEST LODGING *continued*
Bar Harbor Grand Hotel
269 Main St.
Bar Harbor, ME 04609
207-288-5226
www.barharborgrand.com
reservations@barharborgrand.com

CLOSEST CAMPGROUNDS
Blackwoods Campground

Seawall Campground
www.nps.gov/acad/planyourvisit
/camping.htm

CLOSEST RESTAURANTS
The Jordon Pond House
Park Loop Road
Seal Harbor, ME 04675
207-276-3244
www.thejordanpondhouse.com

Café This Way
14 Mount Desert St.
Bar Harbor, ME 04609
207-288-4483
www.cafethisway.com

Side Street Café
49 Rodick St.
Bar Harbor, ME 04609
207-801-2591
www.sidestreetbarharbor.com
info@sidestreetbarharbor.com

Shinbashi
139 High St.
Ellsworth, ME 04605
207-667-6561
www.myshinbashi.com
(Sushi and Japanese)

MUST SEE
Thunder Hole: A small cavern where, when the rush of the wave arrives, air and water is forced out like a clap of distant thunder. Water might spout as high as 40 feet with a thunderous roar! Wheelchair accessible.

NEAREST HOSPITALS/
URGENT CARE CENTERS
Mount Desert Island Hospital
(MDIH)
10 Wayman Lane
Bar Harbor, ME 04609
207-288-5081
www.mdihospital.org

Maine Coast Memorial Hospital
(MCMH)
50 Union St.
Ellsworth, ME 04605
207-664-5311
888-645-8829 (toll free)
www.mcmhospital.org

CELL PHONE SERVICE
Depending upon the carrier, cell coverage is good to excellent most places in and around the park.

EVERYTHING ELSE
For all else, visit
www.nps.gov/acad/index.htm.

Shenandoah National Park

➤ **Location:** Shenandoah National Park is located in the Blue Ridge Mountains of Virginia, just west of Washington, D.C., and stretches 105 miles from its northern entrance at Front Royal to its southern entrance near Waynesboro.

There are four entrances into the park and numerous gateway communities:

Front Royal, accessible via Interstate 66 and Virginia 340
Thornton Gap, accessible via Virginia 211
Swift Run Gap, accessible via Virginia 33
Rockfish Gap, accessible via Interstate 64 and Route 250

Shenandoah National Park begins just south of the city of Front Royal, 72 miles west of Dulles International Airport. The park was formed December 26, 1935 when Secretary of the Interior, Harold Ickes, accepted the deed from the Commonwealth of Virginia conveying 176,429 acres to the federal government. In 1933 and 1934, about 1,000 young men of the newly formed Civilian Conservation Corp (CCC) were stationed in six separate camps. Their primary tasks were to build trails and shelters, to fight fires, reduce fire hazards, control erosion and work on the Skyline Drive.

The Skyline Drive is a meandering road that travels the crest of the park's mountains for about 100 miles providing numerous pull-offs to park and look west into the Shenandoah Valley or east into the sprawling Piedmont area of Virginia, which feathers off to the Atlantic Ocean.

The opening of the Skyline Drive on September 15, 1934 was especially important to anglers because it provided access to the headwaters of the brook trout streams. Today, some of the best fishing is found by parking at the locations noted for each stream. You'll need to hike from one to four miles down the mountains into the streams, and then fish back up the mountain. Even though the Shenandoah National Park is only an hour from our nation's capital, you can still hike into these hollows and fish all day without seeing another angler.

The streams in the Shenandoah National Park provide some of the finest fishing for wild brook trout you could want.

One can often find the brook trout streams in the Shenandoah National Park by standing on top of the mountains and tracing the rising clouds in the mornings. Harry Murray

The wild brook trout in the Shenandoah National Park thrive well in the high-gradient streams. Harry Murray

When the park was formed, the plan was to grow the native brook trout population to allow for recreational angling.

In order to help you find good fishing in the park, we'll look at seasonal angling tactics, aquatic insect hatches, and productive flies. Then we'll cover some of the best streams, showing the best access points.

Good fishing can begin in mid-March when water temperature holds at 40°F for several days. When the aquatic insects begin hatching in numbers, the brook trout start feeding, and the fishing really picks up.

Parking at the trail heads on the Skyline Drive and hiking down to the upper reaches of the streams usually gets you to the finest dry fly fishing the park offers.

➤ **Hatches:** The Epeorus pleuralis mayfly—better known to fly anglers as the Quill Gordon—is the first heavy hatch in these mountains, and the trout feed well on these naturals from mid-March until mid-April. I developed the Mr. Rapidan dry-fly to match this hatch. Both the Quill Gordon and the Mr. Rapidian in size 14 are very effective in the park.

The Paraleptophlebia adoptiva—better-known to fly anglers as the Blue Quill— is our next major hatch, and these are well matched with the Blue Quill dry fly size 16. This hatch starts in late March and lasts until late April.

The Stenonema vicarium—better-known to fly anglers as the March Brown—starts hatching in mid-April and lasts into May. It is the largest mayfly that is present in large numbers. This is well matched with the March Brown dry-fly and the Mr. Rapidan dry-fly, both in size 14.

The Stenonema fuscum and Stenonema canadense—better known to fly anglers as the Gray Fox and the Light Cahill, respectively—follow the March Brown and last through May. However, these hatches are not nearly as heavy as the March Brown hatch.

However, the Ephemerella dorothea—better known to fly anglers as the Sulphur—hatch begins in mid-May, lasts through June, and can be a very heavy hatch.

One specific stonefly hatch, the Isoperla bilineata—better known to fly anglers as the Yellow Sally—holds its own in density with our best mayfly hatches and surpasses them all in longevity. These delicate, little yellow beauties begin hatching

The brook trout in the Shenandoah National Park provide a wonderful challenge in beautiful settings. Jeffrey Murray

Harry Murray enjoys fishing the rising trout he spots in each pool. Harry Murray

in April and can last until July. They are well matched with Murray's Little Yellow Dry Stonefly in size 16.

From June through September, natural terrestrial insects become an important part of these trout's diet. Black ants, a broad variety of beetles, and mountain wasps are all present in great numbers along these streams. The trout feed heavily upon all of them. Flies that are very productive at this time are the Mr. Rapidan Ant in sizes 14-20, Murray's Flying Beetle in sizes 14-18, and Shenk's Cricket in size 16.

The brook trout spawn from early October until late November, and most anglers believe it is best not to stress them by fishing during this time. After early December, the streams become so cold that the trout do not feed well.

➤ **Stream locations:** All stream accesses are keyed to the Potomac Appalachian Trial Club maps (sources on the side bar). Having these maps is strongly recommended before going into the backcountry. The following streams are listed alphabetically with a few minor exceptions that will be self-explanatory. The milepost markers numbered from north

The wild brook trout in the Shenandoah National Park often hold on their feeding stations to feed all day. Harry Murray

to south, are at one-mile intervals along the Skyline Drive and are clearly visible. The trail heads are marked with concrete posts on which metal bands give clear directions and distances for specific trails.

Following are some of the trout streams in the park. For information on many other fine brook trout streams and their access points, refer to *Trout Fishing in the Shenandoah National Park* by Harry W. Murray.

➤ **Big Run:** Many believe Big Run is the finest stream in the park. It is accessible via two trails from the Skyline Drive.

The easiest access is to park at Doyles River Parking on the east side of the Skyline Drive just south of Milepost 81. From the Big Run Overlook, take the Big Run Loop Trail, which connects with the Big Run Portal Trail 2.2 miles down the mountain. The stream is quite small here, so you will probably want to hike down this trail toward Rocky Mountain Run.

The second access point is from Brown Mountain Overlook at Milepost 77. Take the Brown Mountain Trail down 0.7 miles to the Rocky Mountain Run Trail, and follow this 2.7 miles down to Big Run. There is no legal access at the lower end of this stream.

➤ **Conway River:** This stream flows through a portion of the park, meaning that the state portion (outside the park's boundaries) is managed the same as the park's streams, so we include it here.

Route 667 through Fletcher is the main access. Do not park in the two parking lots. Instead, park along the edge of Virginia 667, being respectful to local land owners. The alter-

nate way into the Conway is via Virginia 662 and Virginia 615 across a sometimes very rough road.

➤ **East Branch Naked Creek:** The best access to this stream is from the Naked Creek Overlook just south of Milepost 53 on the west side of Skyline Drive. From the overlook, hike down the left side of the grassy area past the tree line. Swinging left and down the mountain, you might be able to locate an old trail. Though rugged, this is one of the most beautiful parts of the park. There is no legal access at the lower end of this stream.

➤ **Hughes River:** The top of this stream can be reached from two different trails from Skyline Drive.

The Corbin Cabin Cutoff Trail provides good access if you park at the Shaver Hollow parking area just north of Milepost 38. This trail meets the Nicholson Hollow Trail 1.4 miles down the mountain. The latter trail parallels the stream to the lower park boundary.

You can also park at Stony Man Overlook between Milepost 38 and 39. About 100 yards north is the head of the Nicholson Hollow Trail. Follow this 1.8 miles to the stream. To access Hughes River at the lower park boundary, take Route 600 from Nethers to the bus parking lot for Old Rag Mountain. Look for Nicholson Hollow Trail about a half-mile upstream on the right. Take this trail into the Park.

➤ **Jeremy's Run:** Access to this stream is from Skyline Drive at the lower side of the Elkwallow Picnic area at Milepost 24. Park in the second parking area and take the connecting trail for less than 100 yards to the Appalachian Trail. After a short distance, this trail meets Jeremy's Run Trail where the former makes a sharp turn to the left. Jeremy's Run Trail follows the full length of the stream. There is limited parking on the shoulder of Virginia 611 for access to the bottom of this stream.

➤ **North Fork Moormans River:** This stream is managed as a catch-and-release stream, meaning that no trout may be killed. Access to the lower park boundary is available from Virginia 614, also known as Sugar Hollow Road. Park at the upper end of the reservoir and follow this same road along the stream through the park gate. The top of the stream is accessed by parking at the Blackrock Gap parking lot just south of Milepost 87. Walk across Skyline Drive and hike down the North Fork Moormans River Road.

➤ **Piney River:** This stream is accessible from the top by parking at the Piney River Ranger Station on Skyline Drive just south of Milepost 22. Hike down the Range View Cabin Road to where the Piney Branch Trail leads off to the left. This last trail follows the stream to the bottom of the mountain.

You can also access Piney River from the bottom of the mountain via Virginia 600. Parking is a problem here; there is room along Virginia 600 just east of Virginia 653 for one or two cars. Do not block any of the private roads in this area. There is no park land in this immediate area. Hike up the trail to the park boundary before you start fishing.

➤ **Rapidan River:** The lower section of this stream holds the largest trout and produces the best hatches. This section is accessible via Virginia 662 through Wolftown and Graves Mill. Park at the end of this road. A good trail follows this entire section of the Rapidan. The central part of the stream is accessible from Criglersville via Virginia 649/670. Good parking is available where this road meets the stream. Anglers can easily walk downstream to the section holding the large trout or fish upstream from here. The road upstream from here can be very rough. This is a "fish for fun" (no kill stream), meaning catch and release is mandatory.

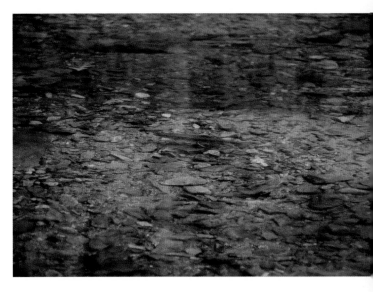

The pure streams and clean stream bottom gravel provide ideal conditions for the brook trout to spawn. Jeffrey Murray

William Downey draws on his experience gained in 65 years of fishing the Shenandoah National Park streams to master these trout. Harry Murray

➤ **Rose River:** Top access is available by parking at the Fishers Gap parking area just south of Milepost 49 and hiking down Rose River Fire Road, which follows the lower two-thirds of the stream to the lower park boundary. An alternate trail to the uppermost part of the river is available by parking at the above area. However, shortly after starting down the mountain on Rose River Fire Road, Rose River Loop Trail splits off to your left. One-half mile down the trail, take a Blue-Blazed Trail to your right for another half-mile to the stream. Top access may also be gained by parking at the Dark Hollow Falls parking area and following the Dark Hollow Falls Trail down to Rose River Fire Road, and then following it down to the river. There is bottom access from Virginia 670, west of Syria. Do not block the road, preventing its use by park rangers.

➤ **Staunton River:** This is a feeder to the Rapidan River, and it can be reached by Virginia 662 from Graves Mill. Park in the parking lot at the end of the road and follow Graves Mill Trail to the Staunton River Trail. This stream is a catch-and-release fishery.

➤ **Thornton River, North Fork:** Virginia 612 provides access to the lower portion of this stream. This road is used by residents with homes in this area, so do not block the road. Park east of the houses and hike up Thornton Hollow Trail into the park. Access into the head of this stream is available via Thornton Hollow Trail, which leaves Skyline Drive halfway between Mileposts 25 and 26. The stream is small here, but hiking down the mountain will get you into more water.

➤ **White Oak Canyon Run:** Many beautiful waterfalls, inspiring scenery, and good trout fishing make this a stream worth visiting. The top access is via parking at Limberlost, just east of Skyline Drive at Milepost 43. Hike one-tenth mile down Old Rag Fire Road to White Oak Canyon Trail. Follow this trail to the right, which will lead you to the stream. This trail provides good stream access all the way to the bottom of the mountain. Virginia 600 west of Syria provides good access to the lower part of the stream. Park in the area beside the stream and follow White Oak Canyon Trail along the stream.

➤ **Tackle and Gear**

Rods and Line: Your rod of choice should be 6-1/2 to 7-1/2 feet long and balance with a 3-weight line. Reels weighing less than 4 ounces are recommended. We also recommend that you choose durable reels that can handle the rough treatment they receive in these streams.

Terminal Tackle and Flies: Fishing Shenandoah's many different hatches requires a well-stocked fly box. We recommend Quill Gordons and Blue Quills for early- to late-spring fishing. March Browns, Gray Foxes and Light Cahills are perfect for mid-spring, while Sulphurs are the ticket for late spring and into early summer. Be sure to pack plenty of Yellow Sallies for mayfly hatches, and terrestrials, including Mr. Rapidian's Ant, Murray's Flying Beetle, and Shenk's Cricket, for summer fly fishing.

The beautiful fall colors in the Shenandoah National Park are just one of the wonderful features that attract anglers. Harry Murray

CLOSEST CITY OR POINT OF ENTRANCE TO THE PARK

There are four entrances into Shenandoah National Park along with numerous gateway communities that offer services:

· Front Royal (a.k.a. North Entrance), accessible via Interstate 66 and Virginia 340.
· Thornton Gap, accessible via Virginia 211.
· Swift Run Gap, accessible via Virginia 33.
· Rockfish Gap (a.k.a. South Entrance), accessible via Interstate 64 and Virginia 250; Rockfish Gap is also the northern entrance to the Blue Ridge Parkway.

CLOSEST AIRPORTS

Washington Dulles International (IAD): 56 miles west to Front Royal; Reagan National (DCA): 70 miles west to Front Royal Full hotel/motel, auto rental, and traveler services is available at both airports.

OPENING AND CLOSING OR FISHING DATES

The park is always open. Portions of Skyline Drive—the only public road through the park—are periodically closed during inclement weather and at night during deer hunting season, which is mid-November through early January.

REGULATIONS

· A State of Virginia fishing license is required.
· A five-day license is available at facilities and camp stores in the park.
· Fishing regulations change, so be sure to get a current copy when you purchase your license.
· You can also visit www.dgif.virginia.gov/licenses or call 866-721-6911.

CLOSEST FLY SHOPS

Murray's Fly Shop
121 S. Main St.
Edinburg, VA 22824
540-984-4212

CLOSEST GUIDES & OUTFITTERS

South River Fly Shop
323 W. Main St.
Waynesboro, VA 22980
540-942-5566

Murray's Fly Shop
121 S. Main St.
Edinburg, VA 22824
540-984-4212

CLOSEST LODGING

Skyland
Mile: 41.7
Late March through November
Information and reservations:
800-999-4714 during season;
December through March: 540-743-5108

Big Meadows Lodge
Mile: 51.3, one mile off the drive
April through November
Information and reservations:
800-999-4714

CLOSEST CAMPGROUNDS

The park has four rustic campgrounds with no hook-ups for electricity, sewage, or water. For information and reservations call 877-444-6777, or visit www.Receration.gov.

Matthews Arm Campground
Matthews Arm is the nearest campground for those entering the park from the north. It is next to a nature trail and the trail to Overall Run Falls, the tallest waterfall in the park. Elkwallow Wayside, with camping supplies and food service, is two miles away.

· The cost is $15 per night. Generator-free and group sites are available. This campground is open from mid-May through October.
· The campground is located at Matthews Arm mile 22.1.
· A map and regulations can be found at https://www.nps.gov/shen/planyourvisit/upload/Mathews_combine.pdf.

Big Meadows Campground
Big Meadows is near many of the major facilities and popular hiking trails in the park. Three waterfalls are within walking distance. The Meadow, with its abundant plant growth and wildlife, also is within walking distance.

· Cost is $20 per night when on the reservation system, and $17 per night during late spring and early fall.
· Generator-free and group sites are available.
· The campground is open from late March through November.
· The campground is located at Big Meadows mile 51.2.
· A map and regulations can be found at https://www.nps.gov/shen/planyourvisit/upload/Lewis_combined.pdf.

Lewis Mountain Campground
Lewis Mountain, the smallest campground in the park, is within seven miles of the popular Big Meadows area.

· There are 31 camp sites available, costing $15 per night, on a first-come, first-served basis.
· The campground is open from mid-April through October.
· The campground is located at Lewis Mountain mile 57.5.
· A map and regulations can be found at https://www.nps.gov/shen/planyourvisit/upload/Lewis_combined.pdf.

Loft Mountain Campground
Loft Mountain is the largest campground in the park, sitting atop Big Flat Mountain with views to the east and west. Two waterfalls and the trails into the Big Run Wilderness area are nearby.

· Cost is $15 per night.
· Generator-free and group rates are available.
· This campground is open from mid-May through October.
· The campground is located at Loft Mountain mile 79.5.
· A map and regulations can be found here: https://www.nps.gov/shen/planyourvisit/upload/combined.pdf.

OTHER ACCOMMODATIONS

Lewis Mountain Cabins and Camp Store
Furnished cabins
Available from April through November
Mile: 57.6
800-999-4714
shenandoah@aramark.com

DINING IN THE PARK

Elkwallow Wayside
Located at mile 24.1
Phone: 540-999-3500
Elkwallow Wayside serves a variety of breakfast selections, as well as sandwiches and grilled items for lunch and dinner. Seating is outside on the patio or at picnic tables. This restaurant is open from April through October.

Skyland Restaurant
Located at mile 41.7 and 42.5.
The Skyland Restaurant serves breakfast, lunch, and dinner and is open April through October.

Big Meadows Wayside
Located at mile 51.2.
Big Meadows Wayside offers a full-service dining room with carryout services and a varied menu of regional favorites and contemporary food. This restaurant is open March through November.

BIG MEADOWS LODGE
Located at mile 51.3.
Big Meadows Lodge serves breakfast, lunch and dinner, and is open from mid-May through October.

Loft Mountain Wayside
Located at mile 79.5
Loft Mountain Wayside has an inside dining room with counter service, as well as seating available outside on picnic tables. Breakfast selections, sandwiches, and grilled items are served here. This eatery is open April through October.

DINING OUTSIDE THE PARK
The Mimslyn Inn
401 W. Main St.
Luray, VA 22835
540-743-5105

The Inn at Little Washington
309 Middle Street
Washington, VA 22747
540-675-3800

Grave's Mountain Lodge
Virginia 670
Syria, VA 22743
540-923-4231

Days Inn
138 Whispering Hill Rd.
Luray, VA 22835
540-743-4521

BEST PLACES TO STAY OUTSIDE THE PARK
Quality Inn Skyline Drive
10 Commerce Ave.
Front Royal, VA 22630
540-635-3161 or 877-424-6423
www.choicehotels.com

Pioneer Motel
541 South Royal Ave.
Front Royal, VA 22630
540-635-4784

Grave's Mountain Lodge
Virginia 670
Syria, VA 22743
540-923-4231
info@gravesmountain.com
www.gravesmountain.com

Holiday Inn
787 Madison Road
Culpeper, VA 22701
540-825-7444 or 800-315-2621
www.holidayinn.com

Comfort Inn
890 Willis Lane
Culpeper, VA 22701
540-547-3374 or 877-424-6423
www.comfortinn.com

Comfort Inn
15 Windi Grove Drive
Waynesboro, VA 22980
540-932-3060 or 877-424-6423

Holiday Inn-Afton Mountain
20 Windi Grove Road
Waynesboro, VA 22980
540-932-7170 or 800-315-2621

BED AND BREAKFAST INNS
The Woodward House on Manor Grade
413 South Royal Avenue
Front Royal, VA 22630
800-635-7011
www.acountryhouse.com

Inn at Little Washington
Middle and Main Street
Washington, VA 22747
540-675-3800
www.theinnatlittlewashington.com

Foster-Harris House
189 Main Street
Washington, VA 22747
540-675-3757 or 800-666-0153
stay@fosterharris.com
www.fosterharris.com

Jo Ann's Bed and Breakfast at Frederick Farm
4629 Bloomer Spring Road
Elkton, VA 22824
540-298-9723
jfrederick@rica.net
www.frederickfarm.com

CAMPGROUNDS OUTSIDE THE PARK
Shenandoah Hills Campground
110 Campground Lane
Madison, VA 22727
540-948-4186 or 800-321-4186
www.shenandoahhills.com

Yogi Bear Jellystone Camp Resort
2250 Lee Highway
Luray, VA 22835
540-743-4002 or 800-420-6679
yogi@campluray.com
www.campluray.com

Swift Run Campground
19540 Spotswood Trail
Elkton, VA 22827
540-298-8086
www.swiftruncamp.com

Waynesboro Campground
U.S. Route 340 North to Interstate 64 (Exit 96)
Waynesboro, VA 22980
540-943-9573

Front Royal RV Campground
P.O. Box 274
Front Royal, VA 22630
540-635-2741
www.frontroyalrvcampground.com

MUST SEE
Numerous Civil War museums and battlefields west of Luray

NEAREST HOSPITAL/URGENT TREATMENT CENTER
Page Memorial Hospital
200 Memorial Dr.
Luray, VA 22835
540-743-4561

Warren Memorial Hospital
1000 Shenandoah Ave.
Front Royal, VA 22630
540-636-0300

Augusta Health
78 Medical Center Drive
Fishersville, Virginia 22939
800-932-0262

Rockingham Memorial Hospital
235 Cantrell Ave.
Harrisonburg, Virginia 22804
540-433-4100

CELL PHONE SERVICE
Cell phones do not work in the park. To use a cell phone, you'll likely need to exit to nearby population centers.

FOR EVERYTHING ELSE
www.nps.gov/shen/index.htm

HARRY MURRAY grew up in Edinburg, Virginia, where he stills lives and owns Murray's Fly Shop, just 20 miles from the Shenandoah National Park. Harry has been fishing the park for 40 years. About 20 years ago, at the request of the Shenandoah National Park's chief fisheries biologist, he wrote *Trout Fishing in the Shenandoah National Park* (Shenandoah Pub, 1989) to help all anglers discover the great fishing in this national park. He conducts fly-fishing schools and guide trips in the park for anglers from all across the country. Harry has designed more than 30 flies especially for the Shenandoah National Park. Harry also designed the Murray's Mountain Trout Rod for the Scott Fly Rod Company. This is considered one of the finest rods made for delicate trout fishing.

The beautiful brook trout streams in the Shenandoah National Park attract anglers from all across the country. Harry Murray

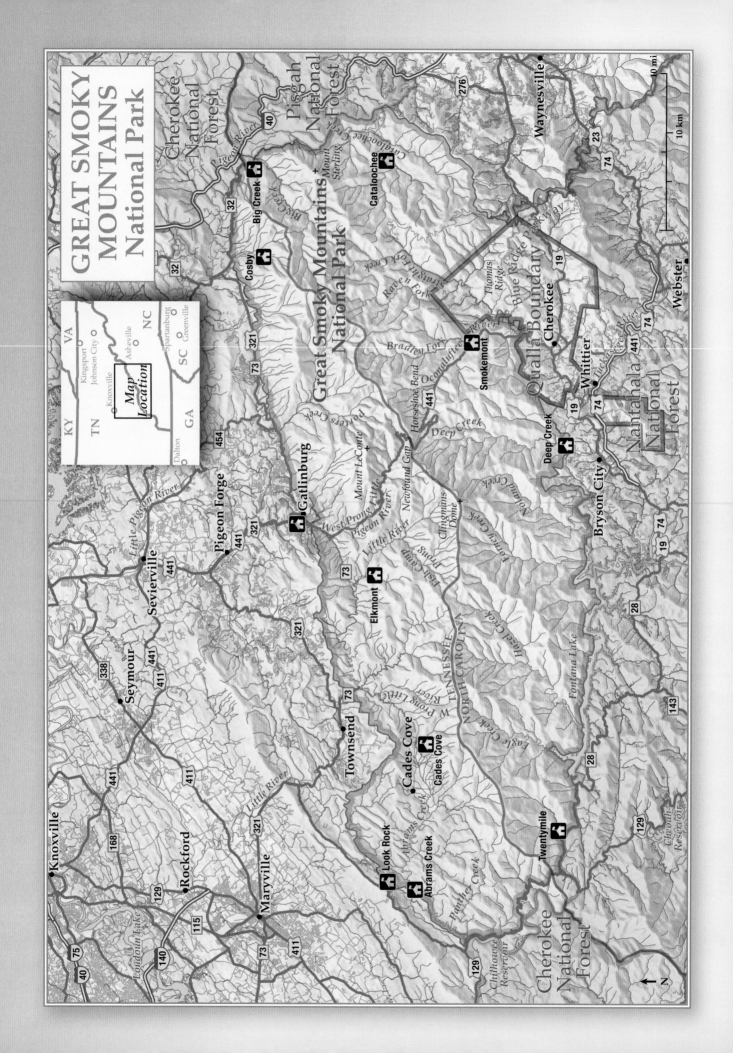

Great Smoky Mountains National Park

➤ **Location:** The Great Smoky Mountains National Park (GSMNP) is in the Southern Appalachian Mountains on the border between North Carolina and Tennessee, and only about an hour's drive from either Ashville, North Carolina or Knoxville, Tennessee. The closest international airport is located in Atlanta, Georgia which is about three hours to the south. Daily jet service is available to Ashville and Knoxville.

The Cherokee Indians were the original inhabitants of what is known today as the Great Smoky Mountain National Park. They settled the fertile river valleys and lived in peace with the European settlers until the early 1800s when gold was discovered in northern Georgia. Because of political pressure, President Andrew Jackson ordered the seizure of the land and the relocation of the Cherokees to the Oklahoma Territory.

A small group of Cherokees hid in the secluded caves of what is today the Great Smoky Mountain National Park, while another small group of Cherokees, known as the Oconaluftee Cherokees, were allowed to remain in the Oconaluftee Valley through a deal established by businessman William H. Thomas. This small group would eventually form what today is the Eastern Band of the Cherokee Nation, which resides in a territory in the western part of North Carolina called the Qualla Boundary. The Qualla Boundary joins the GSMNP on the North Carolina side of the park.

As the European settlers pushed west, they mainly settled in the fertile valleys and plains. Only a few hardy subsistence farmers pushed past what is today known as the GSMNP. However, in the late 19th century and early 20th century, the nation's growing consumption of wood brought the lumber companies and mills to the region. Between 1880 and 1934, when the park was officially established, more than one billion board feet of lumber had been harvested from the region.

Foggy morning in the Great Smoky Mountains. Kevin Howell

*Kevin Howell fishing little Catalochee Creek
in the Smoky Mountains. Kevin Howell*

Fishing has always been one of the major activities in the park, dating back to when the Cherokee who built weir dams to catch fish. The weirs were built to create V-shaped rock pilings in the river. Several families would work together to collect fish by chasing them downstream into the point of the V-shape. Some of the ancient weirs can be still be found in streams surrounding the park today.

The brook trout is the only native trout to the GSMNP. In elevations above 3,500 feet, brook trout have now been displaced by other fish species and degraded water. Rainbow trout were introduced to the region during the heavy logging of the early 20th century. Browns were also introduced in the region during the same period because they could withstand the warmer water temperature and degraded water conditions caused by widespread logging.

Today, fishing still plays a major role in the park, but plenty of other activities, such as hiking, bicycling, orienteering, bouldering, and waterfall tours, are just as common.

The Great Smoky Mountain National Park is a very rough and rugged park that encompasses more than 500,000 acres. Because of its location, visitors will encounter countless weather patterns—often in one day. The lowest elevation in the park is at 850 feet above sea level; the elevation rises rapidly to more than 6,300 feet. The park, for all intents and purposes, is a deciduous rainforest with the Newfound Gap mountain pass and Clingmans Dome receiving 80-100 or more inches of rainfall each year. Even though the park is open year-round, visitors will encounter road closures during the winter months because of snow- and ice-covered roads, especially on the higher peaks. Visitors should always carry a raincoat. Even in the summer months, hypothermia is a real possibility at higher elevations when unsuspecting visitors get caught in one of the daily thunderstorms. These storms can plummet mountaintop temperatures into the upper-40s, and can drop more than an inch of rain in a matter of minutes. Snowfall is a possibility nine months of the year in the higher elevations around Newfound Gap, Clingmans Dome and Mt. Sterling.

Anglers will find brook, rainbow, and brown trout in the park along with smallmouth and redeye bass. Also, anglers will encounter war paint shiners and other coarse fish native to the region. The park is home to about 13 drainage basins and supports hundreds of other minor streams. The park also borders Fontana, Cheoah and Chilhowee Reservoirs.

Anglers should always be vigilant of the water level and weather conditions. A cloud burst that occurs 30 miles upstream on the top of Clingmans Dome can come rushing downstream pushing a two-foot or taller vertical wall of water ahead of it. Unsuspecting anglers can be forced to the bank opposite their normal egress area and end up spending a cold, soggy night with the copperheads and elk while waiting for the waters to recede to a safe level to cross.

Anglers who are planning on camping in the backcountry sites will need reservations and should be mindful of closures as well, often due to rogue black bears. Campgrounds also operate on a reservation-only system, so plan your trip well in advance. During peak fall season, hotels, campgrounds, outfitters and other services will be booked months in advance as far away as Knoxville and Asheville.

Since space limitations of this chapter will not allow me to delve into the more than 700 miles of fishable water in the park in depth. I have chosen to focus the efforts on the more popular and larger drainages.

The Little River System is one of the larger drainages in the park. All three major tributaries offer fishing for rainbow, brook and brown trout. In the main stem—the main or primary river, not a tributary—anglers will also encounter smallmouth bass as far up the river as the Sinks, so named because of its bowl or sink shape. The river fishes well year-round. However, fishing during the summer months on the lower stretches is tough due to the brightly colored "bikini hatch," which occurs daily from around 12-5 p.m. During this time of the year, anglers should fish early or late in the day, or travel higher upstream to where the bikini hatch is not as strong.

Little River is home to the largest trout on the Tennessee side of the park. It is not uncommon for anglers to encounter 4-5-pound brown trout and rainbows that might reach 20 inches. However, Little River is crystal clear and heavily pressured, which will require anglers to use light tippets and cautious approaches.

Vanessa Rollins with a Catalochee Creek rainbow. Kevin Howell

A rainbow trout being released to fight another day. Kevin Howell

Facing. Bull elk feeding in Catalooche Valley in early fall. Kevin Howell

Abrams Creek offers anglers the chance to get away from the road and into the backcountry a little. To access Abrams Creek, fly fishers will need to travel the Cades Cove Loop Road. Be sure to note when the road opens and closes each day before heading to the stream. Anglers walking down the Abrams Falls Trail need to be wary of the Horse Shoe Bend, which offers great fishing, but will take the better part of eight to nine hours to fish completely around the bend. Because Abrams Creek travels a long distance underground through limestone caverns, there is no other way in or out. Once the creek resurfaces near the lower end of the cove, it offers excellent winter-time fishing because it is warmer than other surrounding waters in the park. Abrams Creek is home to some nice smallmouth bass from its mouth at Chillhowee Reservoir, and upstream to Abrams Falls.

Hazel Creek has long been touted as the best stream in the park. The stream is isolated from the majority of park visitors because the only access to the stream is to cross Fontana Reservoir by boat and then hike up the creek to one of the backcountry campsites. Even with its isolation from most park visitors, the stream does receive a considerable amount of fishing pressure. Anglers will encounter all three of the trout species in the creek as well as smallmouth bass and an occasional walleye in the extreme lower reaches of the stream. During the spring, you'll see great caddis fly hatches on Hazel Creek. The drainage has produced several local favorite flies, including the Texas Piss Ant and the Hazel Creek dry fly.

Deep Creek is one of three streams in the park that regularly produces large brown trout (trout that exceed 8 pounds). To access the stream, anglers will need to hike the Deep Creek trail, which is accessible from Deep Creek Campground or via the New Found Gap. I would highly suggest anglers use the lower access because the climb back up Thomas Ridge to Newfound Gap is relentless to those unaccustomed to steep climbs. Deep Creek offers all three trout species although the brook trout are more commonly located in the higher reaches and tributary streams. The lower mile of the stream adjacent to the Deep Creek Campground has an "inner tube hatch" that will rival any river in the world.

Oconaluftee River is second only to Little River when it comes to the largest park drainage. The river can be accessed via U.S. Route 441 for most of its length.

Oconaluftee is well-known for producing trophy trout. I have personally seen three trout weighing more than 10 pounds taken from the deep pools of the river. The river does receive a lot of fishing pressure because anglers can step out of

Below. Davidson River Outfitters guide Dave Bender looks on as Vanessa Rollins fishes the Oconaluftee River. Kevin Howell

Overlooking Deep Creek Valley from Clingman's Dome. Kevin Howell

their cars and right into the river. Bradley and Ravens Forks are large tributaries to the Oconaluftee, and are worthy of fishing in their own right.

There are countless other streams in the park that are well worth the fishing. An angler could literally spend a lifetime fishing the streams just inside the park boundaries. Yet anglers traveling to the area should also check out some of the other streams located in Pisgah and Nantahala National Forests. Anglers also shouldn't overlook streams that are accessible from the Blue Ridge Parkway, which connects the Great Smoky Mountain and Shenandoah National Parks.

Of all the streams in Pisgah and Nantahala National Forests, the Davidson, Nantahala, and Tuckasegee Rivers are the three most notable and historic fisheries in the area. All three of these streams and other surrounding streams are covered in detail in *50 Best Places Fly Fishing the Southeast* (Stonefly Press, 2016).

➤ **Hatches:**
Blue-winged Olive: November-March
Stoneflies: Warm days in November-February
Caddis: March-October
Golden stoneflies: May-July
Black and brown stoneflies: June and July (also after heavy summer thunderstorms)
Terrestrials: Late March to late October, depending on elevation
Dark mayflies: March to mid-April
Light mayflies: Mid-April to mid-June
Yellow Sallies: May-July (these may be Yellow or Chartreuse Green)
Midges: All year
Crayfish: All year

➤ Tackle and Gear

Rods and Line: 6-foot-6-inch to 9-foot rods are standard. Floating lines will range from a 3-weight for the small streams to 5- or 6-weight for the larger rivers. Anglers should avoid brightly colored fly lines such as orange and optic green. Anglers targeting bass might find a 7-weight rod to be a good choice.

Terminal Tackle and Flies: We recommend 9- to 12-foot leaders tapered from 4X to 6X for the larger rivers, and a 7- or 8-foot leader tapered to 5X for the smaller streams. Fluoro-carbon tippet is best unless you are fishing small dry flies. Anglers will find a lot of flies to be very successful, but the Green Weenie, (a.k.a. Green Inchworm) is a must-have fly for every angler venturing into the park. Other really popular flies are the Yallar (Yellow) Hammer, Kevin's Stonefly, and the invaluable Sheepfly.

Turkeys feeding in the fields of Catalochee Valley as fog rises from Mt. Sterling. Kevin Howell

CLOSEST CITY OR POINT OF ENTRANCE TO THE PARK

There are several entrances to the park, but most people enter through Cherokee, North Carolina or Gatlinburg, Tennessee.

CLOSEST AIRPORT

Asheville Regional or McGhee-Tyson Airport (Knoxville) are both are about an hour's drive from the park. Full car rental, hotel/motel, and travel services are available.

OPENING AND CLOSING OR FISHING DATES

· The park is open 24 hours a day, 365 days a year. However, some secondary roads, campgrounds, and other visitor facilities close in winter.
· Fishing is permitted year-round in the park, from 30 minutes before official sunrise to 30 minutes after official sunset.
· Fishing is allowed in all park streams.
· Anglers must possess a valid Tennessee or North Carolina fishing license. (Most anglers use a NC license because it is cheaper.)
· Limit is five brook, brown, rainbow trout, smallmouth bass—or any combination of the above.

FEES

Park entrance and user fees change periodically. For up-to-date fees, free days, and other exceptions, visit www.nps.gov/grsm/index.htm.

CLOSEST FLY SHOPS

Davidson River Outfitters
95 Pisgah Highway
Pisgah Forest, NC 28768
888-861-0111
www.davidsonflyfishing.com
info@davidsonflyfishing.com

Brookings
Chestnut Square Highway 64
Cashiers, NC 28717
828-743-3768
www.brookingsonline.com

Hunter Banks Fly Shop
29 Montford Avenue
Asheville, NC 28801
800-227-6732
www.hunterbanks.com

Little River Outfitters
7807 E. Lamar Alexander Parkway
Townsend, TN 37882
865- 448-9459
www.littleriveroutfitters.com

River's Edge Fly Shop
1235 Seven Clans Lane
Whittier, NC 28789
828-497-9300
www.riversedgeoutfittersnc.com

Curtis Wright Outfitters
5 All Souls Crescent
Asheville, NC
828-274-3471
www.curtiswrightoutfitters.com

3 Rivers Angler
5113 Kingston Pike
Knoxville, TN 37919
865-200-5271
www.3riversangler.com

Orvis Retail Store
136 Apple Valley Rd.
Sevierville, TN 37863
865-774-4162
www.orvis.com

The Smoky Mountain Angler
469 Brookside Village Way
Gatlinburg, TN 37738
865-436-8746
www.smokymountainangler.com

CLOSEST GUIDE SERVICES

Davidson River Outfitters
95 Pisgah Highway
Pisgah Forest, NC 28768
888-861-0111
www.davidsonflyfishing.com
info@davidsonflyfishing.com

Brookings
Chestnut Square Highway 64
Cashiers, NC 28717
828-743-3768
www.brookingsonline.com

Trout Zone Anglers
Crossville, TN
931-261-1884
www.troutzoneanglers.com
TroutZoneAnglers@gmail.com

The Smoky Mountain Angler
466 Brookside Village Way
Gatlinburg, TN 37738
865-436-8746
www.smokymountainangler.com

Fightmaster Fly Fisher
P.O. Box 4146
Maryville, TN 37802
865-607-2886
www.fightmasterflyfishing.com

Frontier Anglers
Maryville, Tennessee
865-719-0227
www.frontieranglerstn.com

R&R Fly Fishing
P.O. Box 60
Townsend, TN 37882
865-448-0467
www.randrflyfishing.com

CLOSEST OUTFITTER

Davidson River Outfitters
95 Pisgah Highway
Pisgah Forest, NC 28768
888-861-0111
www.davidsonflyfishing.com
info@davidsonflyfishing.com

Little River Outfitters
7807 E. Lamar Alexander Parkway
Townsend, TN 37882
865-448-9459
www.littleriveroutfitters.com

Brookings
Chestnut Square Highway 64
Cashiers, NC 28717
828-743-3768
www.brookingsonline.com

BEST PLACE TO STAY IN THE PARK

Mount Leconte Lodge is the only lodging inside the GSMNP. It is only accessible by hiking to the top of Mount Leconte, and is not recommended for those who are not in top physical condition.

Mount Leconte Lodge
865-429-5704
865-774-0045 FAX
www.lecontelodge.com
reservations@lecontelodge.com

KEVIN HOWELL is an author, lecturer, fly-fishing instructor, and guide. He is a member of the Sage Advisory Staff and an Umpqua Signature Fly Designer. Kevin is also the owner of Davidson River Outfitters in Pisgah Forest, North Carolina and is a partner in Andes Drifters in Argentina. Kevin has been guiding the waters of North Carolina, South Carolina, and East Tennessee for 25 years. His newest book, coauthored with Walker Parrett, is *50 Best Places Fly Fishing the Southeast* (Stonefly Press, 2016).

BEST PLACE TO STAY NEAR THE PARK
There are literally hundreds of hotels and cabins just outside of the park entrance, especially in Gatlinburg and Pigeon Forge, Tennessee.

Auntie Belham's Cabins
1024 Charlotte's Ct.
Pigeon Forge, TN 37863
865-436-6618
www.auntiebelhams.com/Gatlinburg

BEST CAMPGROUND IN THE PARK
Cades Cove Campground will give anglers access to both Abrams Creek and Little River with a short drive. All camping in the Smokies is by reservation only. Make reservations well in advance.

Cades Cove Campground
877-444-6777
www.recreation.gov
Open year-round
159 sites
Tents and RVs up to 35 feet

BEST CAMPGROUND NEAR THE PARK
Indian Creek Campground
1367 Bunches Creek Rd.
Cherokee, NC 28719
828-497-4361
www.indiancreekcampground.com

BEST PLACE TO EAT IN THE PARK
There are no dining options within the park boundaries.

BEST PLACE TO EAT NEAR THE PARK
There are hundreds of restaurants in every price category surrounding the park in Gatlinburg, Cherokee, and Pigeon Forge.

CLOSEST AND BEST PLACES TO GET A DRINK
Smoky Mountain Brewery
1004 Parkway #501
Gatlinburg, TN 37738
865-436-4200
www.smoky-mtn-brewery.com

MUST SEE
Cades Cove: Historic homes and churches, wildlife viewing, and mountain scenery make this a popular destination

NEAREST HOSPITAL/URGENT TREATMENT CENTER

North Carolina Side
Cherokee Indian Hospital
75 Paint Town Rd.
Cherokee, NC 28719
828-554-5550

Tennessee Side
LeConte Medical Center
742 Middle Creek Rd.
Sevierville, TN 37862
865-446-7000

CELL PHONE SERVICE
Cell service is not available save for a few fringe locations.

FOR ALL ELSE, VISIT
www.nps.gov/grsm/index.htm

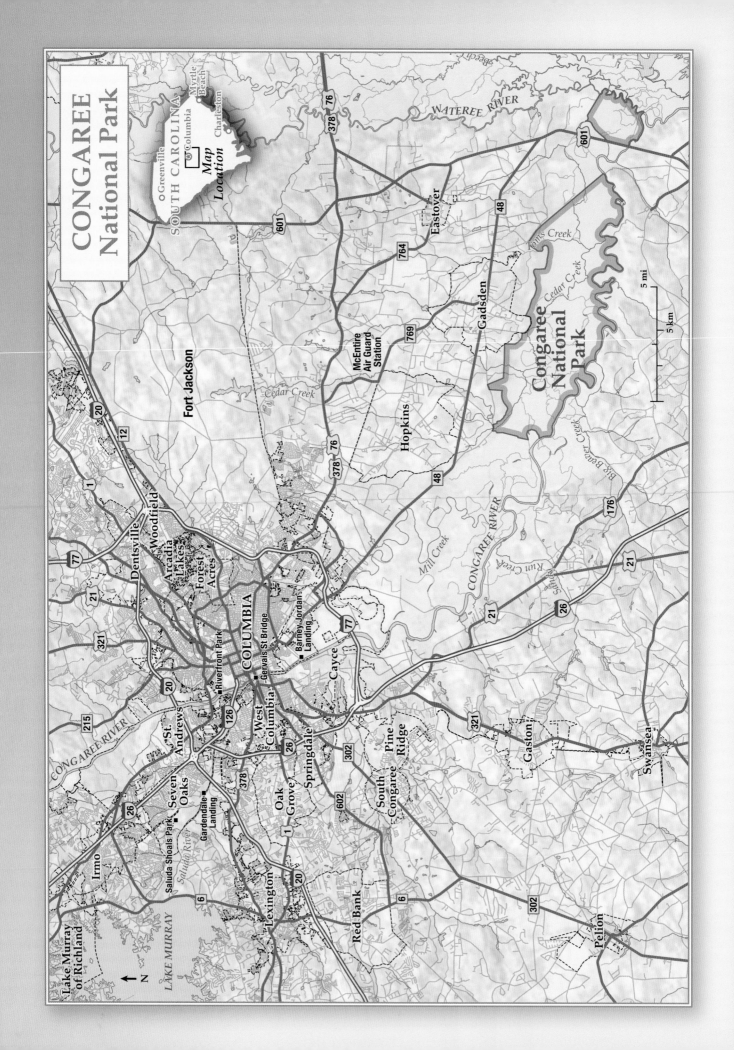

➤ **Location:** Congaree National Park was established in 2003, and is 20 minutes southeast of Columbia, South Carolina.

Saw palmetto, Spanish moss in the cypress, giant pines—all this set in a black water swamp. That's what you will find when you visit the Congaree National Park. Most people do not think of fly-fishing when they think of the area in and around the park, but one visit to the city of Columbia and you will find multiple opportunities for great warm and cold-water fishing. Few places in the world offer a year-round trout fishery lined with Spanish moss-laden hardwoods. Come summer, you'll find smallmouth and striped bass.

The park itself is a beautiful place. Both entry and camping is free with no advance reservations allowed at the two designated campgrounds—Longleaf and Bluff. All sites are first-come, first-served. No RV or car camping permitted—bring a tent.

Hiking is available on the boardwalk that circles through the swamp bottoms or on a few other trails that wind through the swamp. The Weston Lake Loop, part of the Boardwalk Trail, offers fishing opportunities for bass and bluegill. There is no fishing allowed from the overlook or within 100 feet of it.

Another great place to fish is in Cedar Creek. This is the park's paddling trail and is easily accessed via canoe or kayak. Bass and redbreast sunfish will readily take a popper or streamer. A popper/dropper rig is a big producer. Short rods in 3- to 7-weights paired with a floating line are recommended. The swamp is rarely deep enough for sinking lines, and the low-hanging branches make fly casting difficult as it is. Make sure to bring plenty of insect repellent because this is a swamp, and summer is mosquito season.

If you really want to spread your wings, head back to Columbia. The three rivers located in its heart offer world-class fishing that has been kept a secret for a long time.

The Saluda River—a tailwater—flows from the bottom of Lake Murray and offers a coldwater fishery unlike any other in the country.

The Broad River, flowing from the north is a smallmouth bass angler's dream. The Saluda and Broad rivers merge in Columbia to form the Congaree River.

The Congaree River flows easterly and forms the southern boundary of Congaree National Park. The Congaree boasts large numbers of small and largemouth bass. In the spring, stripers up to 40 pounds migrate to spawn in the upper stretches of the Congaree River before moving into the Saluda River for the summer.

Entrance to Congaree National Park. Jake Howard

➤ **Saluda River:** The Saluda River is a unique fishery and well worth your effort. The Saluda River is located about 30 minutes west of the park between the towns of Lexington and Irmo; it flows east from Lake Murray about 13 miles into Columbia. The cold water that comes from the bottom of the lake makes it a prime habitat for trout year-round.

Both browns and rainbows are stocked via helicopter and hatchery truck from December through March. The great news is that once stocked, the trout can grow as much as a half-inch per month. The water stays cold enough in the

Saluda River near Columbia, SC. Jake Howard

summer for the trout to survive, and holdovers up to 26 inches have been caught.

Recent relicensing of the dam has helped regulate flows and water temperature to even allow for limited reproduction by rainbow trout.

Insect life in this tailwater includes midges, caddis, little black stoneflies, Blue-winged Olives and larger mayflies such as cahills and drakes. A good fly selection would include Beaded Pheasant Tails, Hare's Ears and Adams in a variety of sizes. During the stocking period, San Juan worms, egg patterns and large natural or brightly colored nymphs and streamers are the desired patterns. Floating lines are the choice of most local fly-fishers. Rods ranging from 3- to 6-weights are recommended. Intermediate and sink tip lines can come in handy if you're fishing some of the slower and deeper sections of the river.

Five fish of any size may be kept, but only one over 16-inches is allowed.

As the temperatures rise at the end of May and early June, striped bass migrate into the Saluda after spawning in the Congaree River. This congregation of stripers is one of the largest on the east coast and boasts fish more than 40 pounds. They can be caught on most of the popular baitfish imitations such as Clousers, Zonkers, and Craft Fur Minnows, as well as larger musky and saltwater baitfish patterns. Fly rods from 8- to 10-weight with intermediate or sink tip lines are

recommended thanks to the size of fish possible and the size of the river and flies you plan to cast.

From June 1 to September 30, stripers are catch-and-release only. During the remainder of the year, three fish over 26 inches per day may be kept. In the Saluda, the stripers only summer there; fish do not arrive until late May and usually leave at the beginning of September, during the catch-and-release period.

Access is limited for wade fishing and is more accessible with a drift boat, canoe, or kayak. Some wading access is available at Saluda Shoals Park in Irmo. There is a $4 entry fee for the park. Here you will find a walking path and boat ramp in the park to allow easy access to the river. Three-and-a-half miles down you'll find Gardendale Landing, another primitive canoe/kayak takeout. An inflatable drift boat can be loaded and unloaded here with about a 50-yard portage to and from the river. Floating the river can be dangerous and flows over 3,000 cfs should be avoided. If wading, flows less than 1,000 cfs are recommended. All flow information can be found on the USGS water levels site.

➤ **Broad and Congaree Rivers:** The Broad River is a smallmouth bass anomaly with fast-growing fish up to 7-plus pounds. Flowing from Parr Reservoir 17 or more miles into Columbia from the north, the Broad River has extremely difficult access to the public. It would make a great overnight trip. Most day anglers fish from canoes fitted with trolling motors to bring them back upstream.

Other access is available in town at Riverfront Park and the River Walk. From here it is a 4- to 6-hour float into town, where boaters can take out at the Gervais Street Bridge via a primitive takeout or continue floating another 2.5 miles to Barney Jordan Landing. After passing under the Gervais Street Bridge, the Saluda and Broad Rivers merge to form the Congaree River. This entire stretch from the diversion canal dam to Barney Jordan is prime habitat for smallmouth, featuring rocky outcroppings and swift currents with pocket water that often holds bass. This is also the best place to access wade fishing from within the park. Outside the park, access is more readily available via city parks and other public accesses.

Equipment for this stretch depends on the target species. For smallmouth, a 5- to 7-weight will be enough to handle most of the flies you'll use. Clousers, Wooly Buggers, and most other crayfish and baitfish imitations will produce. Good colors include white, browns, olive or chartreuse. Floating lines will work fine most of the time, but deeper sections might require an intermediate or slow-sink tip line. If stripers are the target species then some of the same minnow patterns will work well on an 8- to 10-weight rod. Keep some larger saltwater pattern on hand because the larger flies will reduce the number of smaller fish caught.

The best time to fish for smallmouth begins in March and runs well into September. From March into June, the smallies key on shad, so you'll want to bring a selection of minnow patterns. As the dog days of summer approach, smallmouth start to key on crayfish, making buggers a go-to pattern.

Regulations for smallmouth and largemouth bass have a combined five-fish limit with a minimum length of 12 inches for smallmouth and 14 inches for largemouth. Stripers at least 26 inches in length can be kept from October 1 to May 31 with no more than three stripers per day. Targeting stripers is prohibited on the Congaree River from June 1 to September 30. Check striper fishing regulations on the SCDNR website because they change periodically.

➤ Tackle and Gear

Rods and Line: When fishing within the park, short, 3- to 7-weights with a floating line are recommended. In the Saluda, use floating lines and 3- to 6-weights rods. Intermediate and sink tip lines are good for slower and deeper parts of the river. In the Broad and Congaree Rivers, a 5- to 7-weight will be enough to handle most of the flies you'll use for smallmouth. Floating lines will work fine most of the time, but deeper sections may require an intermediate or slow sink tip line. If you're after stripers, you will want to pack an 8- to 10-weight rod with intermediate or sink-tip lines.

A rainbow from the Saluda River falls for a nymph. Jake Howard

Hayden Dale and a Saluda River rainbow. Jake Howard

Terminal Tackle and Flies: When fishing in the park, poppers and streamers, or a popper/dropper rig are good choices. Keep a good selection of white, brown, olive, or chartreuse Clousers, Wooly Buggers, and crayfish and baitfish imitations when fishing the Broad and Congaree Rivers. When plying the waters of the Saluda River, be sure to pack a selection of Beaded Pheasant Tails, Hare's Ears, and Adams in a variety of sizes. San Juan worms, egg patterns, and large natural or brightly colored nymphs and streamers are the ticket when fishing during the stocking period. Stripers will hit large baitfish imitations such as Clousers, Zonkers, Craft Fur Minnows, and larger musky and saltwater baitfish patterns.

Gorgeous brown trout from the Saluda River. Jake Howard   *Saluda River brown trout released. Photograph by Hayden Dale*

Garrett Jobsis with an average fly-rod striper in the Congaree River. Jake Howard

JAKE HOWARD began teaching himself the art of fly fishing when he was 12-year-old fly-fisher chasing trout on the Saluda River. After high school, he moved west to Colorado. There, he fished the Frying Pan, Blue, Colorado, and Arkansas Rivers. It was not long before he began guiding for a local shop, where he guided guests on upwards of 100 trips each season. While living in Summit County, Colorado, he spent nearly 300 days on the water each year. In 2003, Jake returned to South Carolina. Since then, he has become one of the top performers on the Team Stonefly Competitive Fly Fishing Roster, regularly competing against some of the top fishers in the world. Jake also works full-time at Barron's Outfitters in downtown Columbia, where he has built quite a reputation as the "go-to guy" for tips and gear recommendations for the area. In September 2013, he began a guide service—Saluda Valley Guides LLC—where he guides anglers on the waters he grew up fishing.

CLOSEST CITY OR POINT OF ENTRANCE TO THE PARK
Columbia, South Carolina

CLOSEST AIRPORT
Columbia Metropolitan Airport in Columbia, South Carolina, where full car rental and other transportation services are available.

OPEN/CLOSING PARK DATES OR FISHING
The park is open 24-hours-a-day, every day.
A valid South Carolina fishing license is required.
All South Carolina laws pertaining to licensing, size, and creel limits apply.

FEES
Park entrance and user fees change periodically. For up-to-date fees, free days and other exceptions, visit http://www.nps.gov/cong/index.htm.

CLOSEST FLY SHOPS
Barron's Outfitters
1725 Harden St.
Columbia, SC 29204
803-254-5537
www.barronsoutfitters.com
Note: Barron's is located in downtown Columbia, and offers a variety of services including rod and reel repair and gunsmithing, along with clothing and equipment.

CLOSEST GUIDE SERVICE
Saluda Valley Guides LLC
803-312-2435
www.saludavalleyguidesllc.weebly.com
Full- and half-day float trips are available on the Saluda, lower Broad, and upper Congaree Rivers. You may also take private casting lessons.

BARS AND RESTAURANTS
Saluda's
751 Saluda Ave.
Columbia, SC 29205
803-799-9500
www.saludas.com

Uncle Louie's
1125 Park St.
Columbia, SC 29201
803-933-9833

Carolina Ale House in the Vista
708 Lady St.
Columbia, SC 29201
803-227-7151

Blue Marlin
1200 Lincoln St.
Columbia, SC 29201
803-799-3838

Oyster Bar Columbia
1123 Park St.
Columbia, SC 29201
803-799-4484

Hunter-Gatherer Brewery and Ale House
900 Main St.
Columbia, SC 29201
803-748-0540

HOTELS
Clarion
1615 Gervais St.
Columbia, SC 29201
803-771-8711

Columbia Marriott
1200 Hampton St.
Columbia, SC 29201
803-771-7000

Sheraton
1400 Main St.
Columbia, SC 29201
803-988-1400

NEAREST HOSPITAL/URGENT CARE CENTER
Palmetto Health Richland
5 Medical Park Rd.
Columbia, SC 29203
803-434-7000
www.palmettohealth.org
(Recommended for emergency care)

Providence Hospital
2435 Forest Dr.
Columbia, SC 29204
803-256-5300
www.providencehospitals.com
(Numerous Providence Hospital and health care services are available throughout Columbia and the surrounding area.)

CELL PHONE SERVICE
Available everywhere

FOR ALL ELSE, VISIT
http://www.nps.gov/cong/index.htm

33

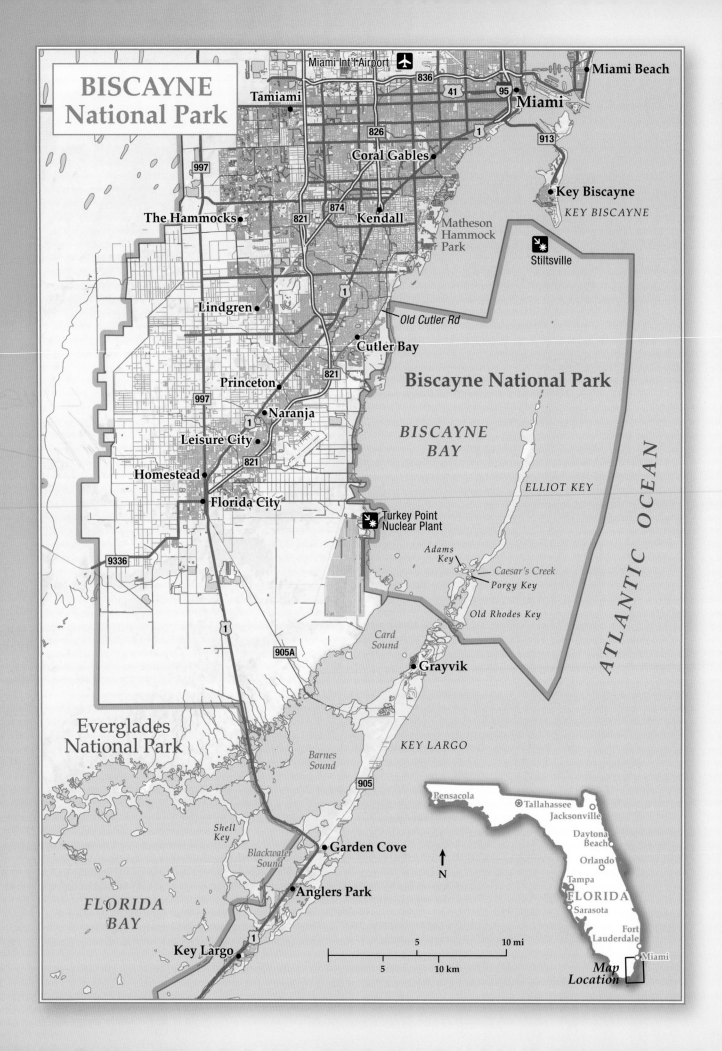

BISCAYNE National Park

Miami Int'l Airport

Miami Beach

Miami

Tamiami

836

41

95

826

1

913

Coral Gables

Key Biscayne

KEY BISCAYNE

997

874

The Hammocks

821

Kendall

Matheson Hammock Park

Stiltsville

Lindgren

Old Cutler Rd

Biscayne National Park

821

Cutler Bay

Princeton

997

821

BISCAYNE BAY

ELLIOT KEY

ATLANTIC OCEAN

1

Naranja

Leisure City

Homestead

821

Florida City

Turkey Point Nuclear Plant

Adams Key

Caesar's Creek

Porgy Key

Old Rhodes Key

9336

Card Sound

1

905A

Grayvik

Everglades National Park

Barnes Sound

KEY LARGO

905

Shell Key

Blackwater Sound

Garden Cove

Pensacola

Tallahassee

Jacksonville

↑
N

Daytona Beach

Orlando

Anglers Park

Tampa

FLORIDA

FLORIDA BAY

Sarasota

1

Key Largo

5   10 mi

5   10 km

Fort Lauderdale

Miami

Map Location

Biscayne National Park

➤ **Location:** The southeast Florida area now known as Biscayne National Park was explored by Spanish explorers as early as 1513. Spanish treasure fleets regularly sailed past the islands now known as the Florida Keys and were often caught in hurricanes. There are 44 documented ship wrecks from the 16th through the 20th centuries in the park.

Following a protracted battle between developers and conservationists over subdivisions and resorts, President Lyndon Johnson declared Biscayne Bay a national monument in 1968. Biscayne National Park came into existence in 1980. Biscayne is a 45-minute drive from Miami, two hours from Naples, and four hours from Orlando. The park is bordered on the north by Key Biscayne, and by Key Largo on the south. The park encompasses 172,924 acres with only five percent of it being land.

In the early 19th century, the first settlements were small farms growing key limes and pineapples. A farmer named Lancelot Jones lived on Porgy Key and traded a farming life to become one of the first bonefish guides at the Cocolobo Club on Adams Key (now the ranger station). In 1932, the settlement of Stiltsville was built on the flats in the north end of the bay. In its heyday, there were 27 structures on stilts. In 1992, Hurricane Andrew destroyed most of the remaining structures.

Biscayne Bay shines like a turquoise jewel sitting at the doorstep of Miami. Visitors to the park can enjoy a multitude of water-related activities, including fishing, scuba diving, snorkeling, sailing, wind surfing, kite boarding and bird watching. For those who don't want to get wet, there's a hiking trail on Elliot Key.

Most of the park is accessible only by boat. Boaters can launch at one of five public marinas run by Miami-Dade County. Boaters can either pay a daily launch fee of $16 or buy an annual pass for $173.50. Anglers wishing to wade from shore can gain access to bonefish flats at Matheson Hammock Park on Old Cutler Road. It would be in the best interest of first-time visitors to hire a professional guide. The complex relationship of tides and fish can leave a first-timer bewildered and discouraged—or worse!

The species that can be targeted in Biscayne is almost endless, with the most sought after being The Big Three:

· Tarpon
· Bonefish
· Permit

Tarpon begin to show around the downtown skyline of Miami in the winter. Cold fronts in the north push tarpon down the Florida coast and into the greater Miami area. These fish take up residence along the beaches and bridge channels. The outgoing tides in the evenings often carry loads of

Legendary Captain Bill Curtis spent so much time on this flat outside Broad Creek fishing for tarpon that local anglers now call it "Curtis Point." Pat Ford

shrimp out of the bay and the silver kings are there to take advantage of the buffet. Anglers position themselves along the shadow lines of the bridges to get shots at cruising and busting fish. Fly rods from 8- to 12-weight are common, with a 10-weight or bigger being the best choice. Fish exceeding 100 pounds are always a possibility. Floating lines are a good choice when the fish are high in the water column. An intermediate or sink tip line can be used to dredge fish that are laying deeper in the current.

Mid-April kicks off consistent sight-fishing for migratory tarpon swimming the entire length of the Florida Keys. Great sight-fishing spots abound on the ocean side flats of Biscayne. Anglers pole or stake out on points to ambush swimming fish.

Captain Bob Branham is on the pole while Tony Nobregas is making the cast. Pat Ford

These fish get plenty of flies thrown their way, and over the years fly patterns have become smaller. Many anglers scale down their bite tippet to 40-pounds to get bites in calm, clear conditions. These tarpon average 60- to 80-pounds, with plenty of fish well over 100 pounds taken each season.

When it comes to fly rods, 11- and 12-weights are the weapon of choice. The new clear floating lines give anglers the ability to present flies to multiple fish in a school without spooking them.

Summer and fall finds smaller resident fish along the bay's islands and mangrove shorelines. High water temperatures often cause oxygen levels in the water to deplete overnight. When this happens, tarpon will be found on these calm mornings gulping air and blasting shrimp on the surface! Topwater flies such as Gurgler patterns draw violent strikes. You'll want 8- to 10-weight rods and floating lines.

Biscayne Bay is a worldwide destination for anglers looking to catch double-digit bonefish. Fish can be caught year round in Biscayne, with the peak season being March through

October. Anglers should not expect to post high catch numbers, but you have a shot at quality fish averaging 7 pounds or more.

Larger flies in natural shrimp and crab patterns work well in Biscayne. Anglers will have many different shot scenarios from tailing fish to "mudders" in three feet of water. Flies with bead chain to heavy dumbbell eyes should be carried. Rods from 7- to 10-weight coupled with floating lines will cover most fishing situations.

Permit fishing in Biscayne Bay can be stellar. If the weather cooperates, February and March can be a great time to take permit. In late April, the majority of the fish head offshore to spawn, returning to the flats in early June. The summer months offer great fishing until the water cools with the first cold fronts. Biscayne Bay is loaded with small strip banks with great current flow.

Permit cruise the edges of these bars and push up on the crowns to feed. Crab flies with heavy lead eyes are ideal for these situations. Often, schools of smaller permit are encountered swimming close to the surface. Shrimp-style patterns thrown tight to the school and quickly stripped away often elicit jack-like bites. On slick, calm days, permit like to float on the surface. A floating crab drifted in the current will do the trick for these fish. Fly rods in 8- to 10-weight with floating lines are the ticket.

The north end of the bay has numerous channels connecting the bay and ocean. Anglers who just want to bend a rod can have great action in these channels. Yellow jacks, jack crevalle, blue runners, cobia, barracuda, many species of snapper and grouper, pompano, and Spanish mackerel can be caught. The typical drill is to anchor the skiff and chum with live bait or frozen block chum. Your best bet is to use 8- and 9-weight rods with intermediate sinking lines. Clouser minnows and baitfish flies are a great choice.

Shark fishing is always a fun thing to do. Biscayne Bay is home to numerous lemon, blacktip, spinner and bull sharks. The first order of business is to catch a barracuda for chum. You then partially fillet the 'cuda and hang it off the side of the boat. Setting up a drift along the edge of a flat with the wind against the current is the ideal situation. Any sharks in the area will smell your chum and rush the boat. A big, bright-colored fly cast in front of the shark can draw a strike.

Depending on the size of the fish, 9- to 12-weight rods with floating lines are recommended.

East of the park boundary lies some spectacular offshore fly fishing. Sailfish, wahoo, blackfin tuna and mahi-mahi (a.k.a. dorado or dolphinfish) can be targeted. Bait-and-switch trolling and live bait chumming works well. Floating or sinking lines are used with 10- to 12-weight rods.

In all cases, you'll need reels that are saltwater anodized with suitable drag and plenty of backing capacity.

➤ Tackle and Gear

Rods and Lines: If tarpon are your quarry, you'll want to arm up with a 10-weight or bigger rod. Pack both floating lines (for shallower fish) and intermediate or sink-tip lines for deeper fish. Using 40-pound bite tippet helps stir strikes in calm, clear conditions, while clear floating lines are great for dropping flies without spooking the fish. When fishing for other species, such as yellow jacks, jack crevalle, blue runners, barracuda, snappers, groupers, pompanos, and Spanish mackerels, 8- and 9-weight rods with intermediate sinking lines are a good choice. When shark fishing, 9- to 12-weight rods with floating lines are the best choice. In all cases, you'll

This school of tarpon is heading south just off Elliot Key. Pat Ford

need reels that are saltwater anodized with suitable drag and plenty of backing capacity. If sailfish, wahoo, blackfin tuna and dorado are on your hit list, make sure you're using 10- to 12-weight rods with sinking lines.

Terminal Tackle and Flies: When targeting tarpon, use topwater flies such as Gurgler patterns to elicit vicious strikes. Larger natural shrimp and crab patterns work well, too. Be sure to pack flies with bead chain to heavy dumbbell eyes. When fishing for permit, pack crab flies with heavy lead eyes and shrimp-style patterns. Floating crab patterns are great for permit that are floating on the surface. Clouser minnows and baitfish flies are great flies for fish such as yellow jacks, jack crevalle, blue runners, barracuda and snappers. When shark fishing, chuck large, brightly colored flies.

Above. There are still double digit bonefish around. Pat Ford

Left. Giant tarpon migrate down Florida's east coast from April through June on their way to the Keys. Pat Ford

Facing. CNN meteorologist Jennifer Gray shows off a 10-pound bonefish on the outside of Sands Key. Pat Ford

Sunrise on the flats—perfect time for tarpon. Pat Ford

It is amazing how many permit there are in the park during the summer months. Pat Ford

CAPTAIN ANDY THOMPSON grew up in Homestead, Florida where he developed a passion for fishing. Andy spent countless hours of his childhood with his father and friends exploring every creek and bay in south Florida that holds a fish. In 1995, Andy took his first paying customer and quickly developed a reputation of being a patient, hard-working guide. Andy has been very successful in Florida Keys tournaments and has put together an impressive tournament resume. Andy has been featured in numerous nationally televised fishing shows with hosts Bill Dance, Mark Sosin, and other notable celebrity anglers.

CLOSEST CITY OR POINT OF ENTRANCE TO THE PARK
Homestead, Florida

CLOSEST AIRPORT
Miami International Airport—Full transportation and rental car services are available.

FEES
Park entrance and user fees change periodically. For up-to-date fees, free days and other exceptions, visit http://www.nps.gov/bisc/index.htm.

CLOSEST FLY SHOPS
Fly Shop of Miami
8243 S. Dixie Hwy
Miami, FL 33143
305-669-5851
www.flyshopofmiami.com
theflyshop02@bellsouth.net

CLOSEST GUIDE SERVICES
Captain Andy Thompson
Salt Air Outfitters
786-473-3185
www.saltairoutfitters.com
skiffguide1@yahoo.com

Captain Bob Brahnam
South Florida Flats Fishing
10206 NW 6th Ct.
Plantation, FL 33324
954-370-1999
www.southfloridaflatsfishing.com
phishpeople199@aol.com

Captain Carl Ball
4000 Crandon Blvd.
Key Biscayne, FL 33149
and 1784 SE 15th Street

Fort Lauderdale, FL 33316
954-383-0145
www.awolfishingguide.com
CaptBall@bellsouth.net

Captain Joe Rodriguez
www.captjoerodriguez.com

CLOSEST LODGING
Check with your guide for preferred closest lodging.
Hampton Inn
2855 NE Ninth St.
Homestead, FL 33033
305-257-7000
www.homesteadhamptoninn.com

CLOSEST CAMPGROUND
Long Pine Key Campground
Everglades National Park
40001 Florida 9336
Homestead, FL 33034
305-242-7700
www.nps.gov

BEST PLACES TO EAT
Capri Restaurant
935 N. Krome Ave.
Florida City, FL 33034
305-247-1544
www.dinecapri.com
thecapri@bellsouth.net

Casita Tejas
27 N. Krome Ave.
Homestead, FL 33030
305-248-8224
(Mexican)

Alabama Jack's
58000 Card Sound Rd
Key Largo, FL 33037
305-248-8741
(Great conch fritter and cold beer)

Black Point Ocean Grill
24775 SW 87th Ave.
Cutler Bay, FL 33032
305-258-3918

FISHING REGULATIONS
· Fishing is permitted all year.
· Park regulations are available at www.myfwc.com.
· Entry into Biscayne National Park is free.
· The cost to launch a vessel at the Dade County public boat ramps is $16.
· A Florida saltwater license is required if you are fishing on your own. The license can be purchased online at www.myfwc.com.
· Jet skis and Wave Runners are prohibited in Biscayne National Park.

MUST SEE
Old Lancelot Homestead in Caesar's Creek Lighthouse at Boca Chica Key

CLOSEST MEDICAL SERVICES
Homestead Hospital
975 Baptist Way
Homestead, FL 33033
786-243-8505
www.baptisthealth.net
For additional information and emergency care facilities visit https://baptisthealth.net/en/pages/home.aspx.

CELL PHONE SERVICE
Cell service is spotty or nonexistent throughout the park.

FOR ALL ELSE, VISIT
http://www.nps.gov/bisc/index.htm

41

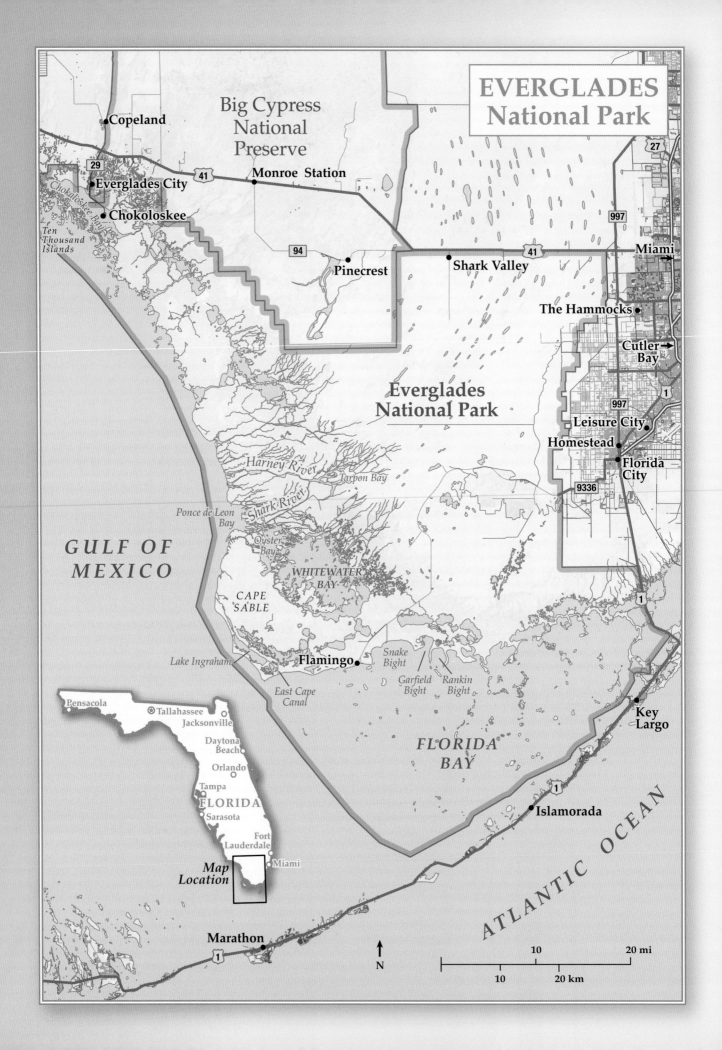

EVERGLADES National Park

Copeland

Big Cypress National Preserve

29

Everglades City

Chokoloskee

Chokaloskee Bay

Ten Thousand Islands

Monroe Station

41

94

Pinecrest

Shark Valley

41

Miami →

27

997

The Hammocks

Cutler Bay →

997

Leisure City

Homestead

Florida City

1

9336

Everglades National Park

Harney River

Tarpon Bay

Shark River

Ponce de Leon Bay

Oyster Bay

WHITEWATER BAY

CAPE SABLE

GULF OF MEXICO

Lake Ingraham

East Cape Canal

Flamingo

Snake Bight

Garfield Bight

Rankin Bight

Key Largo

FLORIDA BAY

Pensacola

Tallahassee

Jacksonville

Daytona Beach

Orlando

Tampa

FLORIDA

Sarasota

Fort Lauderdale

Miami

Map Location

Islamorada

1

ATLANTIC OCEAN

Marathon

1

N

10   20 mi

10   20 km

➤ **Location:** There are only two ways to access park waters by car—on the west coast at Everglades City, and through the park's main entrance in Florida City. The Florida City entrance includes a 38-mile trek from the park entrance to Flamingo's boat ramps. Some might call Flamingo a mini-town, but it's really just a ranger station with a general store, a gas station, and a few park offices and campgrounds. If you are in the Keys, it's about a 25-mile run across Florida Bay to Flamingo, with plenty of fishing available before you get there.

Everglades National Park was established in 1934 to protect the quickly vanishing Everglades. The park covers 1,509,000 acres at an elevation of 0- to 8-feet above sea level.

President George H. W. Bush signed the Everglades National Park Protection and Expansion Act in 1989 that added 109,506 acres to the eastern side of the park, closed the park to airboats, and directed the Department of the Army to restore water to improve the ecosystems within Everglades National Park.

There are a number of ways to fish the park, but they all require a boat and a guide. From Everglades City, you fish the area known as Ten Thousand Islands. Traveling down the west coast, you enter the most productive waters through bays and rivers, which snake inland through an endless maze of mangrove islands, oyster bars and creeks. Most days you will never see another boat once you leave the Gulf, and every turn looks the same as the last. Without an experienced guide, there is no way you can fish this area safely or effectively. There are thousands of shorelines, flats, channels, lakes, bays and oyster bars—some of which hold fish while others are as barren as the Sahara. The trick is knowing the difference (and knowing how to get home)!

When fishing from Flamingo, your best bet is start from Miami around 4:30 a.m. so you can be leaving the dock just as the first traces of gray pierce the black veil of the night. Within minutes, you will be able to see the markers as the pinks of dawn creep over the eastern horizon.

To the east of Flamingo are miles and miles of flats known as Snake, Garfield and Rankin Bights. In certain spots, there are patches of deeper water that will allow a flats skiff access to shorelines where small tarpon feast on shrimp and glass minnows at daylight. This is spectacular fishing. You can see pods of tarpon from 5- to 30-pounds busting bait or gulping air. They will pounce on a properly placed shrimp imitation, cast on an 8- or 9-weight rod. At times, snook and redfish will join the fun, but at daylight, tarpon are the prime target.

However, the trick to tarpon fishing is finding them. Sometimes they are simply not where they are supposed to be. Often, they are visible in areas that are simply too shallow

World record holders Marty and Martini Arostegui with a nice tripletail taken on one of the park's boundary markers. Pat Ford

to be accessible to a standard flats skiff. Many of the guides actually have johnboats for fishing Snake Bight and its shorelines, but you still have to know where to go and what the tide is doing. There are many places that you can get into on a high tide, but you will be stranded there for a few hours until the tide recedes.

Leaving Flamingo at sunrise can make your day even before you start fishing. Pat Ford

When the sun clears the horizon, the tarpon disappear—at least the small ones do. Everyone has an opinion on where they go, but most agree that the "daylight bite" is over by 8 a.m. That means your attention should shift away from the shorelines and onto the flats themselves. Most of the vast area east of Flamingo is very shallow, with acres of turtle grass thriving in a mud bottom. If you were to step out of the boat, you would sink up to your waist instantly. However, the redfish, sea trout and snook don't care. They work their way onto the flats with the incoming tide foraging for shrimp, crabs and baitfish such as pilchards and mullet. The redfish can be spotted tailing while the snook and trout are usually lying in potholes or cruising around the open areas. Both species readily hit a well-placed weedless fly, but the cast has to be perfect. Too far away and they won't see it; too close and they will spook.

Some days, the redfish will race over to where they heard the fly land and suck in anything that moves. On other days, you won't be able to rent a strike. Years ago, the flats were more consistent, but recent fishing pressure, moon phases, salinity changes, and God knows what else have made the eastern bights run hot and cold. Fortunately, this is only one stop on a long list of special places.

South of Flamingo lies Florida Bay—one of the best shallow-water fisheries in the world. Florida Bay is a complex maze of channels and flats, making it a dangerous place to navigate in any vessel. However, Keys guides know it like their backyards. On the surface, the area seems endless, but you can go from 6 feet to 6 inches of water in a microsecond. At cruising speed, you can find yourself high and dry in no time at all. The Islamorada guides fish this area on a daily basis and are a necessary investment.

Florida Bay holds its share of redfish and snook, but also has its own bonefish, shark and tarpon populations. As you move further south from Flamingo, you will encounter more bonefish; unlike the giant "downtown" Islamorada bones, these guys will actually eat a fly if they see it before they see you.

Early in the season, tarpon appear in the park when water temperatures reach 72 degrees. Initially, they can be found at the river mouths all along the west coast, as well as the inland bays. The north launching ramp at Flamingo leads directly into the backcountry. Many feel that the shallow inland bays warm up faster due to the runoff from the shallower inland areas of the Everglades and their mud bottoms, which absorb the sun's warmth quicker and hold it longer. Whatever the reason, in February and March, tarpon can usually be found north of Flamingo in areas such as Whitewater Bay. These early season fish are huge—consistently more than 100 pounds, and sometimes topping 150.

Right. Tarpon in the Whitewater Bay area of the park take on a brownish coloring due to the tannic water. Pat Ford

Below. Most everyone who fly fishes the Everglades releases their catch. Pat Ford

During the winter months, thousands of white pelicans flock to the park...sometimes with a chaperone. Pat Ford

If warm weather sticks around for a few days after mid-February and the tarpon show up in Whitewater Bay, you can be pretty confident that you will also find them in Florida Bay. There is nothing better on a fly rod than a 6-foot Florida Bay tarpon. They arrive in good numbers in April and stay through July. The earlier in the season, the more susceptible they are to weather changes and drops in temperatures, but if conditions are right and you can find them cruising the edges of the flats or up along shorelines, you are in for the thrill of a fly-rod lifetime. These fish will eat! You might only get a half dozen shots a day, but if you put the fly in the right spot, you're gonna get bit. On the Atlantic side of the Keys, you can cast to one thousand fish in a day and never put one in the air.

If you launch out of Flamingo, you can also run to the west toward and into the Gulf of Mexico. The shorelines just west of the harbor hold snook, redfish, tarpon, tripletail, ladyfish, jacks, trout and sharks. When you reach East Cape Canal, you can head north to Ingraham Lake, which is a fishery all to itself.

It is a huge lake with one narrow channel running down its middle. On either side, you will find mud flats that are totally exposed at low tide. There are a few almost invisible gullies that a skilled guide can use to creep into patches of deeper water along the shorelines. However, one small error

in judgment could leave you stranded for quite some time. There is no getting out of the boat to push in Ingraham Lake. However, if you can stay afloat, you'll find reds, snook, and, at times, some monster tarpon. The creeks running into the canal and Ingraham Lake are also home to the largest population of crocodiles in Florida.

If you were to continue west past East Cape Canal, you will find that the southwestern tip of the Florida peninsula is quite charming. The coastal vegetation has been decimated by several hurricanes over the last decade, and there are about 100 yards of dead trees between the pristine beach and the normal Everglades forests. Campers pitch tents on the beaches during the winter months when the insect count is reasonably low, but as the temperatures rise, snook can be found cruising the beaches early in the morning, driving schools of baitfish right up onto the sand. It's a real challenge to get your fly into the school of skipping baitfish, but when you do, a strike is pretty much guaranteed. These west coast snook can run up to 20 pounds, but the real prize during the spring months are the tarpon.

From late April thru June, pods of 50- to 150-pound tarpon enter Florida Bay and also cruise up and down the west coast of the park. Along the Gulf, they can be found rolling in the bays and river mouths. However, for reasons unknown, they move more slowly—just under or even at the surface. In some areas, the water is clear enough to spot them, but more often you will see a fish roll in the distance and be forced to watch for wakes or fins to know when it gets into casting range. The schools move slowly several hundred yards off the beach, and the key is to discern the depth and direction that they are traveling on that particular day. During the "Big Three" tarpon tournaments, you will see guide boats from Islamorada lined up along the west coast of Everglades National Park as far north as the Harney River.

There is something to fish for in the park year-round, but the prime season is April through November. Even though temperatures can get pretty high in July and August, it doesn't dampen the fishing. Tarpon, redfish and snook thrive in water temperatures that would boil a bonefish. It always helps to be on the water at first light. If daybreak brings warm temps, calm water, plenty of sweat, and clouds of mosquitoes that are forcing you to spray on insect repellant, just relax—those conditions are perfect. It does pay to get out of the vehicle and into a moving boat as quickly as possible, however, and you never want to be in a vessel that can't move faster than mosquitoes can fly.

On a normal spring, I'll carry three fly rods—all with weight-forward floating lines. I prefer

· A 9-weight for baby tarpon and the shallow flats
· A 10-weight for casting the bigger flies
· A 12-weight for the big tarpon

Even if you're flats fishing in the middle of Ingraham Lake or Snake Bight, there's a chance that you will run into a 100-pound tarpon. There is also a healthy supply of sharks throughout the park's shallows, and when all else fails they can be lured into casting range by chumming with a stringer of sliced-up ladyfish or jacks. Sharks strike a big orange fly and provide an exhilarating fight on fly tackle. You don't want to tangle with one over 5-feet on anything less than a 12-weight. A shock tippet of 45-pound steel or piano wire is all you need to win the battle, just don't count on the guide getting your fly back for you.

Shark fishing can be exceptional in February, March and April when the huge females move onto the flats to spawn. You can count on finding lemons and bulls way up on the flats and blacktips, tigers and hammerheads in the channels. Your reel will need to have a first-class drag and at least 300

yards of 50-pound braid backing—exactly the same outfit that you would use for tarpon. Small sharks are everywhere and they make excellent casting targets, but they will rarely take a fly unless it is placed directly in front of their nose. It really is necessary to have some scent in the water to fire up the sharks, but it's something you definitely should try before leaving park waters.

During the winter months, it can get chilly running around park waters before the sun comes up, but most of the time conditions will warm up nicely. In late spring and summer, you will need light weight "flats" clothing: long pants and long sleeve shirt, polarized sun glasses, a wide-brimmed hat and

There are few places in the park to wade fish. In most spots, you will sink to your waist in mud. Pat Ford

lots of serious sun screen. A Buff face mask and sun gloves are also very helpful. If you have never experienced the tropical sun, you are in for a shock—one hour of overexposure can ruin an entire trip. You cannot be too careful with the sun, and be sure to drink lots of water throughout the day. If you're on a three-day trip, you want to be able to fish all three days.

To find a guide to fish the park, do a web search for "Everglades National Park fly-fishing" or call The Fly Shop of Miami (305-669-5851) or Florida Keys Outfitters in Islamorada (305-664-5423), or go to Chokoloskeecharters.com for fishing the Ten Thousand Islands area.

To fish out of Flamingo, stay in Homestead. However, Islamorada is much more scenic, and it takes about the same amount of time to get to the fishy waters—you're just traveling by boat rather than car. To fish the Ten Thousand Islands, stay in Everglades City. However, your guide will be able to set you up with accommodations.

Dr. Deborah Longwill shows off a nice Everglades sea trout. Pat Ford

If I could only bring one fly into Everglades National Park it would be shrimpy and weedless. Pat Ford

➤ **Tackle and Gear**

Rods and Line: The best all-around rod for fishing the Florida Bay/Flamingo flats is a 9-weight rod with a weight-forward floating line, a 10- to 12-foot leader and a weedless fly unless you are after the big tarpon or sharks. If sharks are your target, don't use anything less than a 12-weight with a shock tippet of 45-pound steel or piano wire. Your reel should have a first-class drag and at least 300 yards of 50-pound braid backing (which is the same rig you'd use for tarpon).

Terminal Tackle and Flies: Guides all have their "tricks" to tame tarpon, bonefish and permit based on years of experience, the time of year, color of the bottom, and the feed that the game fish are focused upon. Before investing in typically expensive flats fly patterns, check with your chosen guide for recommendations.

In general, however, you'll be using the following:

Bonefish—Crazy Charlie, white, pink, tan and chartreuse, 4-8; Blind Charlie, same colors and sizes; Gotcha, same colors and sizes plus pearl; Clouser Minnows, same colors and sizes.

Sunset in the park. Pat Ford

Permit—Bauer's Flats Crab, olive and tan, 4-6; Money Crab, same colors and sizes; Permit Crab, 2-6, variety of colors light to darker; Zonker Shrimp, 4 to 8, pink, tan and white.

Tarpon—Deceiver, 4/0, 2/0, 2, black; Cockroach, 1/0, 3/0; Deer Hair Deceiver, 1/0; squid patterns in pink, white, tan, brown, 3/0; Whistler or Whizzer patterns in black or red/black.

Shark—Squid, pink or orange, 3/0 or larger.

Capt. Richard Black puts his angler on a nice redfish in Snake Bight. Pat Ford

Everglades National Park is one of the few places you can regularly come across the American Crocodile. Pat Ford

CLOSEST CITY OR POINT OF
ENTRANCE TO THE PARK
· Homestead, Florida (for fishing out of Flamingo)
· Everglades City, Florida (for fishing the Ten Thousand Islands)

CLOSEST AIRPORT
Miami International Airport
2100 NW 42nd Ave.
Miami, FL 33126
Full transportation and rental car services are available.

OPENING/CLOSING PARK DATES
OR FISHING DATES
Everglades National Park is open 365 days a year. Park entrance and user fees change periodically. For up-to-date fees, free days, and other exceptions, visit http://www.nps.gov/ever/index.htm.

FISHING PERMITS
· A separate park fishing license is required.
· If you fish with a guide, he or she will be permitted by the park as a licensed guide and will have a blanket license that covers all anglers.
· If you fish on your own, you will need a fishing license issued by the State of Florida, which may be purchased at www.myfwc.com. Fishing regulations can be obtained at the park entrance.

CLOSEST FLY SHOPS
Fly Shop of Miami
8243 S. Dixie Hwy.
Miami, FL 33143
305-669-5851
www.flyshopofmiami.com
theflyshop02@bellsouth.net

LOCAL GUIDES
Captain Andy Thompson
Salt Air Outfitters
786-473-3185
www.saltairoutfitters.com
skiffguide1@yahoo.com

Captain Eric Herstedt
www.tarponfly.com/
capterichersted@bellsouth.net
954-592-1228

Captain Rick Murphy
www.sportsmansadventures.com/
rick@captainrickmurphy.com

CLOSEST LODGING
Check with your guide for preferred closest lodging.

Hampton Inn
2855 NE Ninth St.
Homestead, FL 33033
305-257-7000
www.homesteadhamptoninn.com

PAT FORD grew up in the New York-New Jersey area, fishing for most anything he could find. His talent for sports photography became apparent during his years as a journalism major at Notre Dame. He wrote his first article for *Salt Water Sportsman* magazine in 1969, and has continued to provide stories and photos to literally every sportfishing publication ever since. Over the years, Pat has held more than two dozen IGFA World Records, and for a decade, he was the chairman of the Golden Fly Invitational Tarpon Tournament, which is held annually in Islamorada. He is a Founding Member of the Bonefish Tarpon Trust and is a member of the Board of Trustees of the American Museum of Fly Fishing in Vermont. Now, as a retired Miami trial attorney, he is the author of *The Best Fly Fishing Trips Money Can Buy* (Stackpole, 2006); and *Fly Fishing Daydreams* (Skyhorse, 2011). Pat's tarpon photography is displayed in Andy Mill's *A Passion for Tarpon* (Wild River Press, 2010). To see more of Pat's work, view his website: www.patfordphotos.com.

BEST CAMPGROUNDS
IN THE PARK
Flamingo Campgrounds in Long Pine Key has tent sites and RV hook-ups.

BEST PLACES TO EAT AND DRINK
Capri Restaurant
935 N. Krome Ave.
Florida City, FL 33034
305-247-1544
www.dinecapri.com
thecapri@bellsouth.net

Casita Tejas
27 N. Krome Ave.
Homestead, FL 33030
305-248-8224
(Mexican)

Alabama Jack's
58000 Card Sound Rd.
Key Largo, FL 33037
305-248-8741
(Great conch fritter and cold beer)

Black Point Ocean Grill
24775 SW 87th Ave.
Cutler Bay, FL 33032
305- 258-3918

MUST SEE
Old distillery in Shark River and the beaches of Cape Sable

CLOSEST MEDICAL SERVICES
Homestead Hospital
975 Baptist Way
Homestead, FL 33033
786-243-8505
www.baptisthealth.net

For additional information and emergency care facilities visit baptisthealth.net/en/pages/home.aspx.

CELL PHONE SERVICE
Cell service is spotty throughout the park, so plan on having no service.

FOR ALL ELSE, VISIT
www.myfwc.com

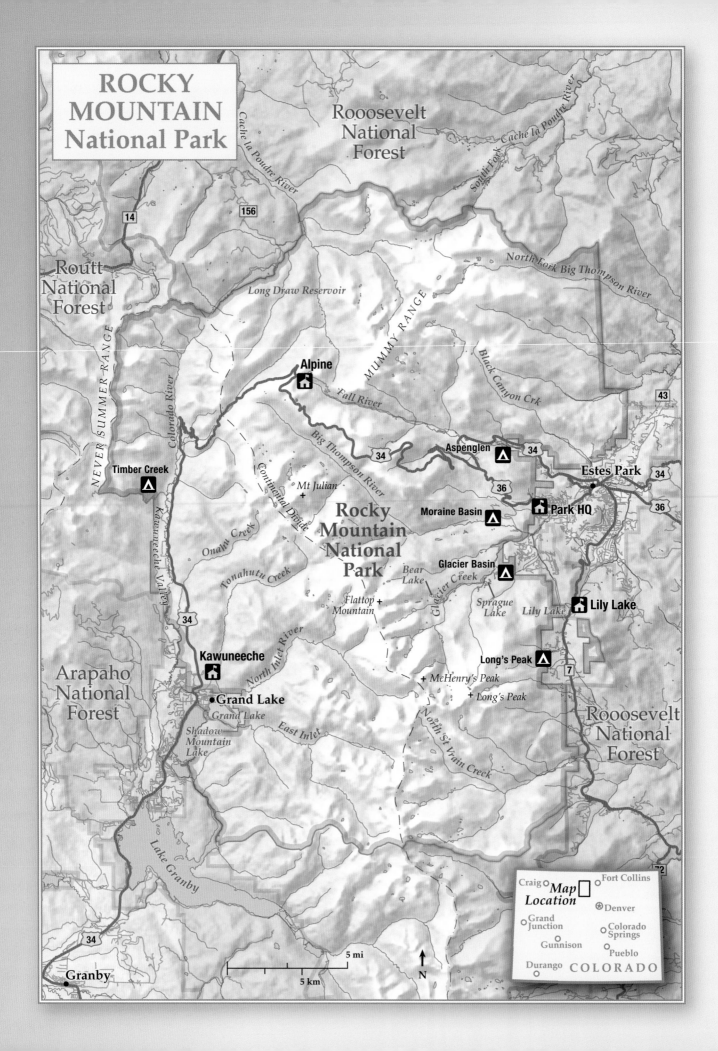

Rocky Mountain National Park

> **Location:** Rocky Mountain National Park is in north central Colorado, with the town of Estes Park serving as the eastern gateway into the park. Grand Lake serves as the western gateway.

The park is accessible from a number of routes:

· From Denver via Boulder/Colorado 36—Interstate 25 north to Exit 217, U.S. Route 36 west to Estes Park
· From Denver via Colorado 66—Interstate 25 north to Exit 243, Colorado 66 west to Estes Park
· From Denver via the Peak to Peak Scenic Byway—Interstate 70 west to Exit 244, U.S. Route 6 to Colorado 119 to Nederland.
· From Nederland, take Colorado 72 to Colorado 7 to Estes Park
· From Loveland via Colorado 34—Route 34 west to Estes Park

Rocky Mountain National Park (RMNP) became the Nation's eleventh national park when it was signed into law on January 26, 1915 by President Woodrow Wilson. If it weren't for the relentless efforts of Enos Mills, the "father" of the park, the land would have most likely fallen in the hands of mining and water moguls at the turn of the 20th century. Hundreds, if not thousands, of years prior, the land was used as hunting grounds by the Ute and Arapaho people. Remnants of hunting "mounds" where the Ute and Arapaho would hide to ambush prey are still seen on the top of Trail Ridge Road, which is the highest continuously paved road in the U.S. at 12,183 feet.

The Continental Divide splits the park into parts, which are generally referred to as the east and west slopes. The east slope contains roughly two-thirds of the acreage in RMNP. The village of Estes Park is the cultural epicenter and jumping off point for almost everything on the east side of the park. The classic western town of Grand Lake serves as the hub for enjoying the year-round activities on the west slope.

The winter months offer little in the way of fishing, but the park's trails are busy with snowshoers and cross-country skiers. Trails that lead to the high country lakes are often covered with 10 feet or more of snow. Come March, if the weather has been unseasonably warm, some of the lowest altitude streams could open for some pre-ice-out fishing, but the trek in requires snowshoes and can be difficult at times. Black stoneflies sizes 16-26 and an occasional size 20 Blue-winged Olive are early-season favorite flies.

Area guide Dick Shinton works a small pocket for hungry ice-out trout prior to full spring run-off. S. B. Schweitzer.

When the longer days of April and May shine on the park, waters begin to open and fishing is possible up to 9,500 feet or so. While the days warm to 50°F and above, unseasonably cold weather can still be the norm, so you should prepare for the worst. Blue-winged olives, size 18 and 20, hatch with regularity and bring fish to the surface. Toward the end of May, hardcore fishing junkies will begin to seek epic ice-out opportunities on some of the lakes under 10,000 feet. When fishing for ice-out fish, use sizes 20 or 22 midge dries, or a Griffith's Gnat.

The view around The Loch, seated at the foot of 13,153-foot Taylor Peak, is unparalleled in the Park. S. B. Schweitzer

By June, run-off is beginning and the trails will become slushy and slick. Waters at lower altitudes will become off-color and frigid cold as the snowpack melts. The days will warm to the 70s. Through mid-to-late June, run-off is in full-swing and most park waters become difficult to fish. Locals tend to turn their attention to many of the tailwaters around the state. If you fish during run-off, focus on nymphing tight to the shorelines on rivers and streams with size 10 or 12 Dark Brown and Golden stoneflies. By the end of June, summer conditions are in full-swing and wet-wading is the norm. Expect air temperatures to be consistently in the 60s and 70s in the high country.

The rivers and lakes yield a smorgasbord of insect activity—caddisflies, Blue-winged Olives, Pale Morning Duns of all colors, and terrestrials are the go-to patterns in a high-country fly box.

Most all the cutthroat varieties in the park are preparing to spawn during the first few weeks of July and regale in spectacular colors. A fish caught in July will most certainly be a photo-worthy high-altitude fish. As July sets in, terrestrial fishing is the ticket. Dark-colored hoppers, ants and beetles in sizes 12 to 18 work well. When the days begin to shorten in August and September, caddis and terrestrial fishing is prime. The fish sense the shorter days and feed voraciously, sometimes recklessly, to a fly fisher's amazement. Mid-September is when the snow starts flying and the days can get dark and blustery, yet the fishing can still be spectacular on both lakes and streams. Come October, the occasional 70-degree day offers a pleasant fall fishing experience. However, those days are rare in the high country. The skies again turn blustery, and the chill of winter begins to set in. While there are some fishing opportunities in November, most all water tightens up and is frozen by Thanksgiving.

With 54 lakes and 203 stream miles containing fish, there's no shortage of high-altitude fishing fun. Of those 54 lakes, 42 of them are above 10,000 feet, which means a good hike is required to fish them. More than 40 trails provide stream or lake fishing access of some kind. Hikes to fishing water range from roadside fishing (no hiking required) to more than 10 miles one way. But the length of the trail isn't the killer; it's the altitude gain. While most trailheads start around 8,500 feet, a hike to over 10,000 feet in just a few miles is not uncommon. Fifteen fishable lakes are above 11,000 feet, meaning those hikes typically require hikes of 5-6 miles or more—each way. Those coming from lower altitudes to fish the high country should drink plenty of water the day before a hike and keep hydrated during the hike to avoid the classic symptoms of nausea and headaches characteristic of altitude sickness.

Nearly half the lakes have populations of endangered native greenback cutthroat, but only on the east side of the Continental Divide. Native Colorado River cutthroat are found on the west slope. Brook trout, also native, are the most common species of fish found across all waters, inhabiting more than 30 percent of the lakes and streams. Brown and rainbow trout can be found in many of the lower altitude (9,500 feet) lakes and streams. In Glacier Creek, for example, it's possible to catch the Rocky Mountain Grand Slam in one day—a rainbow trout, a brookie, a brown and a greenback cutthroat.

Spawning greenback cutthroat stage in the crystal clear waters of a small feeder stream near Fern Lake. S. B. Schweitzer

The crystal clear waters of Glacier Creek hold plenty of hungry trout if you look close enough to find them. S. B. Schweitzer

Fishing high-altitude streams requires short casts and a stealthy approach. During the summer, dry fly fishing upstream with a high-floating size 16 Parachute Adams or a size 12-14 Royal Wulff will entice water slapping strikes often enough to make beginners beg for more. High-altitude stream fish are open-minded, opportunistic eaters that will take most any well-presented fly that resembles a bug they eat. However, sloppy casts will put the fish into scatter mode. Fishing small feeder creeks and streams at 11,000 feet demands smaller flies, with size 16 or 18 dries being the norm.

➤ Tackle and Gear

Rods and Line: A short 3-weight fly rod or an 11-foot to 13-foot Tenkara rod is ideal for high-mountain streams. A 9-foot, 5-weight rod is handy for those windy days on the lakes. Weight-forward lines are preferred, as double taper lines offer little muscle for windy days and sink-tip lines are not necessary.

Terminal Tackle and Flies: A 7-foot to 9-foot leader tapered to 5X tippet is sufficient for any stream or lake; some prefer to use 6X for picky cruising fish. See the earlier part of this chapter for specific fly recommendations.

Cutthroat trout align perfectly in a feeding lane anticipating the next ant or grasshopper to float past. S. B. Schweitzer

Author Steve Schweitzer casts to cruising Yellowstone cutthroat trout in Haynach Lake. S. B. Schweitzer

Above. A male brook trout in vibrant fall spawning colors fell prey to the classic elk hair caddis pattern. S. B. Schweitzer

Below. Area guide Mike Kruise casts to wary trout deep in the backcountry of the park. S. B. Schweitzer

CLOSEST CITY OR POINT OF ENTRANCE TO THE PARK
· Estes Park, Colorado is the eastern entrance and is about 70 miles from Denver via Colorado 66
· Grand Lake serves as the western gateway and is some 60 miles west of Denver via I-70
· Numerous other longer scenic routes are available

CLOSEST AIRPORT
Denver International Airport provides commercial shuttle service from the airport to Estes Park.

PARK FEES
· $20 daily use
· $30 per week
· $50 annual
· America the Beautiful senior passes apply.
· For up-to-date use, campground fees, and fee-free dates, visit http//www .nps.gov/romo/planyourvisit/fees.htm.

OPENING/CLOSING PARK DATES OR FISHING DATES
· Rocky Mountain National Park is open 24 hours a day year-round.
· A Colorado fishing license is required for all persons 16 years of age or older.
· No other permit is necessary.
· There are numerous park closures, rules, and regulations regarding species, possession limits, and tackle.
· For current regulations and licenses, visit http//cpw.state.co.us/thingstodo/ Pages/Fishing.aspx.

CLOSEST FLY SHOPS
Estes Angler
338 W. Riverside
Estes Park, CO 80517
800-586-2110

Kirk's Fly Shop
230 E. Elkhorn Ave.
Estes Park, CO 80517
877-669-1859
Kirksflyshop@aol.com

Laughing Grizzly Fly Shop
10675 Ute Hwy.
Longmont, CO 80504
303-772-9110

Elkhorn Fly Rod and Reel
3121 W. Eisenhower Blvd.
Loveland, CO 80537
970-227-4707

CLOSEST GUIDE SERVICES
Estes Angler
338 W. Riverside
Estes Park, CO 80517
800-586-2110

Kirk's Fly Shop
230 E. Elkhorn Ave.
Estes Park, CO 80517
877-669-1859
Kirksflyshop@aol.com

Laughing Grizzly Fly Shop
10675 Ute Hwy.
Longmont, CO 80504
303-772-9110

Elkhorn Fly Rod and Reel
3121 W. Eisenhower Blvd.
Loveland, CO 80537
970-227-4707

BEST PLACES TO STAY IN THE PARK
There are no overnight accommodations within the park.

BEST PLACES TO STAY NEAR THE PARK
River Stone Resorts & Bear Paw Suites
1 River Rd.
Estes Park, CO 80517
970-586-4005

Alpine Trail Ridge Inn
927 Moraine Ave.
Estes Park, CO 80517
970-586-4585

Rocky Mountain Park Inn
101 S. St. Vrain Ave.
Estes Park, CO 80517
970-586-2332

Rocky Mountain Resorts
2760 Fall River Road
Estes Park, CO 80517
970-586-2528
(Multiple resort properties in the area)

Spirit Lake Lodge
829 Grand Ave.
Grand Lake, CO 80447
970-627-3344

Western Riviera Lakeside
419 Garfield St.
Grand Lake, CO 80447
970-627-3580

Black Bear Lodge
12255 Colorado 34
Grand Lake, CO 80447
970-627-3654
800-766-1123

BEST CAMPGROUNDS IN THE PARK
Moraine Park Campground
Campground reservations 877-444-6777
www.reserveamerica.com or
www.recreation.gov
The park's only year-round campground is in a ponderosa pine forest above the meadows of Moraine Park on Bear Lake Road. It is located about 2-1/2 miles south of the Beaver Meadows Entrance Station.

Aspenglen Campground
U.S. Route 34
Just west of the Fall River Entrance Station

Glacier Basin Campground
Bear Lake Road
About six miles south of the Beaver Meadows Entrance Station

Timber Creek Campground
Along the Colorado River in the Kawuneeche Valley on U.S. Route 34
About 10 miles north of Grand Lake
(Only campground on the park's west side)

BEST CAMPGROUNDS OUTSIDE THE PARK
Jellystone Park of Estes
5495 U.S. Route 36
Estes Park, CO 80517
970-658-2536

Manor RV Park
815 Riverside Dr.
Estes Park, CO 80517
970-586-3251

Estes Park Campground at Mary's Lake
2120 Mary's Lake Rd.
Estes Park, CO 80517
970-577-1026

Winding River Resort
P.O. Box 629
Grand Lake, CO 80447
970-627-3215
trailboss@windingriverresort.com

Elk Creek Campground
143 County Road 48
Grand Lake, CO 80447
970-627-8502

STEVE SCHWEITZER was born and raised in Ohio, and he spent his younger years fishing his parents' farm pond for bass and bluegill with poppers. When he was seven, his grandfather taught him the craft of lure-making and he has been hooked since. Now, an avid fly-fisherman and noted fly tier, Steve enjoys backpacking, hiking and writing about fly-fishing and fly tying. Steve is author of the award-winning *A Fly Fishing Guide to Rocky Mountain National Park* (Pixachrome Publishing, 2011), and he co-authored, *A Fly Fishing Guide to Colorado's Indian Peaks Wilderness Area* (Pixachrome Publishing, 2014) with Mike Kruise. He is a frequent contributor to leading fly-fishing periodicals, and he is a contributing author and illustrator to *Drag-Free Drift—Leader Design and Presentation Techniques for Fly Fishing* (Stackpole Books, 2001) by J. Kissane. Steve resides in northern Colorado.

Camp Riverside
681 Meredith Manor
Grand Lake, CO 80447
970-627-3046

BEST PLACES TO EAT
INSIDE THE PARK
There are no dining facilities inside the park.

BEST PLACES TO EAT NEAR THE PARK
Dunraven Inn
2470 Colorado 66
Estes Park, CO 80517
970-480-0396
(South of U.S. Route 36 intersection)
(upscale Italian)

Rock Inn
1675 Colorado 66
Estes Park, CO 80517
970-586-4116
(South of the U.S. Route 36 intersection)
(Steaks, burgers, pasta, pizza)

River Rock Grilling
1690 Big Thompson Ave.
Estes Park, CO 80517
970-586-6969

Estes Park Brewery
470 Prospect Village Dr.
Estes Park, CO 80517
970-586-5421
epbrewery.com
(pub grub)

Sagebrush BBQ & Grill
1101 Grand Ave.
Grand Lake, CO 80447
970-627-1404
(family-style barbeque)

Fat Cat Café
916 Grand Lake Ave.
Grand Lake, CO 80447
970-627-0900
(breakfast, lunch and brunch)

Rapids Lodge Restaurant
210 Rapids Lane
Grand Lake, CO 80447
970-627-3707
(Dinner reservations recommended)

MUST SEE
Trail Ridge Road and Old Fall River Road—herds of elk in the meadows.

NEAREST HOSPITAL/URGENT CARE
CENTER
Estes Park Medical Center
555 Prospect Ave.
Estes Park, CO 80517
970-586-2317

Saint Anthony Granby Hospital
340 Peak One Dr.
Granby, CO 80443
970-668-3300
(About 15 miles from Grand Lake)

CELL PHONE SERVICE
Cell service is excellent in population centers in and around Estes Park and Grand Lake but is spotty to non-existent in the park itself.

FOR ALL ELSE, VISIT
http//www.nps.gov/romo/index.htm
/index.htm

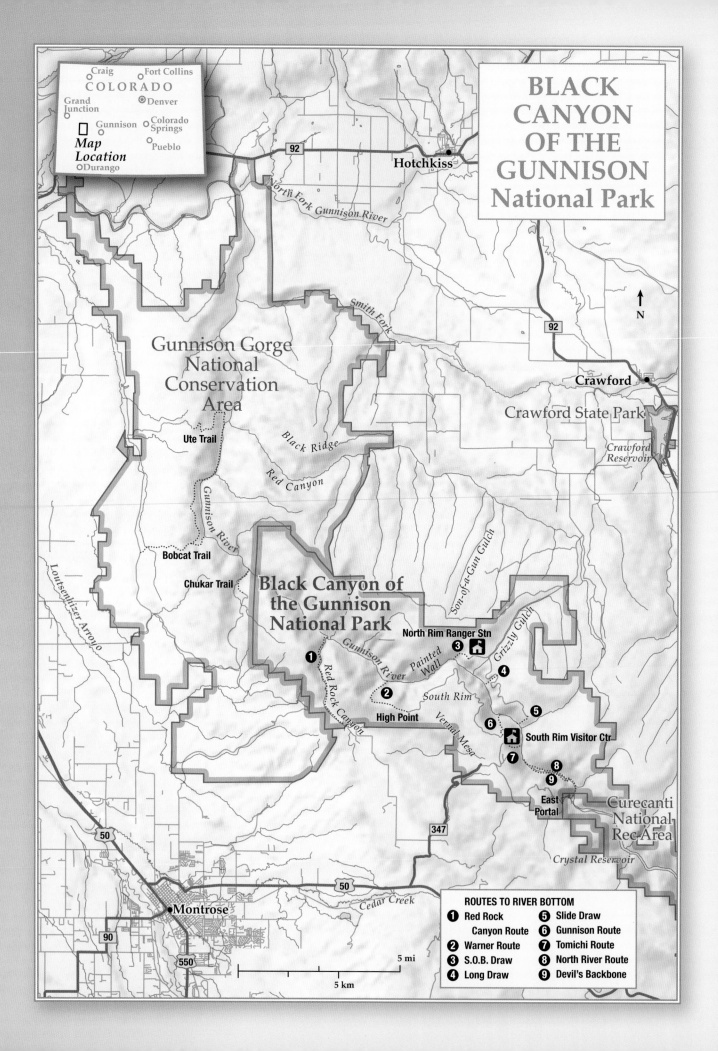

BLACK CANYON OF THE GUNNISON National Park

COLORADO

Craig · Fort Collins
Grand Junction
○ Denver
□ Gunnison ○ Colorado Springs
Map Location
○ Pueblo
○ Durango

N

Hotchkiss

Crawford

Crawford State Park

Crawford Reservoir

North Fork Gunnison River

Smith Fork

Gunnison Gorge National Conservation Area

Black Ridge

Red Canyon

Ute Trail

Gunnison River

Bobcat Trail

Chukar Trail

Black Canyon of the Gunnison National Park

Red Rock Canyon

Gunnison River

Painted Wall

Son-of-a-Gun Gulch

North Rim Ranger Stn ❸

Grizzly Gulch

❹

South Rim

High Point

Vernal Mesa

❺

❻

South Rim Visitor Ctr

❼

❽

❾

East Portal

Curecanti National Rec Area

Crystal Reservoir

Louiseuliizer Arroyo

❶

❷

Montrose

Cedar Creek

50

90

550

50

347

92

92

5 mi

5 km

ROUTES TO RIVER BOTTOM

❶ Red Rock Canyon Route	❺ Slide Draw
❷ Warner Route	❻ Gunnison Route
❸ S.O.B. Draw	❼ Tomichi Route
❹ Long Draw	❽ North River Route
	❾ Devil's Backbone

➤ **Location:** The Black Canyon of the Gunnison National Park (BCNP) was established as a national monument on March 2, 1933 and a national park on October 21, 1999. BCNP is 250 miles from Denver in southwestern Colorado. The entrance to the south rim of the park is seven miles east of Montrose from U.S. Route 50 then eight miles north on Colorado 347. The north rim is accessed from Colorado 92, two miles south of Crawford then nine miles on county roads.

Two other federally protected areas within the park are important to note here:

· Curecanti National Recreation Area (CNRA) (175,852 acres) also is managed by the National Park Service. It encompasses three dams, which are referred to as the Aspinall Units.
· Blue Mesa, Morrow Point, and Crystal Reservoirs are located immediately upstream and to the east of the park.

Downstream of the park is the Gunnison Gorge National Conservation Area (62,844 acres) managed by the Bureau of Land Management. The Gunnison River flows through the reservoirs (45 miles), the park (12 miles), and the GGNCA (14 miles).

In the heart of the Black Canyon of the Gunnison National Park is an abyss—one unmatched by other canyons in its combined depth, narrowness, and sheerness of drop. It commands a profound respect having claimed the lives of seasoned hikers, kayakers, and climbers. Fly fishers, in reverence, refer to the canyon as "the crack" and the Gunnison River as "the Gunny."

Early inhabitants were the Ute Indians. Although they probably avoided the rugged canyon, there is evidence that they camped and hunted along the rims. The Utes were driven out by white settlers in the 1870s when gold and silver were discovered in the nearby San Juan Mountains. In the 1870s, after the Utes had been moved to a reservation, the west quickly became settled and an east-west continental railroad was being explored. Surveyors considered a route through the Black Canyon. However, after spending time in the rugged environment,

they advised the railroad promoter it would be impossible to construct a railroad due to the narrow 48-mile canyon. Eventually, the route did pass through the upper 12 miles before exiting. The fertile valleys surrounding the park were popular for homesteaders, but the mining was short-lived due to the silver crash of 1873.

In 1999, after the ceremony designating it as a national park, President Bill Clinton called the Black Canyon a "true natural treasure," and added, "Its nearly vertical walls, rising a half-mile high, harbor one of the most spectacular stretches of wild river in America."

The deep slash in the earth was created by two million years of erosion. The gorge ranges in depth from 1,300 to 2,700 feet and, at the narrowest point called "the narrows," it is only 40 feet wide. In some places the canyon receives sun-

Tailhead of the Warner Point Trail leading to the Gunnison River 2,722-feet below. Pat Oglesby

light only 33 minutes of the day, creating deep shadows— thus the name, Black Canyon.

It took nearly two billion years for the Gunnison River to carve its way through the Precambrian formations. One of the favorite views is from the Painted Wall overlook where pink streamers of pegmatite animate the 2,250 feet vertical cliff.

The famed Painted Wall in the Black Canyon of the Gunnison National Park. Pat Oglesby

The elevation of the park varies from 5,400 feet at the lower boundary to 9,040 feet at Poison Springs Hill. Because of the varying elevation and seasonal changes, temperatures can vary from a summertime high of 100°F to a winter low of -10°F. Because of the differences in elevation, a variety of flora and fauna is visible within the park. A wide variety of recreation opportunities are available for visitors to enjoy: hiking, technical rock climbing, challenging kayaking, winter snowshoeing, cross country skiing, biking, and, of course, fly fishing in Gold Medal waters.

The Gunnison River has its origin at the confluence of the Taylor and East rivers in the West Elk Mountains, north of Gunnison at Almont. It flows through a variety of private and public lands for 14 miles before it enters 20-mile-long Blue Mesa Reservoir in the CNRA. From there, it flows downstream 12 miles to Morrow Point Reservoir and directly below into Crystal Dam at the upper boundary of the park. Although the river is a tailwater with regulation, the flows can fluctuate from 300 cubic feet per second in the winter to 10,000 cfs during spring runoff. At flows above 3,000 cfs, fishing can be difficult and wading is dangerous if not impossible.

Flows can be checked online at www.waterdata.usgs.gov/co/nwis/current/?type=flow.

Fishing within BCNP requires a hike. Most of the trails are rated difficult, and they all require a free inner canyon wilderness permit. The upper park boundary and the river can be reached by negotiating the hairpin turns of the steep (16 percent grade) six-mile East Portal Road. Vehicles longer than 22 feet are prohibited. The two-mile tailwater fishery below Crystal Dam is paralleled by the road and is easily accessible. The scenery is indescribable: immense vertical granite canyon walls, a gently flowing river, prolific vegetation along the shore, and abundant wildlife. Access anywhere into the canyon below the East Portal requires a hike. This is the beginning of the white water section and is restricted to expert kayakers. This section also requires numerous portages. Rafts and boats cannot negotiate the difficult white water.

Hatches are mostly the same for the BCNP and the GGNCA depending on the time of year. Many of the hatches occur initially downstream and gradually move upstream as the weather and water warms. The world famous Salmonfly (*Pteronarcys californica*) starts its emergence on the lower

The Gunnison River is known for crimson-streaked rainbows. Brad Befus

Below. Sharon Lance fishing the heavy water in the Black Canyon of the Gunnison National Park. Mark Lance

river near the North Fork of the Gunnison confluence in late May or early June. The hatch moves upstream a few miles each day depending on the air temperature and river flows. June is the busiest month on the river, and there can be competition for campsites.

The rainbow trout found in the Gunnison River are progeny of McCloud River rainbows transported by rail from Northern California in 1888. The landlocked strain flourished in waters that were once home to native Colorado River cut-throats. Brown trout were introduced to the Gunnison country when a shipment of Loch Leven fingerlings arrived from Scotland in 1893. The cutthroats suffered from the effects of mining and agriculture, leaving way for the browns and rainbows to replace them. In 1993, whirling disease was detected, and the rainbow population crashed. The brown trout population flourished, and although the average size is 12- to 16-inches, anglers do report trophy size in the 20-plus range. During the decline of the rainbows, Colorado Parks and Wildlife, with the help of Trout Unlimited, heavily stocked a whirling-disease-free strain of rainbows that provided anglers with a sport fish, but they just didn't have the breaking-water, hard-pulling strength of the original stock. Also, because these rainbows were a domesticated strain, they didn't survive or reproduce well in the wild. The good news is some of the original Gunnison River rainbows did have a natural resistance to whirling disease, survived, and are now reproducing in surprising numbers. Sixteen-to 20-inch, red-slabbed rainbows are caught, with 12- to 14-inches being the average. A few even top 20 inches. Each year, there is an increase in the number, and size, of rainbows.

Browns are the dominant species of trout and make up 90 percent of the trout population. Average size runs 12- to 16-inches with frequent catches in the 20-inch range.

The Devil's Backbone Route (below the parking area) is located on the south side of the river. The first half-mile of fishing requires scrambling over boulders along a trail.

Morning light bathes the Gunnison River in the inner-gorge. Mark Lance

Beyond that is a technical "up and over" hike to access water for the next 1-1/2 miles and leaves one exposed above a steep cliff. A primitive two-mile trail—the North River Route—along the river below the East Portal, requires crossing the river but leads to spectacular deep runs, pocket water and riffles beneath the towering granite canyon walls. The river crossing is not wader friendly because of flows exceeding 800 cfs, making watercraft necessary to cross. The hiking can be strenuous and difficult over large boulders and scree fields, but the effort can result in some exciting fishing and spectacular scenery.

➤ **South rim trails:** All the trails, with the exception of the Red Rocks Route, originate within the BCNP boundaries.

Gunnison route—While strenuous, this is the most popular route. However, it is still very strenuous. It begins at the South Rim Visitor Center. A short distance upstream, there's an outhouse and campsites.

Descent: 1.5 hours
Distance: 1 mile
Vertical Drop: 1,800 feet
Ascent: 2 hours
River Access: .75 mile
Campsites: 3

Tomichi route—This route is considered the steepest of the South Rim trails. Access is from the parking area near the South Rim Campground.

Descent: 1.5 hours
Distance: 1 mile
Vertical Drop: 1,960 feet
Ascent: 4.5 hours
River Access: .5 miles
Campsites: 2

Warner route—This is the longest route and overnight travel is recommended. Access is from the Warner Point Nature Trail.

Descent: 2 - 2.5 hours
Distance: 2.75 miles
Vertical Drop: 2,722 feet
Ascent: 4 hours
River Access: 1 mile
Campsites: 5

Red Rock Canyon route—The Red Rock Canyon Route is unique, popular, and is limited to eight people per day, selected through a lottery system. Also, the season is limited—late-May through early October. Contact the National Park Service for more details and directions to the trailhead.

Rocky Mountain big horn sheep are residents of the Black Canyon of the Gunnison National Park. Carol Oglesby

➤ **North rim trails:** SOB Draw—This route is recommended for the first-time inner canyon hiker. Access is from the North Rim Ranger Station. Also, the route is infamous for the copious amounts of poison ivy. Long pants are recommended. Travelers may park near the campground registration board in the pull-through. Parking also is available at the North Rim Ranger Station. In the canyon, campsites are located a short distance downstream.

Descent: 2 hours
Distance: 1.75 miles
Vertical Drop: 1,800 feet
Ascent: 3 hours
River Access: 2 miles
Campsites: 6

Long Draw—When hiking the Long Draw, hikers will find themselves in one of the narrower parts of the canyon. The canyon's steep walls and the fast-moving Gunnison River below make for a spectacular view. Access is from the park at Balanced Rock Overlook.

Distance: 1 mile
Vertical Drop: 1,800 feet
Ascent: 3 hours
River Access: .25 mile
Campsites: 1

Slide Draw—Loose rock along this route makes for unsure footing. The route is extremely steep and dangerous. First,

you'll need to park at Kneeling Camel View and walk east where you'll eventually reach the head of the draw. Then, you'll need to navigate a 30-foot climb down to start the route. Be very careful because the loose rock can be extremely dangerous. Eventually, the draw brings you to the river where you'll also find an area to camp.

Descent: 1.5 hours
Distance: 1 mile
Vertical Drop: 1,620 feet
Ascent: 4 hours
River Access: .75 mile
Campsites: 2

A typical summer-time brown trout from the Gunnison River. Rigs Fly Shop

Tyler Befus with a colorful red-sided rainbow from the East Portal section of the Gunnison National Park. Brad Befus

➤ **Other Trails:** Downstream and north of the park is the NCA and 14 miles of floatable river to the confluence with the North Fork of the Gunnison, known as Pleasure Park. Although there are up to class IV rapids, it is a popular float for recreational rafters and kayakers as well as anglers. Wading anglers will find several miles of pools, slicks, and some riffles that are readily accessible from the hiking trails. Day use and camping permits are required and available at the trail heads.

The Chukar Trailhead—the upper access to the NCA—is reached by taking Falcon Road east from Colorado 50 between Montrose and Olathe. The river launch is accessed by a 1.1-mile maintained trail from the trailhead. All gear must by carried by hand or transported by hiring the permitted horse packer. The takeout for the 14-mile float is at Gunnison Forks Recreation Site (a.k.a. Pleasure Park), west of Hotchkiss and off Colorado 92.

Three additional trails—Bob Cat, Duncan, and Ute—provide hiking access downstream of Chukar Trail and are accessed off the Peach Valley Road.

The stretch in the Gunnison Forks Recreation (GFR) site is easily accessible and is the most popular fishing on the lower Gunnison River. Four miles above the GFR site, at the confluence with the Smith Fork, the river exits the gorge, widens, and provides easy wading. A gentle hiking trail follows the east side of the river nearly to the Smith Fork. The river rarely freezes during the winter and provides year-round angling. The outfitter located near the Gunnison Forks Recreation site is permitted to operate a jet boat on the lower four miles and will transport anglers and their rafts to Smith Fork. This section of the Gunnison River is recommended for a great day of fishing without the experience of a strenuous hike.

Our candid description of the Black Canyon National Park is not intended to discourage anglers, but rather to emphasize the ruggedness of a canyon that can be demanding yet unparalleled by other national parks. The experience is like few others.

➤ **Hatches:** Recommendations for fly patterns to match the hatch are about as consistently accurate as trying to guess when a cold day will follow a colder night—or predict a snow storm on Mother's Day. It can happen. It has happened! But here's an approximation to consider when planning your trip:

Annelids, sizes 10-12, all year
Midges, sizes 18-22, all year
Scuds, size 16, all year found only in the tailwater below Crystal Reservoir at the East Portal
Blue-winged Olives, sizes 14-20, March-May
Eggs, sizes 14-16, April-May and October-November
Caddis, sizes 10-18, April-October

Streamers, sizes 4-8, May-November
Golden stones, sizes 6-10, May thru mid-July
Salmonflies, sizes 4-8, mid-May thru June
Yellow Sallies, sizes 8-12, June thru mid-July
Pale Morning Duns, sizes 14-20, mid-June thru mid-August
Terrestrials, sizes 6-10, July-October

➤ **Tackle and Gear**

Rods and Line: We recommend 9-foot, 5- or 6-weight rods, and floating lines for dry flies, nymphs, streamers. A sink-tip line can be used for streamer fishing.

Terminal Tackle and Flies: We recommend 9-foot leaders in 4X and 5X, and tippet spools from 4X to 6X. Fluorocarbon can be used but isn't necessary. Using a tandem fly rig is effective. Flies for the canyon section include large dry stonefly patterns from early to mid-June, such as foam or other high-vis bodies, orange/tan elk hair wings, and rubber legs. Stonefly Nymphs, Prince Nymphs, Pheasant Tails, Hares Ears, midge patterns in red, black, brown and olive, and soft hackled flies work year-round. Use hoppers, ants and beetles in high summer, with a nymph or midge dropper. Orange scuds and small nymphs can be effective in the East Portal section of the river.

The giant stonefly hatch occurs each June, providing great opportunities for fly fishers. Rigs Fly Shop

*Rubber rafts are required to navigate the
whitewater of the Gunnison River. Rigs Fly Shop*

CLOSEST CITY OR POINT OF ENTRANCE TO THE PARK
Montrose, Colorado

CLOSEST AIRPORT
Montrose Regional Airport; full auto rental and transportation services.

OPEN/CLOSING PARK DATES OR FISHING DATES
- The South Rim is open every day.
- The visitor center closes only on Thanksgiving, Christmas, and New Year's Day.
- The North Rim and the ranger station are closed in winter, typically from late November through mid-April.
- The East Portal road is closed in winter, typically from mid-November to mid-April, depending on weather.
- Fishing is open year-round with the exception of the East Portal, which is inaccessible in the winter.

FEES
National park passes are available at the park headquarters just inside the park boundary on the South Rim.
- Annual Black Canyon Park passes are $30.
- Daily vehicle passes are $15.
- Daily bikers and pedestrian passes are $7.
- Senior passes are $10 with an additional $10 processing fee.

Park entrance and user fees change periodically. For up-to-date fees, free days, and other exceptions, visit www.nps.gov/blca/index.htm.

REGULATIONS
- The Gunnison River within the Black Canyon of the Gunnison National Park is designated as Gold Medal Water and Wild Trout Water, meaning artificial flies and lures only.
- Gold Medal Waters begin 200 yards downstream of Crystal Dam and continue to the North Fork of the Gunnison River.
- All rainbow trout are catch-and-release.
- Daily bag limits for brown trout are four browns 12 inches or less, or three browns less than 12 inches and one more than 16 inches.
- A Colorado fishing license is required.
- For waters outside the park, refer to the Colorado Parks and Wildlife Fishing Regulations.
- A Wilderness Permit is required for all inner-canyon activity, such as rafting, wade fishing, or hiking.
- Taking ANYTHING from the park is prohibited.

CLOSEST FLY SHOPS
CJ's Fly Shop
428 E. Main St.
Montrose, CO 81401
970-249-5588
www.cjsflyshop.com

RIGS Fly Shop & Guide Service
565 Sherman St.
Ridgway, CO 81432
888-626-4460
www.fishrigs.com

Toads Guide Shop
309 E. Main St.
Montrose, CO 81401
970-249-0408
www.toadsguideshop.com

CLOSEST GUIDE/OUTFITTER SERVICES
Black Canyon Anglers
7904 Shea Road
Austin, CO 81410
970-835-5050
www.blackcanyonanglers.com
info@blackcanyonanglers.com

Dvorak's Expeditions
Bill Dvorak
17921 Route 285
Nathrop, CO 81236
719-539-6851 or 800-824-3795
www.dvorakexpeditions.com
info@dvorakexpeditions.com

Gunnison River Expeditions
Alan DeGrange
14494 F Road
Delta, CO 81416
Phone 970-874-8184
www.gunnisonriveroutfitters.com
gre@sopris.net
(Also permitted vehicle shuttle service)

RIGS Adventure Co.
Tim Patterson
565 Sherman St.

P.O. Box 2086
Ridgway, CO 81432
Phone 970-626-4460
www.fishrigs.com
info@fishrigs.com

Scenic River Tours
Matt Brown
703 W. Tomichi Ave.
Gunnison, CO 81230
970-641-3131 or 970-641-4205
www.scenicrivertours.com
info@scenicrivertours.com

PERMITTED HORSE PACKER FOR GUNNISON GORGE
Larry Franks
J & Ray Guides and Outfitters
8310 6400 Road
Montrose, CO 81401
970-323-0115
www.sportsmansdream.com/gray/
wbarx@aol.com

CLOSEST FULL-SERVICE LODGES
Black Canyon Anglers/Gunnison River Farms
P.O. Box 180
7904 Shea Road
Austin, CO 81410
970-835-5050
info@blackcanyonanglers.com

BEST CAMPGROUND, IN THE PARK
South Rim campground
- This campground includes 88 sites, electricity (in Loop B), three accessible sites, and RV spots.
- There are no showers or dump stations.
- Sites in Loop A and B may be reserved three days in advance online through the National Park Service.
- Loop A does not have electricity.
- The campground is open year-round, but drinking water is available only from late-May through mid-September.

BEST CAMPGROUND NEAR THE PARK
The best campground is available near the North Rim is Crawford State Park, two miles south of Crawford, Colorado on Colorado 92.

Two areas are available:
- Iron Creek Campground is located near the boat ramp, with 45 sites offering electricity, water hookups, hot showers, flush toilets and a dump station.

70

PAT AND CAROL OGLESBY—Pat and Carol Oglesby are avid fly fishers, and are actively involved in the fly-fishing industry. As members of the International Federation of Fly Fishers (IFFF), both are Certified Casting Instructors and conduct fly-casting and fly-fishing classes. Pat is involved locally and nationally, while Carol writes the Women's Outlook column for the IFFF *Flyfisher* magazine and was awarded Woman of the Year in 2006. Pat is also involved locally and nationally with the IFFF and writes for the magazine, photographing and covering the annual Fly Fishing Fair. Both are volunteers for Project Healing Waters and were recognized as the regional Volunteers of the Year in 2014. Pat and Carol both are outdoor writers and contribute to the *Grand Junction Daily Sentinel* located in Grand Junction, Colorado. Their writing and photographs have appeared in the *Drake, The Flyfisher,* and local publications.

As life members of Trout Unlimited, Pat is a past president of their local TU Chapter, Grand Valley Anglers, and Carol is the newsletter editor. In 2015, they were presented with the "Silver Trout" award, Colorado Trout Unlimited's highest honor for contributions to coldwater conservation in Colorado.

· Clear Fork Campground has 21 sites without hookups, and includes potable water, showers, flush toilets and vault toilet.

Call the Park Service 970-921-5721.

BEST PLACES TO STAY NEAR THE PARK

Days Inn Montrose
1417 E. Main St.
Montrose, CO 81401
970-642-3564
www.daysinn.com

Hampton Inn Montrose
1980 N. Townsend Ave.
Montrose, CO 81401
970-252-3300
www.hamptoninn3.hilton.com

Holiday Inn Express & Suites Montrose
1391 S. Townsend Ave.
Montrose, CO 81401
970-240-1800
www.hiexpress.com

Red Arrow Inn & Suites
1702 E. Main St.
Montrose, CO 81401
970-249-9641
www.redarrowinn.com

BEST PLACE TO EAT NEAR THE PARK
There are no places to eat in the park.

Camp Robber
1515 Ogden Road
Montrose, CO 81401
970-240-1590
www.camprobber.com

Pahgres
1541 Oxbow Drive
Montrose, CO 81401
970-249-6442
www.pahgres.com

Stone House
1415 Hawk Parkway
Montrose, CO 81401
970-240-8899
www.stonehousemontrose.com

Ted Nelson's Steakhouse
103 Rose Lane
Montrose, CO 81401
970-252-0262
www.montrosesteakhouse.com

CLOSEST AND BEST PLACE TO GET A DRINK

Horsefly Brewery
846 East Main
Montrose, CO 81401
970-249-6889
www.horseflybrewing.com

MUST SEE
The 2,000-foot-tall, narrow canyon walls that drop almost vertically to the Gunnison River

NEAREST HOSPITAL/URGENT TREATMENT CENTER

Montrose Memorial Hospital
800 S. Third St.
Montrose, CO 81401
970-249-2211

CELL PHONE SERVICE:
Cell phones don't work in the canyon, but they do work intermittently on the rim.

FOR ALL ELSE, VISIT
www.nps.gov/blca/index.htm

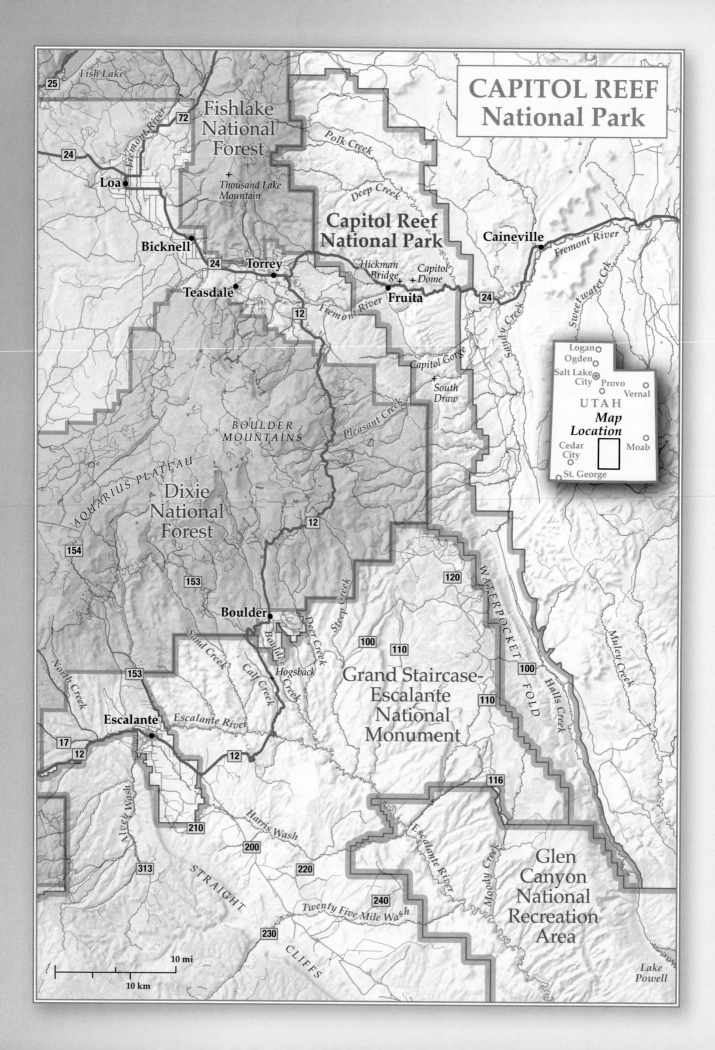

CAPITOL REEF
National Park

➤ **Location:** The park is located in south central Utah. It is open year-round and is usually accessed from Salt Lake City, a three-hour drive from the north. From Las Vegas, it's a 4.5-hour drive from the south. Visitors may also travel through Grand Junction, Colorado, which is a 3.25-hour drive.

Capitol Reef was designated a national monument in 1937 and reclassified as a national park in 1971. The park is a 100-mile-long narrow strip of land with its northern border near Highway 70 and its south-easterly border near Lake Powell. CRNP was named for two geological formations, so there are two parts to the story.

First, the "Capitol" part of the name is derived from a stretch of rounded sandstone cliffs called "Capitol Dome," which look similar to the rotunda on the U.S. Capitol.

Secondly, the "Reef" part of the name comes from the nautical term, "reef," which is a barrier for sea navigation.

In this case, the "reef" is a formidable rock barrier. More specifically, the reef is a monocline (a blend of sand and rock that dips horizontally, making it impossible to pass from one side to the other. The monocline found in Capitol Reef is called the Waterpocket Fold, which is a 65-million-year-old warp in the earth's crust. It is the largest exposed monocline in North America. In this fold, newer and older layers of earth folded over each other, forming an S-shape. This warp, probably caused by the same colliding continental plates that created the Rocky Mountains, has weathered and eroded over millennia to expose layers of rock and fossils.

The Fremont River meanders its way through Capitol Reef National Park and eventually runs into the Colorado River through Lake Powell. Fly fishing near the park is breathtaking and scenic to say the least. Most importantly, fly fishers can get away from crowds found in many national parks, and get lost in this truly remote location. Capitol Reef, com-

*Iconic pioneer cabin with velvet ridge
as a backdrop. Shawn Saunders*

Old Wagon Trail Bridge near Torrey, Utah. Shawn Saunders

pared to other southern Utah national parks, receives far less tourist travel, rewarding visitors who are searching for serenity.

Capitol Reef National Park is larger than both Bryce and Zion National Parks combined. The park lies in Utah's south-central desert, an oasis of colorful sandstone cliffs, impressive domes, and soaring monoliths. Early inhabitants referred to the area as the "land of the sleeping rainbow" because of its beautiful contrasts. This magnificent park treats visitors to multicolored sandstone surrounded by lush green riverbanks and arid desert vegetation, all tucked under deep blue skies.

Another area icon is scenic Byway Highway 12 and The Hogsback. This section of the Escalante Grand Staircase is just an hour from Capitol Reef and could entertain an explorer for weeks. Stream waters that drain the Boulder Mountains Aquarius Plateau pass through here, and quality small stream fishing is abundant with prolific hatches. The Boulder, Calf, and North Creeks and the Escalante River are regularly explored by anglers, but they require some hiking and

know-how. In fact, the last river system mapped in the United States was the Escalante River.

Mormons were sent from Salt Lake City to find and settle other areas of Utah. Many in Wayne County and Capitol Reef National Park trace their existence to these pioneer people. Butch Cassidy and the Wild Bunch frequented the area as they ran from the law in search of a hideout. They found many hidden canyons as well as local establishments in which they could still enjoy some socializing. Butch attended dances and boxing matches in Torrey at the old schoolhouse. The Robbers Roost is commonly known as "Butch Cassidy's Hideout" and Torrey, Utah is the hub for exploring this area.

Torrey is eight miles from CRNP's west entrance and is located at 6,800 feet above sea level, offering tourists pleasant summer weather, proximity to canyons, trails, and parks and wholesome small town fun. The annual Cowboy Music and Poetry Festival and the Big Apple Outdoor Dance Hall are two of the reasons tourists are attracted to Torrey's tree-lined streets. With restaurants, a bookstore and café, two art galleries, a general store, gift shops, RV campgrounds, numerous

Big trout in small water is the name of the game near Capitol Reef National Park. Shawn Saunders

The Wayne Community Health Center is at 100 South in Bicknell. The area's only full-service grocery store, Royal's, is found in Loa. Both of these towns are within a 30-minute drive from the west entrance of the park.

Most of the fishable waters will be found at 5,500 feet or higher. Streams drain from the Aquarius Plateau (Boulder Mountains) and Fishlake Mountain. More than 50,000 acres of rolling forest and meadowlands on the Aquarius Plateau provide the water needed to support wild self-sustaining trout populations. Several small springs and creeks high on Fishlake Mountain form the headwaters of the Fremont River.

Trout can be found within park boundaries on Pleasant Creek, a small drainage with its source in the high elevations of the Aquarius Plateau. Over the past few decades, populations of cutthroat and rainbows have been managed on Pleasant Creek within Capitol Reef, but they have been very inconsistent. From the western boundary of the park, access requires a high clearance vehicle and some good, "old-fashioned know-how" at the wheel. Also, Pleasant Creek on the east park boundary is a fly-fishing option.

Just like the small size of the Colorado River, cutthroat caught there are small, too. However, the sandstone cliffs and canyons will make those small cutthroats worth the effort.

lodging options and one fly shop, Torrey is a convenient gateway town to fly-fishing exploration.

Travelers use Torrey as a base camp for exploring the park, discovering the red sandstone canyons and aspen forests of Thousand Lake Mountain, and hiking and fishing at Boulder Mountain, just minutes away. Torrey is also an excellent access point for Utah's Scenic Byway 12.

Private waters near park boundaries. Shawn Saunders

Monster tiger trout are not uncommon on the west slope of Boulder Mountain. Shawn Saunders

Follow these directions for the most reasonable access:

Drive several miles in a 4x4 on Pleasant Creek road.

Hike downstream on the west side of the canyon.

From there, drive south for 10 miles from the visitor's center on the Scenic Loop to Capitol Gorge where the paved road ends.

Follow the unimproved dirt road through South Draw until you cross the creek.

From here, remember to put your camera in your backpack, fill up your filtration bottle, and have fun exploring.

The trout in Pleasant Creek are more plentiful in waters that lie outside the park, nearer the Boulder Mountains to the west.

Anglers who want to visit "the reef" will find most of the quality waters outside the park boundaries. Though the Fremont River runs through the park, these waters are mostly home to various species of sucker, dace, shiners and chub.

Brown and rainbow trout become more catchable upriver from the visitor's center as you approach park boundaries. This area is remote and requires an energetic hike. Bring plenty of water and some snacks and enjoy the solitude of the remote canyon. Large brown, rainbow, and a few cutthroats are found in abundance upstream and outside the park nearer to Torrey and Bicknell. From the Capitol Reef Visitor's Center, world-class fly-fishing is only 15 minutes away and 1,500 feet higher in elevation. Much of this water is private, but can be accessed through the local outfitters and guides.

The Fremont River flows through the town of Torrey, considered by locals to be the hub for the best fly-fishing, restaurants and lodging. Guides regularly rendezvous with clients in Torrey for excursions to streams and lakes in the nearby Boulder Mountains, Fishlake Mountain, Thousand Lakes Mountain, as well as other waters. Non-anglers can entertain themselves at art galleries, gift stores and restaurants.

Many other fishing options abound near the park. More than 50 fishable lakes can be accessed on the Boulder Mountains, but anglers should be prepared for some adventure including 4x4-required vehicles, short hikes and float tubes for the best results. Fishlake, famous for trophy-sized splake and Mackinaw, is close enough for a day trip. Rainbow trout are stocked by the tens of thousands for bank fishermen and float tubers to enjoy. Visitors can expect to find everything needed to stay and fish for a day during the summer months including improved campgrounds, RV parks, daily cabin rentals, and restaurants.

The fly-fishing season in southern Utah is extended somewhat because it is a bit further south. Unlike many other Rocky Mountain areas, the mountains near the Capitol Reef region typically experience runoff in April or early May. This runoff period is short, and it generally has an effect only on streams draining the south slope of the Boulder Mountains. In particular, the Boulder Creek and Escalante River systems are affected for about a week, usually in mid-May.

Prime fishing conditions on most of the local streams will start in early April. Water temperatures rise from irrigation water being diverted into area canals in preparation for the growing season. And as these temperatures rise weekly, the hatches get more prolific by the day until late May and early June, when the best conditions prevail. These prime conditions will continue through early October. In July or August, due to monsoon storms, valley streams might experience cloudy water. In this case, guides typically move to higher elevation streams or water below dams where fishing continues to be excellent.

As with many western waters, April brings great midge and Baetis activity as well as dry fly fishing at its finest. Fly fishers should continue to use streamers and subsurface patterns except when water temperatures are high enough to trigger hatches. The best success is had in the tail of pools by slow stripping streamers or in very slow eddies where midges and mayflies ride the foam as they emerge.

Expect Yellow Sallies in mid-May as well as golden stoneflies and salmon flies by the second week of June. Grasshoppers and other terrestrials will already be in full swing by early June. Fishing is great throughout the day and be prepared for a plenitude of surface opportunities all at once.

July and August is time for smaller bugs. Water temperatures will reach the upper 60s—perfect for Tricos (*Tricorythodes*) in the morning and prolific evening caddis emergences. A headlamp as well as an afternoon nap in preparation for skating caddis after 9 p.m. is a must. Large numbers of trout will form pods as they engulf mayflies and caddis both early and late in the day.

During September and early October, Blue-winged olives and midges will re-surface, and middle-of-the-day fishing will be most productive. Browns will spawn, meaning your streamers boxes will come out again. November is a great month to find some tranquil angling and even some calm, sunny weather. This is the most under-fished month of the year when many other activities distract anglers from some awesome opportunities near Capitol Reef National Park.

Because the area streams are smaller in size and flow, stealth is a must. Walk slowly and use banks to spot trout and hide as you figure out your game plan. Trout are not particularly picky to specific patterns for the most part, but these wild trout notice tippet and presentation. Another very sought-after talent is the ability to land flies softly to wary trout in the 20- to 25-inch range. In most western waters of comparable size, anglers don't expect to catch fish in the 20-inch class. On the Fremont River and other local waters, expect to locate browns and rainbows that will exceed three pounds.

The middle section Fremont River near Torrey, Utah. Shawn Saunders

High-elevation Colorado River cutthroat daisy chain. Shawn Saunders

Boats and float tubes will not help you on the moving waters, but in the lakes of the Boulder Mountains you are at a big advantage. Some lakes can be fished from the banks and many are much more fishable from floatation. Smaller float tubes can be packed into the best natural lakes, but any float tube or pontoon can help anglers access some drive-in locations. Many seemingly remote lakes on the Boulder are reachable by 4x4 vehicle, UTV, ATV, and short hikes of two miles (or sometimes less).

When fishing the higher elevation lakes as well as valley streams in mid-summer always beware of quick moving monsoon storms that can bring with them aggressive thunderstorms and lightning. A good rain-jacket and light fleece can come in handy when the temperatures drop from 85 to 50 degrees in minutes. Anglers should come prepared to fish the Boulder Mountains with a day pack, a water filter bottle, and snacks.

Nature and animal lovers will find an over-abundance of critters. From one side to the other in Capitol Reef Country, birds and game can easily be viewed without even leaving town. Deer often bed down in parks and back yards. Antelope, elk, moose, mule deer, mountain lions, coyote, black bear, beaver and many others can be seen in Wayne County. Various birds of prey, including bald eagles, hawks, falcons and others, are regulars as well.

Even though these canyons are somewhat easy to access, you can get lost in the beauty of your surroundings. Also, during the summer months of July to early September, flash floods can result from just a little rain.

The streams mostly call for 3- and 4-weight rods with varying lengths for open meadow areas as well as densely forested, high-elevation moving waters. Dry flies are the norm during summer months, but small indicators for shallow nymph rigs are needed, too.

Trout are more easily spooked by the anglers than they are by the flies and tippets. On the lighter side, 5X-6X tippets are a good choice, and 4X is best for big dries and nymphs. Big trout on the Fremont as well as the high mountain lakes will require a 6-weight rod and stronger pound test.

Long, tapered leaders are not the rule here, but stealth is, and anglers should bring their best presentations to the trophy fish that can be found in these waters. Floating lines will be most useful, and sinking lines might come in handy on stillwaters, reservoirs, and other impoundments found here.

It is recommended to bring waist-high waders for fishing in streams during spring and fall, and chest waders as for the lakes.

➤ Tackle and Gear

Rods and Line: Pack 3- and 4-weight rods with varying lengths. Big trout on the Fremont as well as the high mountain lakes will require a 6-weight rod and stronger pound test. On the lighter side, 5X-6X tippets are a good choice, and 4X is best for big dries and nymphs. Floating lines will be used most often, though sinking lines do come in handy. Waist-high waders for fishing in streams during spring and fall, and chest waders as for the lakes are recommended.

Terminal Tackle and Flies: Dry flies are the norm during summer months, but small indicators for shallow nymph rigs are needed, too. In early spring, dry fly fishing is prime, though your best bet is to use streamers and subsurface patterns except when water temperatures are high enough to trigger hatches. Yellow Sallies and Golden stoneflies are great for mid-June. Grasshoppers and other terrestrials are hot during the summer months. July and August is your cue to break out the Trico imitations in the morning and caddis patterns for the prolific evening caddis emergences. During the fall, be sure to pack Blue-winged Olives and midge patterns. The Brown trout spawn means you'll be reaching for your streamer boxes again.

Above. What, no crowds? Fly-fishing heaven at Capitol Reef National Park.

Right. Famous Boulder Mountain brook trout. Shawn Saunders

One of more than
50 fishable lakes in the
Boulder Mountains.
Shawn Saunders

CLOSEST CITY OR POINT OF ENTRANCE TO THE PARK

Torrey, Utah is eight miles west of Capitol Reef National Park's visitors' center on Utah 24.

CLOSEST AIRPORT

The closest airport is Richfield Municipal Airport in Richfield, Utah, where auto rental and other transportation services are available.

FEES

· The park is open year-round with no entry fees (except for the 10-mile scenic loop found south of the visitors' center).
· Park entrance and user fees change periodically.
· For up-to-date fees, free days and other exceptions, visit www.nps.gov/care/index.htm.

OPEN/CLOSING PARK DATES OR FISHING DATES

· Fishing is available year-round.
· A Utah fishing license is required and Utah regulations apply throughout the park.

· Some Boulder Mountain lakes are closed November 1 through the third Saturday in April.

CLOSEST FLY SHOPS

Fremont River Guides & Fly Shop
135 East Utah 24
Torrey, UT 84775
435-425-3999 Store
435-491-0242 Mobile
www.flyfishingsouthernutah.com

Quiet Fly Fisher
17 East 200 North
Loa, UT 84747
435-616-2319
www.quietflyfisher.com

CLOSEST GUIDE SERVICES

Fremont River Guides
435-425-3999 Store
435-491-0242 Mobile
www.flyfishingsouthernutah.com

Quiet Fly Fisher
435-616-2319
www.quietflyfisher.com

CLOSEST LODGES

The Lodge at Red River Ranch
2900 West Utah 24
Teasdale, UT 84773
435-425-3322
www.redriverranch.com

Cougar Ridge Lodge
Cougar Ridge Road
Torrey, UT 84775
801-699-6665
www.cougarridgelodge.com

Austin's Chuckwagon Motel
12 W. Main St.
Torrey, UT 84775
435-425-3335
www.austinschuckwagonmotel.com

CLOSEST, BEST HOTELS

The Rim Rock Inn
2523 Utah 24
Torrey, UT 84775
435-425-3398
www.therimrock.net

Broken Spur Inn
955 E. Utah 24
Torrey, UT 84775
435-25-3775
www.brokenspurinn.com

SHAWN SANDERS—Shawn has been teaching others about the many types of western trout waters for more than 25 years. His true love is fly fishing for big trout in small waters. While growing up on the banks of the Big Wood River and Silver Creek in southern Idaho, he became an outdoor addict and never recovered. Family lured him to southern Utah as a kid; he eventually returned to open Fremont River Guides & Fly Shop in 2001. Through his quarter century of guiding, Shawn has acquired a lot of stories to tell. He has hosted destination trips to Alaska, the Bahamas, Belize, Mexico and elsewhere. *The Fly Fishing Masters* television series western regional qualifier hosted its national competition on his private waters on the Fremont River in 2006. Over the past 10 years, other television shows, *Hooked On Utah* and *Reel Outdoors,* have also showcased his southern Utah waters on the Sportsman Channel. He now enjoys most of his leisure time in the outdoors with his wife and kids.

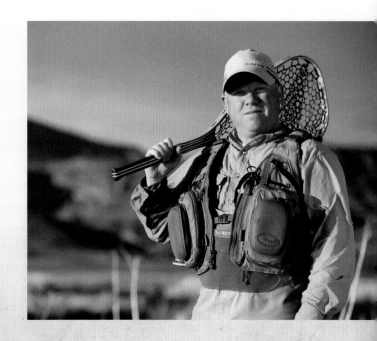

Capitol Reef Resort
2600 E. Utah 24
Torrey, UT 84775
435-425-3761
www.capitolreefresort.com

CLOSEST, BEST CAMPGROUNDS
OUTSIDE THE PARK
Boulder Mountain
· Singletree
· Lower Bowns
· Pleasant Creek
· Oak Creek

Fishlake National Forest
Multiple developed and undeveloped camping areas are available.
115 East 900 North
Richfield, UT 84701
435-896-9233

CLOSEST, BEST CAMPGROUND
INSIDE THE PARK
Fruita Campground
435-425-3791

CLOSEST AND BEST RESTAURANTS
The Rim Rock Restaurant
2523 Utah 24
Torrey, UT 84775
435-425-3388
www.therimrock.net

Café Diablo
599 W. Main St.
Torrey, UT 84775
435-425-3070
www.cafediablo.net

Broken Spur Steakhouse
955 E. Utah 24
Torrey, UT 84775
435-425-3775
www.brokenspurinn.com

CLOSEST AND BEST PLACES
TO GET A DRINK
The Rim Rock Patio
2523 Utah 24
Torrey, UT 84775
435-425-3389
www.therimrock.net

The Saddlery Cowboy Bar & Steakhouse
422 Utah 24
Torrey, UT 84775
435-425-2424
www.saddlerycowboybar.com

MUST SEE
Hickman Bridge (a moderate one-mile hike)

NEAREST HOSPITAL/URGENT
TREATMENT CENTER
Wayne Community Health Center
128 North 300 West
Bicknell, UT 84715
435-425-3744
www.waynechc.org

CELL PHONE SERVICE
Cell phone service is fair to good throughout park and adjacent areas, depending on the carrier.

FOR ALL ELSE, VISIT:
www.nps.gov/care/index.htm

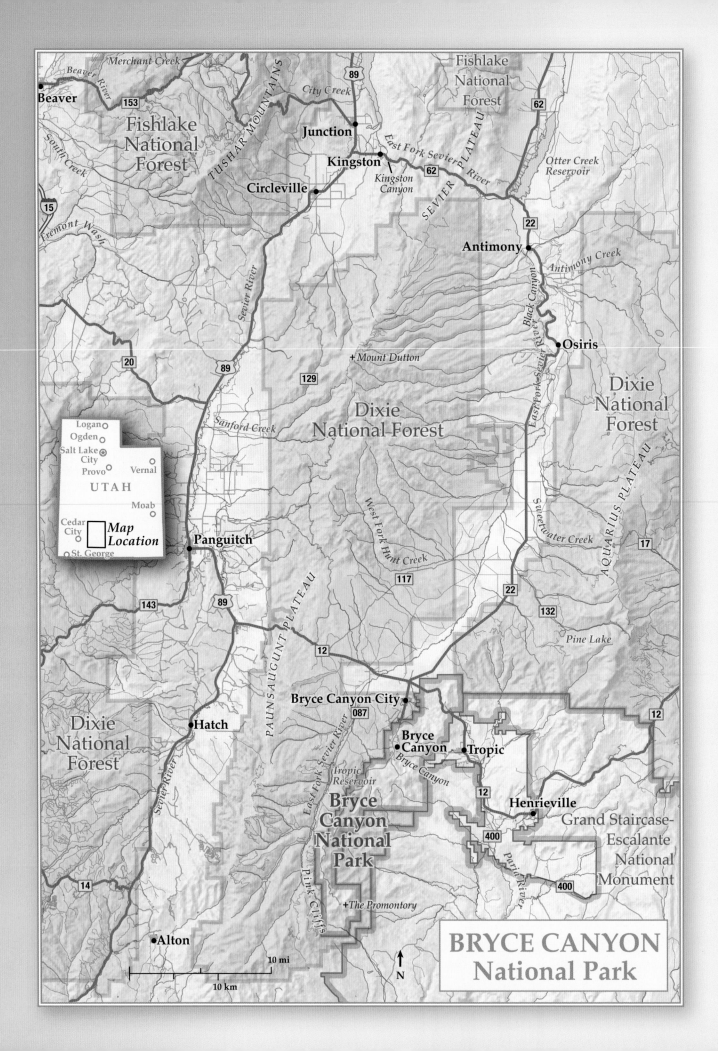

Beaver

Merchant Creek

Beaver River

153

Fishlake
National
Forest

South Creek

TUSHAR MOUNTAINS

City Creek

89

Junction

East Fork Sevier River

Kingston

62

Circleville

Kingston
Canyon

SEVIER PLATEAU

Fishlake
National
Forest

62

Otter Creek
Reservoir

22

Antimony

Antimony Creek

15

Fremont Wash

Sevier River

20

89

129

Sanford Creek

+ Mount Dutton

Dixie
National Forest

Black Canyon

East Fork Sevier River

Osiris

Dixie
National
Forest

Logan ○
Ogden ○
Salt Lake ⊕
City
Provo ○   Vernal ○

UTAH

Moab ○

Cedar
City ○   Map
          Location
○ St. George

Panguitch

West Fork Hunt Creek

117

Sweetwater Creek

AQUARIUS PLATEAU

17

22

132

Pine Lake

143

89

12

PAUNSAUGUNT PLATEAU

Bryce Canyon City

087

Hatch

Sevier River

East Fork Sevier River

Tropic
Reservoir

Bryce
Canyon

Bryce Canyon

Tropic

12

Henrieville

12

Grand Staircase-
Escalante
National
Monument

Dixie
National
Forest

14

Bryce
Canyon
National
Park

Pink Cliffs

+ The Promontory

400

Paria River

400

Alton

10 mi

10 km

N

BRYCE CANYON
National Park

Bryce Canyon National Park

➤ **Location:** The park is open year-round and is usually accessed from Salt Lake City, which is a three-hour drive from the north, or from Las Vegas, a 4.5-hour drive from the south. Visitors can also travel through Grand Junction, Colorado, which is a five-hour drive.

The Bryce Canyon area was settled by Mormon pioneers in the 1850s and named after Ebenezer Bryce, who homesteaded in the region in 1874. The area around Bryce Canyon became a national monument in 1923 and was designated a national park in 1928. The park sits at elevations between 8,000–9,000 feet and covers 35,835 acres. Bryce Canyon is distinctive because of geological structures called hoodoos, formed by frost weathering and stream erosion of the river and lake bed sedimentary rocks. The red, orange, and white colors of the rocks provide spectacular views.

Anglers should be aware that all fly-fishing waters are located outside of park boundaries, but they're nearby and convenient for partial day excursions that begin in the Bryce Canyon area itself. The most important waters—ranging from 6,500–8,500 feet above sea level—are the East Fork (Sevier River), Tropic Reservoir, Antimony Creek, the main stem of the Sevier River, and Kingston Canyon

Most fly-fishing addicts can find the nearest water, get their feet wet, and somehow forget about everything else, including most of the surroundings. Even the most avid angler will lose themselves in the fairyland-style rock and geologic formations. While dry fly fantasies dance in our heads, big, wild trout are looking up and waiting just a few short miles from park boundaries.

Closest to the park entrance are the headwaters of the East Fork of the Sevier River upstream of Tropic Reservoir. The stream, though very small, is playful and healthy with wild browns and cutthroat. Shorter lightweight rods are a must to pinpoint casts into stretches you could jump across. Fishing below the reservoir is not recommended as it is dewatered for irrigation most of the season.

Sunrise at Bryce Point lights up manzanitas.
Brian B. Roanhorse, NPS

This angler found southern Utah's fly fishing Mecca. Shawn Saunders

The Sevier River drainage surrounds the area in its different forks and makes up the most important water for fly fishers. The main stem near Hatch, the East Fork near Antimony, and Kingston Canyon will offer extensive opportunities and varied water types. Anglers visiting for the first time should give ample attention to all of them as they are home to wild brown, cutthroat and rainbow trout and, more importantly, some "blue ribbon" fly-fishing habitat.

Though the small town of Hatch was not named after its epic and famous aquatic insect life, it could have been. Rather, the name comes from the prominent Utah family name recognized in the political arena. There is an expectation that when you hear about the main stem of any river it's going to be substantial water requiring wading ability and a heavier rod. In this case, neither would be true—and that goes for all the waters near Bryce Canyon. Average flows around 50 cubic feet per second or less are most common during good conditions. Pay close attention to the many private posted sections of the Sevier River.

Plentiful undisturbed sections are at your rod's tip and it would take several days to experience all of it. Most of the wild fish are browns or cutthroat, but rainbows are stocked regularly on specific stretches. Don't let the small waters fool you since bruisers exceeding 20 inches are a regular occurrence. Prolific mayfly, caddis, midge and terrestrial hatches are to be expected here just as you would find anywhere else with the perfect mid-summer temperatures in the 80s and elevations around 6,500 feet.

The most extensive and fishable public access is the East Fork, located due north from the junction of Utah 12 and Utah 63 near the town of Antimony. Pine Lake is on your way and only 15 minutes from Bryce. This small west slope of the Boulder Mountain lake is a wonderful opportunity for a float tube. This stretch of water is lined by pine trees and mountains and is easily accessed by car, truck or RV. If you continue driving north on Utah 63 past the Pine Lake access road, you will first see the uppermost stretches of the canyon. As you lose elevation, it widens, and the stream's flow slows

*Chasing rainbows outside Bryce Canyon
National Park. Shawn Sauders*

down and pools into varied pocket water and slow moving meadow areas.

Above the mill are narrow canyon walls, which create pocket water that is perfect habitat for stoneflies. Downstream are slow moving riffles and some runs where breathtaking spinner falls will choke out even the best of nose breathers. Willows, rabbit brush, sage and cedar trees provide ample cover for trout to grow large. This section is also known as Black Canyon due to its abrupt canyon walls of basalt rock.

Antimony Creek—a feeder stream of the East Fork whose headwaters flow from the Boulder Mountains—is a stunningly beautiful freestone stream found just north of Black Canyon. Its waters are smaller, and typically the fish are, too. However, concentrations of rainbow, brown and cutthroat trout are sure to put a grin on your face. Nothing seems to be a secret anymore, but on weekdays, Antimony Creek sure seems like a secret since you'll usually see more deer than anglers.

*Below. One of more than a dozen trophy
trout lakes on Boulder Mountain. Shawn Saunders*

Above. Green Lake mid-summer splendor.
Shawn Saunders

Inset. Big brown trout are commonplace
near Bryce Canyon. Shawn Saunders

Further north on Utah 63, passing through the town of Antimony, is Otter Creek Reservoir. This is float-tube fishing at its finest! Otter Creek Reservoir is a large impoundment, that's home to consistent numbers of rainbows ranging from 16-18 inches. Otter Creek is famous for tempting anglers to keep a fish or two. Downstream is Kingston Canyon, an eight-mile section passing mostly through once privately held land that is now contracted or purchased by the state of Utah for public access. It is also designated as a Blue Ribbon Fishery. Don't forget your camera as Kingston Canyon won't disappoint for scenery or size of fish.

➤ **The Season:** The fly-fishing season near Bryce Canyon is similar to other Rocky Mountain states except that runoff here ends earlier in May instead of June. The Tushar Mountains drain the upper stretches of the Sevier River and unless snowpack is much higher than average, anglers can expect good conditions the first few days in June or earlier. The Boulder Mountains feed lower sections of the East Fork and Antimony Creek, and runoff is seldom substantial enough to pay any attention to after April.

In any case, prime fishing conditions on many of the local waters can be had during March and April before the typical uneventful runoff. Once waters are diverted into dry canals in preparation for growing hay, main-stem flows drop, water temperatures rise and hatches commence. As these temperatures rise weekly, the hatches get more prolific by the day until late May and early June when the best conditions prevail.

Bad weather patterns in southern Utah are very rare in early summer as dry warm air from the south prevails. Blue skies and daytime temperatures in the upper 70s to low 80s are most common. Rain is not the subject of conversation until mid-July. During mid-July through mid-September, monsoonal flows can create havoc on lower elevation streams because of thunder showers. During this rainy period, guides typically move to higher elevation streams and creeks where waters remain clear and cool.

➤ **The Hatches:** Similar to most western states, April brings great midge and Baetis activity as well good dry-fly action. Fly fishers should continue to use streamers and subsurface patterns except when water temperatures are high enough to trigger hatches. The best success is in deep pools as well as tail-outs. Slow stripping streamers works well. Also, look closely at back eddies where midges and mayflies ride the foam and emerge.

Expect Yellow Sallies in late May as well caddis and continued Blue-winged Olive mayflies. Salmon-flies pop up in late May or as late as early June in some areas. Through most of June and early July, Golden stoneflies are the biggest players during the day. If you stay until dark, you're likely to see a mind-boggling evening caddis emergence spread the whole area.

Grasshoppers and other terrestrials will already be in full swing by early June. On the lakes and reservoirs, there are damsel, dragonfly, midge, mayfly and caddis hatches, too. Fishing is great throughout the day, and you should be prepared for a plenitude of surface opportunities all at once.

July and August is time for smaller bugs. Water temperatures will reach the upper 60s, perfect for tricos (*Tricorythodes*) in the morning and prolific evening caddis emergences. Restock your headlamp with batteries and take an afternoon nap in preparation for skating caddis after 8 p.m.

Large numbers of trout will form pods as they engulf mayflies and caddis early and late in the day. Early morning or late evening lake fishing will require increased depth and sink-tip lines.

During September and early October, Blue-winged Olives and midges will re-surface, and middle of the day fishing will be most productive. Browns will spawn, which means the streamer boxes come out of the closet again. November is a great month to find some tranquil angling and even some calm sunny weather. This is the most under-fished month of the year when many other activities distract anglers from some awesome opportunities for fly fishing southern Utah.

➤ **Practical Knowledge:** Stealth is the best ruler for measuring success. Because the area streams are smaller in size and flow, wading slowly and targeting prime holding lies are imperative. Walk slowly and use banks to spot trout and hide behind as you figure out your game plan. Trout are not particularly picky to specific patterns most of the time, but these wild trout notice tippet and presentation. Landing a fly softly is a lost art in this day of ultra-fast action fly rods and

Put the tiger trout at the top of your bucket list. Shawn Saunders

seemingly distance-crazed fly-casters. Wary trout in the 20- to 25-inch range are catchable with short soft presentations. In most western waters of comparable size, anglers don't expect to catch fish in the 20-inch class regularly. In southern Utah, this would be a mistake if you're not ready for it.

Boats and float tubes will not help you on any stream waters of southern Utah, but in the nearby lakes and reservoirs you are at a huge advantage.

When fishing the valley streams and higher elevation lakes in mid-summer months, always beware of quick moving monsoonal storms that can bring with them aggressive thunderstorms and lightning. A good rain-jacket and light fleece can come in handy when the temperatures drop from 85 to 50 degrees in just minutes.

➤ **Animal Life:** Bryce Canyon National Park and the surrounding areas are a nature and animal lover's paradise. From one side to the other, birds and big game can easily be viewed without even leaving city limits. City folk are largely outnumbered by hundreds of river-bottom deer, high mountain elk herds, and beavers splashing their tails in the evening. Antelopes, elk, moose, mule deer, mountain lions, coyotes, black bears, beavers and many others can be seen in Canyon Country. Various birds of prey, including bald eagles, hawks, falcons and others, are regulars, too.

Keep in mind that even though these canyons are somewhat easily accessible, you can get lost in the beauty of your surroundings. Flash floods can result from very little rainfall during the summer months of July to early September.

➤ Tackle and Gear

Rods and Line: Streams mostly call for 3- and 4-weight rods between 7 and 9 feet. Consider longer ones for open meadow areas as well as shorter rods for densely forested, high-elevation moving waters. Rods bigger than a 5-weight are seldom needed. Perhaps the rod of choice would be an 8-foot, 4-weight.

Terminal Tackle and Flies: Dry flies are the norm during summer months, but small indicators for shallow nymph rigs are needed here as well. Trout are mostly wary to anglers, and not so much to specific flies or tippets. On the lighter side, 5X and 6X tippets are usually what you need. You'll want some 4X tippet for use with big dries and nymphs. Long-tapered leaders are not the rule here, but stealth is very important. Anglers should bring their best presentations to the trophy fish that can be found in these waters. Floating lines will be most useful, and sinking lines might come in handy on still-waters, reservoirs and other impoundments. Bring waders for spring and fall lake wading. Waist highs are most comfortable and practical for streams, though chest waders are needed for the lakes. Wet wading is popular among the guides, and is the most comfortable option for hiking around the large expanses of rivers and streams.

*The picturesque secluded
"Boulder Creek." Shawn Saunders*

**CLOSEST CITY OR ENTRANCE
TO THE PARK**
Cedar City, St. George, and Provo, Utah
Flagstaff, Arizona

CLOSEST AIRPORT
Cedar City Regional Airport, where auto rental and other transportation services are available. The airport is about a 90-minute drive from the park.

FEES
Park entrance and user fees change periodically. For up-to-date fees, free days, and other exceptions, visit www.nps.gov/brca/index.htm.

FISHING REGULATIONS
See Utah fishing regulations at www.wildlife.utah.gov/fishing-in-utah/.

CLOSEST GUIDE SERVICES
Fremont River Guides & Fly Shop
135 East Main St.
Torrey, UT 84775
435-425-3999 Store
435-491-0242 Mobile
www.flyfishingsouthernutah.com
info@fremontriverguides.com

Circle Valley Anglers
350 U.S. Route 89
Circleville, UT 84723
435-577-2168
www.circlevalleyanglers.com
circlevalleyanglers@gmail.com

CLOSEST LODGES
Stone Canyon Inn
1380 W. Stone Canyon Ln.
Tropic, UT 84776
435-679-8611
www.stonecanyoninn.com

Ruby's Inn
6 S. Main St.
Bryce Canyon, UT 84764
435-834-5341
www.rubysinn.com

The Lodge at Bryce Canyon
Bryce Canyon National Park
Bryce Canyon, UT 84764
435-834-8700

CLOSEST, BEST HOTELS
Bryce Canyon Resort
13500 E. Utah 12
Bryce Canyon, UT 84764
435-834-5351
www.brycecanyonresort.com

Bryce Canyon Pines
Utah 12, mile marker 10
Bryce Canyon, UT 84764
435-892-7923
www.brycecanyonmotel.com

SHAWN SANDERS—Shawn has been teaching others about the many types of western trout waters for more than 25 years. His true love is fly fishing for big trout in small waters. While growing up on the banks of the Big Wood River and Silver Creek in southern Idaho, he became an outdoor addict and never recovered. Family lured him to southern Utah as a kid; he eventually returned to open Fremont River Guides & Fly Shop in 2001. Through his quarter century of guiding, Shawn has acquired a lot of stories to tell. He has hosted destination trips to Alaska, the Bahamas, Belize, Mexico and elsewhere. *The Fly Fishing Masters* television series western regional qualifier hosted its national competition on his private waters on the Fremont River in 2006. Over the past 10 years, other television shows, *Hooked On Utah* and *Reel Outdoors,* have also showcased his southern Utah waters on the Sportsman Channel. He now enjoys most of his leisure time in the outdoors with his wife and kids.

Bryce View Lodge
105 E. Center St.
Bryce Canyon, UT 84764
435-834-5180
www.bryceviewlodge.com

CLOSEST, BEST CAMPGROUND
OUTSIDE THE PARK
Both campgrounds are in close proximity to the visitor's center and amphitheater, and are surrounded by Ponderosa pines. Sites fill up early, so make advanced reservations.

Bryce Canyon Pines
435-834-5441

Ruby's Inn
435-834-5301

CLOSEST, BEST CAMPGROUND
INSIDE THE PARK
Sunset Campground
This campground is located about 1.5 miles south of visitor center, west of Sunset Point. It sports 80 RV and tent sites (first-come-first-served) and 20 specific tent camping sites (first-come-first-served), restrooms with flush toilets, and drinking water.
877-444-6777
www.recreation.gov

North Campground
This campground is located just east of the visitor center. A general store includes coin-operated laundry and showers. This campground includes restrooms with flush toilets, drinking water, 13 RV sites (by advanced reservation), and 86 RV and tent camping sites (all first-come-first-served).
877-444-6777
www.recreation.gov

CLOSEST RESTAURANT AND
BEST RESTAURANT
Stone Hearth Grille
1380 W. Stone Canyon Ln.
Tropic, UT 84776
435-679-8923
www.stonehearthgrille.com

Ebenezer's Barn & Grill
110 Center St.
Bryce Canyon City, UT 84764
435-834-5341
www.ebenezersbarnandgrill.com

Canyon Diner at Ruby's Inn
26 S. Main St.
Bryce Canyon, UT 84764
435-834-8030
www.rubysinn.com

CLOSEST AND BEST PLACES
TO GET A DRINK
Stone Hearth Grille
Tropic, UT 84776
435-679-8923
www.stonehearthgrille.com

Ebenezer's Barn & Grill
Bryce Canyon City, UT 84764
435-834-5341
www.ebenezersbarnandgrill.com

Canyon Diner at Ruby's Inn
435-834-8030
www.rubysinn.com

MUST SEE
Sunrise Point—Less than a half-mile walk

NEAREST HOSPITAL/URGENT
CARE CENTER
Garfield Memorial Hospital
200 N. 400 E.
Panguitch UT, 84759
435-676-8811

CELL PHONE SERVICE
Cell service is generally good with a few dead spots.

FOR ALL ELSE, VISIT:
www.nps.gov/brca/index.htm

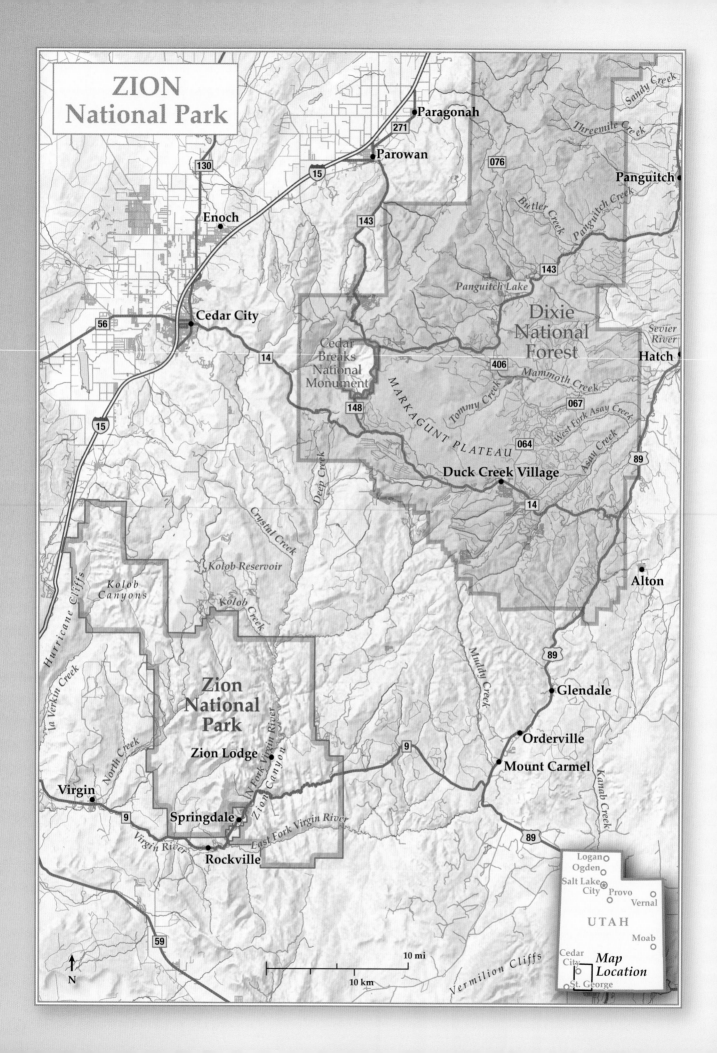

ZION
National Park

Paragonah

271

Parowan

130

15

076

Panguitch

Enoch

143

Butler Creek

Panguitch Creek

Threemile Creek

Sandy Creek

143

Panguitch Lake

Dixie
National
Forest

Sevier
River

Cedar City

14

56

15

Cedar
Breaks
National
Monument

148

406

Mammoth Creek

Hatch

067

West Fork Asay Creek

Asay Creek

89

MARKAGUNT PLATEAU

Tommy Creek

064

Duck Creek Village

14

Deep Creek

Crystal Creek

Kolob Reservoir

Kolob
Canyons

Kolob Creek

Alton

Hurricane Cliffs

La Verkin Creek

North Creek

Zion
National
Park

Zion Lodge

N Fork Virgin River

Zion Canyon

Muddy Creek

9

89

Glendale

Orderville

Mount Carmel

Virgin

9

Springdale

East Fork Virgin River

Kanab Creek

Virgin River

Rockville

89

59

N

10 mi

10 km

Logan
Ogden
Salt Lake
City
Provo
Vernal

UTAH

Moab

Cedar
City

*Map
Location*

St. George

Vermilion Cliffs

➤ **Location:** Zion National Park is in southwestern Utah on Utah 9 in Springdale. Drive distances from major Utah cities are

- Las Vegas, Nevada: 163 miles
- Mesquite, Nevada: 80 miles
- Saint George, Utah: 40 miles
- Salt Lake City, Utah: 307 miles
- Cedar City, Utah: 57 miles

Zion is six hours from Phoenix, Arizona. The closest International airport is McCarran in Las Vegas. Commuter air service is available to and from most small cities around Zion. Interstate 15 borders the west boundary of the park, and U.S. Route 89 borders the east.

The earliest known inhabitants of the Zion Area were the hunter-gatherer groups of the early Anasazi culture thousands of years ago. They gave way to the Virgin Anasazi who settled in permanent communities along with what many consider a splinter group of the Anasazi, the Parowan Fremont Indians. Together, they occupied Southern Utah and the Zion area from about 200 CE through about 1300 CE (Common Era). Their petroglyphs and pictographs are a record of their stay.

The Anasazi were the first to bring primitive irrigation for crop cultivation to the area. They were followed by several different tribes of Southern Paiute Indians who occupied the Zion area between 1300 and 1800. When Mormon pioneers

Temples and Towers of the Virgin. John Fowler

Sunrise in Zion Canyon. Stuart Seeger

began settling the area in 1858, the Southern Paiute Indians cohabitated the area with their new neighbors.

Zion entered national prominence in 1909 when President William Howard Taft dedicated it as Mukuntuweap National Monument (Mukuntuweap translates from the Paiute Indian word meaning "straight canyon"). Zion has the distinction of being Utah's first national park. It was dedicated in November, 1919 by President Woodrow Wilson, based on its magnificent geological formations, canyons and sandstone cliffs.

A wide variety of recreational activities await park visitors: hiking, mountain biking, off-road Jeep tours, guided tours, orienteering, trekking, rock climbing and, of course, fly fishing.

We are going to let you in on a secret. Aside from the sheer beauty and historical significance of Zion, it performs one more important task: Zion is the Southern Gateway to a vast area of presently untapped fly-fishing opportunity. This is truly one of the last underutilized fly-fishing areas in the world. Imagine spending the entire day on the stream without seeing another angler. Instead, you see lots of trout, deer, turkeys and other wildlife. These are not the typical large Western Rivers

that can be so intimidating. These are small, easily waded rivers and streams. Southern Utah fly fishing should be on your bucket list.

Just west of the Zion Park entrance, several warm water fisheries offer anglers a chance at largemouth bass, bluegill, crappie and sunfish. Within a short drive of Zion, fishing opportunities expand to hundreds of miles of coldwater streams and high mountain reservoirs. Several Blue Ribbon fisheries are located within a short drive of the park. These fisheries offer a unique outdoor experience:

· High fishing quality
· Exceptional fish habitat
· Public access

Most of these fisheries have undergone extensive habitat restoration or are scheduled for restoration. Utah has invested millions of dollars in stream restoration for the southern part of the state.

Dixie National Forest borders Zion to the north and is home to several excellent fishing destinations. The headwaters of the Sevier River begin high up on the Markagunt Plateau with the Asay flowing into the Sevier River upstream of where the Mammoth enters. These two streams combine to become one of the top fishing destinations in southern Utah. Asay is easily accessed along Utah 89, and access to Mammoth begins at the confluence of these two streams. Several miles of public access are available as Asay winds its way through an open meadow.

Casting is stress-free in this wide open area, and the easy wading makes this stream a great choice for a quick trip. Rainbow and brown trout inhabit this stream along with mountain whitefish. To the delight of both fish and angler, there are prolific western insect hatches, including Blue-winged Olives, black and golden stoneflies, and numerous caddis hatches.

Mammoth Creek is one of the gems of Southern Utah. It is a classic high mountain stream with extremely fertile aquatic insect populations. All of the western hatches come off like clockwork on this beautiful stream.

Mammoth begins its journey in a pristine alpine setting and ends in a high desert meadow. Mammoth is predominantly a brown trout fishery with brook and cutthroat trout available in some of the high tributaries. Mammoth has one of the best Western Green Drake hatches in southern Utah, and the best part of that is the giant Salmonfly hatch occurs at about the same time. There are more than nine miles of public access, most of which are posted artificial fly- and lure-only, and are subject to slot limits. On the negative side, access on the stream is not well marked. The stream borders large portions of private property, so to get the most out of your outing on Mammoth, it is advisable to hire a guide.

Panguitch Lake, located in this area of Dixie National Forest, is another good-to-excellent fishery. Panguitch (from the Paiute word meaning big fish) is truly what its name implies. Each year, some of the largest Bonneville cutthroat, rainbows and tiger trout are landed on this body of water. The reservoir covers more than 1,200 surface acres with public access available around most of the lake. Float tubers and those with small pontoon boats seem to do the best on the lake. However, shore fishing can be highly productive. Callibeatis are the lone mayfly on the lake, but damsels and midges pick up the slack. Don't forget your chironomid patterns.

A 9-foot, 5-weight will do most of the work here, but Panguitch is an excellent spot to break out a 6-, 7- or 8-weight.

Note that all cutthroat and tiger trout from 15- to 22-inches must be immediately released.

Desert bighorn sheep are a common sight in and around Zion. Terry Gunn

Panguitch Creek exits the lake on the northeast. This tailwater stream is predominantly a brown trout fishery. With more than 15 miles of public access, the stream begins with a steep gradient and transforms into a winding meadow stream at its lower elevations. The Blue Ribbon section of the stream is artificial fly- and lure-only. This section begins at the confluence with Butler Creek and ends at the irrigation diversion near the town of Panguitch. Good populations of rainbows, browns and cutthroat inhabit this area of the stream. Panguitch is an extremely fertile small stream, and trout can grow as large as 20 inches. Abundant summer hatches make Panguitch a top dry fly-fishing destination.

The closest Blue Ribbon fishery to Zion is Kolob Reservoir, located just outside the Zion boundary to the west. Kolob sits in a gorgeous alpine setting at an elevation of just over 8,100 feet. Bonneville cutthroat and large rainbows are found here.

Anaszi petroglyphs, which are more than a thousand years old, document that the Anaszi were once here. Terry Gunn

93

Above. A tiger trout is a cross between a brown trout and brook trout, and can reach weights of more than 10 pounds. Shawn Saunders

Inset. Brown trout are the most common stream-dwelling trout in the region. Shawn Saunders

Bald eagles circle the sky above the reservoir and do a little fishing of their own. Shore fishing is productive throughout the spring, especially after ice off.

When temperatures start to warm up and fish move to the deeper water, a float tube or small pontoon boat is suggested. Most of Southern Utah's reservoirs have large populations of crayfish, and Kolob is no exception. That means you should stock up on buggers and other crayfish imitations. Tie one on and hold on tight, because these cutts and bows get huge. Fish up to and over 24 inches are not out of the ordinary.

For a fly angler, no trip to Southern Utah would be complete without a side trip to two of our favorite locations:
· East Fork of the Sevier in Kingston Canyon
· Beaver River/Merchant Creek, which flows
    down the west slope of the Tushar Mountains

The East Fork of the Sevier in Kingston Canyon is another good choice for a day trip. With more than nine miles of

public access make this section of the East Fork a popular fishing destination. Large populations of brown, rainbow and cutthroat trout inhabit this partial tailwater. A majority of the East Fork flows into Otter Creek Reservoir and is then released back out into the Kingston Canyon section. One small irrigation canal from the upstream section of the East Fork acts as a tributary and can add to the turbidity after a rain storm.

The river is mainly used for irrigation purposes between May and September. From mid-September through early spring, this is by far the best trout water in Southern Utah. Fish grow fast and large here due to the large crayfish population, so streamer fishing is the name of the game. That's not to say that dry-fly enthusiasts can't have the time of their lives, too. Most of Utah's streams and reservoirs allow primitive camping, and there is no better place than along the East Fork. The Kingston Canyon camping area is a short drive north of Zion National Park on U.S. Route 89.

Above. Alpine lakes near the park can offer great fishing into the late fall. Shawn Saunders

Inset. The Bonneville cutthroat trout is the state fish of Utah. Shawn Saunders

The Beaver River/Merchant Creek area is just east of the town in the Tushar Mountains. More than 12 miles of stream access await you on this small river. At 8,400-feet, Merchant Creek starts its trip down the mountain with abundant populations of small rainbows and browns—and all of them have no objection to a well-presented dry fly. Large summer hatches keep these fish looking up all season long, and the river below offers countless pocket water opportunities— the classic riffle, run, and pool topography that we all look for—with fish up to 18 inches populating the lower sections. Scenery along the creek and the river below will enhance your fishing experience. Pullouts are located throughout the canyon along with picnic areas and campsites.

➤ Tackle and Gear

Rods and Line: We recommend 7- to 9-foot, 3- to 5-weight rods for most stream situations. A 7- to 8-weight is an asset on most of the reservoirs. Use floating lines for streams and for some reservoir fishing. Make sure to have sink-tip and full-sink lines for the reservoirs, too.

Terminal Tackle and Flies: We recommend 3X to 6X tippets, and 7.5- to 12-foot leaders. Fluorocarbon is helpful, but not necessary, though fluorocarbon tippet material is recommended. Flies are covered within the chapter text above.

CLOSEST CITY OR POINT OF ENTRANCE TO THE PARK

The park is best accessed via Springdale, Utah.

CLOSEST AIRPORTS

- St. George Airport (SGU)—Less than an hour's drive. Daily non-stop service to Salt Lake City (SLC) and Los Angeles (LAX)
- Las Vegas McCarran International Airport (LAS)—About 160 miles from Zion
- Bryce Canyon Airport (BCE)—In Bryce Canyon
- Salt Lake City International Airport (SLC)—About 290 miles from Zion
- Cedar City Airport (CDC)—About 70 miles from Zion

See more at http://www.travelwest.net /zion-transportation#sthash .y4HkAlAg.dpuf.

OPEN/CLOSING PARK DATES OR FISHING DATES

The park is open 24 hours a day, every day of the year. Some services and facilities might close or reduce hours during parts of the year. All park visitors are required to purchase a recreational use pass upon entering Zion National Park.

FEES:

- Seven-day admission pass—$25
- Annual National Park Pass—$80
- Senior pass—$10 plus a $10 processing fee
- Entrance, parking and use-fees can change annually.
- Visit http://www.nps.gov/zion/planyour-visit/fees.htm.

FISHING REGULATIONS

Fishing is permitted all year.
For more information, please visit http://wildlife.utah.gov/fishing-in-utah.

CLOSEST FLY SHOPS

Circle Valley Anglers
350 S. Utah 89
P.O. Box 268
Circleville, UT 84723-0268
435-577-2168
circlevalleyanglers@gmail.com
www.circlevalleyanglers.com

LOCAL STORES THAT CARRY SOME FLY-FISHING EQUIPMENT

Sportsman's Warehouse
2957 E. 850 North
Saint George, UT 84790
435-634-7300
www.sportsmanswarehouse.com

Hurst's Ace Hardware & Sporting Goods
165 S. Main St.
Cedar City, UT 84720
435-865-9335
www.hurstacecc.com

Beaver Sport & Pawn
91 N. Main S.
Beaver, UT 84713
435-438-2100
www.beaversport.com

CLOSEST GUIDES / OUTFITTER SERVICES

Circle Valley Anglers
350 S. Utah 89
P.O. Box 268
Circleville, UT 84723-0268
435-577-2168
circlevalleyanglers@gmail.com
www.circlevalleyanglers.com

Fremont River Guides & Fly Shop
135 E. Main St.
Torrey, UT 84775
435-425-3999 Store
435-491-0242 Mobile
fremontguide@gmail.com

BEST PLACE TO STAY IN THE PARK

Zion Lodge
Zion National Park
P.O. Box 925
Springdale, Utah 84767
435-772-7700

BEST PLACES TO STAY OUTSIDE THE PARK

Angler's Inn
350 S. Utah 89
Circleville, UT 84723-0268
435-577-2168
circlevalleyanglers@gmail.com
www.circlevalleyanglers.com
(Closest to all waters)

Cottonwood Meadows Lodge
Mile marker 123, U.S. Route 89
Panguitch, UT 84759
435-676-8950
www.cottocmeadowlodge.com

Blue Springs Lodge
120 W. Utah 143
Panguitch, UT 84759
800-987-5634
www.bluespringslodge.com

CLOSEST TO ZION WITH LODGING, DINING, AND DRINK

Bumbleberry Inn and Theater
97 Bumbleberry Ln.
Springdale, UT 84767
800-828-1534
www.bummbleberry.com

Flanigan's Inn / Villas & Restaurant
428 Zion Park Blvd.
Springdale, UT 84767
800-765-7787
www.flanigans.com

BEST PLACES TO EAT NEAR THE PARK

Maria Cocina
1419 E. Canyon Rd.
Beaver, UT 84713
435438-5654

Painted Pony
2 West St. George Blvd.
Saint George, UT 84770
435-634-1700
www.painted-pony.com

Milt's Stage Stop
3560 E. Utah 14
Cedar City, UT 84721
435-586-9344
www.miltsstagestop.com

Centro Wood-fired Pizzeria
50 W. Center St.
Cedar City, UT 84720
435-867-8010

BEST CAMPGROUNDS IN THE PARK

South Campground and Watchman Campground
These campgrounds are near the south entrance at Springdale. This part of the park is desert, and there are few trees.

EMMETT DOANE AND MICHELLE KAMPER
have owned and operated Circle Valley Anglers Fly
Shop and Anglers Inn Lodging since 2005. The shop
and lodging are located just a short drive from three
national parks—Zion, Bryce Canyon and Capitol
Reef. Emmett has been fly fishing and tying flies
for more than 40 years, and is a long-time member
of Trout Unlimited, the International Federation
of Fly Fishers, and the Federation of Fly Fishers
Guide Association.

BEST CAMPGROUNDS NEAR THE PARK

Zion River Resort
551 E. Utah 9
Virgin, Utah 84779
800-838-8594
www.zionriverresort.com

Bear Paw Fishing Resort
905 S. Utah 89
Panguitch, UT 84759
888-553-8439
www.bearpawfishingresort.com

*Best Western Town & Country Motel /
Campground*
189 N. Main St.
Cedar City, UT 84720
888-347-2319
Info@bwcountry.com
(Yes, there is a small RV park tucked
behind the motel.)

CLOSEST PLACE TO GET A DRINK

Majestic View Steakhouse and Saloon
2400 Zion Park Blvd.
Springdale, UT 84767
435-772-0665
www.majesticviewlodge.com

Bit and Spur Restaurant and Saloon
2400 Zion Park Blvd.
Springdale, UT 84767
www.bitandspur.com

Wildcat Willies Grill and Saloon
897 Zion Park Blvd.
Springdale, UT 84767
435-772-0115

MUST SEE
· The massive sandstone cliffs of
  cream, pink, and red.
· If you are a bird watcher, note that
  about 300 species visit the park
  each year.

NEAREST HOSPITAL/URGENT
TREATMENT CENTER

Dixie Regional Medical Center
1380 E. Medical Center Dr.
St. George, UT 84790
435-251-1000

Garfield Memorial Hospital
200 N. 400 East
Panguitch, UT 84759
435-676-8811

Valley View Medical Center
1303 N. Main
Cedar City, UT 84721
435-868-5000

CELL PHONE SERVICE
Cell service is intermittent at best. In
Springdale, service is fair to good,
depending on your carrier.

FOR ALL ELSE, VISIT
http://www.nps.gov/zion/index.htm

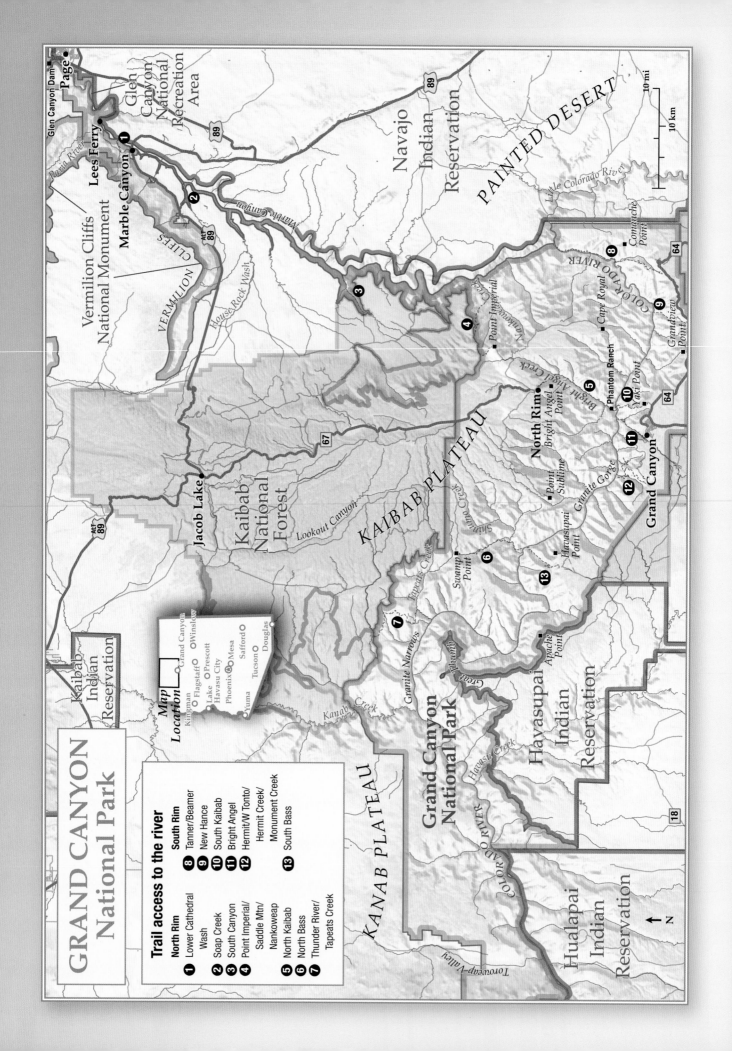

GRAND CANYON
National Park

Trail access to the river

North Rim		South Rim	
1 Lower Cathedral Wash		**8** Tanner/Beamer	
2 Soap Creek		**9** New Hance	
3 South Canyon		**10** South Kaibab	
4 Point Imperial/ Saddle Mtn/ Nankoweap		**11** Bright Angel	
5 North Kaibab		**12** Hermit/W Tonto/ Hermit Creek/ Monument Creek	
6 North Bass		**13** South Bass	
7 Thunder River/ Tapeats Creek			

Map Location

Grand Canyon
Winslow
Flagstaff
Prescott
Kingman
Lake Havasu City
Phoenix
Mesa
Safford
Tucson
Douglas
Yuma

Page
Glen Canyon Dam
Lees Ferry
Marble Canyon
Paria River
Vermilion Cliffs National Monument
VERMILION CLIFFS
ALT 89
Glen Canyon National Recreation Area
89
House Rock Wash
Marble Canyon
Navajo Indian Reservation
89
PAINTED DESERT
Little Colorado River
Nankoweap Creek
Point Imperial
Comanche Point
64
Cape Royal
COLORADO RIVER
Grandview Point
Bright Angel Creek
Phantom Ranch
North Rim
Bright Angel Point
Yaki Point
64
Point Sublime
Grand Canyon
Granite Gorge
Havasupai Point
Shinumo Creek
Swamp Point
Kaibab National Forest
Jacob Lake
67
Lookout Canyon
KAIBAB PLATEAU
Tapeats Creek
Apache Point
Granite Narrows
Kanab Creek
Grand Canyon National Park
Great Thumb
Havasupai Indian Reservation
Havasu Creek
KANAB PLATEAU
Kaibab Indian Reservation
ALT 89
Toroweap Valley
COLORADO RIVER
18
Hualapai Indian Reservation
N

10 mi
10 km

1
2
3
4
5
6
7
8
9
10
11
12
13

Grand Canyon National Park

➤ **Location:** The park is located in northern Arizona adjacent to Utah. The South Rim of the Grand Canyon is open year-round and is located on the Arizona side of the Canyon, while the North Rim is on the Utah side.

The Grand Canyon National Park was established as a national park in 1919 and is about 230 miles long, 18 miles wide and 5,000 feet deep.

The North Rim of the park is more remote and receives just 10 percent of the park's visitors. Lodging, restaurants and shops are open from May 15 through October 15. The entrance to the North Rim is 30 miles south of Jacob Lake on Utah 67. (The actual rim of the Grand Canyon with visitor services is an additional 14 miles south of the entrance station.) There is no airport or rail service to the park from the North Rim.

The South Rim sees the majority of tourists—about 90 percent—and thus has an airport and rail service. It is a 90-minute drive from Interstate 40 and the transportation centers of Williams and Flagstaff; it's a four-hour drive from Phoenix.

While the Grand Canyon might not be the first national park that comes to mind when considering fly-fishing destinations, it should be high on any angler's list. Catching wild trout at the bottom of the Grand Canyon is an experience like no other.

No photo, travel brochure or television travelogue can prepare you for your first glimpse from the edge of the Grand Canyon. Take in a sunrise at Yaki Point along the South Rim, or a sunset from the patio at the North Rim Lodge, and you're sure to see the canyon in a different light.

Natural beauty aside, there is much to learn about the Grand Canyon. A tour of the canyon rim with a knowledgeable guide is a great introduction to the canyon's fascinating geology, its human history, and its ecosystems. Armed with such experiences, along with a few souvenirs from the gift shop, most visitors leave the Grand Canyon having had a wonderful trip—yet they've barely scratched the surface of what the canyon has to offer.

Because it's located far from any population center, it's hard to believe that more than five million people visit the Grand Canyon annually, but just a small fraction of them venture below the rim. Those who do explore the canyon's depths are rewarded with an entirely different perspective. Hiking a short distance down the South Rim's Bright Angel Trail is often all it takes to provide visitors with a sense of scale, and a better understanding of the sheer magnitude of the canyon. Explorations deeper into the canyon will reveal incredible vistas, hidden waterfalls, a lush oasis, signs of ancient civilizations, lessons in geology, and a greater appreciation of its very existence.

The Colorado River through the Grand Canyon harbors good numbers of wild rainbow trout. Will Jordan

The Grand Canyon has been home to trout since the 1920s when the National Park Service (NPS) began stocking select coldwater tributaries with browns and rainbows. At that time, the pre-dam Colorado River was too warm to support trout. In the 1960s, Glen Canyon Dam was completed, transforming the river below the dam into a cold, clear tailwater, famously known amongst anglers as Lees Ferry. Those tailwater conditions continue downstream through the Grand Canyon and link the once-isolated tributaries to a vast network of quality, coldwater habitat.

Today, river runners and backpackers catch trout throughout the Grand Canyon. Rainbows predominate, but browns are caught throughout the park and can be found in higher densities in particular areas. Specimens stretching beyond the first ferrule of a four-piece fly rod are encountered, but

A backpacking angler near the Bright Angel Trailhead. Will Jordan

during March, April, July, and August. The USGS gauge on the lower LCR is a useful resource for anglers planning a trip.

Anglers fortunate enough to take part in a 5- to 20-day private or guided raft trip through the Grand Canyon will have access to the entire river. That is not the case for backpacking anglers, who are limited to well-established, rim-to-river trails, and the relatively short stretches of river available along those routes. Beginning upriver and progressing downriver, the following trails provide access to the Colorado River from the South Rim:

- Jackass Canyon (located on Navaho land and requires a Navaho hiking permit)
- Tanner Trail to Beamer Trail
- New Hance Trail
- South Kaibab Trail
- Bright Angel Trail
- Hermit/W Tonto/Monument/Hermit Creek (Hermit Trail only gets you part way down. Hermit Trail connects with West Tonto Trail; turn right to get to Monument Trail, or go left to get to Hermit Creek Trail, which will take you to the river.)
- South Bass Trail

Trails accessing the river from the North Rim (side) include the following:

- Lower Cathedral Wash Trail
- Soap Creek
- South Canyon
- Point Imperial/Saddle Mountain/Nankoweap Trail (To get to Nankoweap Trail, use Saddle Mountain and Point Imperial trails.)
- North Kaibab Trail
- North Bass Trail
- Thunder River/Tapeats Trail (Tapeats Trail gets you to the river, but at the top of the trail is Thunder River Trail, which provides access to the edge of Kaibab National Forest, where there is a trailhead.)

The Colorado River is daunting water to prospect with a fly rod. It is characterized by powerful rapids, huge eddies, and long stretches of flat water. Most successful anglers focus on the pocket water adjacent to rapids, side channels, tributary mouths, and— more often than not —wherever they happen to camp for the night on a river-raft trip.

➤ **The Tributaries:** A fly-fishing trip through GCNP can be planned to include a visit to one of the Grand Canyon's trout streams, some of which are destinations in their own right. The Colorado River's tributaries offer a much different trout-fishing experience as compared to the Colorado River

the majority of the catch consists of trout ranging from 12- to 16-inches.

➤ **The River:** The Colorado River through GCNP offers more than 200 miles of water to explore. The river is a fickle beast. It's massive—commonly running anywhere from 5,000 cfs (cubic feet per second) to 20,000 cfs. The dam-controlled river is managed first and foremost for energy generation, resulting in drastic daily and seasonal flow fluctuations. Within a given 24-hour period, it is commonplace for flows to fluctuate by 5,000 cfs or more. Sheer size, and disruptive flow regimes aside, the river presents other challenges for anglers. Along its upper 61-mile run, from Lees Ferry to the Little Colorado River (LCR), the river is relatively predictable and consistently productive for anglers. However, below the river's confluence with the LCR, all bets are off. From this point downstream, the river's clarity is at the mercy of the LCR, a largely ephemeral desert river that carries a significant sediment load at high flows. The LCR historically runs high itself. The tributaries provide a more approachable, familiar, and intimate fishing environment, and, perhaps more to the point, the best of the tributaries offer catch rates exceeding those typically experienced on the Colorado River.

Over the course of a Grand Canyon float trip, there are about a dozen perennial tributaries worth stopping to explore with a fly rod. Some of them are longshots, but if the timing is right, many will produce trout. From a backpacker's perspective, there are two, maybe three, tributaries worth the considerable effort required to reach them:

· Bright Angel Creek
· Tapeats Creek
· Shinumo Creek (a distant third)

The remainder are too much of a gamble if fishing is the trip's goal.

The most famous of Grand Canyon trout streams is Bright Angel Creek. It has long offered excellent fishing and is relatively easy to access. Anglers arrive at Bright Angel Creek by foot, raft, and mule. The North Kaibab Trail, South Kaibab Trail, and Bright Angel Trail converge in the vicinity of Phantom Ranch and lower Bright Angel Creek. All three trails are major travel corridors, resulting in a disproportionately high percentage of backcountry use in this region of the Grand Canyon. Even so, it's rare to see another angler on the creek.

Bright Angel Creek is home to good numbers of browns and rainbows, with a strong resident population that is augmented seasonally by migratory fish from the Colorado River. The creek provides excellent spawning habitat and is heavily utilized for that purpose. The brown trout run begins in late fall and has historically included some impressive specimens from 20 to 25 inches, with fish up to 30 inches occasionally. During spring, the creek hosts a run of rainbows with most in the 14- to 18-inch range.

In recent years, the Bright Angel Creek fishery has suffered the effects of a trout-reduction project implemented by the NPS. The middle- and upper-reaches of the creek—from Ribbon Falls and on upstream—remain largely unscathed by the trout-reduction efforts. Anglers will find good numbers of resident browns and rainbows to Roaring Springs and beyond. Access to the creek can be found along the North Kaibab Trail, and backpacking anglers will find that Cottonwood Campground serves as an excellent base camp for exploring the drainage.

Tapeats Creek is another excellent trout fishery. The creek is arguably Arizona's finest wild trout stream. Few anglers have so much as heard of the creek, let alone fished it. In their defense, it's about as remote and difficult to access as they come. The trailhead is located on the North Rim where snow begins piling up in early fall and lingers well into spring. A

Bright Angel Creek near Phantom Ranch. Will Jordan

Rainbow trout comprise the bulk of the Colorado River catch through the Grand Canyon, but brown trout are found throughout the system. Will Jordan

An angler hooks up on the Colorado River. Will Jordan

summer backpacking trip is inadvisable due to the triple-digit heat of the inner canyon and the lack of water and shade along the extremely demanding Tapeats Creek Trail.

The creek is more commonly accessed via the Colorado River. River runners regularly stop at the mouth of Tapeats Creek and hike upstream to see Thunder River, a stunning waterfall bursting from caves in the canyon wall. Few of these visitors linger long enough to fish the creek, which receives very light angling pressure.

All in all, Tapeats provides a precious few miles of stream to explore, but the pockets and plunge pools along its course are teeming with resident and migratory rainbows that average 12 inches and range up to the vaunted 20-inch mark.

➤ **Fisheries Management:** Beginning in 2002, the NPS, in conjunction with cooperating agencies, began an experimental trout reduction project within the Grand Canyon. These efforts have been focused on the Colorado River in the vicinity of the LCR confluence, as well as in Bright Angel and Shinumo creeks. The rationale for trout reduction efforts is that non-native brown and rainbow trout are thought to have a detrimental impact upon native fish populations, particularly the endangered humpback chub.

The fact is that trout are the least of the chubs' problems. The fundamental issue is that the post-dam Colorado River no longer provides suitable habitat. The original ecosystem has been radically altered. The Colorado River is now too cold for humpback chubs to successfully spawn, as are most of the river's tributaries. The last bastion of quality humpback chub habitat within GCNP is the warm, perennial flow of the lower LCR. In an effort to establish additional self-sustaining populations, humpback chubs have recently been relocated into Havasu and Shinumo creeks, with plans to do the same in Bright Angel Creek soon. Whether or not these populations will prove successful in spawning has yet to be determined.

Only a small portion of the GCNP trout fishery has been affected by trout reduction efforts. Biologists have stated that the system is currently supporting an estimated one million trout. The Colorado River and its tributaries provide a large, complex and high-quality trout habitat. Short of completely poisoning the system, trout will be present as long as Glen Canyon Dam continues to release cold, clear water.

► **Notable Nearby Water:** Anglers visiting the Grand Canyon will find themselves near one of the Southwest's (and the world's) finest tailwater fisheries, Lees Ferry. The large expenditure of time and effort required to fish deep within GCNP is often prohibitive for travelling anglers. Not so at Lees Ferry, where anglers will find relatively quick, easy access to the water.

Lees Ferry is a historically important location that provided a critical crossing point of the Colorado River. Today, it continues to provide access, serving as the launch point for all downstream Grand Canyon river trips and all upstream trout-fishing expeditions.

The Lees Ferry fishery encompasses approximately 16 miles of the Colorado River, from the base of Glen Canyon Dam downstream to the mouth of the Paria River and the upper boundary of GCNP. The majority of the river here is flanked by towering canyon walls that form a dramatic backdrop, but impede access to the water.

There is no public boat launch on the river's upper end. Instead, access to the upper river is most commonly achieved by utilizing a jet boat to motor upriver from the Lees Ferry boat ramp. Once upriver, there are numerous sandbars and shallow riffles that offer productive wade fishing when the river is flowing at low to moderate levels.

Also, there is a productive stretch of river known as the "walk-in" that is accessible to anglers on foot. This reach of the river is loosely defined as beginning at the mouth of the Paria River and extending upstream to the Lees Ferry boat ramp. Walk-in access is available upriver from the boat ramp, but most anglers focus on the productive boulder pockets, ledges, and riffles found downriver. Anglers should use caution when wading the walk-in, particularly in the vicinity of the Paria River confluence where deep drop-offs and heavy silt beds can be treacherous. Convenient access to the walk-in can be found from the parking areas and pullouts along Lees Ferry Road.

From top to bottom, the Lees Ferry fishery provides anglers with the opportunity to catch high numbers of fish per rod, with the bulk of the catch consisting of 12- to 16-inch stream-born rainbows (Lees Ferry hasn't been stocked since the 1990s). The majority of the fishing here is done subsurface. Dead-drifting tandem nymph rigs beneath an indicator is the go-to tactic. Midges, scuds, worms, and eggs are the primary fly patterns used. Opportunities to take fish on dry flies are sporadic, but do occur during times of midge emergences and during summer when cicadas are present along the riverbanks.

Lees Ferry is approximately a two-hour drive from the Grand Canyon's North Rim or South Rim. This productive year-round fishery is a destination that can easily be included in a travel itinerary built around a trip to the Grand Canyon.

► **Tackle and Gear**

Rods and Line: We recommend 9-foot, 6- and 7-weight rods anywhere on the Colorado River, with shorter 4- and 5-weight rods for the tributaries.

Terminal Tackle and Flies: Nymphing with an indicator is the primary technique here, with long leaders tapering to 3X. Leaders typically need to be heavily weighted for the big water of the Colorado. BB- and AB-size split shot is essential to success. If streamer fishing is your preference, a minnow pattern affixed to a short, stout leader and a 200- to 300-grain sink-tip line is a productive setup. When fishing the tributaries, a leader of 8- or 9-feet, tapering to 3X, is ideal for the pocket water conditions. Midges, blackfly larva, dobsonfly larva, aquatic worms, roe, and minnows are the bulk of the trout diet within the river. Nymph and streamer tactics take the vast majority of trout here. Consider a Zebra Midge or Gold Bead Head Olive Wooly Bugger.

A backpacking angler high above the Colorado River. Will Jordan

Colorado River at Lees Ferry, the last free-flowing remnant of Glen Canyon. Terry Gunn

CLOSEST CITY OR ACCESS TO THE PARK
Flagstaff, Arizona

CLOSEST AIRPORT AND/OR CAR RENTAL
· Flagstaff Pulliam Airport is the closest small commercial airport to Grand Canyon National Park South Rim; it's a 90-minute drive from the park.
· Sky Harbor Airport in Phoenix is about a 3.5-hour drive from the park. Car rental, hotel and transportation services are available at both airports.

FEES
· Park entrance and user fees change periodically.
· For up-to-date fees, free days and other exceptions, visit http://www.nps.gov /grca/index.htm.
· Golden Eagle, other senior, and special use fees apply.
· All overnight backcountry use within GCNP requires a permit administered by the park's backcountry office.

· South Rim park access: Year-round.
· North Rim park access: April-October (weather permitting).

FISHING LICENSES AND/OR REGULATIONS
· An Arizona fishing license is required.
· For fishing regulations, see www.nps.gov /grca/learn/nature/fish.htm.

CLOSEST FLY SHOPS
Lees Ferry Anglers
HC 67 Box 30
Marble Canyon, AZ 86036
800-962-9755
www.leesferry.com

Peace Surplus
14 West U.S. Route 66
Flagstaff, AZ 86001
928-779-4521
www.peacesurplus.com

Orvis – Scottsdale
7012 E. Greenway Parkway
Scottsdale, AZ 85254
480-905-1400
www.orvis.com

CLOSEST GUIDES/OUTFITTERS
Lees Ferry Anglers
HC 67 Box 30
Marble Canyon, AZ 86036
800-962-9755
www.leesferry.com

Marble Canyon Outfitters
P.O. Box 3646
Page, AZ 86040
800-533-7339
www.leesferryflyfishing.com

CLOSEST LODGE
Cliff Dwellers Lodge
HC 67 Box 30
Marble Canyon, AZ 86036
800-962-9755
www.leesferry.com/cliff-dwellers-lodge

BEST PLACE TO STAY NEAR PARK
El Tovar Hotel
P.O. Box 699
Grand Canyon, AZ 86023
888-297-2757
www.grandcanyonlodges.com

WILL JORDAN is a Montana-based freelance writer and photographer. He attended Northern Arizona University and holds a BS in Finance and Economics. After college, Will lived and worked within Grand Canyon National Park for four years. He is the author of *Flyfisher's Guide to Arizona*, a comprehensive guidebook covering the state's angling opportunities. His work has appeared in a number of publications including *The Drake, Montana Outdoors, TROUT, Northwest Fly Fishing*, and *Southwest Fly Fishing*. Will was a founding partner of *Montana Sporting Journal* and served as the magazine's Associate Publisher from 2006-2012. He currently works for Simms Fishing Products in Bozeman, where he resides with his wife and daughter. More of Will's work can be found at www.willjordanphoto.com.

CAMPGROUNDS IN PARK

North Rim Campground
877-444-6777
· http://www.recreation.gov/
· Reservations are available from May 15 through October 31.
· Winter camping (November 1 through May 15) at the North Rim Campground is allowed with a backcountry use permit. See www.nps.gov/grca/planyourvisit/backcountry-permit.htm.

Mather Campground (South Rim)
Call 1-877-444-6777
www.recreation.gov/
(No RV hook-ups)

Trailer Village
(adjacent to Mather Campground)
100 Market Plaza Road
Grand Canyon, AZ 86023
877- 404-4611 (advance reservations)
928-638-3047 (for same-day reservations)
(RV hook-ups available)

Grand Canyon Village
877-444-6777
www.recreation.gov
· Open year-round
· Reservations are recommended March 1 through mid-November
· More than 300 sites available
· Tent and RV camping

NPS Desert View Campground
· Campsites are first-come, first served
· No reservations accepted
· 50 campsites available
· Small RVs and travel trailers accepted (30 feet or less)

Bright Angel Campground
(The campground is located at the bottom of the canyon, nearly 10 miles from the South Rim, and 14 miles from the North Rim.)
https://www.nps.gov/grca/planyourvisit/campsite-information.htm

CLOSEST RESTAURANT, BEST PLACE TO GET A DRINK

Phantom Ranch Canteen
www.grandcanyonlodges.com/dining/phantom-ranch-canteen

MUST SEE
Sunrise and sunset from either the North Rim or South Rim

NEAREST HOSPITAL/URGENT TREATMENT CENTER

North Country Community Health Center
1 Clinic Rd.
Grand Canyon, AZ 86023
928-638-2551
www.northcountryhealthcare.org

CELL PHONE SERVICE
Wireless service is very limited within the canyon. Landline service is available at Phantom Ranch, and emergency phones are located along the Bright Angel Trail and at Ranger Stations. Raft parties typically have satellite phones for emergency use.

FOR ALL ELSE, VISIT
www.nps.gov/grca/index.htm

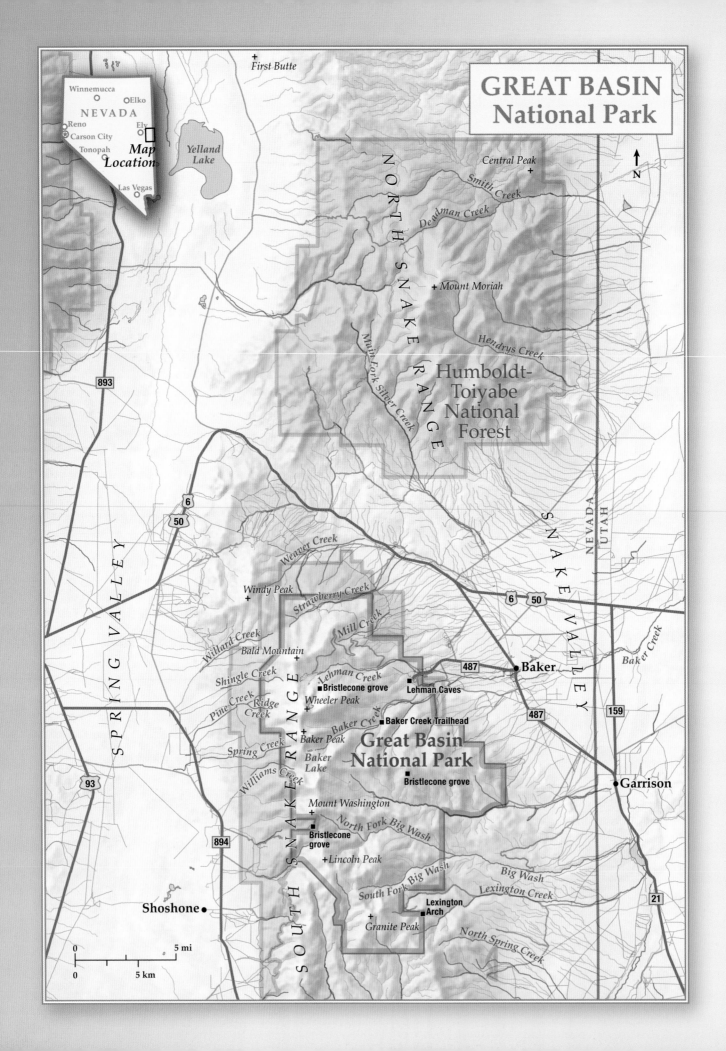

GREAT BASIN
National Park

N↑

+ First Butte

NEVADA

Winnemucca
Elko
Reno
Carson City
Ely
Tonopah
Map Location
Yelland Lake
Las Vegas

NORTH SNAKE RANGE

+ Central Peak
Smith Creek
Deadman Creek

+ Mount Moriah

Humboldt-Toiyabe National Forest

Main Fork Silver Creek

Hendrys Creek

SNAKE VALLEY

NEVADA UTAH

893

6
50

6 50

Weaver Creek

+ Windy Peak

Strawberry Creek

Mill Creek

Willard Creek

Bald Mountain

Shingle Creek

Pine Creek

Ridge Creek

SOUTH SNAKE RANGE

Lehman Creek
■ Bristlecone grove
+ Wheeler Peak

+ Baker Peak

Baker Creek
■ Lehman Caves

487 ● Baker

Baker Creek

487

159

Baker Creek

■ Baker Creek Trailhead

Great Basin National Park

■ Bristlecone grove

● Garrison

Spring Creek

Baker Lake

SPRING VALLEY

93

894

Williams Creek

+ Mount Washington

■
● Bristlecone grove

+ Lincoln Peak

North Fork Big Wash

South Fork Big Wash

Big Wash

Lexington Creek

● Shoshone

Lexington Arch ■

+ Granite Peak

North Spring Creek

21

0   5 mi
0   5 km

➤ **Location:** Great Basin National Park is located in eastern Nevada along the Nevada-Utah border south of U.S. Route 6/50, just west of Baker, Nevada.

The park is accessible by auto and air via several routes:

Via auto:

· From the east or west—U.S. Route 6/50, turn south on Nevada 487 and travel five miles to Baker, Nevada. In Baker, turn west on Nevada 488, and travel five miles to the park.

· From the south (Utah)—Travel north on Utah 21 through Milford and Garrison, which will become Nevada 487 as you cross the state border. Turn west on Nevada 488 in Baker, and travel five miles to the park.

· From the south (Nevada)—Travel north on Route 93 (Great Basin Highway). At U.S. Route 6/50, drive east to Nevada 487 and turn south. Travel five miles to Baker. In Baker, turn west on Nevada 488 and travel five miles to the park.

Via air:

· The nearest airports are located either in Ely, Nevada, 70 miles away, or Cedar City, Utah, 142 miles away.

· Major airports are found in Salt Lake City, Utah (234 miles) and Las Vegas, Nevada (286 miles).

No public transportation is available to, or in, Great Basin National Park.

Great Basin National Park (GBNP) was established in 1986 to serve as a representative symbol of the vast region known as the Great Basin covering a large portion of the arid west. Roughly bordered by the Sierra Nevada on the west, the Wasatch Mountains on the east, and the Snake River Plain on the north, the 200,000-square-mile Great Basin is a unique portion of our country in which none of its water ever reaches an ocean.

All water from streams, rivers, and precipitation flows inward to terminus lakes, or it simply evaporates in sinks

A view of Mt. Wheeler as seen from Mt. Moriah. Chris Crookshanks

Fly fishing Baker Lake. Gretchen Baker

and playas. The roughly 77,000 acres of GBNP encompass nearly the entire south Snake Mountain Range in White Pine County, Nevada. Elevations range from about 5,000 feet on the valley floor to more than 13,000 feet atop Wheeler Peak. Visitors are treated to a multitude of habitats, from salt desert scrub to a high alpine environment.

Leave your bigger rods at home. Pack a sturdy pair of boots, a 3-weight, and prepare for a backcountry stream fly-fishing adventure for native trout in one of the numerous creeks that flow in and around GBNP.

However, before we get into fishing, a little background info is in order. Nearly 10,000 years ago, much of what is the current-day state of Utah was covered by ancient Lake Bonneville. The extreme western shore of this lake was located in Snake Valley, adjacent to the park. As the climate warmed and the lake desiccated, its sole native trout species, the Bonneville

cutthroat, became isolated in mountain streams and creeks fed by snowmelt runoff. At one time, it can be presumed that all streams flowing from the east flank of the Snake Mountains (both north and south ranges) into Snake Valley contained Bonneville cutthroat trout.

Now, let's fast forward to modern times. Not long after the region was settled in the late 1800s and early 1900s, these native survivors were largely lost as a result of stream diversions and the stocking of non-native species such as rainbow, brook, and brown trout, which outcompete and/or readily hybridize with the Bonneville cutthroat trout.

However, a cooperative effort initiated in the 1990s between the National Park Service, Nevada Department of Wildlife, Bureau of Land Management, U.S. Forest Service, conservation organizations such as Trout Unlimited, and private landowners has resulted in the restoration of the Bonne-

ville cutthroat trout to nearly every stream in both the north and south Snake Range where it once resided. Among various other attractions, park visitors are offered the rare treat of catching wild, native trout within their historic range.

As recently as 1998, there were only four streams in Nevada that held Bonneville cutthroat trout: two within historic range (Hendry's and Hampton Creeks) and two outside the Bonneville cutthroat's native habitat (Goshute and Pine / Ridge Creeks). Nearly 20 years later, the hard work of many dedicated fisheries professionals has resulted in the species inhabiting 12 streams in Nevada. In fact, Bonneville cutthroats currently inhabit all but four streams in their native range in Nevada, with two of these creeks currently undergoing restorations to bring back the cutthroats.

Waters within GBNP are open year-round, and any hour of the day or night. A Nevada fishing license is required for those 12 years and older. Annual licenses also require a trout stamp. Fishing is usually best throughout the warmer months

Left. The upper reaches of Hendry's Creek. Chris Crookshanks

A Bonneville cutthroat trout from Smith Creek. Chris Crookshanks

(June-October) once the springtime runoff has subsided and continues through fall before the snow flies. Catch-and-release fishing is encouraged.

If you have visions of standing in a drift boat, matching the hatch, and making a perfect presentation, your bubble might be quickly burst. Although the scenery in GBNP might rival some of the more popular national parks, these creeks require a technique with which many fly fishers are not accustomed. Keep in mind that what is called a "stream" in Nevada—the driest state in the nation—would often not even warrant a name in other locales. The creeks in and around GBNP are small, fast moving, high gradient waters fed by snowmelt runoff. Most can be jumped across with little effort. This is close-quarters fly-fishing. Adult fish are found in habitats where expected, namely the plunge pools between high velocity riffles. Because these streams are so small, stealth when approaching and casting is paramount. Fish will often dart out of sight simply from footsteps felt on the stream bank. Don't be afraid to approach on hands and knees or bust through sometimes thick riparian vegetation along these streams to reach pools that hold trout. Solitude is the norm as you'd be hard pressed to encounter another angler when fishing most of these streams.

Waders are not needed. However, for battling the vegetation, sturdy boots, long pants, a long-sleeved shirt, hat, and sunglasses are highly recommended. A 2- or 3-weight rod with a floating line will suffice; the shorter the rod the better. Strong leaders and tippets are also not necessary as most streams in and around GBNP receive such little fishing pressure; you'll find that these trout are eager to eat almost anything offered. Caddis and mayfly hatches of various species occur throughout the summer, but resident trout will readily take smaller-sized Elk Hair Caddis, Pale Morning Duns, Parachute Adams, Coachmen, and Wulffs. For those who want to drag nymphs, Pheasant Tails, Copper Johns, and Prince Nymphs are recommended (no indicator needed). Don't forget the terrestrials throughout the warmer summer months. Ants, beetles, and hoppers will drive these fish crazy!

Casting—if it can be referred to as such—takes some ingenuity. Although there are undoubtedly some open areas on most of the streams you'll encounter, it is certainly the exception rather than the rule. In close quarters with streamside vegetation, back casting is simply not an option in most places. Be prepared to use a modified roll cast, bow-and-arrow, or slingshot type cast to get your fly into a desired pool.

Although you won't find 20-inch fish, and these are not classified as Blue Ribbon fisheries, the real trophy lies in the opportunity to catch beautiful native cutthroats in their historic habitat with scenery and solitude that is unmatched.

Facing. A Great Basin bristlecone pine. Chris Crookshanks

➤ **Waters within GBNP (south Snake Range):** Flowing eastward into Snake Valley

Snake Creek: Access is via Snake Creek Road (NF-448) off Nevada 487 (high-clearance vehicle recommended). The upper reaches of Snake Creek within GBNP were slated for chemical renovation in 2016, with reintroduction of Bonneville cutthroat trout to follow. Note: The lower reaches of the stream (below the park boundary) contain populations of brown, brook, and rainbow trout.

South Fork of Big Wash: Access is via the Big Wash Canyon Road (White Pine County Road 42) in Garrison, Utah (four-wheel drive vehicle mandatory). The south fork of Big Wash contains a population of Bonneville cutthroat trout. Note: A very long, strenuous hike is required to access this stream. Please ask GBNP officials for directions.

Baker Creek: Access is via Baker Creek Road (graded gravel road, open May-November) off Lehman Cave Road (Nevada 488). The main stem of Baker Creek contains populations of brook and rainbow trout. The South Fork of Baker Creek (hiking access via the Baker Creek Trailhead) contains a population of Bonneville cutthroat trout.

Lehman Creek: Access is available at various points from the Wheeler Peak Scenic Drive (paved, upper portion above Upper Lehman Creek Campground, which is open June-October). Lehman Creek contains populations of brown, cuttbow, and rainbow trout.

Mill Creek: Access is via dirt road south of Strawberry Creek Road (NF-456) which is off U.S. Route 6/50. Please ask GBNP officials for directions (four-wheel-drive vehicle mandatory). Mill Creek contains a population of Bonneville cutthroat trout.

Strawberry Creek: Access is via the Strawberry Creek Road (high-clearance vehicle recommended) from U.S. Route 6/50. Strawberry Creek contains a population of Bonneville cutthroat trout.

Pine and Ridge Creeks: Access is via a two-track road from Nevada 894 from U.S. Route 93 in Spring Valley. Please ask GBNP officials for directions (four-wheel-drive vehicle mandatory). Although not within native range, Pine and Ridge Creeks (Ridge is a small tributary to Pine) contain populations of Bonneville cutthroat trout. Note: The road into Pine / Ridge Creek is extremely rough and rocky.

Williams and Shingle Creeks: Access is via various two-track roads from Nevada 894 off U.S. Route 93 in Spring Valley. Please ask GBNP officials for directions (four-wheel-drive vehicle mandatory). Williams and Shingle Creeks contain populations of rainbow and brown trout. Note: Roads into these streams are extremely rough and rocky.

A Bonneville cutthroat trout from upper Snake Creek. Chris Crookshanks

➤ **Other GBNP Waters: Baker Lake:** Access is via a 12-mile roundtrip hike from the Baker Creek Trailhead. At four surface acres, Baker Lake contains populations of brook trout and Lahontan cutthroat trout (introduced, not native).

➤ **Nearby Waters Outside GBNP:** Flowing eastward into Snake Valley

Big Wash: Access is via the Big Wash Canyon Road (White Pine County Road 42) in Garrison, Utah. Big Wash contains a population of Bonneville cutthroat trout. Note: Because the entire reach of fishable stream is private, access is by permission only.

Flowing westward into Spring Valley

Willard Creek: Access is via the Osceola Road from U.S. Route 6/50 in Spring Valley (high-clearance vehicle recommended). Although not within native range, Willard Creek contains a population of Bonneville cutthroat trout. Note: Please be aware of and respect private property boundaries.

➤**The North Snake Range**
Note: Much like the south Snake Range is comprised of the Great Basin National Park, most of the north Snake Range is

made up of the Mt. Moriah Wilderness Area. One could argue that the Mt. Moriah Wilderness Area is just as impressive as GBNP. All waters recommended here represent streams where restoration projects for Bonneville cutthroat trout have occurred. All listed waters are within native range and flow eastward into Snake Valley.

Hendry's Creek: Access is via the Silver Creek Road (White Pine County Road 41) just west of the junction of U.S. Route 6/50 with Nevada 487. Travel northeast for about 12.5 miles and turn west at the Hendry's Creek sign (NF-429) and continue to the trailhead. Hendry's Creek contains the only known remnant population of Bonneville cutthroat trout in Nevada. Fish can be found from the trailhead upstream for approximately 7 miles (high-clearance vehicle recommended).

Smith Creek: Access is via the Silver Creek Road (White Pine County Road 41) just west of the junction of Route 6/50 with Nevada 487. Travel northeast about 20 miles, turn west on Smith Creek Road (NF-460) and continue to the Smith Creek Trailhead (high-clearance vehicle recommended). Smith Creek contains a population of Bonneville cutthroat trout. Fish distribution begins about two miles upstream from

Releasing a Bonneville cutthroat trout. Gretchen Baker

the trailhead. The headwaters of Smith Creek can also be accessed from Spring Valley on White Pine County Road 37 (East Spring Valley Road) from U.S. Route 6/50 in Spring Valley. Head east at the 4-Mile Road turnoff (NF-460 – Marble Wash Road) and follow the two-track to the top of the mountain (four-wheel-drive vehicle mandatory). Smith Creek can be found by following signs to Mud Springs Wash (NF-469).

Deadman and Deep Canyon Creeks: Access is via the Smith Creek Trailhead (see above). From the trailhead, hike about 2.2 miles up Smith Creek and then turn south along the trail. Deep Canyon Creek becomes a tributary to Deadman Creek approximately one-half mile above the Smith Creek confluence. Both Deadman and Deep Canyon Creeks contain populations of Bonneville cutthroat trout. Note: Some of the best fishing and habitat for Bonneville cutthroat trout can be found in the half-mile stretch of stream from the Deadman / Deep Canyon confluence downstream to the confluence of Smith Creek.

Silver Creek & Silver Creek Reservoir: Access is via the Silver Creek Road (White Pine County Road 41) just west of the junction of U.S. Route 6/50 with Nevada 487. Travel north and turn northwest at White Pine County Road 40. Follow this road along Silver Creek until it ends. Hiking from the end of the road upstream. Silver Creek is a stream that was chemically renovated in 2013. Reintroduction of Bonneville cutthroat trout was initiated in 2015. Also, Silver Creek Reservoir contains a population of tiger trout.

➤ Tackle and Gear

Rods and Line: A 2- or 3-weight rod with a floating line is recommended—the shorter the rod the better. Strong leaders and tippets are also not necessary as most streams in and around GBNP receive such little fishing pressure; you'll find that these trout are eager to eat almost anything offered.

Terminal Tackle and Flies: Caddis and mayfly hatches of various species occur throughout the summer, but resident trout will readily take smaller-sized Elk Hair Caddis, Pale Morning Duns, Parachute Adams, Coachmen, and Wulffs. For those who want to drag a nymph, Pheasant Tails, Copper Johns, and Prince Nymphs are recommended (no indicator needed). Don't forget the terrestrials (ants, beetles, and hoppers) throughout the warmer summer months.

113

CLOSEST CITY OR POINT OF ENTRANCE

- Baker, Nevada (population 68), which offers very limited services, is about five miles from the entrance to GBNP.
- Ely, Nevada is about 70 miles away on Nevada 6/50. Full services are available there.

CLOSEST AIRPORTS

- Salt Lake City, Utah: 234 miles
- Las Vegas, Nevada: 286 miles

OPEN / CLOSING DATES FOR THE PARK

- GBNP is open year-round, as is the fishing season.
- There is no access fee.
- Some access roads are closed seasonally.
- Check with park headquarters or http://www.nps.gov/grba/index.htm.

FISHING REGULATIONS

- Nevada fishing regulations apply.
- All waters are open year-round, any hour of the day or night.
- There is a 10-trout limit.
- Catch and release is strongly encouraged.
- For those 12 years and older, a Nevada fishing license is required.
- Annual licenses require an additional trout stamp.
- Fishing licenses can be purchased in Ely, NV at Sportsworld, the Hotel Nevada & Gambling Hall, the Ely Field Office of the Nevada Department of Wildlife, or online at www.ndow.org.

CLOSEST FLY SHOP

Sportsworld
1500 Aultman St.
Ely, NV 89301
775- 289-8887
www.sportsworld-ely.com

BEST PLACE TO STAY IN THE PARK

- The park has developed camping ($12 per night) at various locations including Strawberry, Upper Lehman, Lower Lehman, and Baker Creeks, Wheeler Peak, and Grey Cliffs (group site, reservations only) campgrounds.
- All camping is on a first-come, first-served basis.

- Primitive, free campsites can be found along Snake and Strawberry Creeks.

BEST CAMPGROUND NEAR THE PARK

Cave Lake State Park
U.S. Route 93 – Success Summit
775-296-1505
www.parks.nv.gov/parks/cave-lake-state-park/

LODGING NEAR THE PARK

The Border Inn
Eight miles northeast of Baker, Nevada on Route 6/50 at the Nevada/Utah border
775-234-7300
www.borderinncasino.com/
Gas, diesel, mini-mart, gift shop, ATM, motel, restaurant, bar, and small casino

Hidden Canyon Ranch
P.O. Box 180
Baker, NV 89311
775-234-7172
Hidden Canyon Ranch offers a bed and breakfast in a luxurious lodge with breathtaking scenery and wildlife galore. Rooms include private baths, king beds, refrigerators, and a fully cooked breakfast. Hiking, wildlife viewing, and fishing for native Bonneville cutthroat trout is available on site.

Whispering Elms Motel, Campground, and RV Park
775-234-9900
www.whisperingelms.com/
This motel/campground is open from spring to late November, and offers a bar, lounge, and grassy spot for tents, 25 partial- and full-RV sites, and six motel rooms. Laundromat and showers are available, and motel guests have free Wi-Fi and satellite TV.

Silver Jack Inn & LectroLux Café
14 Baker Ave.
Baker, NV 89311
775-293-0189
www.silverjackinn.com/
This inn offers seven rooms with kitchenettes along with five RV spots. Sports equipment rentals include bikes and snowshoes.

BEST PLACE TO EAT IN THE PARK

There is only one place to eat within GBNP: Lehman Caves Café and Gift Shop in the Lehman Caves Visitor Center. Breakfast, lunch, and snacks are available from April-October. An adjacent gift shop offers souvenirs and books, as well as camping and travel items.

BEST PLACES TO EAT NEAR THE PARK

The Border Inn
Eight miles northeast of Baker on U.S. Route 6/50 at the Nevada / Utah border
775-234-7300
www.borderinncasino.com/
Gas, diesel, mini-mart, gift shop, ATM, motel, restaurant, bar, and small casino

Silver Jack Inn & LectroLux Café
14 Baker Ave.
Baker, NV 89311
775-293-0189
www.silverjackinn.com/
Open spring through November. Breakfast, lunch, and dinner are served, and a specialty bakery/deli offers pastries, pies, deli wares, and groceries. Also a Sunday brunch is served. Be sure to view the art, crafts, sculptures, jewelry, books, furniture, and other offerings.

PLACES TO GET A DRINK

Silver Jack Inn & LectroLux Café
14 Baker Ave.
Baker, NV 89311
775-293-0189
www.silverjackinn.com/
Open spring through November
Espresso, wine, and a full bar

The Border Inn
Eight miles northeast of Baker on Route 6/50 at the Nevada-Utah border.
775-234-7300
www.borderinncasino.com/
This in offers a full-service restaurant, bar, and small casino.

CHRIS CROOKSHANKS and his family are a fly-fishing enthusiasts. Their best times are those spent on the water doing what they love. Whether it's experiencing nature, having a good laugh, or catching fish, the Crookshanks are all at home on the water. Chris's family includes his beautiful wife, Chelise, and his two wonderful children—son, Cade, and daughter, Chloe. Chris and his wife learned early on that their best times together were with others on a river, lake, stream, or reservoir. Each year, they dedicate special trips to remind them how important this time is for their family. Chris is a fisheries biologist with the Nevada Department of Wildlife. One of his proudest accomplishments was spending 15 years in White Pine County, Nevada, and taking part in the restoration of Bonneville cutthroat trout to their native range.

MUST SEE

Lehman Caves: Near the GBNP visitor's center, Lehman Caves is one of the nation's most spectacular marble caves, featuring formations such as stalactites, stalagmites, helictites, flowstone, popcorn, and more than 300 rare shields. Guided tours include the Lodge Room Tour (60 minutes) and Grand Palace Tour (90 minutes). The tours are offered multiple times daily (except holidays). Tickets can be purchased at the main visitor's center.

Wheeler Peak: At 13,065 feet, Wheeler Peak is the second highest peak in Nevada. Breathtaking views of the mountain and surrounding valleys are afforded on the Wheeler Peak Scenic Drive. You can also take in views of its glacial cirque and the only existing glacier in Nevada. For the more adventurous, Wheeler Peak can be summited via the Wheeler Peak Trailhead. The hike is roughly 4.0 miles with an elevation gain of approximately 3,000 feet. Views from the summit are magnificent.

Bristlecone Forest: Bristlecone pines are the oldest living organisms known; some are older than 4,900 years. Access the Bristlecone Forest from the Bristlecone Pine Trailhead. The hike is roughly 2.8 miles round trip. Some of the trees you'll see were growing at the time the Egyptians built the pyramids!

Lexington Arch: Accessed via the Lexington Canyon Road at the south end of GBNP, the hike to view the arch is 1.7 miles (one way) with an elevation gain of 820 feet. At more than 60 feet high, Lexington Arch is unique in that fact that it is comprised of limestone and not sandstone like most others. This is one of the largest limestone arches in the western U.S.

NEARBY HOSPITAL/URGENT CARE FACILITY

William B. Ririe Hospital
1500 Ave. H
Ely, NV 89301
775-289-3001
www.wbrhely.org/

CELL PHONE SERVICE
Most cell phones do not work within GBNP. The closest, reliable service can be obtained by driving west on U.S. Route 6/50 into Spring Valley.

FOR ALL ELSE, VISIT
http://www.nps.gov/grba/index.htm

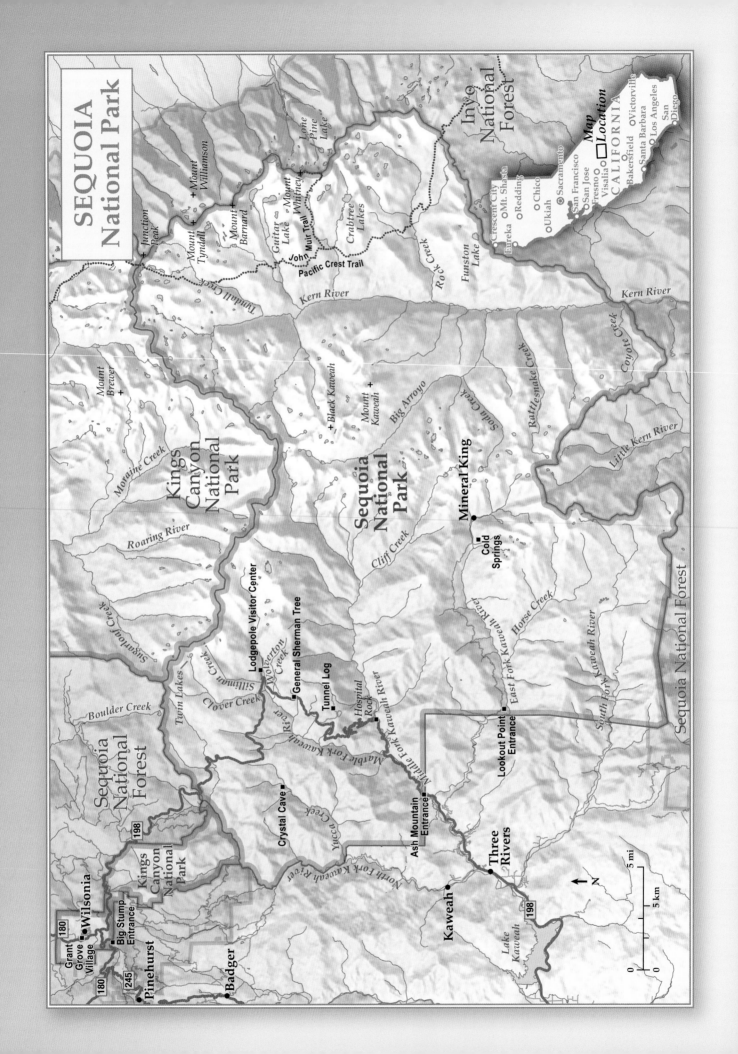

SEQUOIA National Park

Map Location

CALIFORNIA

Crescent City
Eureka ○   Mt. Shasta ○
Redding ○
Ukiah ○   Chico ○
                Sacramento ⊛
        San Francisco ○   San Jose ○
                    Fresno ○   Visalia ○
                        Bakersfield ○   Victorville ○
                            Santa Barbara ○   Los Angeles ○
                                        San Diego ○

Inyo National Forest

Kings Canyon National Park

Sequoia National Park

Sequoia National Forest

+ Junction Peak
+ Mount Williamson
+ Mount Tyndall
+ Mount Barnard
Lone Pine Lake
Guitar Lake
Mount Whitney
John Muir Trail
Crabtree Lakes
Pacific Crest Trail

Tyndall Creek
Kern River
Rock Creek
Funston Lake
Kern River

+ Mount Brewer
+ Black Kaweah
+ Mount Kaweah
Big Arroyo
Soda Creek
Rattlesnake Creek
Little Kern River
Coyote Creek

Moraine Creek
Roaring River
Cliff Creek

Mineral King ●
Cold Springs ●

Sugarloaf Creek
Twin Lakes
Clover Creek
Silliman Creek
Wolverton Creek

■ Lodgepole Visitor Center
■ General Sherman Tree
■ Tunnel Log

Boulder Creek

East Fork Kaweah River
Horse Creek
South Fork Kaweah River

■ Hospital Rock
Marble Fork Kaweah River
Middle Fork Kaweah River

■ Crystal Cave
Yucca Creek

■ Lookout Point Entrance

■ Ash Mountain Entrance

● Three Rivers

North Fork Kaweah River

Sequoia National Forest

Kings Canyon National Park

[180]
Grant Grove Village ■
Wilsonia ■
Big Stump Entrance

[180]
[245]
Pinehurst ●

Badger ●

Kaweah ●

Lake Kaweah
[198]

N ←

5 mi
5 km
0
0

➤ **Location:** Sequoia National Park is located in the south-central area of California's Sierra Nevada range. Sequoia and Kings Canyon National Parks are commonly referred to as "SEKI" by both locals and the National Park Service, though they are administered as one park. Combined, the two are 120,000 acres larger than Yosemite, its neighbor to the north. Kings Canyon is covered in detail in the next chapter.

The northern entrance is a 90-minute drive east of Fresno on California 180. You'll first enter a portion of Kings Canyon National Park—at the Big Stump Entrance—which provides access to both parks. Two miles inside this entrance is a junction with the northern end of California 198, also known as The General's Highway. The northern boundary of Sequoia National Park is just a 30-minute drive south on California 198.

The southern entrance is an hour east of Visalia on California 198. Both Fresno and Visalia are on north/south California 99. Both cities have airports, with Fresno's Yosemite International airport being the larger of the two.

Native Americans tribes such as the Monache and the Western Mono called this area home 6,000-7,000 years ago. The first Europeans didn't lay eyes on it until the late 1700s. Not long afterward, trappers, miners and loggers poured into the area. Sequoia was incorporated as a national park in 1890. Additional portions of the Sierra have been annexed, giving the park its present size of 404,063 acres. Kings Canyon National Park was created in 1940 and encompasses 461,901 acres.

All of the fly-fishing opportunities within Sequoia National Park are provided by two river drainages:
· The Kaweah River in the west
· The Kern River in the east

➤ **Kaweah River:** The Kaweah River is a much smaller drainage than that of the Kern River, though all five forks of the Kaweah contain trout. The North, South, East, Middle and Marble forks contain both rainbows and browns in their lower and middle elevations. As you climb higher, you'll find brook trout and even some golden trout making up a larger percentage of the fish population.

The Lodgepole area is a great jumping off point for fishing the northern section of Sequoia. Four different streams are located within a four-mile drive of the Lodgepole Visitor Center. The visitor center is the primary location of visitor services, including a campground, store, and restaurant.

➤ **Clover Creek:** Starting in the north is Clover Creek, which originates in Twin Lakes and flows north to south into the Marble Fork of the Kaweah River. Clover has a good population of brook, rainbow and rainbow-golden hybrids. Most fish are in the 6- to 8-inch range, with a fair number up to the 10-inch range. Easy access can be found at the California 198 bridge. Effective fly patterns during May and June include size 16-18 Little Yellow Sally stoneflies. Spring through fall, you'll have better luck with a smaller, darker caddis in sizes 16-18. A foam black ant in size 16 is a season-long go-to fly.

➤ **Silliman Creek:** Silliman Creek is located a half-mile east of Clover Creek and offers nearly identical fishing conditions, species and sizes as Clover. Access here is also from California 198. Because this stream and Clover Creek are nearly identical in nature, and are located only a half-mile apart, fly patterns are basically the same in both creeks.

Jimmie Morales fishing the Kings River during a strong spring Salmonfly hatch. Andrew Maurer

Working upstream on the East Fork Kaweah River in Mineral King. Andrew Maurer

➤ **Marble Fork Kaweah River:** Access to the Marble Fork from the Lodgepole area is found from the Highway 198 bridge upstream through the visitor center and all along the campgrounds, including the trail upstream to Tokopah Falls. For the stealthy angler, fish are abundant everywhere. However, as is typical, the further you can move in either direction away from the more populated areas, the better the fishing will become. A majority of trout here are rainbow and brook, in addition to numerous brown trout. Sizes range up to 12 inches, with the larger fish usually being browns.

Useful early season (May-June) fly patterns here include Little Yellow Sallies and some Golden Stones. Caddis, small mayfly and carpenter ant patterns work all season long. The Marble Fork has been designated Wild Trout Water, meaning you may only use single, barbless hooks, and is catch-and-release only.

Because all trout in the park are wild fish, an emphasis on presentation over imitation will be far more productive.

➤ **Wolverton Creek:** Wolverton Creek, located just south of Lodgepole, is a much smaller stream than the waters covered earlier in this chapter. Wolverton Creek begins in Wolverton Meadow and flows west, crossing under California 198, and then plunging steeply down to the Marble Fork, with little to no access downstream of the highway.

The upper meadow sections are primarily brook trout waters. As the stream leaves the meadow, the brookies are replaced by brown trout. It is not an easily fished stream because of the rugged terrain and heavy brush. Small black stoneflies, in addition to early-season Yellow Sallies, will hatch throughout spring and summer. Heavy stream-side vegetation lends to the effective use of terrestrial patterns such as ants, beetles, and even small hoppers.

➤ **East Fork Kaweah River, Mineral King:** Mineral King is a more recent addition to the southern end of Sequoia National Park. It is unique in that access to this area is separate from the main section of the park and has limited visitor services. Entrance to Mineral King is on Mineral King Road from California 198 (between the town of Three Rivers and the southern entrance to the main park at Ash Mountain). Mineral King Road is by no means a "highway." It is a 25-mile drive, consisting of very steep, winding, sometimes a rough one-lane road, negotiable by any vehicle, but requiring about 90 minutes to cover, one way.

Most of the Kaweah East Fork is inaccessible because it lies in the bottom of an extremely deep gorge, thousands of feet below the roadway. First fishing access is in the Atwell Mill area, where a mile hike leads down into the river, where abundant rainbows and browns reside in this section of the river. Browns reaching 16 inches can be found here.

Next access is upstream at the Cold Springs campground area. Access here is much easier, from the campground to road's end—a distance of about two miles. Brook trout, rainbow and rainbow-golden hybrids populate this section, with many of the hybrids leaning strongly to the golden side of the mix.

At an elevation of nearly 8,000 feet, the insect life—as measured by obvious hatches—is minimal. The upper meadow is open and grassy, meaning it produces huge numbers of

Who doesn't enjoy the brilliant colors of a wild brook trout? Kaweah Marble Fork. Andrew Maurer

Below. Even during modest, higher springtime flows as pictured, Kaweah Marble Fork runs clear, with many small fish that will rise to dry fly patterns such as small (#16-18) Elk Hair Caddis. Andrew Maurer

grasshoppers through the warmer days of the summer and fall seasons. Effective flies include your favorite hopper patterns in sizes 12 to 16. Most other attractor patterns, including small caddis, ants, Adams, and Stimulators can also be productive with careful presentation.

➤ **Kern River:** The upper Kern River drainage within Sequoia National Park is only accessible by foot or horseback, and it's primarily out of reach by short day-hikes. The numerous lakes and streams of the backcountry can offer terrific fly-fishing opportunities to those with the time and stamina to make the longer trips required to reach them.

The waters of the upper Kern are also the ancestral home of the California State Fish, the golden trout. While the distribution of the native golden trout has been extended through years of efforts by fishing enthusiasts and the Department of Fish & Wildlife, their original home waters were confined to certain small tributaries of the upper Kern headwaters.

Below. Six-year old Maddie with one of her first trout on a dry fly, taken from East Fork Kaweah River in Mineral King. Andrew Maurer

120

Facing. A golden-rainbow hybrid from the Mineral King region of Sequoia National Park. Jay Dunkley

Above. A pretty, speckled Marble Fork brown trout. Andrew Maurer

➤ **Flora and Fauna:** The elevation of the two parks varies from below 2,000 to the 14,494-foot peak of Mt. Whitney on the eastern border of Sequoia—the highest point in the lower 48 states. Within that range you will find a great number of habitats supporting a wide variety of plant and animal species. Species that most deserve your respect are black bears, rattlesnakes, and poison oak.

Black bears—during the summer season—range from the lowest to nearly the highest elevations. Problems with bears have been greatly reduced over the past decade or so by strict regulations regarding food storage for both campers and backpackers. The installation of metal bear-proof storage boxes in campsites and at trailheads have helped keep food and trash away from bears and your campsite. Current regulations are readily available both online and at all park offices and visitor centers.

Rattlesnakes are an indigenous species throughout the Sierra and are most frequently found at elevations between 1,000 and 7,000 feet. They are not often encountered within the parks, but awareness and caution should be exercised whenever hiking in the regions they most favor, which include the bottom of Kings Canyon proper and the area around Crystal Cave.

Sequoia Poison Oak is usually found below 4,000 feet. Its oak-like appearance in shiny three-leaf groupings (that turn reddish in the later summer and fall) make it fairly easy to recognize once you've been familiarized with it. Sequoia Poison Oak also is present in the lower elevations of Kings Canyon.

➤ Tackle and Gear

Rods and Line: A 9-foot, 4- or 5-weight rod is appropriate for most of the park's waters. The main Kings River does have some deeper pools and runs where a sink-tip can come in handy for pulling streamers. Floating lines will get you by for most of the season.

Terminal Tackle and Flies: A 7.5- to 9-foot, 3X to 5X leader will cover most situations. Fly patterns are covered in the text above.

Other Gear: Mosquito repellent is a necessity in spring and early summer. A windbreaker/rain jacket and sun protection are valuable all year, as Sierra weather can change rapidly. When selecting a mosquito repellant, be aware that those composed of a high percent of DEET, though highly effective, will "eat" fly lines and some plastic fly boxes. There are brands that come with an applicator that allows you to use the repellant on exposed skin, but avoid touching the chemicals with your hands.

Silver Spring Resort in the Mineral King area of Sequoia—quiet, attractive, rustic cabins and delicious home-made pies! Andrew Maurer

CLOSEST CITY OR POINT OF ENTRANCE TO THE PARK

· Fresno, California: 45 miles to Big Stump on California 180
· Visalia, California: 42 miles to Ash Mountain on California 198

CLOSEST AIRPORT

· Fresno, California: Fresno Yosemite International Airport
· Visalia, California: Visalia Municipal Airport

Both offer car rental and traveler services, but Fresno is considerably larger.

PARK FEES

· $30 Vehicle Entry Pass (valid for seven days)
· $15 Individual Entry Pass (valid for seven days)
· $20 Motorcycle Entry Pass (valid for seven days)
· Sequoia National Park Annual Pass - $50

Note, the price for motorcycle entry is increasing to $25 starting Jan. 1, 2017. Park entrance and user fees change periodically. For up-to-date fees, free days and other exceptions, visit www.nps.gov/seki/index.htm.

OPENING/CLOSING PARK DATES OR FISHING DATES

The park is open for sight-seeing, photography, hiking and activities other than fishing year-round. There might be some minimal closures during heavy snows in the winter and early spring. These are normally quickly cleared by the park's road crews.

FISHING REGULATIONS

· A California fishing license is required to fish in Sequoia.
· California Fish and Wildlife regulations apply.
· Park open and close dates vary. See https://www.nps.gov/seki/planyourvisit/hours.htm.
· Artificial, barbless catch-and-release is in effect at 9,000 feet and below, if fishing for rainbow trout.
· The Kaweah drainage is open year round with the Marble Fork reserved as Wild Trout water and restricted to artificial flies, barbless catch-and-release.
· Sequoia is open for sight-seeing, photography, hiking and activities other than fishing year-round.
· Mineral King Road is closed in mid-winter while the rest of the park might be subject to some minimal closures during heavy snows in the winter and early spring. These are normally quickly cleared by the park's road crews.

CLOSEST FLY SHOPS

Yosemite Rivers Fly Shop
40827 California 41
Oakhurst, CA 93644
559-641-7788
www.sierraflyfisher.com

Herb Bauer Sports
6264 N. Blackstone Ave.
Fresno, CA 93710
559-435-8600

CLOSEST GUIDE SERVICE

Sierra Fly Fisher
559-683-7664
www.sierraflyfisher.com

BEST PLACES TO STAY IN THE PARK

Wuksachi Lodge
64740 Wuksachi Way
Sequoia National Park, CA 93262
886-807-3598
www.visitkingscanyon.com

JIMMIE MORALES grew up in Fresno, California, which is the heart and soul of the San Joaquin Valley but isn't usually thought of as one of the great hubs of fly fishing in California. However, he begs to differ. With Yosemite to the north, Kings Canyon and Sequoia National Parks to the east, the Sierra National Forest to the northeast, O'Neal's Forebay, and San Luis Reservoir to the west, and great surf fishing over on the Monterey coastline, what more could a nine-year-old fly fisher want? He started fly fishing 41 years ago and hasn't put down his fly rod since. After helping teach casting in his early teens and later taking people out unofficially for years, he started guiding as a profession in 1995.

Silver City Mountain Resort
Mineral King Road
Three Rivers, CA 93271
558-561-3223
www.silvercityresort.com

BEST CAMPGROUND IN THE PARK
Atwell Mill Campground
Three Rivers, CA 93271
559-565-3341
· Nine miles from California 198 on Mineral King Road adjacent to the East Fork of the Kaweah River
· 21 sites at the 6,650-foot elevation
· Campgrounds are open late May to late October
· No RVs
· Tents only

BEST CAMPGROUND OUTSIDE THE PARK
Princess Campground Sequoia National Forest
California 180
Miramonte, CA 93633
877-444-677
· 10- to 15-minute drive from Grant Grove via California 180
· Based next to a large meadow at the 5,900-foot elevation

BEST PLACE TO EAT INSIDE THE PARK
Silver City Mountain Resort
Mineral King Road
Three Rivers, CA 93271
550-561-3223

BEST PLACE TO EAT NEAR THE PARK
School House Restaurant
(New American fare)
1018 S. Frankwood Ave.
Sanger, CA 93657
559-787-3271
(Historic brick schoolhouse established in 1921)

MUST SEE
· Hospital Rock: A massive quartzite rock, located on California 198 along the Kaweah River's middle fork.
· General Sherman Tree: This Sequoia is the largest tree (by volume) in the world; it measures about 52,500 cubic feet.
· Grant Grove Village: The is the base camp to both Sequoia and Kings Canyon national parks.
· Tunnel Log: Located on Moro Rock-Crescent Meadow Road, this fallen Sequoia has been cut to allow cars to pass through it; see http://www.road sideamerica.com/story/21675.

NEAREST HOSPITAL/URGENT TREATMENT CENTER
Community Regional Medical Center
2823 Fresno St.
Fresno, CA 93721-1324
559-459-6000
(793-bed hospital with full emergency, surgical and cardiac facilities)

Mountain View Medical Clinic
468 N. Vermont Ave.
Dinuba, CA 93618
559-591-6200

Immediate Care Center
215 E. Caldwell Ave
Visalia, CA 93277
559-622-9800

Sequoia Prompt Care
1110 S. Ben Maddox
Visalia, CA 93292
559-624-4800

CELL PHONE SERVICE
Cell service is good around population centers, but is spotty at best within the park.

FOR ALL ELSE, VISIT
www.nps.gov/seki/index.htm

123

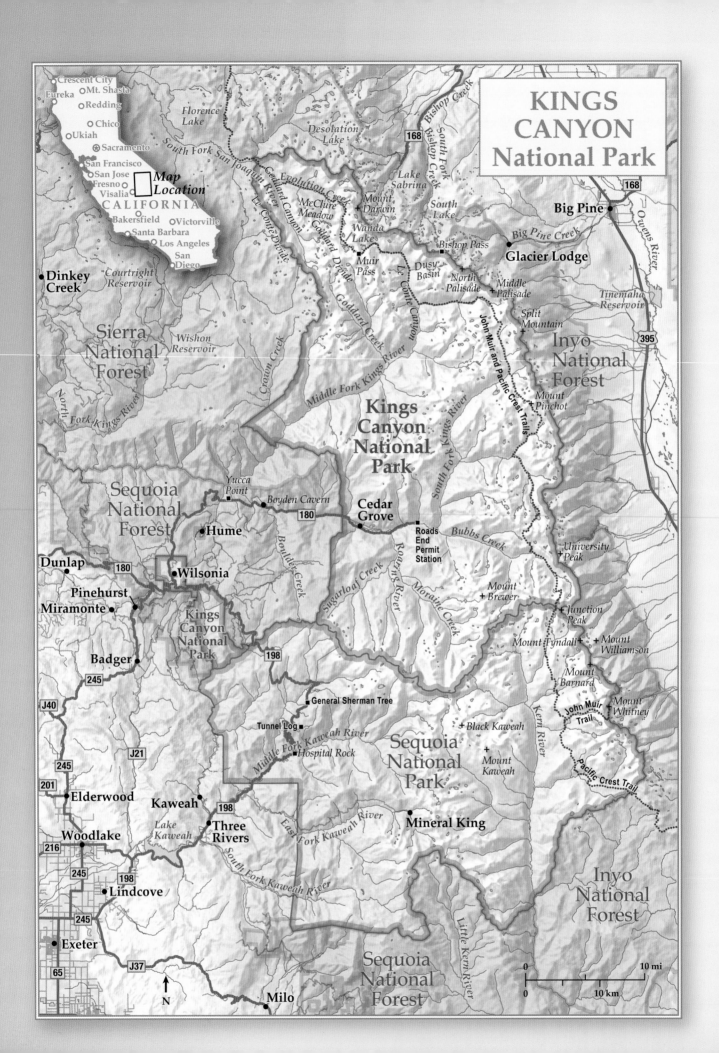

KINGS CANYON National Park

Crescent City
Eureka
Mt. Shasta
Redding
Chico
Ukiah
Sacramento
San Francisco
San Jose
Fresno
Visalia
CALIFORNIA
Bakersfield
Santa Barbara
Victorville
Los Angeles
San Diego

Map Location

Florence Lake
Desolation Lake
Bishop Creek
South Fork Bishop Creek
168

South Fork San Joaquin River
Evolution Creek
McClure Meadow
Mount Darwin
Lake Sabrina
South Lake
Le Conte Divide
Goddard Canyon
Wanda Lakes
Bishop Pass
Big Pine Creek
Big Pine
168

Glacier Lodge
Dinkey Creek
Courtright Reservoir
Muir Pass
Le Conte Canyon
Dusy Basin
North Palisade
Middle Palisade
Owens River
395

Goddard Creek
Goddard Divide
Split Mountain
Tinemaha Reservoir

Sierra National Forest
Wishon Reservoir
Middle Fork Kings River
Inyo National Forest

North Fork Kings River
Crown Creek
Mount Pinchot

Kings Canyon National Park
South Fork Kings River
John Muir and Pacific Crest Trails

Sequoia National Forest
Yucca Point
Boyden Cavern
Cedar Grove
180
Roads End Permit Station
Bubbs Creek
University Peak

Hume
Boulder Creek
Roaring River
Moraine Creek
Mount Brewer
Junction Peak

Dunlap
180
Wilsonia
Sugarloaf Creek
Mount Tyndall
Mount Williamson

Pinehurst
Miramonte
Kings Canyon National Park
Mount Barnard

Badger
198
Kern River
Mount Whitney
John Muir Trail

245
J40
General Sherman Tree
Pacific Crest Trail

J21
Tunnel Log
Black Kaweah
Middle Fork Kaweah River
Hospital Rock
Sequoia National Park
Mount Kaweah

245
201
Elderwood
Kaweah
198
East Fork Kaweah River

Woodlake
Three Rivers
Mineral King

216
Lake Kaweah
Inyo National Forest

245
198
South Fork Kaweah River

Lindcove
Little Kern River

245
Exeter

65
J37
Sequoia National Forest
Milo

N

0   10 mi
0   10 km

➤ **Location:** Kings Canyon National Park is located in the south-central section of California's Sierra Nevada range. The western entrance is a one-hour drive east of Fresno on California 180. The southern entrance is a two to two-and-a-half-hour drive east of the city of Visalia and through Sequoia National Park on California 198. These are the only two entrances to the park. Both Fresno and Visalia are on north/south California 99 corridor. Both cities have airports, with Fresno's Yosemite International airport being the larger of the two.

Sequoia and Kings Canyon national parks are commonly referred to as "SEKI" by both locals and the National Park Service. Combined, the two are 120,000 acres larger than Yosemite, their neighbor to the north. They are administered as one park, but for the purposes of this book, they will be discussed separately. (Sequoia National Park was covered in the previous chapter.)

Spectacular backdrops and crystalline water add to the pleasure and challenge of coaxing a strike on the Kings. Andrew Maurer

Native Americans tribes such as the Monache and Western Mono called this area home 6,000-7,000 years ago. The first Europeans didn't see it until the late 1700s. Not long after, trappers, miners and loggers poured into the area. Kings Canyon National Park was created in 1940 and encompasses 461,901 acres.

When it comes to fly fishing in Kings Canyon, the Kings River and a portion of the San Joaquin River are home to good populations of rainbow, brown, brook and golden trout.

➤ **The San Joaquin River:** The headwaters of the south Fork of the San Joaquin drain the northernmost section of the park. Evolution Creek and the waters of Goddard Canyon are the two main water sources.

Goddard Canyon and the highest lakes of Evolution Valley are golden trout country. Lower in the McClure Meadow area of Evolution Valley, rainbow, brook and brown trout take over the population. The confluence of the two streams marks the northern boundary of the park.

➤ **The Kings River:** The South and Middle Forks of the Kings are separated from the San Joaquin by the Goddard Divide and the 11,955-foot Muir Pass. Golden trout abound in the upper drainages. Brook trout are also found in many of the lakes and streams. Rainbow and rainbow/golden hybrids are found wherever the two are able to mingle.

This area can be most easily reached from the wilderness hiking trailhead that enters the park from the east side of the Sierra at South Lake, west of the town of Bishop on California 395. The route enters Kings Canyon Park over Bishop Pass and through Dusy Basin. It contains a beautiful series of small lakes and connecting streams that also are full of golden trout and which constitutes a part of the headwaters of the Kings River. Getting to the San Joaquin drainage of Evolution Valley means descending the trail from Bishop Pass down into Le Conte Canyon to the John Muir Trail on the Kings River. Next, you will go up upstream and over Muir Pass,

Left. A Kings River rainbow's aerial display rewards a careful mid-river approach, good cast, and perfect drift of a caddis dry fly. Andrew Maurer

Below. Approaching a nice hole using shade and rocks for cover. Andrew Maurer

Kings River browns such as this one can make any fly fisher's day a memorable one! Jay Dunkley

eventually reaching the San Joaquin drainage. When hiking here, be prepared for long, steep climbs, descents, and rugged rocky terrain. It takes strong legs and an equally strong back to access these areas.

The South Fork of the Kings River becomes highly accessible as it enters Kings Canyon itself. Here, California 180 runs right along the river from Boyden Cavern to Road's End, and is 15 miles of one of the "fishiest" rivers you will ever see. The catch rate here seems to be about half-and-half rainbow to brown trout. The average trout here will be around 9 inches, but we do see some very nice fish caught every year. Brown trout of well over 20 inches inhabit this section of the river. Other tributaries to the South Fork include Bubbs Creek and the Roaring River, beyond Road's End.

Trailheads depart from Road's End into the backcountry wilderness, but even day hikes upstream can be most rewarding with respect to both fishing and terrific scenery.

The descent of California 180 into Kings Canyon from above provides a number of impressive scenic overlooks into the canyon and a spectacular view down into the confluence of the middle and south forks of the Kings River at Yucca Point. After the highway meets and follows the south fork upstream to Road's End, nearly any area where parking can be found off the road can provide fine fishing opportunities (depending on season and stream flows).

Cedar Grove is the sole source of commercial services along the river in the bottom of Kings Canyon itself. Cedar Grove offers lodging, food, and provisions. Upstream, between Cedar Grove and Road's End, are three large campgrounds, all of which lie adjacent to the river and provide easy access to it. Fishing prospects, again, will improve with the distance traveled away from those areas of heaviest usage.

As with most high-country fisheries, the higher in elevation you travel along the Southern Sierra Nevada, the starker and more sterile the environment becomes. Above 10,000 feet, there are some caddis in both the lakes and streams, but not many. This usually reflects in the size of the trout you will catch. One fly that always attracts trout at higher elevation are ant patterns—carpenter ants are found at elevations up to 11,000 feet and beyond. They can be fished dry or wet.

The 15 miles of road along the south fork in the canyon offer a great variety of water types, including beautiful pools, long and fast riffles, and ideal pocket water. Andrew Maurer

We prefer to fish the alpine lakes by sight-fishing—that is, approaching the water slowly and sighting the fish before casting. The water is usually very clear and the trout are quite visible. They often appear to stake out a claim on a certain piece of shoreline and will cruise back and forth through that area. Cast to them when their backs are to you, then let them turn and "come upon" the fly. A slight twitch can sometimes induce a strike as well. In fact, the "twitch" is a valuable tactic when fishing most any high alpine Sierra lake with a dry fly. After a minute or so of unnoticed floating on a lake, a brief slight twitch of your dry fly can be just the thing to draw the attention of a nearby passing fish.

Grasshoppers can be found up to the 9,000-10,000-foot mark. Heavy winds, which are common in the afternoons, can knock the poor-flying insects into the water. Some smaller (12-16) hopper patterns are always good to have in the fly box. Early season, many fly fishers love to fish mosquito patterns. The pesky insects begin showing up right after the snow melts and can sure put a damper on your trip if you are unprepared. The truth is that very few trout know what a mosquito is because the bugs mostly prefer the stagnant water from which they came. The trout take the mosquito patterns as just another insect that's trapped in the surface of the lake or stream.

Another local "secret" fly for the highest elevation Sierra lakes is the Sierra Bright Dot—a small, fore-and-aft style grizzly-hackled pattern tied with a bright red-orange thread body—that will often take fish when nothing else seems to work.

Springtime can be great at higher elevations. The snowmelt will usually start sometime during the first part of April with the 10,000-foot level usually becoming accessible around July 4th. This is spawning time for the rainbows and goldens. Any moving water where these trout are known to live will see concentrations of the fish posting up to move into the running water. This lasts from a couple of weeks to perhaps a month. If you're looking for that large golden, this is the time of the year to catch one.

As the tributaries converge and drop in elevation, they turn into larger streams and rivers where the aquatic insect life becomes heavier and more diverse. Mayflies and stoneflies join with the caddis. At elevations from 1,000-7,000 feet, the angler will see mayflies such as the Blue-winged Olive in sizes 18-22, March Browns in size 12, Pale Morning Duns in sizes 16-18, as well as others throughout the season.

Stoneflies include the Golden stonefly in sizes 12-16, the Yellow Sally in sizes 14-18, and the Giant Salmon Fly in sizes 4-6. The ever-present caddis runs in sizes 14 to 18 throughout the season with the October Caddis size 8 showing in the month it's named after. Terrestrials are always a good bet during the heat of summer.

➤ Flora and Fauna: The elevation of the two parks varies from below 2,000 to the 14,494-foot peak of Mt. Whitney on the eastern border of Sequoia—the highest point in the lower 48 states. Within that range you will find a great number of habitats supporting a wide variety of plant and animal species. Species that most deserve your respect are black bears, rattlesnakes, and poison oak.

Black bears—during the summer season—range from the lowest to nearly the highest elevations. Problems with bears have been greatly reduced over the past decade or so by strict regulations regarding food storage for both campers and

Author Jimmie Morales with a fine rainbow. Andrew Maurer

backpackers. The installation of metal bear-proof storage boxes in campsites and at trailheads have helped keep food and trash away from bears and your campsite. Current regulations are readily available both online and at all park offices and visitor centers.

Rattlesnakes are an indigenous species throughout the Sierra and are most frequently found at elevations between 1,000 and 7,000 feet. They are not often encountered within the parks, but awareness and caution should be exercised whenever hiking in the regions they most favor, which include the bottom of Kings Canyon proper and the area around Crystal Cave.

Sequoia poison oak is usually found below 4,000 feet. Its oak-like appearance in shiny three-leaf groupings (that turn reddish in the later summer and fall) make it fairly easy to recognize once you've been familiarized with it. Sequoia poison oak also is present in the lower elevations of Kings Canyon.

➤ **Tackle and Gear**

Rods and Line: A 9-foot, 4- or 5-weight rod is right for most of the park's waters. The main Kings River does have some deeper pools and runs where a sink-tip can come in handy for pulling streamers. Floating lines will get you by for most of the season.

Terminal Tackle and Flies: A 7.5- to 9-foot, 3 to 5X leader will cover most situations. Fly patterns are covered in the text above.

Other Gear: Mosquito repellent is a necessity in spring and early summer. A windbreaker/rain jacket and sun protection are valuable all year, because Sierra weather can change rapidly. When selecting a mosquito repellant, be aware that those containing a high percentage of DEET will "eat" fly lines and some plastic fly boxes. There are brands that come with an applicator that allows you to use the repellant on exposed skin, but not touch the chemicals with your bare hands.

CLOSEST CITY TO POINT OF ENTRANCE TO THE PARK
· Fresno, California: 45 miles to Big Stump on California 180
· Visalia, California: 42 miles to Ash Mountain on California 198

CLOSEST AIRPORTS
· Fresno, California: Fresno Yosemite International Airport
· Visalia, California: Visalia Municipal Airport
Both offer car rental and traveler services, but Fresno is considerably larger

OPEN/CLOSING DATES OR FISHING DATES
· A California fishing license is required to fish in Sequoia.
· California Fish and Wildlife regulations apply.
· Park open and close dates vary. See https://www.nps.gov/seki/planyourvisit/hours.htm.
· Artificial, barbless catch-and-release is in effect at 9,000 feet and below, if fishing for rainbow trout.

· The Kaweah drainage is open year-round with the Marble Fork reserved as Wild Trout water and restricted to artificial flies, barbless catch-and-release.
· Sequoia is open for sight-seeing, photography, hiking and activities other than fishing year-round.
· Mineral King Road is closed in mid-winter while the rest of the park might be subject to some minimal closures during heavy snows in the winter and early spring (these are normally quickly cleared by the park's road crews).

CLOSEST FLY SHOPS
Yosemite Rivers Fly Shop
40827 California 41
Oakhurst, CA 93644
559-641-7788
www.sierraflyfisher.com

Herb Bauer Sports
6264 N. Blackstone Ave.
Fresno, CA 93710
559-435-8600
www.herbbauersportinggoods.com

CLOSEST GUIDE SERVICE
Sierra Fly Fisher
559-683-7664
www.sierraflyfisher.com

BEST PLACES TO STAY IN THE PARK
John Muir Lodge
86728 California 180
Kings Canyon National Park, CA 93633
866-807-3598
www.visitsequioa.com

Cedar Grove Lodge
Kings Canyon National Park, CA 93633
801-559-4714

Wuksachi Lodge
64740 Wuksachi Way
Sequoia National Park 93262
866-807-3598
www.visitkingscanyon.com

Silver City Mountain Resort
Mineral King Rd.
Three Rivers, CA 93271
558-561-3223
www.silvercityresort.com

JIMMIE MORALES grew up in Fresno, California, which is the heart and soul of the San Joaquin Valley, but isn't usually thought of as one of the great hubs of fly fishing in California. However, he begs to differ. With Yosemite to the north, Kings Canyon and Sequoia National Parks to the east, the Sierra National Forest to the northeast, O'Neal's Forebay, and San Luis Reservoir to the west, and great surf fishing over on the Monterey coastline, what more could a nine-year-old fly fisher want? He started fly fishing 41 years ago and hasn't put down his fly rod since. After helping teach casting in his early teens and later taking people out unofficially for years, he started guiding as a profession in 1995.

BEST CAMPGROUND IN THE PARK

Atwell Mill Campground
Three Rivers, CA 93271
559-565-3341
· Nine miles from California 198 on Mineral King Road adjacent to the East Fork of the Kaweah River
· 21 sites at the 6,650-foot elevation
· Campgrounds are open late-May to late-October
· No RVs
· Tents only

BEST CAMPGROUND OUTSIDE THE PARK

Princess Campground Sequoia National Forest
California 180
Miramonte, CA 93633
877-444-677
· 10- to 15-minute drive from Grant Grove via California 180
· Based next to a large meadow at the 5,900-foot elevation

BEST PLACE TO EAT INSIDE THE PARK

Silver City Mountain Resort
Mineral King Rd.
Three Rivers, CA 93271
559-561-3223

BEST PLACE TO EAT NEAR THE PARK

School House Restaurant
(New American fare)
1018 S. Frankwood Ave.
Sanger, CA 93657
559-787-3271
(Historic brick schoolhouse established in 1921)

MUST SEE

· Hospital Rock: A massive quartzite rock, located on California 198 along the Kaweah River's middle fork.
· General Sherman Tree: This Sequoia is the largest tree (by volume) in the world; it measures about 52,500 cubic feet.
· Grant Grove Village: The is the base camp to both Sequoia and Kings Canyon national parks.
· Tunnel Log: Located on Moro Rock-Crescent Meadow Road, this fallen Sequoia has been cut to allow cars to pass through it; see http://www.roadside-america.com/story/21675.

NEAREST HOSPITAL/URGENT TREATMENT CENTER

Community Regional Medical Center
2823 Fresno St.
Fresno, CA 93721-1324
559-459–6000
793-bed hospital with full emergency, surgical and cardiac facilities

Mountain View Medical Clinic
468 N. Vermont Ave.
Dinuba, CA 93618
559-591-6200

Immediate Care Center
215 E. Caldwell Ave
Visalia, CA 93277
559-622-9800

Sequoia Prompt Care
1110 S. Ben Maddox
Visalia, CA 93292
559-624-4800

CELL PHONE SERVICE

Cell service is good around population centers but is spotty at best within the park.

FOR ALL ELSE, VISIT
www.nps.gov/seki/index.htm

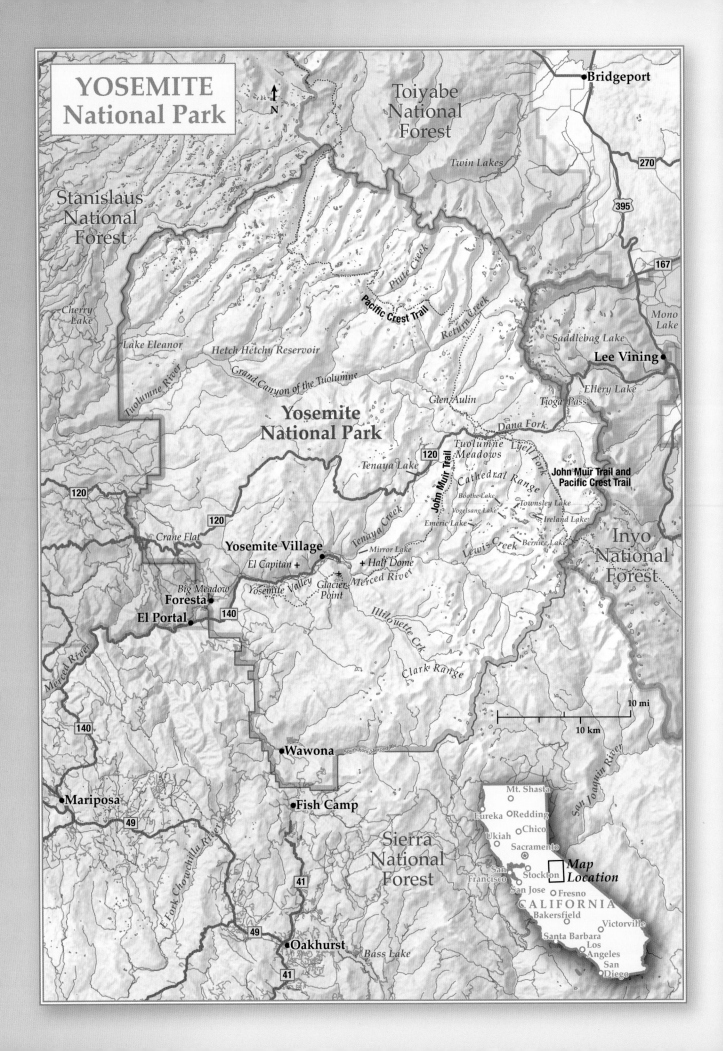

Yosemite National Park is set within California's Sierra Nevada Mountain range. It's famed for its giant, ancient sequoias, for Tunnel View scenic vista, the iconic vista of towering Bridalveil Fall, and the granite cliffs of El Capitan and Half Dome. In Yosemite Village, you'll find shops, restaurants, the Yosemite Museum, and the Ansel Adams Gallery, which offers prints of the photographer's renowned black-and-white landscapes of the area.

The park is most easily accessed via the following routes:

- **San Francisco/Bay area:** Interstate 580 east to Interstate 205 east to California 120 east (Manteca), or California 140 east (Merced) into Yosemite National Park.
- **Sacramento:** California 99 south to California 120 east (Manteca), or California 140 east (Merced) into Yosemite National Park.
- **Los Angeles area:** Interstate 5 north (or Interstate 405 north to Interstate 5) to California 99 north to California 41 north (Fresno) into Yosemite National Park.

In 1890, Yosemite became our third national park following Yellowstone and Sequoia. It is one of our most popular and highly visited parks due both to its scenic grandeur and its location. During peak season—from May through September—the park can fairly be described as "crowded," with a visitor count that generally runs about four million every year.

Yosemite's high visitor count might reasonably produce lowered expectations for quality fly fishing. Funny thing, but nothing could be further from the truth. In fact, Yosemite offers some of the most varied and attractive fly-fishing opportunities anywhere, ranging from the sublime to the spectacular. It's nearly impossible for an experienced fisher to have a "bad day" with a fly rod anywhere in the park. (Although it would be ill-advised to put that statement to the test by waving a graphite rod in the air during a not-uncommon summer lightning storm!) And for novice or beginner fly-fishers, the park also abounds with ideal waters for honing new skills.

An appreciation for the range and abundance of Yosemite fly-fishing opportunities can be understood with a look at a few of the park's physical statistics:

- 1,169 square miles in size
- Elevation ranging from 3,000 to more than 13,000 feet
- 214 miles of paved roads
- 800 miles of hiking trails, including large sections of the John Muir and Pacific Crest Trails
- Hundreds upon hundreds of streams and lakes

Almost 95 percent of the park consists of backcountry wilderness. As much beautiful water as there is readily acces-

The Merced River in the lower end of Yosemite Valley can provide better fishing than more crowded areas upstream—along with some mighty fine scenery. Andrew Maurer

sible to anyone in a vehicle, it is a tiny fraction of what awaits just beyond the next ridge, around the next bend, 70 feet down into that granite gorge, or 30 miles up the hiking trail.

In other words, as is so often true in any attractive fly-fishing destination, even just a short walk away from the road or the nearest campground can bring great rewards, which will likely come in the form of both fish *and* scenery!

The park encompasses the headwaters of two major watersheds—the Tuolumne River to the north and the Merced

Tenaya Lake, 13,000-foot Mt. Conness in the background, viewed from Olmstead Point. Andrew Maurer

River to the south. Yosemite Valley was the only region of the park with an original resident population of native rainbow trout in the Merced River, which served historically as the end of the road for spawning salmon or steelhead from the Pacific Ocean via San Francisco Bay and the San Joaquin River.

Originally, Yosemite was home to the Awhaneechee tribe of Americans Indians. Not long after its discovery by early explorers of European descent, and its glowing descriptions by the famed writer and explorer John Muir, its popularity grew rapidly among the new Californians eager for adventure and wild, scenic environments.

Soon, the sportsmen among them began pursuing the introduction of a variety of trout species into the many waters of the park, which had formerly held none. Between the late 1800s and the 1940s, most of the park's waters became populated with a variety of introduced trout species, including rainbow, brook, brown, golden, and others that no longer remain.

The trout thrived in the optimal conditions of most Yosemite waters, and for the following several decades, reg-

ular stocking continued throughout the park, in service to the expectations of the fishing public. However, by 1991, a change in attitude toward non-native species began to take root when a new environmental consciousness was embraced by the National Park Service. In 1991, all stocking of trout within the park ceased. The end of trout stocking brought an end to fish populations in only a few of the high wilderness lakes, which lacked access to suitable spawning streams. At the same time, it also insured that the excellent spawning conditions on countless other park waters would henceforth go on to continue sustaining healthy populations of self-propagating wild trout.

Fly fishing in Yosemite offers a wide range of water types and species of trout. The park's two watersheds, Tuolumne and Merced, are similar in fish, fishing, and habitat variety, which vary more with changes in elevation than by location in either the north or south.

Tuolumne Meadows, on the Tioga Road, lies at about 8,600 feet in the upper eastern side of Yosemite, about a 90-minute drive from Yosemite Valley. It is worth visiting as much for its splendid scenery as it is for the abundant access to beautiful fly-fishing waters. It also provides the nearest access to the headwaters of both of the park's watersheds:

· The Tuolumne River to the north
· The Merced River headwaters that begin about 10 miles to the south of Tuolumne Meadows

The upper Tuolumne River flows through large meadows of the same name and is fed by several of its other forks that converge in the immediate area, including the Lyell Fork, Dana Fork, and other nearby creeks—nearly all of which hold fish. The trout species include rainbow, brown and brook trout, with the brookies holding a slight edge in numbers. The browns in the area are often the largest of the three species (by a slight margin). Average sizes in most of these streams are from 6 to 9 inches, although a few larger (and wiser) fish can be found on occasion, up to a foot or more.

There is one large campground in Tuolumne Meadows and lodging is available at the Tuolumne Meadows Lodge, consisting of rustic but comfortable tent-cabins and tent-covered dining room. Reservations are strongly advised for both. It is also a major trailhead area for numerous backcountry destinations, both north and south.

Like most alpine habitats, the shorter season and the lower numbers of insects produce trout that are hungry, not terribly selective, and willing to grab nearly any well-placed and well-presented fly of a reasonable pattern and size. Any vari-

ety of standard patterns of caddis such as Elk Hair, X-Caddis, EC-Caddis, many mayfly patterns, Pale Morning Duns, Blue-winged Olives, and the all-around Adams in sizes 16 to 18 will serve quite well.

Terrestrials such as ants, small hoppers, and beetles often work well. The same can be said for nymphs, although dry

A nice Merced River rainbow on a March Brown dry during a strong spring hatch below the park. Andrew Maurer

Below. Casting to undercut banks and overhanging brush can bring rewards in open spaces with little cover, which are common around Tuolumne Meadows. Andrew Maurer

Above. A longer cast improves your odds with skittish trout when natural cover is scarce in areas of the Lyell Fork. Andrew Maurer

Inset. A brilliant brookie in fall spawning colors from Gardisky Lake just outside Yosemite's eastern Tioga entrance. Andrew Maurer

flies are usually taken so readily that there's little reason or need to fish beneath the surface. Exceptions can occur at periods of higher water in spring or following heavy rainfall, and in a few of the deeper pools and runs, when a caddis pupa, Pheasant Tail, midge larva or pupa, small stonefly, or similar can be effective. Nymphs can be fished alone or as a dropper beneath a dry fly. Fishing nymphs might also tempt any larger brown trout that might be hugging the bottom.

All of Yosemite's high elevation streams share crystal water clarity, frequently bordered by wide open meadows and/or smooth granite. And—as in most small- to medium-size streams—the fish can be easily spooked. Success in fly fishing will be much improved by stealthy, accurate, and delicate presentations in casting and good drag-free drifts.

Most streams are easily waded and not often more than thigh deep. Moving slowly, staying low, taking advantage of any cover or shade to hide your presence are all helpful advantages. As flows and water levels decrease later in the season, such cautions become even more important, as is the ability to make longer accurate casts to fish that spook so easily. The up-side of fishing in the region is the forgiving lack of obstacles to casting— fewer trees and much wide-open space, making it a great area for new fly fishers. In the open meadows, many fish will hug the deeper undercut banks beneath overhanging brush, which can present the biggest challenge to casting while avoiding twig snags.

Rods of 7- to 9-feet, 3- to 5-weight with floating lines, 9- to 11-foot leaders and 5X tippet will work just fine in most of the high country. On the larger waters of the Merced and Tuolumne at lower elevations (3,000 feet), where the fish can be larger and more selective, a 9-foot, 5-weight rod is ideal, with 9- to 11-foot leaders and tippets of 4X to 6X.

If current multi-year drought conditions continue in California, they might increasingly affect trout populations because of low, warm stream flows in later season. Judicious consideration should be applied to fishing on any waters where the health of the fishery itself could be in question.

While the majority of annual visitors to Yosemite will enjoy the park from its paved roadways and day-hiking trails, the 95 percent of the park consisting of wilderness can only be accessed on foot or horseback. Backpacking is one of the best ways to get away from the crowds and find some of the most rewarding fishing in Yosemite. Wilderness Permits are required for overnight pack trips. These are available from any of the park ranger stations, or if you're starting from outside the park, you can get your permit from any U.S. National Forest District station.

Tuolumne Meadows has major trailheads leading in every direction of the park, as does Yosemite Valley. However, starting from the valley involves dramatically long, steep climbs to reach the much higher backcountry.

A series of "High Sierra Camps" spread in a loop through the backcountry at easy hiking distances offer comfortable overnight stays and meals in tent cabins. They are very popular with hikers who enjoy the amenities and freedom of hiking without heavy camping gear. Reservations are required well in advance. The camps are well-placed for access to good fishing in nearby streams and lakes.

Vogelsang High Sierra Camp: This camp is located about seven miles south of Tuolumne Meadows by trail, and offers great choices among streams and lakes. Ireland, Boothe, Emeric, Vogelsang and Bernice Lakes can all offer

The Tuolumne's Lyell Fork sports more than 10 miles of beautiful, varied trout water, which are easily accessed from nearby John Muir/Pacific Crest trails. Andrew Maurer

Mt. Dana at sunset near the eastern park entrance, dusted by early fall snow. Andrew Maurer

good fishing for rainbows, brooks, or browns, and Fletcher and Townsley Lakes have golden trout. Summer evenings can bring terrific fun casting dry flies to sometimes large numbers of rising fish. Further to the south are countless more opportunities, including several miles of Lewis Creek, another good producer.

Glen Aulin High Sierra Camp: North of Tuolumne Meadows about six miles by trail is Glen Aulin High Sierra Camp on the river at Glen Aulin Falls, where fishing for larger rainbows and browns gets better and better as you continue downstream. A few days' hiking further into the northern end of the park brings more fishing opportunities in streams and lakes than can be mentioned here. But for those with a full backpack, fly rod, and the motivation, great pleasures await the intrepid angler in the Yosemite backcountry, north or south.

Lake Tenaya: This lake is located about 10 miles west of Tuolumne Meadows, and is very popular because it's the only lake in the park accessible by vehicles. It also has a lovely sand beach. The lake holds a population of rainbows that are not easy to catch because of the popularity of the lake and its depth. No motors are allowed on the lake, but float tubes, kayaks and paddle craft are useful, especially if rising fish are seen in the mornings or evenings. It's also worth trying throwing and stripping a black or olive Wooly Bugger, streamer or Zug-Bug on a sink-tip line.

Merced River's South Fork: The south fork is another stream of boulder-strewn runs, deep pools, and cobble riffles holding a healthy population of rainbow and brown trout up to 14 inches. The river can drop quite low later in the season, but earlier it offers fine fly fishing, with dry fly caddis patterns, nymphs or emergers being the go-to flies during typical warm weather. Also, here is the Wawona hotel, which is located just a few miles inside the park's southern entrance on California 41, at 4,000 feet. It is popular for its beautiful, historic hotel, golf course, stables, and numerous campgrounds. The warmer climate at that elevation makes swimming popular, so a little extra driving and/or hiking along the river, either up- or downstream of the Wawona commercial area, will bring quiet solitude and undisturbed fish.

Merced River Tributaries: The longer stretches of highway connect primary park destinations, such as California highways 120, 41, and the Glacier Point Road. Along the way, these roads cross many small creeks throughout the park, mostly tributaries of the Merced River. Nearly all of them that still flow all season (and even some that don't) hold trout for the adventurous fly fisher willing to do some bushwhacking and negotiate sometimes steep and rugged terrain. Similar flies to those already mentioned will work, and the rewards can include some beautiful and feisty trout that have seen surprisingly little fishing pressure.

Yosemite Valley: This area is far and away the most crowded region of the park during peak season. The valley's Merced River can challenge a fly fisher's hopes for good fishing opportunities. To be sure, its gliding slicks, pools and gravel riffles are exquisitely beautiful, but the numbers of park users can be daunting. There are, however, rainbows and browns in the river, and they can be coaxed to take a fly with careful selection of time and place.

Tenaya Creek: There are other options for fishing in the general area. Tenaya Creek, the source of Mirror Lake at the east end of the valley, descends from Tenaya Lake to merge with the Merced below Mirror Lake. It holds a population of small rainbows, brooks and browns that can be found above Mirror Lake along a trail that follows the creek upstream.

Crane Creek: This creek flows through Big Meadow near Foresta, and is promising for small rainbows and browns in the early season. To get there, take the Foresta Road to the west off Big Oak Flat Road between Yosemite Valley and the Crane Flat junction with California 120.

Tuolumne River: This river below O'Shaughnessy Dam (Hetch Hetchy Reservoir) holds larger resident rainbows and browns, making it attractive to fly fishers. Also, the greater variety and abundance of insects thriving at lower elevations contribute to the increased growth of the trout. However, the increased number of hatches requires that the angler be more mindful of insect hatches and their timing. Recognizing and matching the hatch with the correct fly pattern is of greater importance here than in most other areas of the park.

As a tailwater, the Tuolumne below O'Shaughnessy Dam has the added advantages of consistently cold water and extra-prolific insects. Access to the O'Shaughnessy tailwater is from just outside the northern park entrance on California 120, by taking Evergreen Road (becoming Hetch Hetchy Road) which leads to the river below the dam.

Hatches to look for through the season include
· Blue-winged Olives from January-March.
· Golden stones in March.
· March Browns from March-April.
· Salmon flies in April.
· Pale Morning Duns, caddis, and Yellow Sallies throughout the season after spring water levels have stabilized and into September.
· Big October Caddis after September.
· Stoneflies, hoppers and ants can be effective through the mid-season, and midge patterns such as the RS2, WD-40, and Johnny Flash can prove their value, too.

Merced River: This stretch of the river outside and below the western park entrance on California 140 near El Portal is very similar to the Tuolumne River, which is described above. Fish here can reach 18 inches and up.

The Merced River outside of the park differs from the Tuolumne tailwater by being subject to detrimental warming during the low flows of late summer in drought years.

➤ **Lodging:** Each of the four entrances to Yosemite has lodging, camping and restaurant services within 10-15 miles of the highway. Just outside the eastern entrance, at Tioga Pass, are two attractive lakes—Tioga and Ellery—with small, pleasant campgrounds and nice populations of rainbow trout, including some larger stocked fish.

In between the Tioga and Ellery Lakes is a turn-off to the north side of California 120. It's a good gravel road that leads to Saddlebag Lake, with several additional nice campgrounds along the way and a small, rustic "resort" and cafe at the lake. Saddlebag is stocked regularly with rainbows, and contains some fish up to 20 inches that can be caught on dry flies or streamers from the shore. At the north end of Saddlebag Lake is the "Twenty Lakes Basin," most popular with overnight and day hikers. It is an especially fun place to explore with a fly rod, for its many varied, scenic and easily accessible small- to modest-sized lakes and streams containing good numbers of trout, including some goldens.

Note that on March 1, 2016, the names of many Yosemite attractions and accommodations changed with a new concessionaire taking charge of sales and services, including
· The Awahanee Hotel, established in the 1920s, is now the Majestic Yosemite Hotel
· The former Wawona Hotel is now Big Trees Lodge
· Curry Village has been renamed Half Dome Village
· Yosemite Lodge at the Falls is now Yosemite Valley Lodge

➤ **Tackle and Gear**

Rods and Line: Rods of 7- to 9-feet, 3- to 5-weight with floating lines, 9- to 11-foot leaders and 5X tippet will work just fine in most of the high country. On the larger waters of the Merced and Tuolumne at lower elevations (3,000 feet), where the fish can be larger and more selective, a 9-foot, 5-weight rod is ideal, with 9- to 11-foot leaders and tippets of 4X to 6X.

Terminal Tackle and Flies: Standard patterns of caddis such as Elk Hair, X-Caddis, EC-Caddis, many mayfly patterns, Pale Morning Duns, Blue-winged Olives, and the all-around Adams in sizes 16 to 18 are recommended. Terrestrials such as ants, small hoppers, and beetles often work well. Nymphing (fished alone or as a dropper beneath a dry fly) can produce during periods of higher water in spring or following heavy rainfall, and in a few of the deeper pools and runs, when a caddis pupa, Pheasant Tail, midge larva or pupa, small stonefly, or similar can be effective.

CLOSEST CITY OR POINT OF ENTRANCE TO THE PARK

Central west slope, Sierra Nevada Range, California—This entrance is accessible from four directions on three state highways:

- California 120 from the northwest (Groveland) and east (Lee Vining), which ascends Tioga Pass (10,000-feet) and is closed for the winter due to snow (late November to mid- to late May).
- California 140 from the west (Mariposa).
- California 41 from the south (Oakhurst).
- Entrance to the park is available via wilderness trails by back- and horse-packers from numerous trailheads in the surrounding National Forests. (Free Wilderness Permits are required and are available from Park Ranger Stations or National Forest offices nearest the park's entrances.)

APPROXIMATE DRIVING TIMES

- San Francisco: 4 hours
- Sacramento: 3 hours
- Fresno: 1.5 hours
- Los Angeles: 6 hours

CLOSEST AIRPORTS

- Mammoth Yosemite Airport (Mammoth Lakes)
- Fresno Yosemite International (Fresno)
- Merced Regional Airport
- Modesto City-County Airport

INTERNATIONAL AIRPORTS

- San Francisco International Airport
- Oakland International Airport
- San Jose International Airport
- Sacramento International Airport
- Fresno Yosemite International Airport
- Reno-Tahoe International Airport

OPEN/CLOSING PARK DATES OR FISHING DATES

- Open year-round.
- California 120 Tioga Pass closed during winter.
- Other temporary road closures, tire-chain and 4-WD restrictions are possible in the winter.
- Fishing season: last weekend in April to November 15.

REGULATIONS

We strongly encourage catch-and-release fishing on all park waters to preserve wild trout populations.

- Standard California Department of Fish and Wildlife regulations for Sierra trout: Five-fish bag limit, no live bait.
- California fishing license required for anglers ages 16 and older.

Merced River in Yosemite Valley, from Happy Isles to Foresta Bridge below the park:

- Catch-and-release for rainbow trout, artificial lures or flies only.
- No bait.
- Five-fish bag limit on browns only.

Tuolumne River below O'Shaughnessy Dam (Hetch Hetchy Reservoir):

- Artificial lures or flies only
- Barbless hooks
- Two-fish bag limit
- 12-inch maximum size limit
- 0-fish limit (no fish may be kept) from November 16 to opening date the following season (in April)
- No motors allowed in park

For up-to-date closures and regulations, please visit http://www.nps.gov/yose/plan-yourvisit/fishing.htm.

CLOSEST FLY SHOPS

Yosemite Rivers Fly Shop
40827 California 41
Oakhurst, CA 93644
559-641-7788
www.sierraflyfisher.com

The Trout Fitter
3011 Main St.
Mammoth Lakes, CA 93546
760-924-3676
info@thetroutfitter.com

CLOSEST GUIDE SERVICES

Sierra Fly Fisher
Bass Lake/Oakhurst
559-683-7664
www.sierraflyfisher.com

CLOSEST OUTFITTERS

Southern Yosemite Mountain Guides, Inc.
42997 E. Mountain View Lane
Oakhurst, CA 93644
800-231-4575
info@symg.com

LODGING/CAMPING

- Yosemite has a large number of lodging and campground options.
- Lodging choices range from modest

"tent-cabins" up to the renowned Majestic Yosemite (formerly Ahwahnee) Hotel. Campgrounds range from RV spaces to tents only.

- A number of campgrounds are available on a first-come, first-served basis, but the majority are by reservation, as is all of the lodging.
- Reservations are strongly advised, well in advance (6 months-1 year) for peak season, due to the park's popularity. There are also numerous campgrounds and lodging options not far outside the park's four entrances.

BEST PLACE TO STAY IN THE PARK

Majestic Yosemite
(pricey, good food, amazing dining room)
1 Ahwahnee Dr.
Yosemite National Park, CA 95389
801-559-4884

BEST PLACE TO STAY NEAR THE PARK

Tenaya Lodge
1122 California 41
Fish Camp, CA 93623
Reservations: 888-514-2167
Hotel: 559-683-6555
tenayareservations@dncinc.com

BEST CAMPGROUND IN THE PARK

Tuolumne Meadows Campground
877-444-6777
www.recreation.gov
(Located at Tuolumne Meadows on Tioga Road, about 90 minutes northeast of Yosemite Valley, at 8,600 feet elevation)

BEST CAMPGROUND NEAR THE PARK

Junction Campground
Saddlebag Lake Road
760-647-3044

- Located at the intersection of Tioga Pass and Saddlebag Lake Road
- Small meadow campground with 13 sites, pit toilets, and available on a first-come, first-served basis
- Campground is about two miles from Saddlebag Lake

Saddlebag Lake Campground
877-444-6777
From Bishop, California:

- At the intersection of U.S. Route 395 and California 168, take California 168 west 15.3 miles to South Lake Recreation sign. Turn left and go one mile to the campground, which will be on the left.

ANDREW MAURER was born and raised in central California, not far from Yosemite. He has been fly fishing in the Sierra and throughout much of the West for 37 years. The waters and wilderness of Yosemite National Park have held a huge portion of his passion for fly fishing.

Following retirement from a 30-something-year career in graphic design and a little part-time community college teaching, he began guiding in 2008. He focused on the same waters that he's known, fished and loved for so long. While he was motivated primarily by his passion for the sport, he hadn't anticipated the extreme pleasure, satisfaction, and just plain fun that he discovered in sharing the sport with others of all levels of experience. Men, women, kids, groups of all kinds, expert fishers and absolute "newbies," young and old—he's never ceased to be amazed at how much fun it is to share this thing. To watch it take hold of so many others, as he still remembers it doing to him, is the sweetest of pleasures.

Andrew's photographs have appeared in annual reports and calendars for *Trout Unlimited* and *California Trout,* travel and fishing magazines, including *Trout,* the quarterly magazine of *Trout Unlimited,* fishing industry advertising, research reports, festivals and events for conservation groups.

BEST PLACE TO EAT IN THE PARK
Majestic Yosemite (pricey, good food, amazing dining room)
1 Ahwahnee Dr.
Yosemite National Park, CA 95389
801-559-4884

BEST PLACE TO EAT NEAR THE PARK
Tioga Pass Resort
(Casual, rustic, great food)
85 California 120 West
Lee Vining, CA 93541
209-372-4471
tiogapassresortllc@gmail.com

CLOSEST PLACES TO GET A DRINK
Yosemite Valley Lodge
9006 Yosemite Lodge Dr.
P.O. Box 578
Yosemite National Park, CA 95389
209-372-1403
(formerly known as Yosemite Lodge at the Falls)

BEST PLACES TO GET A DRINK
Majestic Yosemite Bar
1 Ahwahnee Dr.
Yosemite National Park, CA 95389
888-413-8869

MUST SEE
· The view of Yosemite Valley from Glacier Point.
· El Capitan: A majestic rock formation found in the north side of Yosemite Valley and one of the world's most popular places for rock climbing and BASE jumping.
· Half Dome: A famed rock formation found on the eastern side of Yosemite Valley, which has one sheer face, making it appear as a dome that has been halved.
· Inside of the Majestic Yosemite Hotel: This grand hotel was built in 1927 and still contains many original paintings, rugs and tapestries.

NEAREST HOSPITAL/URGENT TREATMENT CENTER
Yosemite Medical Clinic
9000 Ahwahnee Drive
Yosemite National Park, CA 95389
209-372-4637

OTHER MEDICAL CENTERS
John C. Fremont Healthcare District
5189 Hospital Rd.
Mariposa, CA 95338
209-966-3631

Mercy Medical Center Merced
333 Mercy Ave.
Merced, CA 95340
209-564-5000

Mammoth Hospital
85 Sierra Park Rd.
Mammoth Lakes, CA 93546
760-934-3311

Memorial Medical Center
1700 Coffee Rd.
Modesto, CA 95355
209-526-4500

CELL PHONE SERVICE
· Cell service is either not available or is very limited. You might be able to get a signal at the roadside in the middle of Tuolumne Meadows—move around until you get a signal.
· Sometimes you can get a signal at the at junction of California 140 and Big Oak Flat Road.
· The nearby towns of El Portal and Lee Vining also have cell service.

FOR ALL ELSE, VISIT
http://www.nps.gov/yose/index.htm

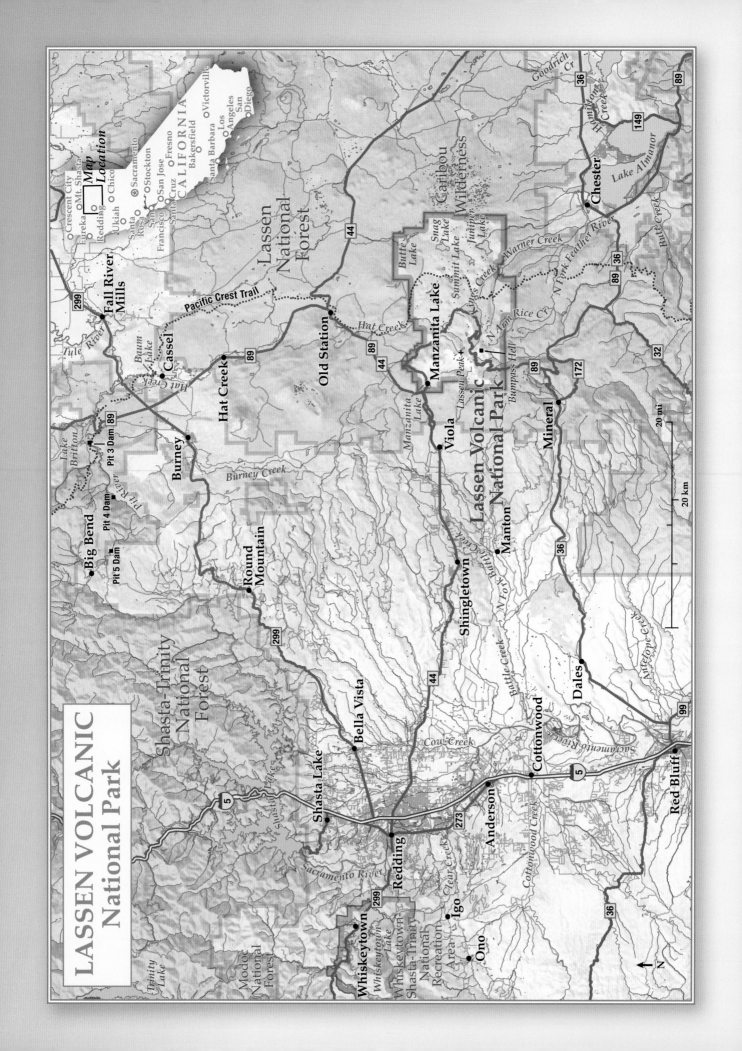

LASSEN VOLCANIC
National Park

Map Location

CALIFORNIA

Crescent City
Eureka   Mt Shasta
          Redding
Ukiah   Chico
Santa   Sacramento
Rosa   Stockton
San   San Jose
Francisco Santa Cruz
          Fresno
Santa Barbara Bakersfield
          Los Angeles
          San Diego
Victorville

Lassen National Forest

Shasta-Trinity National Forest

Modoc National Forest

Lassen Volcanic National Park

Caribou Wilderness

Pacific Crest Trail

Chester
Lake Almanor
Goodrich Cr
Hamilton Cr
Butte Creek

Fall River Mills
Tule River
Baum Lake
Cassel
Hat Creek
Burney
Hat Creek
Old Station
Manzanita Lake
Snag Lake
Summit Lake
Juniper Lake
Lassen Peak
Viola
Warner Creek
Kings Creek
Bumpass Hell
N Fork Feather River
Mineral
Manton
Shingletown
N Fork Battle Creek
Battle Creek
Cottonwood
Anderson
Dales
Cottonwood Creek
Antelope Creek
Red Bluff
Sacramento River

Big Bend
Pit 5 Dam
Pit 4 Dam
Pit 3 Dam
Lake Britton
Pit River

Round Mountain

Burney Creek

Bella Vista

Cow Creek

Shasta Lake
Shasta Lake

Redding

Whiskeytown
Whiskeytown Lake
Whiskeytown Shasta-Trinity National Recreation Area
Trinity Lake

Igo
Ono
Clear Creek

Sacramento River

N Arm Rice Cr

Manzanita Lake

Battle Creek

20 mi
20 km

N

299
36
89
149
44
89
89
36
32
172
36
99
273
5
44
5
299

➤ **Location:** Lassen Volcanic National Park is located in northeastern California:

- 1 hour from Redding, California
- 2.5 hours from Reno, Nevada
- 3 hours from Sacramento, California
- 3.5 hours from San Francisco, California
- 3 hours from Medford, Oregon

Lassen Volcanic National Park, the fifteenth national park established by Congress, was created in 1916 after a series of volcanic eruptions that began in 1914. The park is famous for thermal features such as bubbling mud pots, steaming fumaroles, and boiling springs. Lassen Peak stands at 10,463-feet, and most of the park is located above 6,000-feet elevation.

United Express serves the Redding Airport with flights from San Francisco. Interstate 5 is one hour to the west and U.S. Route 89 runs right through the park. There are five entrances to the park, including Main Park Road, which runs north-south through the park. Main Park Road runs between the northwest (Manzanita Lake) park entrance and the southwest park entrance. Dead-end roads provide access to Butte Lake, Juniper Lake, and Warner Valley areas.

The park is surrounded by the Lassen National Forest and marks the divide between the Cascade Range to the north and the Sierra Nevada to the south. About 400,000 people visit Lassen Volcanic National Park each year.

Driving through the park non-stop takes about an hour. The most popular visitor activities are auto touring, camping, and day hiking. The most heavily trafficked area of the park is the western half, which includes California 89, Manzanita Lake and Summit Lake roadside campgrounds, the Sulphur Works, and the visitor centers. Popular day-hikes in this area include trails to Lassen Peak, Bumpass Hell, and the Manzanita Lake Loop.

Visitors looking for more solitude should consider visiting the eastern half of the park. This area can be accessed by car at Butte Lake, Juniper Lake, and the Warner Valley Road.

These entry points include campgrounds and trailheads for day hikes and backpacking trips. There are 150 miles of hiking trails in the park. Backpackers can combine several of the shorter trails to create a multi-day wilderness trip. The Caribou Wilderness borders the eastern edge of the park and offers options for extending a backpacking trip. The Pacific Crest Trail transects the park from north to south providing even more hiking options.

While the park is technically open year-round, California 89 is typically open only from June or July through early winter. Popular winter activities include snowshoeing, backcountry skiing, and sledding. The park offers a seven-day vehicle pass for $20 and an annual pass for $40.

Sight fishing on foot is a great way to fish the shallow flats at the south end of Manzanita Lake. Andrew Harris

A trip to the park gives the fly angler an opportunity to combine a great national park experience with an excellent trout-fishing adventure. The park is home to Manzanita Lake, a highly regarded stillwater fishery, and there is an abundance of quality trout-fishing destinations within a 90-minute drive. This area offers an amazing variety of water types:

Lassen Peak towers over Manzanita Lake, making this one of the most scenic places to fish in northern California. Andrew Harris

- Giant spring creeks that you can wade or float
- Large tailwater rivers suitable for drift boats
- Rugged freestone streams
- Expansive reservoirs
- Private ponds with trophy trout
- Countless miles of small streams to fish

➤ **Manzanita Lake:** A fly fisher's trip is not complete without spending some time at Manzanita Lake. This mountain gem is home to finicky rainbow and brown trout that provide great sport for fly fishers throughout the summer months. Manzanita Lake is located at the north entrance to the park. At first glance, the lake might appear over-run with picnickers, campers, hikers and kayakers, but take a closer look and you'll see rising fish—lots of 'em.

Sight-fishing is almost always an option at Manzanita Lake. The water is perfectly clear and the trout frequently cruise near the surface looking for midges, *Callibaetis* may-

flies, terrestrials, and damselflies. Manzanita Lake is 26 acres, and the average depth is less than 10 feet. There is something for every type of stillwater angler here.

- There are abundant sight-fishing and dry-fly opportunities.
- Indicator-nymphing is highly productive.
- Streamer fishing and fly trolling work well, too.
- The lake can be fished from shore, by wading, or by watercraft.
- If you don't have your own watercraft, you can rent a sit-on-top kayak at the Manzanita Lake store.
- The shore angler's best bet is to sight-fish to trout cruising near the bank.

Sight fishing from shore is easiest mid-day when the sun is high and the fish are easier to spot. Manzanita Lake rainbows and browns will cruise alarmingly close to shore, especially in areas with dense vegetation. Many are hooked (but seldom landed) on bow-and-arrow casts from shore. These shoreline cruisers are typically interested in terrestrials such as flying ants and beetles.

➤ **Juniper Lake (and Others):** While Manzanita Lake is the best fishery in the park, there are other options to wet a fly. Juniper Lake is the next best stillwater option. Many of the other lakes in the park are devoid of fish, including Summit Lake and Snag Lake.

➤ **The North Fork Feather River:** Rice Creek, Kings Creek, and Warner Creek start inside the park and flow south, merging to create the North Fork Feather River, which flows into Lake Almanor. These streams are very small inside the park boundaries, but they do have little rainbows and brook trout. Fishing improves downstream outside of the park boundaries where the streams increase in size. The North Fork Feather River and its tributaries offer productive small-stream fly-fishing. The best time is in June and July, before they get too low. These tributaries open at the end of May. Some areas of the North Fork Feather River are stocked with hatchery trout during the summer.

➤ **Lale Almanor:** The North Fork Feather River is the primary tributary to Lake Almanor, a vast reservoir situated at 4,505-feet elevation. At roughly 13 miles long by 6 miles wide, this reservoir is popular for water sports and fishing. The most sought-after species are rainbow and brown trout,

Inset. A typical brown trout from Manzanita Lake. The rainbow and brown trout populations in Manzanita Lake are wild and self-sustaining. Andrew Harris

Below. The Pit River is well-known for its robust population of hard-fighting rainbow trout, its rugged scenery, and very difficult wading. Andrew Harris

Large brown trout can be found in nearby Hat Creek to the north of the park. Andrew Harris

Facing. Burney Creek is a scenic and productive fishing spot about an hour north of Lassen Volcanic National Park. Andrew Harris

and smallmouth bass. Trout can be found near the surface fall through spring, but the lake gets quite warm in the summer and the trout move deep or near submerged springs.

One of the most popular fishing attractions here is the Hexagenia or "hex hatch" from mid-June to mid-July. These pinkie-sized mayflies hatch at dusk and attract the attention of big trout and smallies. Other worthwhile options in the Chester/Lake Almanor area include Butt Valley Reservoir, Yellow Creek, and Hamilton Creek (a tributary on the east side of the lake). The Almanor Fishing Company in Chester has information and a local guide service.

➤ **Hat Creek:** Great fly-fishing options can be found just to the north of Lassen Volcanic National Park, including Hat Creek, Burney Creek, and the Pit and Fall Rivers. Hat Creek begins inside the park and flows north toward the Pit River near the town of Burney. It starts as a very small stream, but its volume increases exponentially due to springs near the town of Old Station. The section near Old Station is heavily

stocked during the summer months and is a very popular fishing destination, especially for spinning gear enthusiasts.

Most fly fishers opt for the section closer to Burney that begins at Hat Creek Powerhouse #2. This 3.5-mile stretch between the powerhouse and Lake Britton is designated Wild Trout Water with good fishing for wild rainbows and browns. This is a large spring creek with alternating sections of choppy riffles and flat water. Popular hatches include golden and giant stoneflies in the spring and Pale Morning Duns, caddis flies and Trico spinner falls in the summer. Nearby Baum Lake and Cassel Forebay are also worthwhile destinations.

➤ **Burney Creek:** Burney Creek is just minutes from Hat Creek, near the town of Burney. The best section is inside McArthur-Burney Falls State Park. The 129-foot Burney Falls is a must-see attraction. You can fish above or below the waterfall. There is a large campground at the state park and the creek is heavily stocked above the waterfall. The one-mile section of creek from the base of the waterfall downstream to

Lake Britton has wild rainbows and browns. Fish don't grow large, but it's a great place to take a 3- or 4-weight rod and spend a half day fishing.

➤ **Fall River:** One of the nation's (some say the world's) finest spring creeks can be found about 90 minutes north of Lassen Volcanic National Park near the town of Fall River Mills, just 15 minutes from Hat Creek and Burney Creek. Fall River is a classic meadow spring creek with a twist: All fishing is done from boats. Boat fishing is a must due to privately owned banks and a mucky bottom that is no good for wading. There is a public launch maintained by California Trout. Boats can be rented by guests of Circle 7 and Spinner Fall Lodge, which are two streamside accommodations. Visiting anglers typically hire a guide to fish this destination.

Fall River is famous for predictable hatches, sight-fishing opportunities, and large, wild trout. Vast weed beds provide cover for the river's abundant rainbow trout and serve as a food factory, churning out massive numbers of aquatic insects. Hatches include
· Pale Morning Dun mid-day hatches from May through July
· Callibaetis in the afternoons from July through October
· Hex hatch at dusk during June and July
· Fall Baetis hatches

Above. All fishing on Fall River is done by boat, and most anglers anchor up and fish downstream below the boat. Andrew Harris

Streamer fishing with clear intermediate and fast-sinking lines is another popular technique.

➤ **Pit River:** Fall River, Hat Creek, and Burney Creek are all tributaries to the Pit River, one of the longest rivers in California. The most popular stretch of the Pit River is the roughly 30 miles of water from Lake Britton Dam downstream to the town of Big Bend. Several dams and powerhouses divide this stretch into beats known as Pit 3, Pit 4, and Pit 5.

The Pit River is a wild rainbow trout fishery and has one of the highest catch rates in California. The challenge is in the wading and bushwhacking. The Pit is a very fast river with slippery boulders and few small rocks to fill in the gaps between the big rocks. The best fishing is in the areas with moving water. Avoid the big slow pools as they don't typically hold trout. Studded felt wading boots are best here and a wading staff is a must. Good nymph fishermen can expect to hook four or more fish an hour with a typical fish running 10 to 15 inches. There are plenty of larger fish around, too.

➤ **Lower Sacramento River:** An hour west of Lassen Volcanic National Park is one of the country's best tailwaters—the Lower Sacramento River between Redding and Red Bluff. While drift boating is popular year-round, wading is also a good option during fall, winter and spring when flows are under 7,000 cfs. Anglers using drift boats, rafts, or pontoon boats can select from six different sections of river to float.

There are numerous guide services in the area offering guided trips. Any day of the year can be excellent, with the most popular times being spring and fall. It is typical for anglers fishing with guides to hook a minimum of 10 fish a day. The bigger fish are generally found closer to Redding where a day's catch typically ranges from 14 to 20 inches. The fish get smaller as you move downstream, but the average size is at least 12 inches throughout the entire river system.

There is a seasonal run of steelhead on the lower part of the river from September through March.

There are four runs of Chinook salmon throughout the year, so fish are always looking for egg imitations. The biggest run is the fall run during October and November. That is a great time of year to drift an egg pattern through salmon redds in hopes of hooking a large rainbow trout.

➤ **Pay-to-Play Water:** In addition to the public water, there are numerous quality pay-to-play operations within an hour of Lassen Volcanic National Park.

· The Almanor Fly-fishing Company in Chester books Lassen Meadows Ranch and Goodrich Creek on the south side of the park.
· The Battle Creek drainage to the west of the park is another private water hot spot.
· Confluence Outfitters books Eagle Canyon Trophy Trout Lakes and North Fork Battle Creek.
· The Fly Shop in Redding books Battle Creek Ranch, Rock Creek Lake, and Lake Christine.
· Bailey Creek Lodge and Digger Creek Ranch are other good options.

This area is also known for its vineyards and a down-to-earth wine-tasting experience.

➤ **Tackle and Gear**

Rods and Line: You could do all of your fishing in this area with a 9-foot, 5-weight rod. However, a 3- or 4-weight is nice for the smaller streams, and a 9.5-foot, 6-weight rod is ideal for nymphing the Lower Sac.

Terminal Tackle and Flies: Your best bet is to go with 9-foot leaders and tippet in sizes 3-6X. Floating lines will suffice for all the stream fisheries, but pack a clear intermediate and fast-sink line for the lake fisheries and Fall River. While some of the summertime fishing can be done without waders, bring waders and felt-soled boots if you'll be fishing the Pit River, Hat Creek, or wading on the Lower Sac. A sturdy wading staff and studded felt boots are recommended for the Pit River. Standard trout flies work well on most of these destinations. Visit a local shop for current recommendations.

A large rainbow trout from the lower Sacramento River. Andrew Harris

CLOSEST CITY OR POINT OF ENTRANCE TO THE PARK

· From the south, most travelers drive up Interstate 5 to Red Bluff and take California 36 east to the south entrance of the park, about an hour's drive from Red Bluff.
· The south entrance can also be accessed from the town of Chester on Lake Almanor.
· The north entrance of the park can be accessed from Redding and Shingletown via California 44 East and from Burney and Old Station via California 89 South.

CLOSEST AIRPORT

· The Redding Airport (RDD) is an hour west of the north entrance of the park. Current flight connections are limited to San Francisco (SFO).
· Many visitors fly into Reno-Tahoe International Airport (RNO) or Sacramento International Airport (SMF).
· The south entrance of the park is about two-and-a-half hours by car from RNO and three hours from SMF.

OPEN/CLOSING PARK DATES OR FISHING DATES

· The road through the park is frequently closed well into June and July pending snow removal, but Manzanita Lake is typically accessible by car at some point in May.
· The smaller streams in the park are usually accessible in mid- to late June.
· Most fishing in the park is done from May through October, with the summer months being the most popular.
· The park road usually closes after the first big snow storm, which typically happens sometime between Thanksgiving and Christmas.
· The other fisheries in the area are at a lower elevation and therefore have a longer season. The Lower Sac and Lake Almanor are open to fishing year-round, as are parts of the Pit River.
· Hat Creek, Fall River, and Burney Creek are open from late April through mid-November.
· The upper North Fork Feather River and tributaries are open from late May through mid-November.

· Check the California Department of Fish and Wildlife regulations booklet for information about seasons, gear restrictions, and limits for each particular fishery.
https://www.wildlife.ca.gov/regulations

CLOSEST FLY SHOPS

The Lake Almanor Fly Fishing Company
159 Main St.
Chester, CA 96020
530-258-3944
www.almanorflyfishing.com

The Fly Shop
4140 Churn Creek Rd
Redding, CA 96002
530-222-3555
www.flyshop.com

Shasta Angler
43503 California 299 E
Fall River Mills, CA 96028
530-336-6600
www.confluenceoutfitters.com/Fall-River-Mills.aspx

OUTFITTERS AND GUIDES PERMITTED TO GUIDE INSIDE THE PARK

Confluence Outfitters
888-481-1650
www.ConfluenceOutfitters.com

Lance Grey & Company
P.O. Box 962
1079 Northgate Drive
Willows, CA 95988
530-517-2204
http://lancegrayandcompany.com/

OUTFITTERS AND GUIDES FOR SURROUNDING FISHERIES

Confluence Outfitters
888-481-1650
www.ConfluenceOutfitters.com

The Lake Almanor Fly Fishing Company
159 Main St
Chester, CA 96020
530-258-3944
www.almanorflyfishing.com

The Fly Shop
4140 Churn Creek Rd
Redding, CA 96002
530-222-3555
www.flyshop.com

CLOSEST FULL-SERVICE LODGES

Bailey Creek Lodge
P.O. Box 405
Manton, CA 96059
530-474-4600
www.baileycreeklodge.com

Spinner Fall Lodge
28076 Metzger Rd
Fall River Mills, CA 96028
530-336-5300
www.spinnerfalllodge.com

Clearwater Lodge
24500 Pit One Powerhouse Rd
Fall River Mills, CA 96028
530-336-5005
www.clearwaterlodge.com

BEST PLACE TO STAY IN THE PARK

Drakesbad Guest Ranch
14423 Chester Warner Valley Road
Chester, CA 96020
866-999-0914
www.drakesbad.com

BEST PLACE TO STAY OUTSIDE THE PARK

Highlands Ranch Resort
41515 Hwy 36 E
Mill Creek, CA 96061
530-595-3388
www.highlandsranchresort.com

BEST CAMPGROUND IN THE PARK

Manzanita Lake Campground
877-444-6777
www.Recreation.gov
· 179 sites
· $18 per night

STORE AND KAYAK RENTALS

Manzanita Lake Camper Store
530-335-7557

BEST CAMPGROUND NEAR THE PARK

Hat Creek Hereford Ranch RV Park & Campground
17855 Doty Rd.
Hat Creek, CA 96040
530-335-7171
www.hatcreekherefordrv.com/

ANDREW HARRIS, owner of regional guide service Confluence Outfitters, has guided anglers in northern California since 1997. The guides at Confluence Outfitters focus on the best trout and steelhead fisheries in both northern California and southern Oregon. Andrew and his wife, Katie, also manage Eagle Canyon, a private stillwater fishery near Red Bluff. Andrew authored the book *Plumas National Forest Trout Fishing Guide* and is a regular contributor to *California Fly Fisher Magazine.* Learn more at www.ConfluenceOutfitters.com.

BEST PLACES TO EAT IN THE PARK

Dining options in the park are meager and are limited to the Manzanita Lake Camper Store and the Lassen Café at the visitor center at the South Entrance. You can also make dining reservations at the Drakesbad Guest Ranch (see listing above).

BEST PLACE TO EAT AND GET A DRINK NEAR THE PARK

The closest towns to the north entrance are

· Old Station (14 miles)
· Shingletown (17 miles)

These communities provide markets, burgers, pizza, beer, and gas. For a really good dining experience, you'll need to drive an hour to Redding. Also, the town of Chester has a variety of restaurants and is located less than a 30-minute drive from the south entrance.

MUST SEE

· The view of Mt. Lassen (a.k.a. Lassen Peak) while you fish Manzanita Lake— This is an active volcano located in the Shasta Cascade region of California. The peak rises 2,000 feet above the surrounding area.
· 129-foot Burney Falls—The falls are located outside the Lassen National Park boundaries in nearby McArthur-Burney Falls Memorial State Park, Shasta County, California. In 1954, the falls were designated as a National Natural Landmark.
·

CLOSEST HOSPITAL/URGENT TREATMENT CENTER

SOUTH ENTRANCE TO THE PARK

Seneca Healthcare District

130 Brentwood Drive
Chester, CA 96020
530-258-2151

NORTH ENTRANCE TO THE PARK

Mercy Medical Center

2175 Rosaline Ave.
Redding, CA 96001
530-225-6000

Fall River Mills/Burney area

Mayers Memorial Hospital
43563 California 299 East
Fall River Mills, CA 96028
530-336-5511
info@mayersmemorial.com

CELL PHONE SERVICE

Cell service is spotty at best in the park. Exit the north entrance of the park and drive about two miles toward Shingletown to get a good signal. There is also good cell coverage in the town of Chester near the south entrance of the park.

FOR ALL ELSE, VISIT

http://www.nps.gov/lavo/index.htm

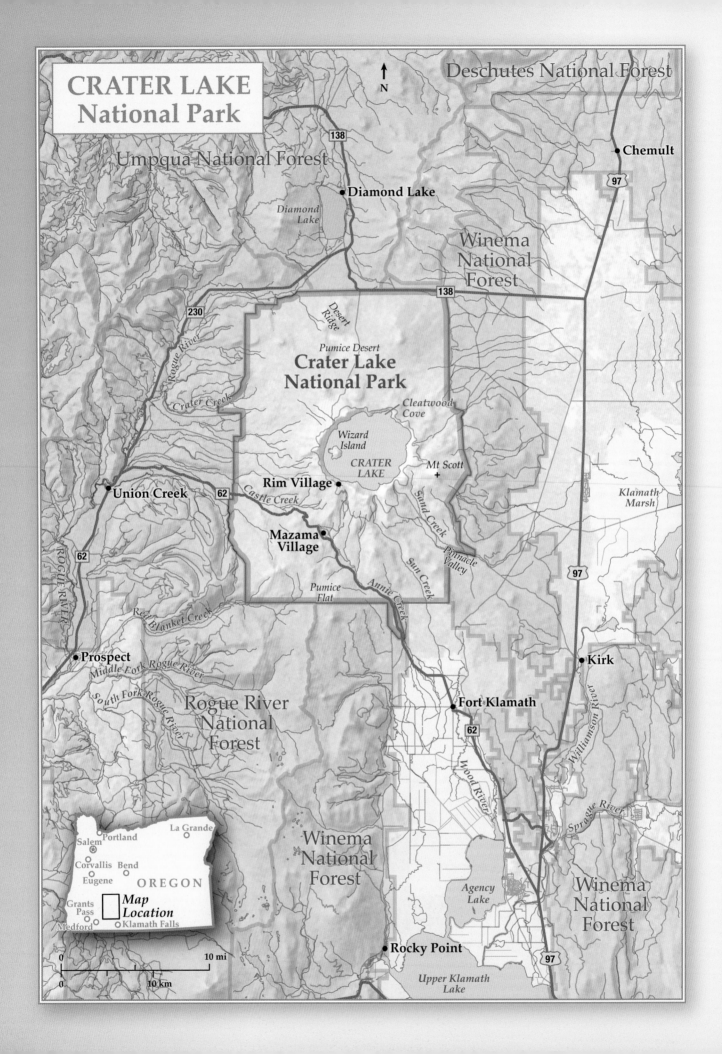

➤ **Location:** Crater Lake is located in southern Oregon, meaning the closest airport is 80 miles away in Medford (although Crater Lake-Klamath Falls Regional Airport is expected to re-establish air service). Car rentals and other services are in Medford.

Following are directions for getting to the park:

Via auto from the south:
- From Medford: Oregon 62 north and east to the park's west entrance
- From Klamath Falls: Oregon 97 north to Oregon 62 north, and west to the park's south entrance

Via auto from the north:
- From Roseburg: Oregon 138 east to the park's north entrance
- From Bend: Oregon 97 south to Oregon 138 west to the park's north entrance
- AmTrak train service to Klamath Falls, about 60 miles from the park

Local native tribes had centuries of interaction with the lake prior to gold prospector John Hillman's first sighting of "Deep Blue Lake" in 1853. It became a national park under President Theodore Roosevelt in 1902. Crater Lake hosts about 500,000 visitors a year in its 183,000 acres. It continues to be a prominent ritual site for the tribes.

If fly fishing the deepest lake in the U.S. or the cleanest, clearest large body of water in the world is on your bucket list, Oregon's Crater Lake is your destination. Crater Lake is located in the Cascade Range of southern Oregon. It was formed 7,700 years ago when then 12,000-foot Mt. Mazama—under intense volcanic pressure—literally blew its top and collapsed, forming a deep caldera—a volcanic crater or cauldron—where the snow-capped volcano once stood. The eruption might have been the largest in North America in the last 640,000 years.

Later activity resulted in emergence of another distinct volcano within the caldera—the iconic Wizard Island. There

Headwaters of Rogue River. Marshal Moser

Wizard Island from the rim. Marshal Moser

are no rivers or streams flowing into the caldera, so the nearly five trillion gallons of water in the lake are exclusively from rain and snow melt. The rim of the volcano is roughly 7,000-feet above sea level with numerous lava-formed peaks, the highest being Mt. Scott (9,000 feet), encircling the intense blue water of the lake far below (6,173 feet above sea level). The deepest point below lake surface is 1,943 feet, making it the deepest lake in the United States.

Any visit to Crater Lake should include the 33-mile trip around the lake. The views from the road and the multiple turnouts are nothing short of spectacular. You can drive, bike or take a park-operated trolley where 100 percent of your attention can be devoted to Crater Lake National Park.

➤ **Crater Lake:** Without river or stream inflows, Crater Lake originally contained no fish. Between 1888 and 1941, however, six species were introduced. Today, only rainbow trout and kokanee salmon remain. Because Crater Lake was originally fishless and the mandate for the national parks is to preserve natural conditions, fishing for the non-native trout and salmon is not regulated. No license. No limit. Rainbow trout average 10 to 14 inches although a few 20-inchers are present. Kokanee salmon are usually small in Crater Lake. Fishing is allowed at the following two locations:

Cleatwood Cove: The bottom of the Cleatwood Cove Trail, where there is access to one-quarter-mile of rocky shoreline. The trail down to Cleatwood is a strenuous 2.2-mile roundtrip—the equivalent of descending and then ascending 65 flights of stairs. The water is crystal clear and the views from inside the caldera are unique and memorable. No waders or floating devices are allowed for fear of contamination. If you keep fish, pack them out and clean them away from the lake.

Wizard Island: The island is reachable only by park tour boats from Cleatwood Cove, and it offers better fishing opportunities. These boats leave in the morning and return in the afternoon at a cost of $42 roundtrip. Reservations are required.

Recommended gear includes 4- to 6-weight rods with a type II clear intermediate line; 12-foot leaders tapered to 5X. Fly patterns are size 10 or 12 leeches and Woolly Buggers along with size 12 to 16 Hare's Ear, Prince, and Bird's Nest nymphs.

➤ **Crater Lake Park Streams:** Most small streams within the park revert to standard state regulations with the exception of requiring a license. Bull trout are present in a number of streams and are protected. No fishing is allowed in Sun Creek because it is one of the few streams in the Klamath Basin with native bull trout.

Streams originating in the park and flowing into the National Forests surrounding Crater Lake National Park mostly contain brook, rainbow, and brown trout. The streams are all small within the park, but some of them quickly get larger and produce large fish a short distance from the park.

Access to these will require an adventurous spirit, hiking boots and some determination (detailed maps are available at the park office).

· Castle and Crater Creeks on the west side
· The famous Rogue River in the northwest
· Sand Creek on the east side
· Annie Creek and its tributaries on the south side

Yamsi Ranch brookie caught in upper Williamson. Brian O'Keefe

Upper Williamson River. Brian O'Keefe

Big Williamson smile. Marlon Rampy

the water begins to boil with voracious trout feeding on butterfly-sized mayflies.

Marlon Rampy, head guide at the Lonesome Duck Lodge, states that there are indeed many successful angling approaches to fishing for the Williamson's large rainbows. His favorite technique is to swing soft hackle patterns in shallow- to medium-depth water. Choosing the correct time of day will also increase the productivity of this technique. Hatches of Blue-winged Olive mayflies or a caddis emergence can move the trout into shallower waters to locate the bugs. He recommends a floating line with a long leader down to 5X tippet and then the soft hackle fly of choice.

"Quarter the cast a bit downstream, a quick mend and the current will do the rest," Rampy said. "As the fly swings across the run it will lift through the water column imitating the emergence behavior of the hatch. The line and leader will be tight to the fly; strikes from the hungry trout can be heavy. An easy lift of the rod as the strike occurs is all you will need—that and a big net."

When gearing up for the smaller streams, we recommend a 3- or 4-weight rod, floating line with 7-foot leader tapered to 5X. Dead-drift standard nymphs in sizes 14-18, or slowly retrieve a small streamer through the bends.

➤ **Williamson River:** The Williamson River is the premier wild trophy trout fishery in the Pacific Northwest, and one of the very best in the United States. It is situated on the eastern side of the Cascades, 20 miles down Oregon 62 from Crater Lake National Park. The volcanic river regularly produces fish in excess of 10 pounds and 26 inches. A boat or floating device is recommended because there are only a couple of public access points on the primary run from Chiloquin down to the Oregon 97 bridge. The season is late May to October 31.

The recommended early-season rig is a 6-weight rod with clear intermediate sink line, 12-foot, 3X or 4X leaders early in season. Later in the season, we recommend switching to 12- to 16-foot leaders in 5X fluorocarbon when spring creek conditions kick in about July 1.

Swinging black, cinnamon and olive leech Woolly Bugger patterns are good go-to tactics. However, if those aren't getting the job done, try size 14 to 18 Flash-Back Pheasant Tail, Hair's Ear, Bird's Nest or a Copper John with both a dead drift and a swing. Late June through July is the best opportunity to catch these massive fish on a dry because it is the Hexagenia hatch! Late evening, as the last light of day fades,

➤ **Wood River:** The Wood River is about 20 miles from gushing spring headwaters to the delta at Agency Lake. The same big, migratory rainbows that move from Klamath Lake into the Williamson River also come into the Wood River and mix with good numbers of browns to make this renowned fishery.

It is about 10 miles east from Crater Lake National Park along Oregon 62. There is very little access to the river as this is predominantly ranch and cattle country. You can drop in smaller floating devices (full-sized boats take local knowledge and practice) at a couple of road crossings; shuttles are necessary.

Floating the oxbow waters and fishing the undercut banks with a hopper delicately placed under the overhanging grasses can produce the splash of success. As with the Williamson, the water will be cloudy until runoff has ended in mid-June, then the lighter tippets (minimum 5X) and stealthy tactics are critical to success.

Look for opportunities 20 to 30 feet downstream and tight to the bank while fishing dries. There are lots of deep pools on the bends that offer a great chance for a hook-up while stripping a black or cinnamon Wooly Bugger on a sink tip or intermediate sink line. Use a 5-weight rod with the dries and a 6-weight for subsurface. If you can only carry one rod, stay with the 6-weight.

➤ **Upper Rogue River:** West of Crater Lake National Park along Oregon 62 (Crater Lake Highway) is the famous Rogue River. It begins its 215-mile journey to the Pacific Ocean on the west ridge of the Cascades, gaining volume from springs and tributary creeks and rivers along the way. It is one of the first rivers where fly fishing for steelhead became popular. Below the dam at Lost Creek Lake is one of the favorite fisheries on the river. Trout, steelhead and salmon all inhabit these waters. "The Holy Water" is a notable fly-fishing-only, mile-long section that holds the largest—in both numbers and size—trout in the system.

Salmonflies, caddis, and mayflies are major surface hatches to imitate while a streamer or a weighted nymph are wet options. Heading downriver, there are numerous public parks and launch points with easy access from the highway. These will provide the best bank-fishing options.

Drifting the river is the most productive technique and the options on the Upper Rogue are many:

· McGregor Park to Rogue Elk
· Rogue Elk to Shady Cove
· Shady Cove to Dodge Bridge

Stalking the North Umpqua. Marshal Moser

Most of these drifts are 6-8 miles in length. Regulations are complex with steelhead open year-round, but trout and salmon have limited seasons.

➤ **North Umpqua:** The North Umpqua begins just outside the north entrance to the park, near the junction of Oregon 138 and 230. It is most revered for its 31 miles of fly-only water beginning above the town of Idleyld Park, and the Rock Creek hatchery. Fly fishers come from all over the world to test their skills on both summer and winter steelhead runs on this swift, boulder-strewn river. Summer runs are a combination of hatchery and wild fish with an average count of 8,000-10,000 per season. Winter runs are primarily wild fish with counts of 4,000-6,000. Cleated boots, floatation vest, wading staff and a whistle are essential as the wading is extremely challenging.

Seven to 10-weight Spey and single-handed rods are standard for swinging a Skunk, Purple Peril or Black Gordon pattern (the local favorites). The famous Steamboat Inn is along this stretch and is a great base for lodging, meals and supplies.

➤ **Tackle and Gear**

Rods and Line: Recommended gear includes 4- to 6-weight rods with a type II clear intermediate line; 12-foot leaders tapered to 5X. Recommended gear for the smaller

streams is a 3- or 4-weight rod, and floating line with 7-foot leader tapered to 5X. When fishing the Williamson River in early-season, we recommend a 6-weight rod with clear intermediate sink line, 12-foot, 3X or 4X leaders. Later in the season, we recommend switching to 12- to 16-foot leaders in 5X fluorocarbon when spring creek conditions kick in about July 1. The Wood River calls for a 5-weight rod for dry flies, and 6-weight for subsurface flies. If you can only carry one rod, stay with the 6-weight. When fishing the North Umpqua, we recommend 7- to 10-weight Spey and single-handed rods.

Terminal Tackle and Flies: Recommended flies for Crater Lake fishing include size 10 or 12 leeches and Wooly Buggers, along with size 12 to 16 Hare's Ear, Prince, and Bird's Nest nymphs. For the smaller streams, try dead-drifting standard nymphs in sizes 14-18, or slowly retrieve a small streamer through the bends. In the Williamson, swinging black, cinnamon and olive leech and Wooly Bugger patterns are good go-to tactics. Also, try size 14-18 Flash-Back Pheasant Tail, Hair's Ear, Bird's Nest or a Copper John with both a dead drift and a swing. In the Wood River, try a black or cinnamon Woolly Bugger on a sink tip or intermediate sink line. In the North Umpqua, try a Skunk, Purple Peril or Black Gordon pattern—the local favorites.

Williamson River redband rainbow returned. Marlon Rampy

Hexagenia mayfly ready for take-off. Marlon Rampy

CLOSEST CITY OR ACCESS TO THE PARK
· Klamath Falls, Oregon is 60 miles southeast
· Medford, Oregon is 80 miles southwest

CLOSEST AIRPORT
· Rogue Valley International in Medford
· Crater Lake/Klamath Regional Airport in Klamath Falls
Auto rental and travel services are available at both.

OPEN/CLOSING PARK DATES OR FISHING DATES
The park is open year-round, but with an average annual snowfall of 44 feet, all roads, except the south entrance (Oregon 62) and Rim Village are closed November to June. Snow shoes and cross-country skis become the manner of travel. Photo ops and viewing are still available at Rim Village. (Check with the Park Service 541-594-3000; www.nps.gov/crla.)
· The park is open year-round, but road closures might occur during winter snows.
· No separate park fishing license is required.
· Oregon opening and closing dates, and all other fishing regulations apply.

PARK ENTRANCE FEE
· $15 per car for a seven-day pass.
· Golden Eagle and other senior and special use fees apply.
· For up-to-date information including "free entrance days" such as holidays, visit the Crater Lake National Park website http://www.nps.gov/crla/index.htm.

CLOSEST FLY SHOPS
The Ledge
369 S. Sixth St.
Klamath Falls, OR 97539
541-882-5586
www.yetiledge.com

Roe Outfitters
5291 Running Y Rd.
Klamath Falls, OR
541-884-3825
www.roeoutfitters.com

The Fishing Hole
21873 Oregon 62
Shady Cove, OR 97539
541-878 4000
www.thefishingholeflyshop.com

Steamboat Inn
42705 N. Umpqua Hwy.
Idleyld Park, OR 97447
541-498-2230
www.thesteamboatinn.com

CLOSEST GUIDE/OUTFITTER SERVICES
Lonesome Duck Ranch
32955 Oregon 97
Chiloquin, OR 97624
541-210-9463
www.lonesomeduck.com

Marlon Rampy
P.O. Box 4222
Medford, OR 97501
541-660 3780
www.flyfishoregon.com
marlon@flyfishoregon.com

Craig Schuman
541-778-1194
http://www.guidedwatersflyfishing.com

Roe Outfitters
5291 Running Y Rd.
Klamath Falls, OR
541-884-3825
www.roeoutfitters.com

CLOSEST LODGING/LODGES
Lonesome Duck Ranch
32955 Oregon 97
Chiloquin, OR 97624
541-210-9463
www.lonesomeduck.com

Crystalwood Lodge
38625 Westside Rd.
Rocky Point, OR 97601
541-381-2322
www.crystalwoodlodge.com

STEVE HILBERT'S love for Oregon started in the late 1960s while attending the University of Oregon and playing football for the Ducks. After graduation, he and Debbie married and spent 30 years in Lake Tahoe, Nevada raising a family and building their interior design business. Lonesome Duck began in 1995 as a dream and some chicken scratches on a yellow pad. With a tremendous amount of work, persistence and dedication, Lonesome Duck is now a premiere Southern Oregon vacation destination for trophy trout fly fishing and Crater Lake excursions.

Crater Lake Lodge
Crater Lake National Park
888-774-2728
www.craterlakelodges.com

Steamboat Inn
42705 N. Umpqua Hwy.
Idleyld Park, OR 97447
541-498-2230
www.thesteamboatinn.com

CLOSEST, BEST CAMPGROUND
Mazama Campground
(Located seven miles from the rim of Crater Lake just inside the south entrance gate)
888-774 2728

CLOSEST, BEST HOTEL
Crater Lake Lodge
Crater Lake National Park
888-774-2728
www.craterlakelodges.com

With its historical exhibits, luxurious dining, and incredible viewing deck complete with rocking chairs, the lodge is a must-see. Camping and RV sites also are available in the park.

CLOSEST AND BEST RESTAURANT
Crater Lake Lodge
Crater Lake National Park
888-774-2728
www.craterlakelodges.com

CLOSEST AND BEST PLACE TO GET A DRINK
Crater Lake Lodge
Crater Lake National Park
888-774-2728
www.craterlakelodges.com

MUST SEE
· The 33-mile trip around the lake—The views from the road and the multiple turnouts are nothing short of spectacular. You can drive, bike or take a park operated trolley.
· Crater Lake Lodge—The massive lodge has 71 rooms. It was originally built in 1915 and was renovated in the 1990s. It is a glimpse at an earlier era in America.
· Phantom Ship as seen from the rim—This is a small island in Crater Lake that gets its name from its resemblance to a ghost ship.

NEAREST HOSPITAL/URGENT CARE CENTER
Sky Lakes Medical Center
2865 Daggett Ave.
Klamath Falls, OR 97601
541-882-6311
http://www.skylakes.org/

Asante Rogue Medical Center
2825 E. Barnett Rd.
Medford, OR 97504
541-789-4900
http://www.healthgrades.com/hospital-directory/oregon

CELL PHONE SERVICE
Within the park, cell service is poor to non-existent.

FOR ALL ELSE, VISIT
http://www.nps.gov/crla/index.htm

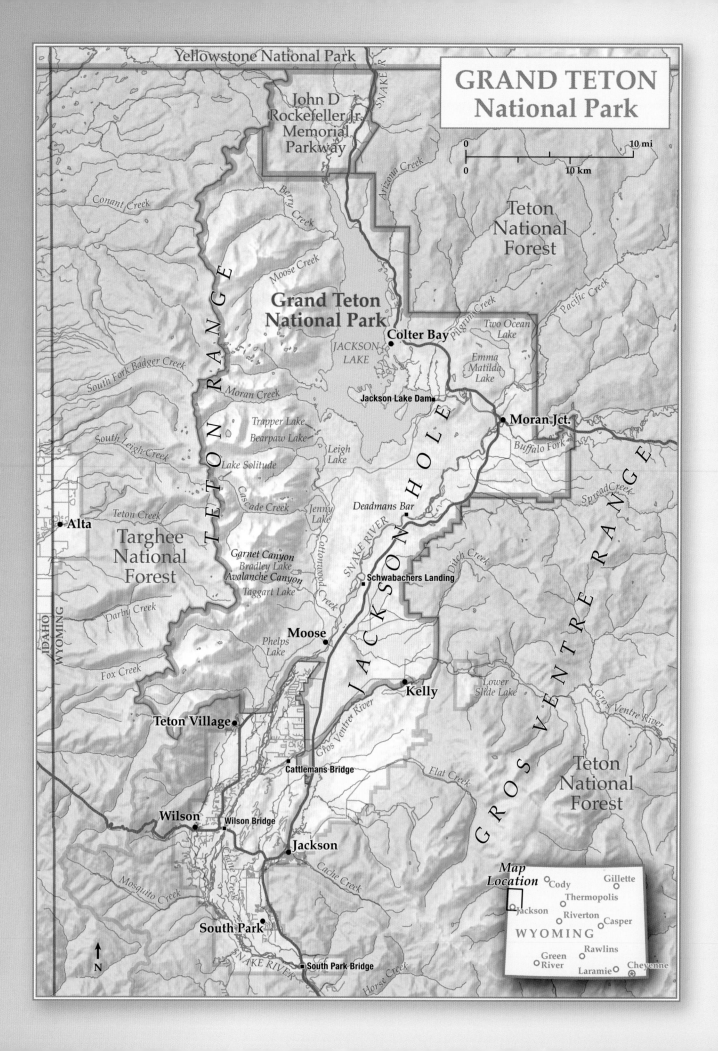

GRAND TETON
National Park

Yellowstone National Park

John D
Rockefeller Jr.
Memorial
Parkway

SNAKE

Arizona Creek

Teton
National
Forest

Conant Creek

Berry Creek

Pacific Creek

Moose Creek

**Grand Teton
National Park**

Pilgrim Creek

Two Ocean
Lake

Colter Bay

*JACKSON
LAKE*

Emma
Matilda
Lake

South Fork Badger Creek

Moran Creek

Jackson Lake Dam

Moran Jct.

Trapper Lake

Buffalo Fork

South Leigh Creek

Bearpaw Lake

Lake Solitude

Leigh
Lake

Spread Creek

Cascade Creek

Jenny
Lake

Teton Creek

Alta

JACKSON HOLE

Deadmans Bar

SNAKE RIVER

Ditch Creek

GROS VENTRE RANGE

Gros Ventre River

TETON RANGE

Garnet Canyon
Bradley Lake
Avalanche Canyon

Cottonwood Creek

Schwabachers Landing

**Targhee
National
Forest**

Taggart Lake

Darby Creek

Fox Creek

Moose

Phelps
Lake

Lower
Slide Lake

Kelly

Gros Ventre River

Teton Village

Gros Ventre River

Teton
National
Forest

Cattlemans Bridge

Flat Creek

Wilson

Wilson Bridge

Mosquito Creek

Fish Creek

Jackson

Cache Creek

South Park

SNAKE RIVER

South Park Bridge

Horse Creek

N

IDAHO
WYOMING

0 ___ 10 mi
0 ___ 10 km

*Map
Location*

Cody
Gillette

Thermopolis

Jackson
Riverton
Casper

WYOMING

Green
River
Rawlins

Laramie
Cheyenne

Grand Teton National Park

Floating the Snake River is the perfect way to enjoy great fishing and spectacular scenery. Scott Sanchez

➤ **Location:** Grand Teton National Park is located in northwestern Wyoming, north of the town of Jackson and south of Yellowstone National Park. The park was created in 1929 with additional lands purchased and donated by John D. Rockefeller. The park was increased to its current size in 1950. It is among the best places in the world to catch native trout in wild, scenic surroundings. The Snake River fine-spotted cutthroat is a fish that is as beautiful as its surroundings and is uniquely adapted to the rugged environment.

With the headwaters in adjacent Yellowstone National Park and the upper drainage in Grand Teton National Park, the Snake River is a special watershed. Fishing in Teton Park is primarily a summer endeavor due to the northern latitude and elevation. Lower Teton lakes are free of ice by late May. For stillwater anglers, a big attraction is Mackinaw or lake trout. Fish weighing more than 20 pounds have been caught in Jackson, Jenny and Phelps Lakes. While the supersize "macks" are usually difficult for the fly angler to reach, spring is the best bet. Lake trout up to 24 inches are relatively easy to fool in fly rod–depth water.

A Teeny or full sink line is necessary for consistent results. Leeches, Woolly Buggers and streamers are the best bet. You can also catch some nice size cutthroats using the same methods.

Hiking is a very popular activity in Teton Park, and this is a good way to watch wildlife and catch fish. Most of the Teton Park streams are sterile because they are too clean and cold, but once they flow into the lakes, higher water temperatures and aquatic invertebrates create fisheries. In Teton Park, there are several great options for a day hike and fishing (Taggart, Bradley, and Phelps Lakes). These three lakes are very good fishing options in June, when rivers are high and muddy.

Taggart and Bradley are accessed from the Taggart Lake Trailhead, three miles from the Moose entrance. The initial section is the same for both, but the trail splits about a mile up. Taggart is 1.6 miles, located at the base of Avalanche Canyon. Bradley is 2.1 miles and is at the base of Garnet Canyon. Both have cutthroat and brook trout.

Taggart has a number of rock points to use as a casting platform, and there is a meadow on the far side that will give you room for a backcast. Leeches, streamers and size 12- to 16-nymphs such as scuds, midge larva or those with peacock bodies, are the best flies. The same is true on most backcountry lakes in Jackson. Floating lines will suffice for much of the fishing, but a favorite backcountry set up is a 5- or 6-weight rod with a clear intermediate line. This allows a fly fisher to cover a wide range of distances and depths. When

161

Flat Creek is a superb spring creek that offers technical fishing for large cutthroats. Scott Sanchez

Below. A large Snake River fine-spotted cutthroat from Flat Creek. Scott Sanchez

fish are on top, generic dries such as Royal Wulffs and Elk Hair Caddis will work.

Backcast room is a little limited on Bradley, but you can work mini bays from the side. Also, casts parallel to the bank are effective. The inlet and outlet are good bets. On Bradley, brookies topping 15-inches have been caught, both using leech patterns.

Phelps Lake is a good-size lake at the base of Death Canyon in Teton Park. You'll find lake trout in the 20-pound range, and cutts up to 27 inches are a possibility. Streamer and leech fishing with sinking lines are generally good techniques, but during summer, ant and beetle patterns can be very effective. The inlet area fishes well most of the year, and wade fishing on the north shoreline for cruisers can also be good. A float tube isn't a bad option. The lake can be accessed from the Rockefeller Visitor Center (a one-mile hike). Leigh, Trapper, Bearpaw and Lake Solitude are other hike-to fishing lakes.

Backcountry hiking and fishing require some basic gear and common sense. A pack with rain jacket, water or a water purifier, food, a flashlight and a map are required gear, and

could save your life. Bear spray is another good idea. You will probably never need it, but you would be one happy camper if you had to use it.

Around the first part of July, Snake tributaries such as the Gros Ventre River, northeast of Jackson, start to clear. You cross the Gros Ventre six miles north of Jackson on Oregon 89 in Teton Park. You can fish it from various pull outs or at the Gros Ventre Campground.

As for the bison: enjoy their company, but keep a safe distance.

After you go through the town of Kelly, turn onto Gros Ventre-Slide Lake Road. Below Slide Lake, you can hike into a nice canyon, which was formed by the largest non-earthquake landslide in the United States. This section has excellent pocket water and is one of the few places in the valley that has rainbows. The cutts dominate, but every once in a while you hook a 'bow. Down-wing dries work well, but a wire nymph can be useful as well. Near the top of Slide Lake, the road turns to dirt. Road conditions can vary, especially with rain. From here and up, the national forest offers 30 miles of fishing access.

Pacific and Spread Creeks are other fishable Teton Park streams. Pacific Creek is just inside the Moran entrance to Teton Park, and Spread Creek is between Moose and Moran on Oregon 89. Both flow into the Snake River in Teton Park but are also accessible upstream in Bridger Teton National Forest. Attractor dry flies such as Stimulators or Convertibles are great for fishing the numerous riffles and pools of these streams.

When the Snake clears— around the second week in July— big attractor dries fish very well. Convertibles, Tarantulas and Chernobyl Ants are good flies, and with the smattering of various stoneflies in the river, they also serve as imitations of these insects. There are also quite a few smaller stoneflies such as Yellow Sallies, and down-wing attractors, such as a Stimulator, Elk Hair Caddis or Trudes, fish well most of the summer.

Fish you catch early will mostly be small, with the larger fish having moved out of the spring creeks. About the first of August, however, you will see start seeing the bigger fish back in the river. Most of the Snake River is braided with channels and side channels of various sizes. This makes it easier to wade fish some sections of the river, and it is like having a bunch of smaller streams instead of just one river.

Phelps Lake is just one of the backcountry lakes in Teton Park and offers fishing for lake trout and native cutthroats. Scott Sanchez

Native Snake River fine-spotted cutthroat on large dry flies are the attraction of Jackson Hole. Scott Sanchez

Larger Teton Park lakes offer the option to catch a lake trout on a fly. Scott Sanchez

Some of the channels are similar to spring creeks. You can get match-the-hatch caddis and mayfly-fishing just minutes after you were fishing a size 6 Chernobyl on the main river. Pale Morning Duns and tan caddis are pretty common, and matching patterns including emergers are helpful. Ants and beetles are the other good side channel flies.

August is a great month on the river. The big fish are back, and terrestrials are in full swing. Another insect, the brown stone, *Claassenia Sabulusa,* starts to hatch this time of year. On the surface, hopper patterns and attractors cross over for the bug, which might explain why fish are eating hoppers

a good distance from the bank. Yuk Bugs along the banks are excellent emergers, especially on rock banks. On rainy August days, you'll also see a hatch of Hecuba mayflies. This is a cousin to the Green Drake and can be imitated with a size 14 Parachute Hare's Ear or a March Brown parachute. Fish seem to key in on them. These patterns—along with generic parachutes and Wulffs—are good searching patterns when the fish ignore the larger flies. The best fishing on the river coincides with water temperature and insect activity (usually between 10 a.m. and 3 p.m., and then from about 6 p.m. on).

September is prime season on the Snake River, and is a favorite time of year among seasoned anglers. As you move into mid-September, skies are autumn's deep blues, and the changing cottonwoods and aspens complete the color spectrum. The cutthroats seem to sense the upcoming winter months and feed aggressively on hoppers, brown stones, caddis, Pale Morning Duns, Baetis and Hecuba mayflies. The best fishing is midday, due to water temperature and insect activity. The fishing will continue into October, but it will slow as the weather cools and temperatures drop.

Due to the size of the Snake, the best access is by drift boat. A good guide will show you the area, put you on fish, and get you down the river safely. You cast from the skillfully rowed boat, but you will also get out and wade productive areas. The guide will also instruct you, which is an excellent chance for beginners to learn how to fly fish. This is great option to take a non-fishing partner: They get a private scenic trip, and you get to fish. A day of fishing the Snake with a riverside lunch is always magnificent.

➤ River Sections: The section below Jackson Lake Dam and Pacific Creek—about four miles—has a spring creek–look to it. This water is available to wade below the dam, at the Pacific Creek boat launch and at Cattleman's Bridge. Good Trico hatches will occur at the beginning of September, and as the month progresses, Baetis will take over. When you first start working a pod of fish, a size 16 or 18 Parachute Adams will produce for both hatches, but after you stick a couple of them, more imitative patterns such as Thoraxes, Compara-duns, spinners and Quigley's Cripples are more effective.

On this section of river, there is a decent population of lake trout and browns, which are Jackson Lake escapees. Try fishing a sinking line with a Double Bunny or Kiwi Muddler. You never know what you might touch. Anglers have reported catching browns nearly 30 inches long on a leech, as well as cuts up to 24 inches on streamers.

Pacific Creek to Deadmans Bar is a 14-mile float. For the wade fisherman, fish the area where Pacific Creek flows in. There are also some wadeable side channels downstream of

Sometimes you need to look up while fishing. Death Canyon above Phelps Lake. Scott Sanchez

The Gros Ventre River is a tributary to the Snake River and offers fishing, hiking and camping opportunities. Scott Sanchez

the Moran entrance to the park where the Buffalo Fork goes into the Snake. Of course you can fish the Buffalo Fork and Pacific Creek. The river increases speed and volume and goes back to its freestone nature as the Pacific Creek and the Buffalo Fork go into it. From this point down, it will become more braided, and after each spring runoff and you can expect a different river. You need to be an experienced boatman to safely float the rest of the Snake through Jackson Hole. At the Deadman's Bar boat launch there is limited wade fishing.

Deadmans Bar to Moose is a fast, high gradient 12-mile section with lots of braids. There are plenty of places to get out of a boat and wade. Smaller braids are almost like streams and will provide some intimate fishing, with visual takes. Try using large dries, streamers or Yuk Bugs for fishing the pockets found along log jams and banks. The bigger flies—such as the Mystery Meat Golden Stone—seem to motivate the fish when they don't have long to decide. If the big stuff isn't happening, try a 12 to 16 Wulff or large beetle. You are dead center

in front of the Tetons here, so look up from your fly every once in a while. This is probably the most dangerous float due to log jams and blocked channels. Schwabachers Landing is about halfway between Deadman's and Moose and is prime wade fishing. The river is braided, and you could spend days exploring. Also for wade fisherman, park at the Moose Bridge or Visitor Center and wade upstream for a short distance. There is also fishing downstream of the bridge on both sides.

A 16-mile float from Moose to Wilson Bridge starts in Teton Park and flows through private and Bureau of Land Management lands. This section has some of the best trout populations with lots of braids, as well as natural and dike banks. The trick to fishing dikes is to find the correct spot for the water flows. It needs to be fast enough to bring trout food and give them overhead cover from raptors, but not so fast they can't hold in it. Due to the length of the section, there is a lot of water to fish, and with the braids and main channels lots of variety.

You'll find plenty of good wade and float access downstream of Teton Park in Jackson Hole at Wilson Bridge:

- On the east side, you can walk about 1.5 miles upstream on the dike and then go down to the river when it looks good.
- On the west side, you can walk downstream for 3 miles.
- A Wilson to South Park float is about 11 miles.
- Downstream of South Park, the River becomes primarily one channel as it flows through the national forest.
- South Park to Pritchard and Pritchard to Elbow are popular floats.
- From West Table to Sheep Gulch is the whitewater section.
- Route 89 parallels the river and offers miles of access in the national forest for the shore angler.

Teton Park and Jackson Hole have great dry fly fishing for Snake River cutthroats, with plenty of public access and outdoor opportunities.

➤ **Tackle and Gear**

Rods and Line: A 9-foot, 5- or 6-weight works well as an all-around rod for the larger streams and lakes. An 8- to 9-foot, 4-weight is best for the smaller streams. For lake trout fishing, use a 7- or 8-weight rod and sinking head to match.

Terminal Tackle and Flies: When it comes to leaders, a 7.5- to 9-foot 3X and 4X leader works well for most fishing. For flat sections during hatches, 9-foot, 5 or 6X leaders are better. Attractor dries work well on the Snake and its tributaries—Convertible, Chernobyl Ant, Stimulator, Trudes, Para Adams, Para Wulffs and Para Hares Ear in sizes 8 to 14. For streamers, try a Kiwi Muddler, Double Bunny or Coffee Minnow.

CLOSEST CITY OR POINT OF ENTRANCE TO THE PARK
- Jackson, Wyoming—Eight miles
- Idaho Falls, Idaho—2-hour drive
- Salt Lake City, Utah—5-hour drive

CLOSEST AIRPORT
- Jackson Airport in Teton Park is three miles from Moose entrance.
- Idaho Falls Regional Airport is a 2-hour drive.

OPEN AND CLOSING PARK DATES
- The park is open 24 hours a day, year-round.
- Park road from Taggart parking lot to Signal Mountain is closed November 1 through April 30.

FEES
- Park entrance and user fees change periodically.
- Golden Eagle and other senior and special use fees apply.
- For up-to-date fees, free days and other exceptions, visit http://www.nps.gov /grte/index.htm.

FISHING REGULATIONS
- A Wyoming license is required.
- Regulations, stream, river, ponds and lakes water openings and closures change year to year, and occasionally during the season.
- Visit http://www.nps.gov/grte /planyourvisit/fish.htm.

CLOSEST FLY SHOPS
JD High Country Outfitters
50 E. Broadway
Jackson, WY 83001
307-733-3270
www.jdhcoutfitters.com
info@jdhcoutfitters.com

Snake River Angler
185 Center St.
Jackson, WY 83001
and
10 Moose St.
Moose, Wyoming 83012
307733-3699
www.snakeriverangler.com
fish@snakeriverangler.com

Westbank Anglers
3670 North Moose Wilson Rd.
Wilson, WY 83014
307-733-6483
www.westbank.com
info@westbank.com

Orvis Jackson
485 W. Broadway
Jackson, WY 83001
307-733-5407
www.orvis.com/s/jackson-hole-wyo-ming-orvis-retail-store

Grand Fly Fishing
3200 W. McCollister Dr.
Teton Village, WY 83025
307-734-9684
www.grandfishing.com

CLOSEST GUIDE SERVICES
JD High Country Outfitters
50 E. Broadway
Jackson WY 83001
307-733-3270
www.jdhcoutfitters.com
info@jdhcoutfitters.com

Snake River Angler
185 Center St.
Jackson, WY 83001
and
10 Moose St.
Moose, Wyoming 83012
307-733-3699
www.snakeriverangler.com
fish@snakeriverangler.com

Westbank Anglers
3670 N. Moose Wilson Road
Wilson, WY 83014
307-733-6483
www.westbank.com
info@westbank.com

World Cast Anglers
485 W. Broadway
Jackson, WY 83001
307-733-6934
www.worldcastanglers.com
GoFish@WorldCastAnglers.com

Grand Teton Fly Fishing
225 W. Broadway Ave,
Jackson, WY 83001
307-690-0910
grandtetonflyfishing.com
info@grandtetonflyfishing.com

Fish the Fly
c/o Jason "JB" Balogh
P.O. Box 42
Jackson, WY 83001
307-690-1139
www.fishthefly.com
jb@fishthefly.com

Grand Fly Fishing
3200 W. McCollister Dr.
Teton Village, WY 83025
307-734-9684
www.grandfishing.com

Jackson Hole Anglers
P.O. Box 9005
Jackson, WY 83002
888-458-7688
www.jacksonholeanglers.com
info@jacksonholeanglers.com

LODGES
Triangle X Ranch
2 Triangle X Ranch Rd.
Moose, Wyoming 83012
307-733-2183
www.trianglex.com
TheRanch@Trianglex.com

Moosehead Ranch
Located on Wyoming 89 south of Moran
307-733-3141
www.mooseheadranch.com
mhreservations@aol.com

Lost Creek Ranch
95 Old Ranch Rd.
Moose, WY 83012
307-733-3435
www.lostcreek.com
ranch@lostcreek.com

BEST PLACE TO STAY IN THE PARK
Jenny Lake Lodge
Moose, WY 83012
307-733-4647
800-628-9988
www.gtlc.com
(high-end)

Jackson Lake Lodge
101 Jackson Lake Lodge Road
Moran WY 83013
307-733-4647
800-628-9988
www.gtlc.com
(mid- to high-end)

Signal Mountain Lodge
Inner Park Road
Moran, WY 83013
307-543-2831
P.O. Box 50 – Moran, WY 83013
www.signalmountainlodge.com
(mid- to high end)

Dornans Rental Cabins
12170 Dornan Road
Moose, WY 83012
307-733-2415
www.dornans.com
timm@dornans.com
(Cabins)

BEST PLACE TO STAY NEAR THE PARK
Cowboy Village Resort
120 S. Flat Creek Dr.
Jackson, WY 83001
307-733-3121
800-962-4988
www.townsquareinns.com
cowboy@townsquareinns.com
Note: There is a wide range of places to stay in Jackson ranging from Motel 6 to the Four Seasons.

BEST CAMPGROUNDS IN THE PARK
Jenny Lake
Inner Park Rd.
Moose, WY 83012
800-628-9988

Gros Ventre
800-628-9988
www.nps.gov/grte
www.gtlc.com
(Usually not full and can accommodate large RVs)

BEST PLACE TO EAT IN THE PARK
Leeks Marina (family fare)
North of Moran
307-543-2546
www.signalmountainlodge.com

Dornan's (Pub food)
12170 Dornan Rd.
Moose, WY 83012
307-733-2415
www.dornans.com
timm@dornans.com

Jenny Lake Lodge (fine dining)
Moose, WY 83012
307-733-4647
800-628-9988
www.gtlc.com

BEST PLACE TO EAT NEAR THE PARK
Trio (fine dining)
45 S. Glenwood
Jackson, WY 83001
307-734-8038
www.bistrotrio.com

Snake River Brewery (pub food)
265 S. Millward
Jackson, WY 83001
307-739-2337
www.snakeriverbrewery.com
beer@snakeriverbrewing.com

Sidewinders (family)
945 W. Broadway
Jackson, WY 83001
307-734-5766
www.sidewinderstavern.com

Abuelito's (Mexican)
385 W. Broadway
Jackson, WY
307-733-1207
www.elabuelitocafe.com

SCOTT SANCHEZ started fly fishing and fly tying at the age of 12. He grew up in Salt Lake City and tried his self-taught fly-fishing skills on the trout of the Wasatch front. At 14, he taught his first fly-tying class. He has worked in the fly-fishing industry for more than 20 years in a variety of positions, including assistant manager at Jack Dennis Sports, wholesale manager at Dan Bailey's, tying flies commercially, helping with video and book production for Snake River Books, guiding, consulting work for Dan Bailey's, working at the Austin Angler and being the Texas sales rep for Scott Rods. He is a member of the Scott Rods Pro Staff, Whiting Pro Staff, is the former fly-tying editor for *Fly Fisherman Magazine* and writes the fly-tying column for *American Angler*. In 1994, he received the Peter Crosby Memorial Sportsmanship Award from the Jackson Hole One Fly, and in 2007 he received the Arnold Gingrich Lifetime Achievement Award from the International Federation of Fly Fishers for literary contributions to fly tying. In 2010, he was awarded the coveted Buz Buszek Award from the IFFF.

Osteria (Italian)
(Located in Hotel Terra)
3335 W. Village Dr.
Teton Village, WY 83025
307-739-4100

Thai Me Up (Thai)
75 E. Pearl Ave.
Jackson, WY 83001
307-733-0005
www.thaijh.com

CLOSEST AND BEST PLACES TO
GET A DRINK

Dornan's
12170 Dornan Rd.
Moose, WY 83012
307-733-2415
www.dornans.com

Signal Mountain Lodge
Deadman's Bar
Inner Park Rd.
P.O. Box 50
Moran, WY 83013
Reservations: 307-543-2831
www.signalmountainlodge.com

MUST SEE

· Schwabachers Landing—About four miles north of Moose on Highway 89. You can drive down to a Snake River side channel. Gorgeous views of the Tetons. Moose, elk and bison frequent the area. Good fishing in the side channels of the Snake as well as the main stem. Carry bear spray.
· The Middle Teton Glacier—You can see this from the Lower Saddle trail.
· Signal Mountain Summit Road—If you are fit enough, take a five-mile climb to the top of Signal Mountain. From here, you will have a spectacular view of Teton Range. In the summer, wildflowers cover the hillsides.

NEAREST HOSPITAL/URGENT
TREATMENT CENTER

Grand Teton Medical Clinic
Jackson Lake Lodge
101 Jackson Lake Lodge Rd.
Moran, WY 83013
307-543-2514
After hours: 307-733-8002

St John's Medical Center
625 E. Broadway
Jackson, WY 83001
307-733-3636
www.tetonhospital.org

CELL PHONE SERVICE
Cell service is good to excellent throughout area.

FOR ALL ELSE, VISIT
http://www.nps.gov/grte/index.htm

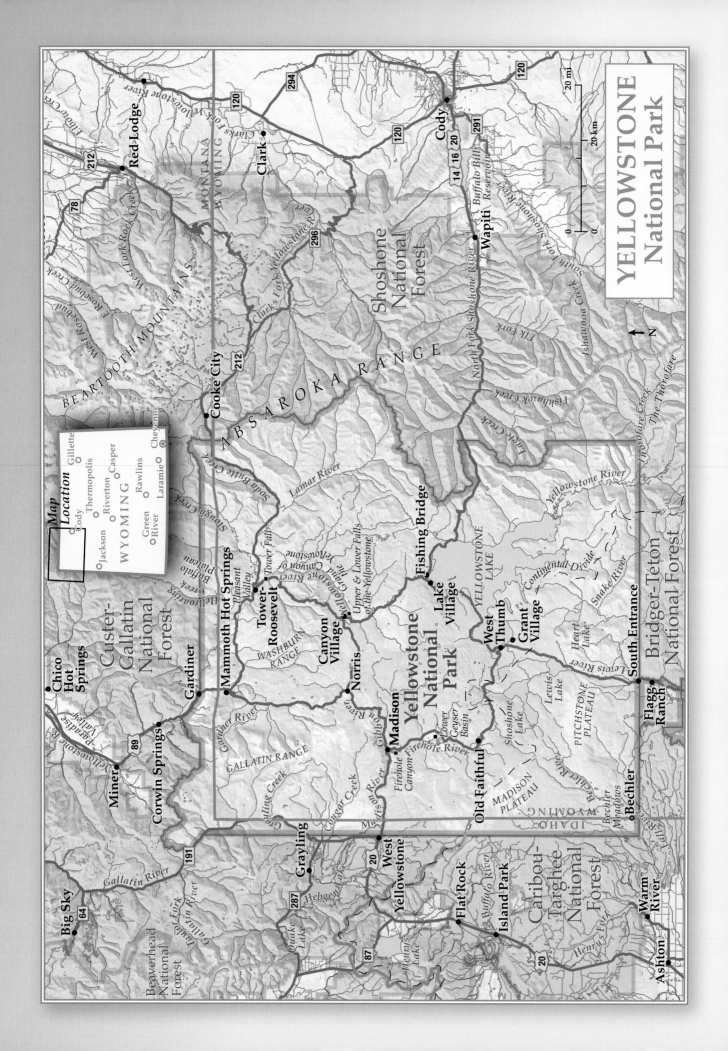

YELLOWSTONE National Park

Map Location

WYOMING
- Gillette
- Cody
- Thermopolis
- Riverton
- Casper
- Jackson
- Rawlins
- Green River
- Laramie
- Cheyenne ★

20 mi

20 km

N

Beartooth Mountains
West Fork Rock Creek
E Rosebud Creek
Elbow Creek
Clarks Fork Yellowstone River

Red Lodge
212
78
120
294
120

Clark
296
120
Cody
14 16 20
291
Buffalo Bill Reservoir
Wapiti

MONTANA
WYOMING

Cooke City
212

ABSAROKA RANGE

SHOSHONE NATIONAL FOREST

North Fork Shoshone River
South Fork Shoshone River
Elk Fork
Ishawooa Creek
Fishhawk Creek
Eagle Creek
The Thorofare
Thorofare Creek

Chico Hot Springs
Custer-Gallatin National Forest

Gardiner

Mammoth Hot Springs
Gardiner River

Soda Butte Creek
Slough Creek
Lamar River

Pleasant Valley
Buffalo Plateau
Hellroaring Creek

Tower-Roosevelt
Tower Falls
WASHBURN RANGE

Grand Canyon of the Yellowstone
Upper & Lower Falls of the Yellowstone
Yellowstone River

Fishing Bridge

Yellowstone River

Continental Divide

Corwin Springs
Miner
89
Paradise Valley
Yellowstone R.

Gallatin Range
Grayling Creek

Norris
Gibbon River

Canyon Village

Madison
Firehole
Firehole River
Canyon

Lower Geyser Basin

YELLOWSTONE LAKE

Lake Village

West Thumb

Grant Village

Heart Lake
Snake River

South Entrance

Bridger-Teton National Forest

Big Sky
64
191
Gallatin River
Taylor Fork Gallatin River

Grayling
287
Hebgen Lake
Quake Lake

West Yellowstone
20
Madison River
Cougar Creek

Old Faithful

Shoshone Lake

Lewis Lake
Lewis River

PITCHSTONE PLATEAU

Flagg Ranch

YELLOWSTONE NATIONAL PARK

MADISON PLATEAU

Bechler
Bechler Meadows
Bechler River

IDAHO
WYOMING

Beaverhead National Forest

87
Henrys Lake

Flat Rock
Island Park
20
Buffalo River
Henrys Fork

Caribou-Targhee National Forest

Warm River
Ashton

➤ **Location:** Yellowstone National Park covers nearly 3,500 square miles in the northwest corner of Wyoming with portions in Montana and Idaho. Yellowstone is open year-round, though some areas of the park are inaccessible by car in the winter.

Because of its sheer size and fly-fishing diversity, we have arbitrarily divided this chapter into five sections—an overall introduction and sections devoted to each quadrant (West, South, East and North). Together, this five-part chapter covers the park and adjacent fly-fishing waters in Montana, Wyoming and Idaho.

Yellowstone was established as a national park by Congress on March 1, 1872 to help preserve the wildlife and to showcase its unique geothermic features. The park encompasses 3,468 square miles comprised of lakes, canyons, rivers, and mountain ranges. There are more than 300 geysers throughout Yellowstone as well as hot springs, mud pots, and fumaroles. Some of Yellowstone's most famous and breathtaking geysers include Old Faithful and Steamboat Springs—the tallest geyser in the world.

In 1988, Yellowstone Park experienced a fire that burned 36 percent (793,880 acres). The fire started out as small, individual fires, but drought and winds caused the fires to combine into one large fire that burned out of control for several months. Fighting the fires cost the U.S. more than $120 million, but it never did stop the fire. It was the snow and moisture that finally brought the fires to an end. The fire burned tens of millions of trees and plants, leaving the park looking desolate and black with ashes. Almost immediately, planes started dropping grass seed throughout the area while crews started replanting trees and other plants.

The closest major city airport is in Bozeman, Montana with seasonal air service (June-September) into West Yellowstone. Additional air service is through Idaho Falls, Idaho. Tourist services including car rentals, hotels, motels, campgrounds, dude ranches, lodges and restaurants abound throughout the area.

➤ **Yellowstone National Park facts and figures:**
· The entirety of the park covers 2,221,766 acres.
· 96 percent of the park is in Wyoming.
· 3 percent of the park is in Montana.
· 1 percent of the park is in Idaho.
· Highest Point: 11,358-feet (Eagle Peak).
· Lowest Point: 5,282-feet (Reese Creek).

· The park is larger than Rhode Island and Delaware combined.
· About five percent of the park is covered by water, while 15 percent is grassland, and 80 percent is forest.
· Park rangers are your best source of information on road and trail conditions, hazards and information about wildlife.
· Yes, there are bears! Yes, bears can maim and kill! However, fly fishers will likely see more bison than any other critter. These gentle giants are deceptively fast and you never want to get between a grazing mother bison and her baby. Never!

➤ **Open and closing park dates or fishing dates**
The general fishing season in Yellowstone opens on the Saturday morning of Memorial Day weekend, and runs through the first Sunday in November. Visit www.nps.gov/yell/planyourvisit/fishdates.htm.

➤ **Regulations**
· Fishing regulations, including closures, can be confusing, so be sure to visit www.nps.gov/yell/planyourvisit/fishdates.htm prior to fishing.
· A Yellowstone National Park Fishing Permit is required to fish in the park. All anglers 16 and older must have a park fishing permit (3-day, 7-day and season permits are available).
· Children under the age of 15 may get a free permit, which must be signed by an adult. This permit allows children to fish without direct adult supervision.
· Yellowstone fishing permits can be purchased at Fishing Bridge Information Center, Bridge Bay Marina, Canyon Information Center, Mammoth Park Headquarters, the Old Faithful Store, and at ranger stations. Note that a Wyoming, Idaho or Montana fishing license will not make you legal inside park boundaries. You must have a park permit.
· No state fishing licenses are required when fishing inside the park.
· Yellowstone National Park (YNP) limits anglers to artificial-only, lead-free fishing tackle.
· The flies you are currently fishing must have barbs flattened. However, flies not in use do not need the barbs squeezed.

- You are allowed to fish a maximum of two flies at a time.
- Articulated flies with two or more hooks are not permitted.
- Native fish (cutthroat trout, grayling, and mountain whitefish) are protected by catch-and-release regulations.
- There is no limit on non-native fish, though we encourage catch-and-release of brown trout.
- Yellowstone general regulations permit the use of float tubes and other human-powered craft on all park lakes.
- All watercraft must undergo an invasive species inspection and operators must purchase and display a license sticker, available at the Mammoth Hot Springs Ranger Station.
- Watercraft of any kind are not permitted on park rivers.
- The Yellowstone River downstream of the park boundary is an ideal driftboat river, and most area fly shops and outfitters focus their guide service on this stretch of the river.
- Regulations change annually as do open and closed waters.
- See https://www.nps.gov/yell/planyourvisit/fishing.htm

➤ **Fees**
- An entrance permit is good for seven consecutive days.
- Fees are $30 vehicle, $12 hiker or bicycle, and $20 snowmobile or motorcycle.
- Persons age 15 and under are admitted free.
- The entry fee is waived if you have a Yellowstone/Grand Teton Pass, Interagency Annual, Senior or Access Pass.
- Passes can be obtained at any national park, monument or recreation area. Yellowstone Passes are available at park entrances.
- Park entrance and user fees change periodically. For up-to-date fees, free days and other exceptions, visit www.nps.gov/yell/index.htm.

We begin our Yellowstone adventure at the West entrance in West Yellowstone, Montana not far from the Gallatin, Gibbon, Madison and Firehole Rivers, Old Faithful Geyser, Old Faithful Lodge and everything you want to see. However, you can begin anywhere.

Just be careful. This isn't an amusement park. Those animals are real—and they're wild.

*Angler working streamers in the lower Grand
Canyon of the Yellowstone. Walter Wiese*

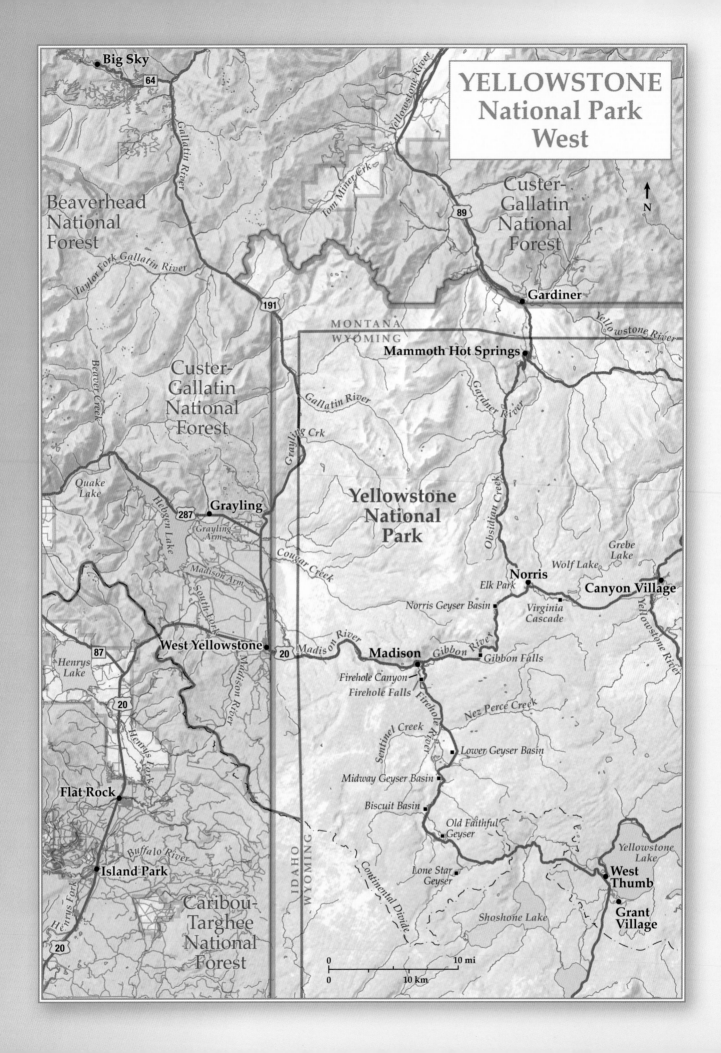

YELLOWSTONE
National Park
West

Big Sky
64

Beaverhead
National
Forest

Gallatin River

Taylor Fork Gallatin River

Tom Miner Crk

Custer-
Gallatin
National
Forest

89

N

191

Gardiner

Beaver Creek

MONTANA
WYOMING

Yellowstone River

Custer-
Gallatin
National
Forest

Mammoth Hot Springs

Gallatin River

Gardner River

Quake
Lake

Hebgen Lake

Grayling Crk

Yellowstone
National
Park

Obsidian Creek

Grebe
Lake

Wolf Lake

287

Grayling

Grayling
Arm

Madison Arm

Cougar Creek

Norris

Canyon Village

Elk Park

Yellowstone River

West Yellowstone

South Fork

Madison River

20

Madison River

Norris Geyser Basin

Virginia
Cascade

87

Henrys
Lake

Madison

Gibbon River

Gibbon Falls

20

Firehole Canyon

Firehole Falls

Firehole River

Nez Percé Creek

Henrys Fork

Sentinel Creek

Lower Geyser Basin

Flat Rock

Midway Geyser Basin

Buffalo River

Biscuit Basin

Island Park

Old Faithful
Geyser

IDAHO
WYOMING

Continental Divide

Lone Star
Geyser

Yellowstone
Lake

West
Thumb

Henrys Fork

20

Caribou-
Targhee
National
Forest

Shoshone Lake

Grant
Village

0   10 mi

0   10 km

➤ **Location:** West Yellowstone, Montana—known to many as "Trout Town West, USA"— is a full-service community on the western border of Yellowstone National Park (YNP). It is the most-used entrance to Yellowstone, the closest to Old Faithful, and the best entrance to the quality rivers, lakes and streams that make up this headwater system of the Missouri River.

Most of the rivers in this area have their beginnings in the park and flow in a northern and westerly direction along the east side of our Continental Divide to Three Forks, Montana where the Gallatin and the Madison join the Jefferson River and form the upper Missouri River. These upper Missouri drainages consist of some of our country's most valued and cherished rivers and fisheries.

➤ **The Firehole River:** The Firehole River gets its start on the high plateau of YNP and meets the Gibbon River at Madison Junction to form the upper Madison River. The Firehole received its name because it looks like the river is on fire with its hundreds of geysers and hot springs both in the water and along its banks. It makes its way down to the Lone Star Geyser, and then all around the Old Faithful area. It then flows downstream through Biscuit Basin, Midway Geyser, the Lower Geyser Basin, over Firehole Falls and through the Firehole Canyon to join the Gibbon at Madison Junction Campground.

Along its warm and gingerly flow, the Firehole is constantly being fed by thousands of small to large geysers and hot springs, each contributing to its size, shape and water temperature. In mid-summer, this high water temperature can have a very serious effect on the trout fishery. However, for all the hot water added to river, there are also large numbers of cold springs and cold tributaries that somehow make the river trout-friendly, and provide very good-to-excellent dry fly fishing.

Originally, the Firehole River above Firehole Falls was fish-less. It was first stocked with trout and various warm water species in about 1890. While the warm water fishery never materialized, the early stocking of brook, brown and rainbow trout caught on, and, in just a few years, the Firehole and its tributaries were being fished for food to supply the new hotels and the visiting public.

The Firehole and others rivers in Yellowstone were stocked off and on through the 1950s. In the late 1960s, catch-and-release and fish-for-fun and enjoyment became more important than catching and killing a limit. Under the direction of Jack Anderson, then superintendent of YNP, all the fisheries in the park were from then on managed as a wild, natural, self-sustaining population of wild trout for the enjoyment of the public, and as a natural food supply for the park's wildlife.

The Lower Falls of the Yellowstone River. Bob Jacklin

The Firehole is one of the first rivers to clear of spring run-off and offers some great hatches of Blue-winged Olives, Pale Morning Duns, and a wonderful little White Miller Caddis. It is a sheer delight to fish along the many hot springs and small geysers while watching rising trout all along the way. The sizes of the natural flies are small, so we keep to a size 16 or 18 fly to match the hatching insects. Small nymphs in sizes 14, 16, and 18—such as the Pheasant Tail, the Gold Ribbed Hare's

The Firehole River along a "Hot Pool" just below the Old Iron Bridge. Bob Jacklin

Ear, and the Bead Head Prince Nymph—will do the trick. Fishing a soft-hackled fly downstream as an emerger will often bring that larger trout to the fly.

The Firehole River has an overabundance of smaller catchable browns and rainbows from 8 to 10 inches with some larger trout mixed in. These trout just love to rise to a well-presented dry fly. The good dry fly fishing lasts until mid-July when the water temperatures rise and the fishing starts to slow. Dry-fly fishing returns in mid-September when the cool air of fall brings the Firehole back to life.

➤ **Access points:** The Firehole River can be accessed from a number of locations.

Start at the Biscuit Basin parking area and fish downstream from this point. Fish downstream from the parking area at Midway Geyser. From Midway, you can fish and hike downstream for miles with great pool and riffle water all the way. Look for the Nez Perce Picnic area, and fish along the Fountain Flat Drive Road.

The Nez Perce Creek is also worth a try. One strategy is to drive along the road from Madison Junction towards Old Faithful and pull off at each turnout and check for rising trout. Most of the river in this area is very flat with a glassy surface—very inviting! Fishing this upper Firehole River is a wonderful and a rewarding experience. Remember to fish with a light rod, a long and fine leader with a 5X tippet. Try fishing dry flies downstream and feed your fly with a natural dead drift into the fish's window from across and above.

The Firehole Canyon below Firehole Falls has a good population of trout, some of which are larger. There is a small salmon fly hatch in mid-June and fishing with a large a Salmon Fly Nymph or the Giant Salmon Fly Dry might bring one of these larger browns up for a grab. This canyon section of the Firehole River requires a larger tippet and flies. What more could you want— an early and late season fishery with rising trout, and the beauty of fishing on the Firehole in Yellowstone, our first national park.

➤ **The Gibbon River:** The Gibbon River starts at the outflow of Grebe Lake, flows through Wolf Lake and travels west down through Virginia Cascades and on to Norris Junction. This upper section of the Gibbon River is very small and has

A nice fall-run brown trout from the Madison River in Yellowstone Park. Bob Jacklin

The Madison River along the West Entrance Road. Bob Jacklin

a mixed fishery of very small brook and brown trout along with some Arctic grayling. There is a good and self-sustaining population of grayling in Grebe Lake, which is just about a three-mile walk from the trail head located along the highway between Norris Junction and Canyon Village.

As the Gibbon River flows past the Norris Campground, it picks up in size and is now a more fishable stream with large pockets, pools, and undercut banks that holds some sizeable brown trout. As the river continues through the Norris Geyser Basin, it flows through two large meadows—Elk Park and the Gibbon Geyser Basin. Both are great open areas with winding pools and undercut river banks. The two meadow areas are divided by a hidden Gibbon Rapids, which flows over a rocky section through a dense forest and past the Gibbon Picnic Area. These two open meadow areas are favored fishing areas on the Gibbon.

The river usually clears by late June and offers great small hatches in the mornings and the evenings. Use a size 16 Pale Morning Dun in the meadow areas and a small Little Yellow or Pale Olive Stone Fly dry size 14 in the riffled areas. In early July, there is a Brown Drake hatch in the evenings in these meadow sections of the river with a good chance to connect to a sizeable brown trout.

When the river passes Beryl Springs, it picks up speed through a canyon area on its way to Gibbon Falls. This canyon section is best fished with a good floating fly as it is mostly pocket water with lots of riffles and some deeper pools. Below Gibbon Falls, the river flows through a very dense-timbered area right along the highway with some off-road parking areas.

As the river gets closer to Madison Junction, it opens up into another good size meadow that some call Gibbon Mead-ows. This section of the Gibbon is very close to the Madison Campground, and is fished quite heavily. However, it is a great late-summer and fall fishery using grasshopper patterns along its winding banks and shallow runs. In late fall, there is some good streamer fishing for the brown trout coming up the river from the Madison River on their fall spawning run.

➤ **The Madison River in Yellowstone Park:** The Madison River gets its start with the confluence of the Gibbon and the Firehole Rivers at Madison Junction Campground. The river runs 14 miles due west along the West Entrance Road to the west entrance of Yellowstone. From there, it skirts the town of West Yellowstone and then flows into Hebgen Lake just north of the town. This upper 14 miles of the Madison River, with its long, glassy, weeded glides, shallow riffles and deeper holding pools, has been classified by some as one of the largest limestone streams in our country. The many limestone rock deposits with deeper areas and heavy-weeded runs offer great cover and feeding areas for a good population of brown and rainbow trout.

There is one setback in this upper section of the Madison River—the general temperature of the surface water in mid-summer is just a little higher than is optimal for a coldwater fish such as trout. This is caused by the Firehole River and the high temperature of its surface water. During mid-summer, the surface temperature in the upper Madison can get as high as 75 degrees, which is a little too warm for trout. Because brown trout are able to tolerate slightly higher water temperatures, they have adapted. Over the course of many years, a world-renowned brown trout fishery has been created.

Bob Jacklin lands a large rainbow trout on the Madison River as it enters Hebgen Lake. Sharyn Jacklin

The rainbow trout also have adapted quite well and, like brown trout, use Hebgen Reservoir as a holding and nursery fishery with fall spawning runs up the Madison River. The rainbows spawn in very early spring or mid-winter when the Madison River in Yellowstone is at its coolest. The Madison also has a good population of wild Rocky Mountain whitefish. Even with these high surface-water temperatures in mid-summer, the Madison has good populations of mayflies, caddisflies, stoneflies and even some Salmonflies in the riffled sections of the river.

Starting in early June (with a normal weather pattern) the Madison will have some hatching insect activity—including that small hatch of Salmonflies in the riffled sections—with hatches upstream all the way to Madison Junction and through the Firehole River and Canyon. Good hatches of Pale Morning Duns and Blue-winged Olives occur, along with a late-June or early-July Gray Drake hatch and a great morning and evening spinner fall. Throughout these 14 miles of placid river, there are fishing accesses all along the road.

The best fishing is during the mornings and evenings through June and well into July. In late July through August, things do slow up, and the trout become a little more sensitive to water temperature. These higher water temperatures have a stressful effect on the fish, especially when they are caught and played out.

The most famous and most-used fishing access points on the Madison are the Barns Pools 1 and 2 just inside the West Gate of Yellowstone. Trout are somewhat equally and naturally distributed through these 14 miles of river. Some of the

better-known fishing accesses are measured by miles from the west gate. The eight-mile fishing/parking area is a prime example. There is a very cold rivulet that enters the Madison across the stream at this access, and the fish tend to stack up there. This is a quite busy fishing area in mid-season and through the fall.

The fall spawning run of brown and rainbow trout starts in early September with the fish moving up the Madison River out of Hebgen Lake. This fall run has become a prime destination and ritual for the fly fisher who wants to challenge these lively 2- to 4-pound trout. Fishing with streamers, Woolly Buggers and soft-hackled wet flies are a sure bet. As the fall season progresses, these spawning trout will work their way up the Madison until late October when there are fish all through the upper 14 miles of the Madison River. This fall run of browns and rainbows will last until the season's end.

➤ **The Gallatin River:** Like the Madison, the Gallatin River starts high on the Yellowstone Plateau and flows west where it meets and parallels U.S. Route 191 at the 22-mile highway marker from West Yellowstone. The Gallatin then flows 40 miles north and through the Gallatin Canyon as it parallels the highway and into the Gallatin Valley where it makes a left turn and heads west to Three Forks. There, it meets the Madison and Jefferson Rivers to create the mighty Missouri River.

Unlike the Madison, the Gallatin is a freestone stream with a very cold water temperature. The headwaters have a good population of cutthroat trout, but most of the river has a good mixture of browns and rainbows. There is a trailhead for the upper Gallatin at the 20-mile highway marker with good dry-fly fishing in mid-summer. The river is clear and cold with many oxbows and deep undercut banks. The cutthroat fishery seems to be doing very well in this headwaters backcountry area. This mid-section of the Gallatin River along U.S. Route 191 is still in Yellowstone Park. Here you can leisurely hike and fish the stream as far as time allows. Here the Gallatin changes from a meadow into a freestone stream.

At the 30-mile highway marker, the river and the highway flow out of Yellowstone Park into Montana. The area around Big Sky is a favorite. There is a good mile of public access just upstream from the Big Sky area. This Gallatin Game Range is open to the public with good fishing. You will need to park along the highway and walk across the open sagebrush to access the river.

This section of the Gallatin River from the Big Sky area down and through the Gallatin Canyon and Valley moves very fast and is highly oxygenated water. This is stonefly water and has a great Salmonfly hatch with lots of lesser stoneflies hatching throughout July and August. The fishing is good in this canyon section, but access is somewhat limited because of the highway running along the river. Late August and on into September is grasshopper time on the Gallatin! When fishing with a hopper pattern, present your fly with a natural, dead drift. A dragged fly will not work very well in this clear and very fast moving river.

➤ **Fishing in Montana:** There are some excellent fisheries outside the park, but still in the West Yellowstone area. Those who fish, guide, live and work in southwest Montana are very proud of the quality and quantity of their trout fisheries. The Montana Department of Fish, Wildlife and Parks has done an excellent job of managing its rivers and streams as a Wild Trout Fishery. There has been no stocking or supplementation of trout in these rivers and streams for well over 40 years.

The quality of these rivers and streams has provided a natural reproduction of wild trout and whitefish, which has made this southwest area of Montana the Trout Capital of the lower 48 states. Some of the lakes are stocked periodically with small rainbow trout to help build up the fishery where needed. The brown trout fishery takes good care of itself providing a quality fishing experience for visiting anglers.

➤ **The Madison River in Montana:** The Madison River flows out of Yellowstone into Montana just three miles north of West Yellowstone where it flows under U.S. Route 191 bridge and downstream into Hebgen Reservoir. This mile-long section of the Madison River is best fished in mid-summer and through the fall. Good hatches of Tricos followed by a good spinner fall happen almost every morning at about 10. The river in this area supports a sizeable number of small rainbows and browns along with Rocky Mountain whitefish. By mid-August, a few larger trout are starting to work their way up the Madison River and will hold and feed in this estuary, which is easy to read and fish.

One of many freestone rivers in Yellowstone Park. Bob Jacklin

Eagle's store, established in 1908, is one of the landmarks at the West entrance. Bob Jacklin

➤ The Madison River "Between the Lakes": "Between the lakes" is a local term for the Madison River as it runs between Hebgen Dam and Quake Lake. This mile-long section of the Madison River is one of the finest trout fisheries in Montana. It has a very healthy population of browns and rainbows, as well as Rocky Mountain whitefish.

This section of the Madison is very popular and sometimes overcrowded. There are several nice campgrounds in the area, including the Camp Fire Lodge, which sits on the river between Hebgen and Quake Lakes. This section of the river is open to fishing all year, and affords some great nymphing through the winter and off-season months.

The giant Salmonfly hatch on the lower Madison River finishes up in this section of the stream around July 4 and offers some great dry-fly fishing. We can only offer a guess as to hatching times since the waters will vary from year to year with the spring runoff. This fast moving section of the Madison has just about all of the insect hatches found in this area of the country:

· Salmonflies
· All the lesser stoneflies
· Western Green Drakes
· Pale Morning Duns
· Blue-winged Olives
· Prolific hatches of caddisflies in all shapes and sizes

As the river flows into Quake Lake, it offers good Callibaetis and Tricos in July and August. The river here has a great run of spawning rainbows in the spring and a great run of browns in the fall.

➤ The Lower Madison River: Those who live and work out of West Yellowstone refer to the Madison River below the Quake Lake outlet as the "Lower Madison." However, the Montana Department of the Fish, Wildlife and Parks has officially named this section of the Madison as the "Upper Madison." The Lower Madison is the river from Ennis Lake to Three Forks.

There are 40 miles of continuous, fast-moving river from the outlet of Quake Lake to Ennis Lake. The late Lee Wulff once referred to this section of the Madison as a "40-mile riffle." The Montana Fish, Wildlife and Parks Department has divided these 40 miles into several sections and floats, with a good number of boat put-ins and take-outs—all with restroom facilities.

· The upper section, from the Quake Lake outlet to Lyons Bridge, is non-fishing from the boat area.
· From Lyons Bridge downstream to Ennis—about 30 miles—is the float area that is used by many of the fly shops and outfitters from West Yellowstone, Big Sky and the Ennis area.

· The upper area from the outlet of Quake Lake down to Lyons Bridge is a great wade-fishing area. This area has a wild and self-sustaining population of wild browns, rainbows and our Rocky Mountain whitefish, and the fishing is generally very good to excellent.

➤ **The South Fork of the Madison River:** The South Fork is a meadow stream and spring creek rolled into one. It crosses U.S. Route 191 four miles west of West Yellowstone, just before the KOA Campground. Upstream from the highway bridge, the river is closed to all fishing where it flows through the private and historic Madison Fork Ranch.

Above the ranch there is some fishable water. The river is small with a population of small brook and brown trout. From the highway bridge downstream, the river offers four miles of public water with some challenging fishing. Here, this placid meadow stream meanders with oxbow after oxbow, deep pools, heavy willow and undercut banks with gin-clear water. The water temperature here in midsummer is about 43 degrees—that is cold!

Before Hebgen Lake was formed in 1910, the south fork was a solid Arctic Grayling fishery. Afterward, it became one of Hebgen's main spawning tributaries for the rainbows and browns that were planted at that time. This clear and cold meadow stream is primarily a spawning stream with a run of rainbows in the spring and a run of browns in the fall. There is a very good population of Rocky Mountain whitefish which love to hit a deeply fished nymph. There are some good-sized resident trout in the stream. Fishing is generally slow, however.

Near where the river enters Hebgan Lake, the water is wide and smooth with an even flow. There is some very good dry-fly fishing using a good Callibaetis parachute dry fly. This lower section of the river also gets a Western Green Drake hatch and lots of Blue-winged Olives and Pale Morning Duns in the spring and through the fall. There is a large pool, and the river opens in to a large estuary where it meets Hebgen Lake. The lake itself is best fished with a boat or a float tube.

➤ **Hebgen, Quake and Henrys Lakes:** These three lakes are within an easy and quick drive from West Yellowstone.

Hebgen Lake: This large lake offers several good access points with boat launches and campgrounds, which are all accessible from U.S. Routes 191, 20 and 287, as well as back roads. Some say the lake is under-fished, though it is one of the prime brown trout fisheries in the state and generates a great fall run of wild browns and rainbows up the Madison River.

Hebgen Lake offers some great fishing just along the shore at ice-out. The fly fisher has a great opportunity casting Woolly Buggers while wading along the shore in the morning and evening. Hebgen also offers some good midge fishing in June, which is followed up with some great Callibaetis dry-fly action in mid-summer.

Earthquake Lake: Earthquake Lake (also called "Quake Lake" by some) was created by the 1959 earthquake, which briefly dammed the Madison River, creating this quality fishery. Like Hebgen, Earthquake Lake is under-fished. It is best fished with a small boat or float tube, and casting up against the timbered banks using Woolly Buggers and, in late summer, grasshopper patterns. Also, you'll find wonderful dry-fly fishing where the Madison River enters the lake. Like Hebgen, Earthquake Lake provides a good fishery of browns and rainbows. Over the years, several browns over 10 pounds have been caught in the Madison River below Hebgen Dam where the river enters Earthquake Lake.

Henrys Lake: This lake is just over the Continental Divide from West Yellowstone in Idaho, and has a long and quality reputation as one of the top fly-fishing lakes in the country. Its history goes all the way back to the late 1800s and very early 1900s when very large native Yellowstone Black-Spotted cutthroat trout were harvested for food in places such as Salt Lake City. Over many years, Henrys provided a quality fishing lake for native cutthroat trout, as well as the introduced hybrid cutthroats and Eastern brook trout. Fly fishers come from all over the world to fish this quality fishery just over the hill, only 10 miles from West Yellowstone.

➤ **Tackle and Gear**

Rods and Line: For the general Yellowstone area, we recommend an 8-½- or 9-foot fly rod with a number 5 line. During the spring, when fishing the Salmonfly hatch or in the fall, when fishing streamer flies, we recommend a 6-weight line [on the 5-weight rod] which simply turns over the larger flies easier and makes fishing more enjoyable. All of your standard trout fly-fishing tackle is recommended along with waders and a good wading staff when wading these high mountain rivers and streams.

Terminal Tackle and Flies: In most cases, your home assortment of trout flies, such as the standard mayflies, caddisflies, and stoneflies, will work very well. The Yellowstone area offers some of the best dry-fly fishing in the lower 48. Soft-hackled flies and a Woolly Bugger often produce when all else fails. It is always a good idea to check with one of the local fly shops for the top flies that are being used during the time you plan your fishing trip.

AROUND THE PARK

Note that opening and closing dates, regulations, and fees are discussed in the Introduction section of this chapter. Specific guides, outfitters, restaurants, and other services listed here apply generally to the area we've labeled Yellowstone National Park, West.

CLOSEST CITY OR POINT OF ENTRANCE TO THE PARK

West Yellowstone, Montana: West Yellowstone is a full-service community that offers accommodations, from large hotels to smaller motels, with a good range of prices. Contact the Chamber of Commerce for a full listing of accommodations and a vacation planner. West Yellowstone has a state-of-the-art visitors center run by the State of Montana, Yellowstone National Park and local Chamber of Commerce.

West Yellowstone Chamber of Commerce
P.O. Box 458
West Yellowstone, MT 59758
406-646-7701
www.destinationyellowstone.com

CLOSEST AIRPORT

- West Yellowstone Airport (seasonal) with connections from Salt Lake City, Utah
- Bozeman, Montana and Idaho Falls, Idaho, each of which roughly is a 100-mile scenic drive

CLOSEST FLY SHOPS, GUIDE SERVICES, AND OUTFITTERS

The fly-fishing shops are all outfitters with quality guide services and cater to teaching fly fishing. Fly fishing is much more than a job or business in West Yellowstone—it is a way of life. Also, there are fly shops and guide services in all the other communities including

Big Sky, Montana
Ennis, Montana
Last Chance, Idaho

Bob Jacklin's Fly Shop
105 Yellowstone Ave.
West Yellowstone, MT 59758
406-646-7336
www.jacklinsflyshop.com

Arrick's Fly Shop
37 N. Canyon St.
West Yellowstone, MT 59758
406-646-7290
www.arricks.com

Bud Lilly's Trout Shop
39 Madison Ave.
West Yellowstone, MT 59758
406-646-7801
www.budlillys.com

Blue Ribbon Flies
305 Canyon St.
West Yellowstone, MT 59758
406-646-7642
www.blue-ribbon-flies.com

Madison River Outfitters
117 N. Canyon St.
West Yellowstone, MT 59758
406-646-9644
www.madisonriveroutfitters.com

Eagle's Store
3 N. Canyon St.
West Yellowstone, MT 59758
406-646-9300
www.eagles-store.com

West Yellowstone Fly Shop
140 Madison Ave.
West Yellowstone, MT 59758
406-646-1181
www.wyflyshop.com

BEST PLACE TO STAY IN THE PARK

Old Faithful Inn Complex (includes Old Faithful Lodge and the Snow Lodge)

The Old Faithful Inn
1 Grand Loop Rd.
Yellowstone National Park, WY 82190
http://www.yellowstonenationalparklodges.com/lodging/summer-lodges/old-faithful-inn/
reserve-ynp@xanterra.com
Reservations for lodging and camping
- Direct: 307-344-7311
- Dinner Reservations: 307-344-7311
- In-Park Lodge/Guest Information: 307-344-7901

Old Faithful Snow Lodge
2305 Old Faithful
Yellowstone National Park, WY 82190
http://www.yellowstonenationalparklodges.com/lodging/winter-lodges/old-faithful-snow-lodge-cabins/
Reservations for lodging and camping
- Direct: 307-344-7311
- Dinner Reservations: 307-344-7311
- In-Park Lodge/Guest Information: 307-344-7901

BEST CAMPGROUNDS IN AND AROUND WEST YELLOWSTONE

- The closest campground is Madison Junction Campground, located 14 miles from West Yellowstone.
- Baker's Hole Campground is a U.S. Forest Service campground on the border of Yellowstone along U.S. Route 191 on the Madison River.
- There are several commercial campgrounds in West Yellowstone as well as the large Yellowstone Grizzly RV Park. Contact the Chamber of Commerce for a listing of services, restaurants, and accommodations: www.distinationyellowsone.com.

BEST PLACE TO EAT IN THE PARK

Old Faithful Inn Restaurant
1 Grand Loop Rd.
Yellowstone National Park, WY 82190
307-344-7311

BEST PLACE TO EAT NEAR THE PARK

West Yellowstone has a large variety of restaurants breakfast to dinner, pizza parlors and family restaurants.

CLOSEST AND BEST PLACES TO GET A DRINK AND EAT IN WEST YELLOWSTONE

Bullwinkle's Saloon and Eatery
115 N. Canyon St.
West Yellowstone, MT 59758
406-646-9664

The Buffalo Bar
335 U.S. Route 20
West Yellowstone, MT 59758
406-646-1176
http://thebuffalobar.com
info@thebuffalobar.com

Slippery Otter Pub
139 N. Canyon St.
West Yellowstone, MT 59758
406-646-7050

Wild West Pizzeria & Saloon
14 Madison Ave.
West Yellowstone, MT 59758
406-646-4400
http://www.wildwestpizza.com

BOB JACKLIN has been a fly-fishing guide and outfitter in the West Yellowstone area since 1969, originally as a guide for Bud Lilly's Trout Shop. He opened Jacklin's Fly Shop in 1974. He is a world-class fly fisher, fly tier and master fly-casting instructor on the IFFF's Board of Governors. He has been tying flies commercially since 1963 and is a past recipient of the IFFF's Buz Buszek Award for his contributions to the art of fly tying. Bob is a charter member of the International Federation of Fly Fishers, on the pro-staff for St. Croix Rods, Ross Reels, Dr. Slick Instruments for Anglers, Cortland Lines and Whiting Farms. On October 23, 2004, at the Catskill Fly Fishing Center and Museum, Bob was inducted into the Fly Fishing Hall of Fame.

MUST SEE
· Old Faithful Geyser—This is the most famous geyser in the world, with an average eruption interval of about 90 minutes. The eruption shoots water as high as 185 feet into the air.
· Lobby of the Old Faithful Lodge—This is the largest log structure in the world. It was built in 1903-04 and includes a massive stone fireplace, wood and wrought iron, and a clock that has been handcrafted from copper.
· Grand Canyon of Yellowstone—This Yellowstone River canyon is 1,200 feet deep in places, and 4,000 feet wide in some spots. You'll have views of two waterfalls—the 300-foot drop of the Lower Falls and the 100-foot drop of the Upper Falls.

NEAREST HOSPITAL/URGENT TREATMENT CENTER
West Yellowstone Clinic
11 S. Electric St.
West Yellowstone, MT 59758
406-646-9441
Note: The closest full-service hospitals are located in Bozeman, Montana and Idaho Falls, Idaho.

CELL PHONE SERVICE
Full cell phone service is available in and around West Yellowstone. In Yellowstone Park, cell phone use is limited but available in places such as Old Faithful, Mammoth Hot Springs, and Fishing Bridge.

FOR ALL ELSE, VISIT
http //www.nps.gov/yell/index.htm

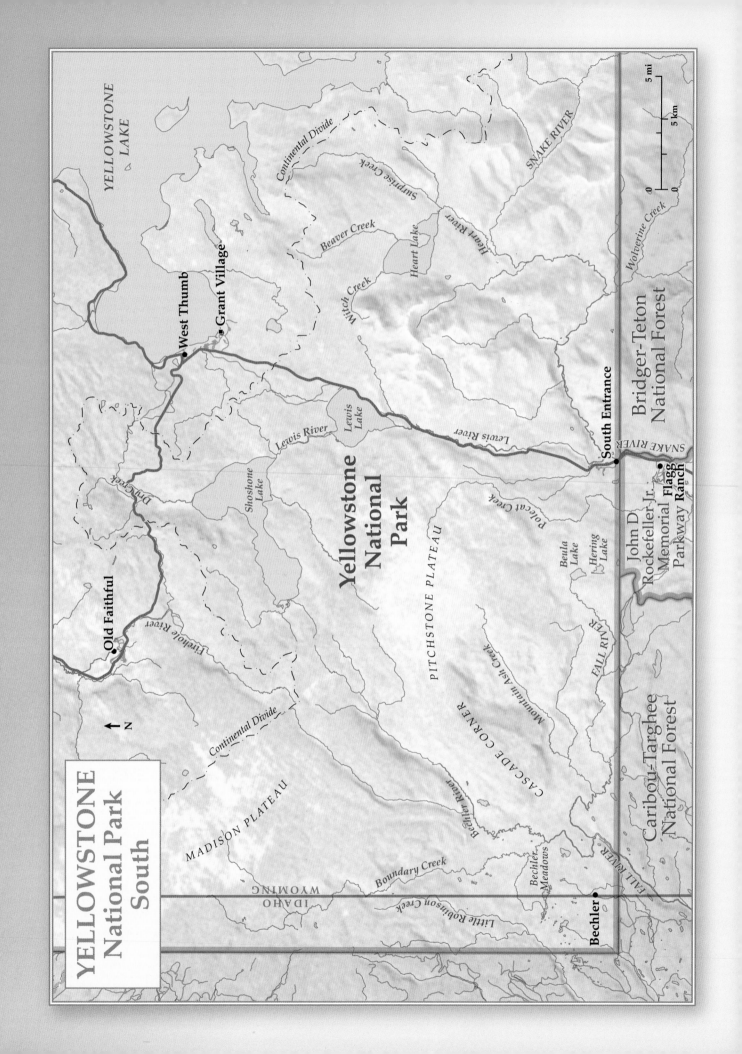

► **Location:** There are essentially two drainages on the Pacific side of the Continental Divide within the park: those of the Snake River, and those of the Fall River. No other part of the park has as many remote quality fisheries as these two combined.

► **Snake River Drainages:**
The only easily approached waters are
· A small portion of the Snake River as it exits the park
· Lewis Lake
· Part of the Lewis River drainage above and below the Lewis River Canyon

These waters are adjacent to the South Entrance Road up to the Continental Divide just south of West Thumb Junction. This road nearly bisects the Snake River drainage on which we will focus.

Shoshone Lake lies at the top of the Lewis River drainage. At 12 square miles, it is the largest road-less lake in the lower 48. Originally devoid of salmonids, the introduced lake trout and lesser populations of brown and brook trout now reach trophy size. There are two practical land routes to reach this lake:
· Shoshone Lake Trail: 4.5 miles beginning just above Lewis Lake
· DeLacey Creek: Three miles beginning at the Grand Loop Road between Old Faithful and West Thumb Junction

The popular water trail is motorized across Lewis Lake, then up the non-motorized Lewis River to the lake. It's a three-mile trip—ideal for canoes—with the last three-quarters mile requiring a portage to the lake. Shoreline fishing on Shoshone Lake is limited and is best in low-light conditions early in the season when juvenile lake trout and brown trout cruise shallows. Fishing from a boat rowed and portaged up the river or from flotation devices packed in on either of the two trails is the best strategy.

The most productive approach is to present leech, scud, and streamer patterns around submerged weed beds. Another productive approach is to troll streamer patterns from June into July and then coming back to do the same by mid-September. Fishing the river—locally called "The Channel"—can be interrupted during summer because of numerous boaters

Bechler Ranger Station, gateway to Fall River Basin. Bruce Staples

ascending to campgrounds along Shoshone Lake. But a late-June Green Drake emergence, terrestrial insect presence, and a few giant stoneflies emerging in the upper river can bring topwater trout action.

Lewis Lake is close to the South Entrance road and hosts a full-service boat dock at Lewis Lake Campground. The lake can be easily fished from a boat or waded around the shoreline. Presenting leech, scud, and streamer patterns around submerged weed beds is a productive approach.

By late June, fish in the roadside meadow reach of Lewis River below the lakes start to respond to a Green Drake emergence, adult stoneflies blown in from the canyon, and to mid-summer terrestrial insects. A hair mouse pattern presented here during evenings can be devastating. In October, mature brown trout from both lakes move into the top three-quarters mile of "The Channel" to spawn. At this time, numerous anglers seeking trophy browns come there by either the trail or by boating across Lewis Lake.

Browns also spawn directly below Lewis Lake in October and in the river below the highway crossing. In both lakes, large lake trout move to rocky shallows to spawn. As with the browns spawning in the river, large streamer patterns attract trophy-sized individuals.

The Lewis River Canyon is mostly inaccessible and dangerous, so we will concentrate on the river below at its

Cave Falls is the water gateway to Fall River Basin. Bruce Staples

confluence with the Snake River, just above the South Entrance. Here, both rivers host brown and cutthroat trout and Rocky Mountain whitefish. The brown trout dwindle in numbers, and the cutthroat seem to diminish in size as you proceed up the Snake River.

In all waters in this area of Yellowstone, cutts respond to the relatively minor mayfly emergences but more readily strike late-day caddisfly activity and summertime terrestrial insects. In late October, a run of brown trout from the river above Jackson Lake ascends here and turns mainly into the lower Lewis River to spawn. In their wake, cutthroat trout, mountain whitefish, and a few juvenile lake trout follow to pick off drifting eggs. Two miles west of the South Entrance ranger station, you can take an easy walk on the South Boundary Trail to Polecat Creek where lightweight tackle is best for its brook, brown, and cutthroat ranging to moderate size.

➤ **Heart Lake Basin:** So much for the relatively easily accessed waters in this part of the park. Heart Lake Basin is part of the Snake River drainage, but considerable effort is required to access it.

Getting to the lake is best accomplished through the trail-head across the South Entrance Road from the northeast corner of Lewis Lake. The trailhead sign notes the 8.5-mile walk to Heart Lake. It is distance enough to discourage most fly fishers, but for those willing to put forth the effort, some of the best early season fishing in the park awaits, but only after a winter of heavy snowfall.

Heart Lake, the most remote large lake in the park, like Shoshone Lake, sits just beneath the Continental Divide. Lake trout were introduced here early in the last century and not only thrive, but co-exist with native cutthroat trout and mountain whitefish.

Fishing in Heart Lake Basin opens on July 1 in order to protect critical grizzly bear habitat, and it can be a fly-fishing paradise. Inform park rangers of your intent, and arrive at the trailhead during first light. Be equipped with

· Lightweight waders
· DEET
· Rain gear
· Bear spray
· Water purifier

186

- High-carb food
- Fly gear, including full sink and floating lines
- Streamer patterns
- Speckled Dun patterns
- Adult Damselfly patterns

Once you reach the lake, you will see Heart Lake Ranger Station, which is sometimes occupied. Forget about fishing adjacent Witch Creek. Cutthroat have left it weeks ago because of its thermal water load.

Go directly to the lake, and observe the nearly half-mile-long beach. Watch for rise forms in the shallows. Speckled Duns and adult Damselflies will be on the surface with salmonids responding. Rig a floating line and a Speckled Dun and adult Damselfly pattern, get into your waders, and walk into the shallows ready for action.

When the wind comes up by late morning, switch to your sinking line and present streamer patterns. Either way, your reward will be cutthroat trout ranging to several pounds and juvenile lake trout. If you do not mind walking two miles further down the Heart Lake Trail, those same cutthroat will still be in the lower end of Beaver Creek to respond to Pale Morning Dun and Yellow Sally patterns. During an

Lewis River brown trout caught and released in summer. Shane Wootan

Boundary Creek at Bechler River Trail crossing. Bruce Staples

187

overnight or multi-day stay in the basin, the same fishing can be experienced, but you will be subject to park backcountry regulations.

Because of its 12.5-mile distance from the trail head, the most practical approach to fish Heart Lake and Beaver Creek is by taking a two-day (at least) trip. During early July, adult stoneflies are blown up from the canyon into the quarter-mile meadow reach of the river outlet. Ravenous cutthroat both there and in the outlet bay will readily respond to floating stonefly patterns.

Plan any of these trips no later than the first week and a half of July because, with warming waters, the largest trout move to lake depth

A late-season Bechler River cuttbow hybrid posing before returning to the river. Everet Evans

and become available only via boat. A fly angler equipped with large streamer patterns and a lead core line can travel by boat out to depths where huge lake trout reside. These fish will come into rocky shallows around the lake by mid-September to spawn and be available to fly fishers equipped with full-sink lines and large streamer patterns. The largest lake trout on record taken from Yellowstone Park waters—42-pound behemoth—came from the depths of Heart Lake. Six- and 7-weight rods with full-sink or floating lines are ideal for fishing lakes in this drainage. Six-weight rods with floating and sink-tip lines are best for fishing the streams, whether presenting dry or wet patterns.

➤ **Fall River Basin:** Fall River Basin holds the other major drainage west of the Continental Divide in Yellowstone National Park. If the basin remained subject to the current park fishing regulations and held a developed road system, its visitation would be equivalent to those on the Madison and Yellowstone Rivers drainages.

Currently, other than the Yellowstone River drainage above the lake, the basin holds the most remote quality waters in the park (arguably anyway). Access to the waters on the west side of the basin—mainly Bechler River and Boundary Creek—is from Bechler Ranger Station, about 25 miles east of Ashton, Idaho. From Ashton, travel east on U.S. Route 20, Idaho 47—also known as The Mesa Falls Scenic Route. After about six miles, the Cave Falls Road proceeds east from the highway to the 1.5-mile-long Bechler Ranger Station Road. The ranger station—fully staffed during park fishing season—

is the best location to start visits to waters on the west side of the basin. However, some access is possible from a trailhead at the end of the Cave Falls Road, which parallels Fall River for a few miles.

Day and overnight trips bring anglers to the river in Bechler Meadows where it is similar to, but larger than, Slough Creek in the first meadow above its campground. Fall River below Mountain Ash Creek is as large as Bechler River in its meadow, but of varying character.

Waters in the east end of the basin are best accessed off the Ashton-Flagg Ranch Road which leaves U.S. Route 20, a mile south of Ashton, to proceed east into Wyoming and end near the Flagg Ranch Resort on the John D. Rockefeller Memorial Parkway. There are a number of trailheads from Ashton-Flagg Ranch Road as it proceeds east going into Fall River, Mountain Ash and Proposition Creeks, and Beula (formerly spelled as Beulah) and Hering Lakes.

The middle section of this road is in near-primitive condition, passable with care by vehicles including family sedans, but it is not passable by vehicles hauling trailers or by large recreational vehicles.

Apparently the basin was originally void of salmonids, but Yellowstone cutthroat were introduced early in the 20th century. How rainbow trout came to Fall River Basin around 80 years ago is unknown, but the result is hybridization with cutthroat to produce a trout similar to those in the Henry's Fork of the Snake River. As in the Henry's Fork, these fish can grow large in certain parts of the five major streams in the basin. No Rocky Mountain whitefish occupy waters in the basin within the park. Brook trout—the only other salmonid resident—came into Fall River and recently spread to Mountain Ash Creek and the beaver ponds on Proposition Creeks after escaping from Fish Lake just outside the park's south boundary. As with any other park, backcountry visits longer than a day trip are subject to park backcountry camping regulations.

Cascade Corner includes the most waterfalls in Yellowstone. Aside from Proposition Creek, the other four major streams in Fall River Basin hold a number of waterfalls, and on each stream, one of these acts as a barrier above which cutthroat-rainbow hybrid trout are not present. Instead, you'll find only Yellowstone cutthroat trout.

The basin and both plateaus above Fall River Basin—Madison Plateau on the northwest and Pitchstone Plateau on the northeast—receive the most snowfall of any location in the park. The resulting melt water determines when it is practical to enter the basin to fish its streams. In many years, this occurs after the general fishing season opens. Snow melt also determines when the Ashton-Flagg Road becomes passable to allow access to Beula and Hering Lakes, both hosting only Yellowstone cutthroat ranging to trophy sizes.

The streams become fishable around July 1, and access to the lakes opens by then. The succession of aquatic insects on both lakes is familiar—Dragonflies followed by Damselflies, then Speckled Duns and Cinnamon caddis—so life cycle patterns of these insects are your best bets. Small leech patterns and midge life cycle patterns always work in both lakes throughout the season. The seasonable progression of aquatic and terrestrial insect emergences for the major streams in the drainage—all of which have substantial meadow reaches—begins with the Giant, Golden, and Isoperla stoneflies, Gray Drakes, and Pale Morning Duns as soon as run-off becomes insignificant.

Wind-blown large stoneflies from canyon to meadow reaches are important then. Soon after come afternoon Green

Lewis River in Meadows is one of few extensive roadside streams for fishing on the Pacific side of Yellowstone National Park. Brown trout grow to large sizes here. Bruce Staples

A well-defined trail system provides access in the fly-fishing heaven of Fall River Basin. Bruce Staples

Drake and evening Brown Drake emergences followed in time by terrestrial insects, Speckled Duns in meadow reaches, and late summer Trico and flying ant activity. The importance of these lasts until a killing frost—usually before the end of October—ending the season in some of the park's best remote waters.

➤ **Tackle and Gear**

Rods and Line: 6- and 7-weight rods with full-sink or floating lines are ideal for fishing lakes in this drainage. Six-weight rods with floating and sink-tip lines are best for fishing the streams in the Snake River Drainages, whether presenting dry or wet patterns. Six-weight rods with floating, sink-tip, and full-sink lines are ideal for presenting dry or wet flies in Fall River Basin waters.

Terminal Tackle and Flies: In the Snake River Drainages, leech, scud, and streamer patterns from Jume into July, and

again in mid-September. Green Drakes, terrestrials, and giant stonefly patterns are good bets in late June. Hair mouse patterns in the evenings can be very successful. In Heart Lake, Speckled Dun and adult Damselfly patterns with floating lines are a good setup. Later in the mornings, switch to sinking lines and streamer patterns. If you can reach deep waters via boat, try large streamer patterns and a lead core line. In mid-September, lake trout return to the shallows to spawn, so switch to full-sink lines and large streamer patterns. In Beaver Creek, try Pale Morning Dun and Yellow Sally patterns. In Fall River Basin waters, dragonfly, damselfly, Speckled Duns, and cinnamon caddis patterns are good early-season bets. Later season go-to patterns include giant, golden, and Isoperla stoneflies, Gray Drakes, and Pale Morning Duns. Later season bets include Brown Drakes, terrestrial insects, Speckled Duns and Tricos.

Both Snake River fine-spotted and Yellowstone cutthroat trout are in waters on the Pacific side of the Continental Divide. Bruce Staples

ALL AROUND THE PARK

Note that opening and closing dates, regulations, and fees are discussed in the Introduction section of this chapter. Specific guides, outfitters, restaurants, and other services listed here apply generally to the area we've labeled Yellowstone National Park, South.

CLOSEST CITY OR POINT OF ENTRANCE TO THE PARK

· Fall River Drainage Idaho Falls, Idaho
· Snake River Drainage Jackson, Wyoming

CLOSEST AIRPORT

· Idaho Falls, Idaho: Municipal Airport, 110 miles
· Jackson, Wyoming: Jackson Hole Airport, 50 miles

Full services and car rentals are available at both airports.

CLOSEST FLY SHOPS
Fall River Side

Jimmy's All Seasons Angler
275 A St.
Idaho Falls, ID 83402
208-524-7160
jimmys@ida.net
www.jimmysflyshop.com

Three Rivers Ranch
P.O. Box 856
Warm River, ID 83420
208-652-3750
www.threeriversranch.com

Henry's Fork Anglers
3340 Idaho 20
Island Park, ID 83429
208-558-7525
info@henrysforkanglers.com

Trouthunter
3327 Idaho 20
Island Park, ID 83429
208-558-9900
http //www.trouthunt.com/

Snake River Side

Snake River Angler
10 Moose St.
Moose, WY 83012
307-733-3699
fish@snakeriveranglers.com

CLOSEST GUIDE SERVICES
Fall River Side

Three Rivers Ranch
P.O. Box 856
Warm River, ID 83420
208-652-3750
www.threeriversranch.com/

Henry's Fork Anglers
3340 Highway 20
Island Park, ID 83429
208-558-7525
info@henrysforkanglers.com

Trouthunter
3327 Idaho 20
Island Park, ID 83429
208-558-9900
http //www.trouthunt.com/

Snake River Side

Snake River Angler
10 Moose St.
Moose, WY 83012
307-733-3699
fish@snakeriveranglers.com

Flagg Ranch Resort
P.O. Box 187
Moran, WY 83013
800-443-2377
info@flaggranch.com

CLOSEST OUTFITTERS
Fall River Side

Three Rivers Ranch
P.O. Box 856
Warm River, ID 83420
208-652-3750
www.threeriversranch.com/

Henry's Fork Anglers
3340 Idaho 20
Island Park, ID 83429
208-558-7525
info@henrysforkanglers.com

Snake River Side

Flagg Ranch Resort
P.O. Box 187
Moran, WY 83013
800-443-2377
info@flaggranch.com

BEST PLACE TO STAY IN THE PARK
Old Faithful Inn Complex (includes Old
Faithful Lodge and the Snow Lodge)

The Old Faithful Inn
1 Grand Loop Road
Yellowstone National Park, WY 82190
http://www.yellowstonenationalparklodges.
com/lodging/summer-lodges/old-faithful-
inn/reserve-ynp@xanterra.com
Reservations for lodging and camping
· Direct: 307-344-7311
· Dinner Reservations: 307-344-7311
· In-Park Lodge/Guest Information:
  307-344-7901

Old Faithful Snow Lodge
2305 Old Faithful
Yellowstone National Park, WY 82190
http://www.yellowstonenationalparklodges.
com/lodging/winter-lodges/old-faithful-
snow-lodge-cabins/
Reservations for lodging and camping
· Direct: 307-344-7311
· Dinner Reservations: 307-344-7311
· In-Park Lodge/Guest Information:
  307-344-7901

BEST PLACE TO STAY NEAR THE PARK
Fall River Side

Three Rivers Ranch
P.O. Box 856
Warm River, ID 83420
208-652-3750
www.threeriversranch.com/

Eagle Peak Lodge
(Formerly Ashton Inn)
164 White Pine Rd.
Ashton, Idaho 83420
208-652-3699

*Guesthouse International Henry's
Fork Inn*
115 South Bridge St.
St. Anthony, ID 83445
208-624-3711

Snake River Side

Flagg Ranch Resort
U.S. Route 89
P.O. Box 187
Moran, WY 83013
800-443-2377
info@flaggranch.com

BEST CAMPGROUND IN THE PARK
Lewis Lake Campground
South Entrance Rd.
Yellowstone National Park, WY 82190
307-344-7381

BEST CAMPGROUND NEAR THE PARK
Cave Falls Campground
Caribou Targhee National Forest
Forest Road 006
Ashton, Idaho 83420
208-524-7500

BEST PLACE TO EAT IN THE PARK
Old Faithful Inn Restaurant
1 Grand Loop Rd.
Yellowstone National Park, WY 82190
307-344-7311

CLOSEST AND BEST PLACES TO
GET A DRINK
Fall River Side

Three Rivers Ranch
1662 Idaho 47
P.O. Box 856
Warm River, ID 83420
208-652-3750

Trouthunter
3327 Idaho 20
Island Park, ID 83429
208-558-9900
http //www.trouthunt.com/

Snake River Side

Flagg Ranch Resort
U.S. Route 89
P.O. Box 187
Moran, WY 83013
800-443-2377
info@flaggranch.com

CLOSEST AND BEST RESTAURANTS
Fall River Side

Chriswells Trail's End Restaurant
213 Main St.
Ashton, ID 83420
208-652-9918

El Jaliciense, Inc.
119 S. Bridge St.
St. Anthony, ID 83445
208-624-1124

BRUCE STAPLEs of Idaho Falls, Idaho, has fly fished the Greater Yellowstone area for 35 years. He began tying flies in the 1970s, and during the 1980s he began writing of his Greater Yellowstone angling adventures. His literary contributions include articles in *Fly Tyer*, *American Angler*, *Fly Fishing the West*, *Yellowstone-Teton Country* and *Fly Fisher* magazines. During the 1990s, he was a columnist for the *Idaho Falls Post Register*. He is currently contracted with Stackpole Books to produce his fifth book, *Fly Fishing the Greater Yellowstone Backcountry*.

Bruce is associated with Jimmy's All Seasons Angler in Idaho Falls and is an advocate for protection and preservation of regional coldwater fisheries. He is active in preserving the fly-fishing heritage of the Greater Yellowstone region and is a recognized authority for fly fishing in Yellowstone National Park.

Bruce is active in the International Federation of Fly Fishers (IFFF) and a recipient of the Western Rocky Mountain Council, IFFF Fly Tyer of the Year award in 1990 and the Charlie Brooks Memorial Life Membership in 1998. In 2001, he was the thirty-second recipient of the IFFF's Buz Buszek Memorial Award for fly-tying excellence. He is a member of the Whiting Farms and Daiichi Pro Staffs.

Trouthunter
3327 Idaho 20
Island Park, ID 83429
208-558-9900
http //www.trouthunt.com

Snake River Side

Dornan's
12170 Dornan Rd.
P.O. Box 39
Moose, WY 83012
307-733-2415

Flagg Ranch Resort
U.S. Route 89
P.O. Box 187
Moran, WY 83013
800-443-2377
info@flaggranch.com

MUST SEE
· Idaho Scenic Highway 32 from Ashton, Idaho to Tetonia, Idaho
· Idaho Highway 47, the Mesa Falls Scenic Route from Ashton, ID to Island Park, ID

NEAREST HOSPITAL/URGENT TREATMENT CENTER

Fall River Side

Eastern Idaho Regional Medical Center
3100 Channing Way
Idaho Falls, ID 83404
208-529-6111

Madison Memorial Hospital
450 East Main St.
Rexburg, ID 83440
208-359-6300

Snake River Side

St. John's Medical Center
625 East Broadway
Jackson, WY 83001
307-733-3636

CELL PHONE SERVICE
Cell service is poor and spotty. Locations near developments within Yellowstone Park or communities at park entrances enjoy reasonable service.

FOR ALL ELSE, VISIT
http //www.nps.gov/yell/index.htm

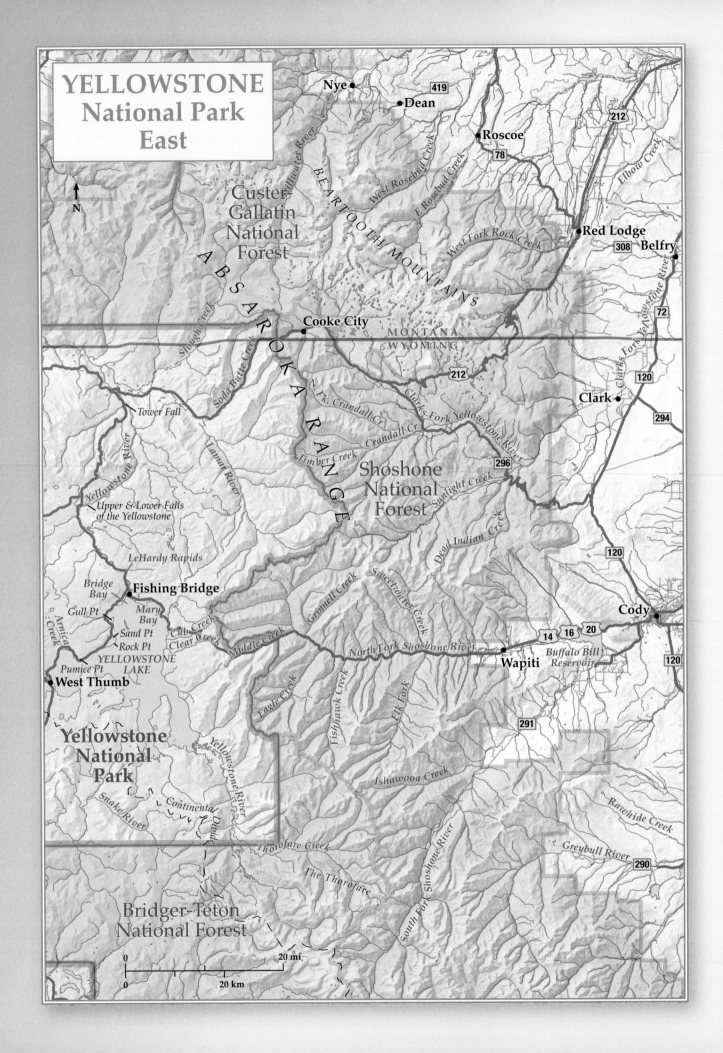

YELLOWSTONE
National Park
East

N

Nye
Dean

419

212

Roscoe

78

Custer-
Gallatin
National
Forest

BEARTOOTH MOUNTAINS

Stillwater River

West Rosebud Creek

E Rosebud Creek

West Fork Rock Creek

Red Lodge
Belfry

308

72

ABSAROKA

Cooke City

MONTANA
WYOMING

212

Clark

120

294

Slough Creek

Soda Butte Creek

Tower Fall

Lamar River

N. Fk. Crandall Cr.

Crandall Cr

Clarks Fork Yellowstone River

296

Elbow Creek

Clarks Fork Yellowstone River

RANGE

Timber Creek

Shoshone
National
Forest

Sunlight Creek

Yellowstone River

Upper & Lower Falls
of the Yellowstone

LeHardy Rapids

Dead Indian Creek

120

Bridge
Bay

Fishing Bridge

Gull Pt

Mary
Bay

Sand Pt

Rock Pt

Cub Creek

Clear Creek

Grinnell Creek

Sweetwater Creek

Cody

Arnica Creek

Pumice Pt

West Thumb

YELLOWSTONE
LAKE

Middle Creek

North Fork Shoshone River

14 16 20

Wapiti

Buffalo Bill
Reservoir

120

Eagle Creek

Fishhawk Creek

Elk Fork

291

Yellowstone
National
Park

Yellowstone River

Continental Divide

Snake River

Thorofare Creek

The Thorofare

Ishawooa Creek

South Fork Shoshone River

Rawhide Creek

Greybull River

290

Bridger-Teton
National Forest

0   20 mi

0   20 km

➤ **Location:** The snow-capped volcanic peaks of the Absaroka Mountains flanking the eastern boundaries of the park are the source for the Yellowstone and Lamar River systems, which are home to native Yellowstone cutthroat trout.

The headwaters of the Yellowstone River begin at Younts Peak, which is located south of Yellowstone Park in Wyoming's vast road-less wilderness area called the Thorofare (made famous by mountain man John Coulter).

The fly fishing is outstanding in this wilderness area. However, access to the Thorofare region requires extra effort, time and planning (backpacking or horse packing) in order to enjoy a successful fishing trip.

Anglers should focus their efforts in the park on Yellowstone Lake and the Yellowstone River in the renowned LeHardy Rapids to Mud Volcano section. Native Yellowstone cutthroat can be found throughout the entire Yellowstone River drainage on the east side of the park, including the lake. Both are accessible by vehicle on what is called the Lower Loop Road.

Yellowstone Lake is the largest body of water in Yellowstone National Park. The lake is 7,732 feet above sea level and covers 136 square miles with 110 miles of shoreline. Also, Yellowstone Lake is the largest freshwater lake above 7,000 feet in North America. There are good hatches of mayflies—especially Callibaetis, damsels and caddis—on the lake. If cutthroats are feeding in shallow water, dries or nymphs that imitate these insects will produce. Anglers have better success fishing streamers such as Woolly Buggers and Conehead Zonkers on the lake itself. Where tributaries such as Arnica, Cub and Clear Creek enter the lake, anglers can expect better results matching the hatch or fishing deep with beadhead nymphs.

The lake and its tributaries open to angling June 20 and close the first weekend in November. Fly rods 9 to 10 feet in line sizes 5 to 7 are recommended for fishing the lake. Sinking or sink-tip lines are not necessary unless one is fishing water depths deeper than 10 feet.

Boats with motors must launch at Bridge Bay. Float tubes, canoes, kayaks and one-man pontoon boats can be launched from shore, within reason. Mary Bay, Gull Point, Sand Point, Rock Point and Pumice Point are good places to float and fish the lake.

The Yellowstone River flows out of the lake at Fishing Bridge, a popular tourist attraction. The river is permanently closed in this area to protect native Yellowstone cutthroat. Legal access begins on the river just upstream from LeHardy Rapids. Here, the river fishes like a large spring creek downstream to the Mud Volcano area. In this section, fly fishers can expect good dry-fly fishing from July 15 (opening day) until the park closes to fishing the first weekend in November. Midges, mayflies, caddis, stoneflies and terrestrial insects hatch, or are on the water, the entire season. Nymphs, soft hackles and streamers perform consistently when the trout are not interested in dry flies.

Anglers can also find good fly fishing by accessing the lower Yellowstone River near Tower Fall where a steep, winding trail leads anglers to the river. During late summer,

Clarks Fork of the Yellowstone—Wild & scenic river inside Shoshone National Forest, Cody, Wyoming. Tim Wade

Fishing with buffalo on Slough Creek, Yellowstone National Park. Tim Wade

enterprising fly fishers can fish downstream to the bridge spanning the road leading to Cooke City, Montana, near Roosevelt Lodge.

This section of the Yellowstone River contains Yellowstone cutthroat, rainbow and brown trout and Rocky Mountain whitefish. Large attractor dry flies—Para-hoppers, Royal Trudes, Royal Wulffs, Parachute Adams, Elk-Hair Caddis, Stimulators and Madam X—consistently perform during summer and fall months. Dropping a beadhead nymph under a dry fly or strike indicator, suspended 24 to 30 inches also works well. Five- or 6-weight fly rods matched with weight-forward, floating fly lines do the job on big trout and afternoon winds.

The Lamar River and its two principal tributaries, Slough and Soda Butte Creek, are located in the northeast corner of the park. All flow into the lower Yellowstone a short distance downstream from the Roosevelt/Cooke City roads in the park near the Lamar Picnic Area. Access to the Lamar and its tributaries is best from Cooke City, Montana or Cody, Wyoming,

through either the Northeast or East Gates into Yellowstone.

Like the Yellowstone River, the Lamar River headwaters are in the rugged Absaroka Mountains in Wyoming created during Yellowstone's volcanism period around 50 million years ago. Soda Butte and Slough Creek are sourced from glaciers high in the Beartooth Mountains that define the park's northern boundaries.

All three watersheds provide miles of good trout water and fish well from Memorial Day until the end of the fishing season. All are easily accessed from the Cooke City Road. The same flies suggested for the upper Yellowstone River are effective throughout the east side of Yellowstone.

Once strictly a native Yellowstone cutthroat fishery, the Lamar River, Soda Butte and Slough Creek now have hybridization occurring between non-native rainbows and native cutthroat trout. The U.S. Fish and Wildlife Service and National Park Service implemented a program to remove non-native trout species that inhabit native cutthroat trout habitat. Anglers must now kill all rainbow and rainbow/cutt

Native Yellowstone cutthroat trout caught and released on Lamar River, Yellowstone National Park. Tim Wade

Releasing a Yellowstone cutthroat on Yellowstone River in the Thorofare Wilderness area. Tim Wade

hybrids when caught in the Lamar, Slough or Soda Butte. No exceptions. Yellowstone cutthroat must be released unharmed upon landing.

These three watersheds can fish well as early as late May and continue to do so until the park closes the first weekend in November. Better water conditions exist after spring runoff ends in early July. Early to mid-July is the time for consistent mayfly and caddis activity, with a few late-emerging golden stones or salmonflies on the water to keep the fly fishing interesting.

Grasshoppers, ants and beetles begin to work well around the first of August. These insects often work when matching the hatch becomes difficult. Beadhead nymphs, soft hackles and the ubiquitous Woolly Bugger will serve the angler well when the trout aren't keying on a hatch or chomping terrestrials when given the opportunity.

There is not space to address the park's prolific aquatic insect hatches. Volumes have been written about the hatches and fly patterns. Read up on the subject prior to your planned fishing excursion. Fly boxes should carry a size range of flies. Local fly shops in Cody and Cooke City are a good place to stock up before fishing. One can also have a lot of fun with 3- and 4-weight fly rods with weight-forward floating lines on Slough and Soda Butte Creeks. Four- through 6-weight fly rods are recommended for the Lamar River due to winds and distances.

➤ **The East Side of Yellowstone:** The angler cannot fish the east side of the park without also sampling the North Fork of the Shoshone or Clarks Fork of the Yellowstone River located, literally, over the Absaroka Mountains, which divide Yellowstone Park from the state of Wyoming.

Like their counterparts inside the park, the Clarks Fork and the North Fork, as they are locally known, provide excellent fly fishing March through November. Peak times on these Wyoming rivers are the same as those inside the park, July through November. These rivers and their tributaries are located within Shoshone National Forest, our nation's first preserve set aside for the enjoyment of the public and managed as multiple use from the beginning. Both rivers offer an extraordinary amount of Forest Service and Bureau of Land Management land on which to fish and enjoy the abundant wildlife and scenery.

➤ **North Fork Shoshone River:** The North Fork of the Shoshone River has been rated one of the top 10 freestone rivers in the Rocky Mountains. You must fish it at some point in your angling career. Public access is 24 miles west of Cody inside the Shoshone National Forest on the road to the east entrance. Thirty miles of the North Fork is yours to enjoy. Rainbow, native Yellowstone cutthroat, Rocky Mountain whitefish and brown trout inhabit the river.

Like the Yellowstone and Lamar Rivers, the North Fork trout are wild and average 16 inches, with many much larger than that. The North Fork also has numerous tributaries that fish well, too. Grab some bear spray and bushwhack up these excellent feeder streams for a great day of fishing on the Elk Fork, Sweetwater, Fishhawk, Grinnell, Eagle or Middle Creeks.

Take note, North Fork trout love to eat big flies, dry or wet. Leader up (2X and 4X leaders and tippets are recommended) and use fast action 5- and 6-weight fly rods to facilitate landing and releasing these hot trout. Floating lines are perfect for all-round use. A fly reel with at least 50 yards of backing, fly line and good drag is advised.

Spring runoff at Pebble Creek, Yellowstone National Park. Tim Wade

➤ **Clarks Fork of the Yellowstone:** The Clarks Fork of the Yellowstone is Wyoming's first Federally Designated Wild & Scenic River. Once seen, it is easily understood why the river has that designation. Surrounded by the Absaroka and Beartooth Mountains, the Clarks Fork is more remote for most of its length than its sister, the North Fork of the Shoshone.

When discussing the Clarks Fork, it's best to divide it into three sections—lower, middle and upper:

Lower: Thirty minutes from downtown Cody on Wyoming 120, the lower Clarks Fork of the Yellowstone can be accessed at a number of angler access points. These are in order:

· Edelweiss, County road 8UC
· County Road 8WC
· County Road 8VE
· Wyoming 294
· County Road 8VC

From these roads, anglers have miles of the lower Clarks Fork to enjoy in relative solitude much of the time. The lower river runs through a wide glacial valley. Here, the river is 30 to 40 yards wide and has riffles, runs, chutes and pocket water. Brown, rainbow, cuttbow hybrids, native Yellowstone cutthroat and Rocky Mountain whitefish reside in the lower river. Browns and rainbows run large, while the other species average 13 inches.

Middle: The middle section of the Clarks Fork is accessed by driving Wyoming 120, turning left onto Chief Joseph Scenic Highway (Wyoming 296) and following the road until arriving at Dead Indian and Sunlight Creeks. These two creeks are fun free-flowing streams with native cutthroat up to 18 inches and lots of brook trout to keep one busy when the cutthroat are inactive. The water is best described as fast with lots of pocket water and downfalls that hold good numbers of brook and native cutts.

· Access to Dead Indian is from Wyoming 296 at Dead Indian Campground.
· Access to Sunlight Creek is from Wyoming 296 onto Sunlight Basin Road, a few miles up the road from Dead Indian Campground. Follow the dirt road to Wyoming Game and Fish Angler access signs, or designated Shoshone Forest campground signs upstream to Little Sunlight Creek, where bear closures limit vehicular travel.

Like Dead Indian Creek, Sunlight Creek is a major tributary to the Clarks Fork of the Yellowstone and provides lots of fly-rod action from brook trout and smaller native cutthroat. Sunlight Creek also has a canyon section, but access is difficult. Good physical condition is a must before tackling the canyon of Sunlight Creek or the canyon of the Clarks Fork River.

Crandall Creek flows into the upper section of the Clarks Fork. Wyoming 296 crosses the creek one mile from the community of Painter Estates. Access to Crandall Creek and some of its tributaries is by foot or horseback via the Crandall Creek Pack Station. The turnout is less than 200 yards north from where the highway crosses the creek. One must hike one mile around private property before it is legal to fish. North Crandall and Timber Creeks are upstream from the pack station as well.

Upper: After exploring Crandall Creek, the upper Clarks Fork section begins at Painter Estates. There are several campgrounds and turnouts from Wyoming 296 that provide relatively easy access to the river. There are also numerous glacial lakes found in the upper Beartooth Plateau, which provide much of the Clarks Fork flow. These lakes provide additional fly-fishing opportunities should the upper river go to sleep or prove difficult to fish. The elevation of the upper river is 7,000 feet and higher. Many of the lakes that drain into the upper river sit at an elevation from 8,000-9,500 feet. The growing season is short at these elevations so the size of the trout goes down compared to the sizes caught at lower elevations. The Clarks Fork is full of small rainbow, native cutthroat and brook trout with the occasional Arctic grayling caught from time to time. Size runs 4 to 16 inches.

Expect lots of 10- to 12-inch trout when fishing the middle and upper sections of the Clarks Fork. The river, its contributing glacial lakes and tributaries, are perfectly suited for 0- through 3-weight rods. Hatches are the same as those found inside Yellowstone or on the North Fork of the Shoshone. Carry a good assortment of dries and nymphs in sizes 10 to 20 to match the insect hatches. Ant, beetle and smaller grasshopper flies might be all one needs July through September.

More than 2.2 million acres of prime fly-fishing real estate has been given an overview within this chapter. It would take a lifetime to fish all of the waters available to anglers on the east side of the park. Study the books and publications that cover these waters in more detail to ensure a quality fly-fishing experience. More importantly, explore and enjoy the many waters available to anglers in our National Park System.

➤ **Tackle and Gear**

Rods and Line: In Yellowstone Lake, 5- to 7-weight rods (9- to 10-feet long) with size 5-7 lines. Sinking or sink-tip lines are great when fishing deep. When fishing the Yellowstone River, we recommend 5- or 6-weight fly rods matched with weight forward, floating fly lines. When fishing the Slough and Soda Butte Creeks, 3- and 4-weight fly rods with weight forward floating lines on . 4-6-weight fly rods are recommended for the Lamar River. In the North Fork Shoshone River, 2X and 4X leaders and tippets are recommended on fast action 5- and 6-weight fly rods. Floating lines are perfect for all-round use. A fly reel with at least 50 yards of backing, fly line and good drag is advised. When fishing Clarks Fork, 0- through 3-weight rods are recommended.

Terminal Tackle and Flies: In Yellowstone Lake, Callibaetis, damsels and caddis imitations are effective for cutthroats. If the cutts are feeding in shallow water, dries or nymphs are the ticket. Wooly Buggers and Cone-Head Zonkers also are solid producers. When fishing the Yellowstone River, Para-hoppers, Royal Trudes or Wulffs, Parachute Adams, Elk Hair Caddis, Stimulators and Madam X are solid producers during summer and fall. Dropping a bead-head nymph under a dry fly or strike indicator, suspended 24- to 30-inches also works well. Terrestrials work well starting in early August. In Clarks Fork, dries and nymphs in sizes 10 to 20 to match the insect hatches are musts. Ant, beetle and smaller grasshopper flies are primary flies July through September.

Angler having fun on north fork of the Shoshone River, Shoshone National Forest. Tim Wade

AROUND THE PARK

Note that opening and closing dates, regulations, and fees are discussed in the Introduction section of this chapter. Specific guides, outfitters, restaurants, and other services listed here apply generally to the area we've labeled Yellowstone National Park, East.

CLOSEST CITY OR POINT OF ENTRANCE TO THE PARK

Cody, Wyoming

CLOSEST AIRPORT

Yellowstone Regional Airport is a few miles east of Cody. Both Delta and United provide daily service to and from Denver and Salt Lake International Airports. The airport is two miles from accommodations and dining in downtown Cody.

Yellowstone Regional Airport
2101 Roger Sedam Dr.
Cody, WY 82414
307-587-5096
For private airplane fuel service, contact Choice Aviation:
307-587-9262
csr@choiceaviation.com

CLOSEST FLY SHOPS

North Fork Anglers
1107 Sheridan Ave.
Cody, WY 82414
307-527-7274
flyfish@wavecom.net
www.northforkanglers.com

Grub Steak Expeditions
2340 Meadowlark Ct.
Cody, WY 82414
307-527-6316
307-899-9234
tour2yellowstone@gmail.com
www.tourtoyellowstone.com
(Tour Yellowstone)

CLOSEST GUIDE AND OUTFITTER SERVICES

North Fork Anglers
1107 Sheridan Ave.
Cody, WY 82414
307-527-7274
flyfish@wavecom.net
www.northforkanglers.com

Grub Steak Expeditions
2340 Meadowlark Ct.
Cody, WY 82414
307-527-6316
307-899-9234
tour2yellowstone@gmail.com
www.tourtoyellowstone.com
(Tour Yellowstone)

Wyoming Adventures
932 Arapahoe
Thermopolis, WY 82443
307-272-6792
anglingadv@yahoo.com
www.flyfishbighorn.com

Rocky Mountain Sports
1526 Rumsey Ave.
Cody, WY 82414
307-527-6071
www.rocky-mountain-sports.com

LODGING, GUEST RANCHES, INFORMATION

Cody has more than 35 motel/hotel properties. The Cody and The Ivy are two of Cody's premier lodging establishments. Both are minutes from Yellowstone Regional Airport and downtown Cody. For lodging, public campgrounds and general information, contact

Cody Visitor Center /
Cody Chamber of Commerce
800-393-2639
www.yellowstonecountry.org

GUEST AND DUDE RANCHES ON ROAD TO EAST ENTRANCE

Bill Cody Ranch
2604 Yellowstone Hwy.
Cody, WY 82414
307-587-2097
billcody@billcodyranch.com
www.billcodyranch.com

Elephant Head Lodge
1170 Yellowstone Hwy.
Cody, WY 82414
307-587-3980
vacation@elephantheadlodge.com
www.elephantheadlodge.com

Shoshone Lodge
349 Yellowstone Hwy.
Cody, WY 82414
307-587-4044
shoshonelodge@gmail.com
www.shoshonelodge.com

Pahaska Tepee
183 Yellowstone Hwy.
Cody, WY 82414
800-628-7791
pahaska@pahaska.com or www.pahaska.com

CAMPGROUNDS

· Campgrounds are open seasonally, generally June-September.
· Contact the Shoshone National Forest to inquire about campgrounds for hard-sided campers and tent campers. Campgrounds in Shoshone National Forest and inside YNP do have restrictions concerning grizzly bears.
· Either agency can answer questions regarding campground reservations.

Shoshone National Forest
808 Meadow Lane
Cody, WY 82414
307-527-6241
www.fs.usda.gov/shoshone

Yellowstone National Park Lodges
Reservation Department
P.O. Box 165
Yellowstone National Park, WY 82190
307-344-7311 or 866-439-7375
info-ynp@xanterra.com
www.yellowstonenationalparklodges.com

CLOSEST/BEST CAMPGROUND

Ponderosa Campground
1815 Eighth St.
Cody, WY 82414
307-587-9203
www.codyponderosa.com

BEST PLACE TO STAY IN THE PARK

Lake Yellowstone Hotel
The Lake Yellowstone Hotel and Cabins opened in 1891 and is listed on the National Register of Historic Places.
866-256-9046

Old Faithful Inn Complex (includes Old Faithful Lodge and the Snow Lodge)

The Old Faithful Inn
1 Grand Loop Rd.
Yellowstone National Park, WY 82190
http://www.yellowstonenationalparklodges.com/lodging/summer-lodges/old-faithful-inn/
reserve-ynp@xanterra.com
Reservations for lodging and camping
· Direct: 307-344-7311
· Dinner Reservations: 307-344-7311
· In-Park Lodge/Guest Information: 307-344-7901

TIM WADE grew up in California and began fishing around the age of five. He spent his formative years fishing the Sierra with his parents and siblings. It was on the Kern River where he caught his first trout on a fly. Since then, he has fished the world for any species of fish that would whack a hook covered with fur and feathers. Fly fishing and fly tying have been Tim's passion since age 16. Gaining a driver's license and receiving a car as a birthday present opened up an entirely different world of fly fishing. Tim is a life member of TU and the IFFF and has been actively involved in both organizations since the early 1970s. He founded several chapters in Wyoming for both organizations to help protect coldwater, warmwater and saltwater fisheries. Tim moved to Cody, Wyoming in 1981. In 1984, he became a licensed fly-fishing outfitter and founded North Fork Fly and Tackle, a mail-order and outfitting business. In 1987, friends and clients talked him into opening a fly shop in downtown Cody. The fly shop and guiding/outfitting operation was subsequently renamed North Fork Anglers.

He has received the Wyoming Outdoor Writers Association award several times for his weekly *Streamside* column in the *Cody Enterprise*. Tim has also been featured on ESPN Outdoors, TU TV, TNN Outdoors, Americana Outdoors, the Outdoor Channel, and most recently a three-year stint on Trout TV.

Old Faithful Snow Lodge

2305 Old Faithful
Yellowstone National Park, WY 82190
http://www.yellowstonenationalparklodges.
com/lodging/winter-lodges/old-faithful-
snow-lodge-cabins/
Reservations for lodging and camping
· Direct: 307-344-7311
· Dinner Reservations: 307-344-7311
· In-Park Lodge/Guest Information:
  307-344-7901

BEST PLACES TO EAT IN THE PARK

Lake Yellowstone Hotel

1 Grand Loop Rd.
Yellowstone National Park, WY 82190
866-256-9046

Old Faithful Inn Restaurant

1 Grand Loop Rd.
Yellowstone National Park, WY 82190
307-344-7311

Fishing Bridge General Store

1 East Entrance Rd.
Yellowstone National Park, WY 82190
The counter restaurant at the Fishing Bridge Store makes a great burger with fries! Topping the meal off with some huckleberry ice cream is one of life's great pleasures.

MUST SEE

Upper and Lower Falls of the Yellowstone and West Thumb Geyser Basin
Must see in Cody: Buffalo Bill's Center of the West, a complex of five museums under one roof

NEAREST HOSPITAL/URGENT TREATMENT CENTER

West Park Hospital

707 Sheridan Ave.
Cody, WY 82414
307-527-7501
800-654-9447

Cathcart Urgent Care

42 Yellowstone Ave.
Suite 120
Cody, WY 82414
307-578-2903

Yellowstone National Park Medical Services

· Emergency medical services are provided by rangers on duty.
· Call 911 in case of an emergency.
· Medical services are available year round, except some holidays, at Mammoth Clinic: 307-344-7965.

· Services are also offered seasonally in the summer at Lake Clinic, 307-242-7241, and at Old Faithful Clinic, 307-545-7325.
· All of the park clinics are open to the public and are staffed and equipped for most medical emergencies as well as for routine care. Services include injury and illness treatment, x-rays, and some lab and pharmacy services.
· If in-patient care or advanced services are required, the clinic staff can stabilize patients and arrange for appropriate transfer to a hospital outside the park.

CELL PHONE SERVICE

Cell phone service is good in the Cody area. Service is spotty at best in the mountains bordering Yellowstone and inside Yellowstone Park itself. Coverage with Verizon and AT&T is good within a 20-mile circle from Cody. There is service at Lake Overlook, Fishing Bridge, Canyon and Lake Hotel.

FOR ALL ELSE, VISIT

www.nps.gov/yell/index.htm

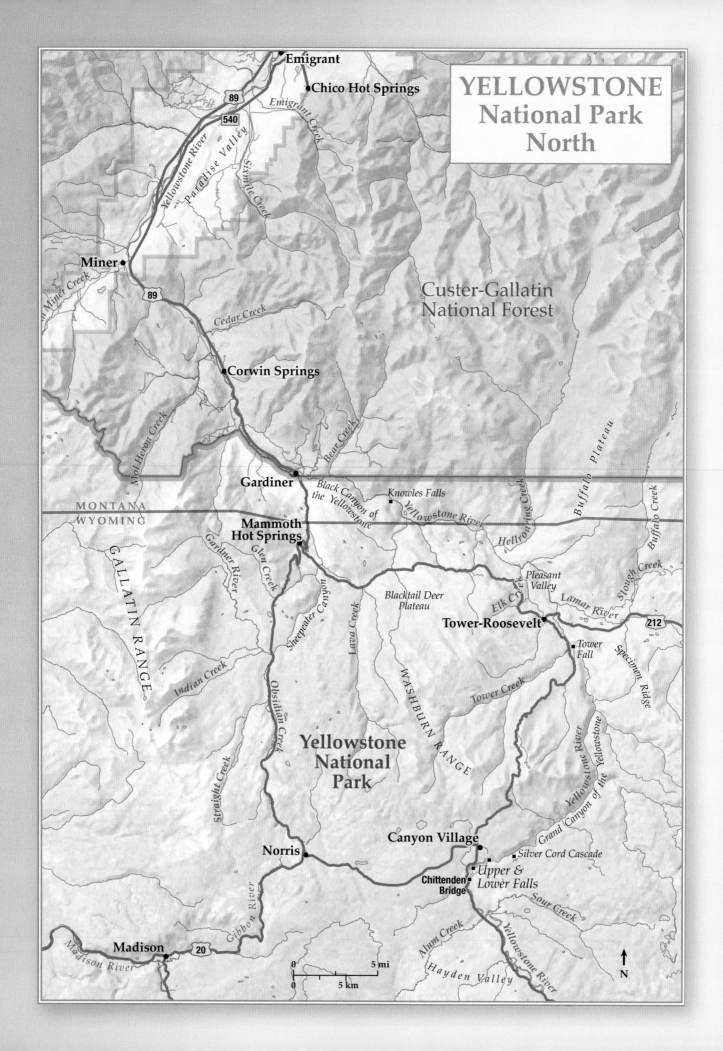

YELLOWSTONE
National Park
North

Emigrant

Chico Hot Springs

89

540

Yellowstone River

Paradise Valley

Sixmile Creek

Emigrant Creek

Miner

Miner Creek

89

Mol Heron Creek

Cedar Creek

Corwin Springs

Custer-Gallatin
National Forest

Bear Creek

Gardiner

*Black Canyon of
the Yellowstone*

Knowles Falls

Yellowstone River

Hellroaring Creek

Buffalo Plateau

MONTANA
WYOMING

Mammoth
Hot Springs

GALLATIN RANGE

Gardiner River

Glen Creek

Sheepeater Canyon

Lava Creek

Blacktail Deer
Plateau

Pleasant
Valley

Elk Creek

Tower-Roosevelt

Lamar River

Slough Creek

Buffalo Creek

212

Indian Creek

Obsidian Creek

Straight Creek

Yellowstone
National
Park

WASHBURN RANGE

Tower Creek

Tower
Fall

Specimen Ridge

Yellowstone River

Grand Canyon of the Yellowstone

Canyon Village

Silver Cord Cascade

Norris

Gibbon River

Chittenden
Bridge

Upper &
Lower Falls

Alum Creek

Sour Creek

Madison

Madison River

20

Hayden Valley

Yellowstone River

0   5 mi

0   5 km

↑
N

➤ **Location:** The north-central part of Yellowstone National Park is drained by the main stem of the Yellowstone River and its tributary, the Gardner River, as well as portions of the Lamar River drainage (discussed in the Yellowstone East section of this chapter). This part of the park offers some of the region's most-varied fishing, from tiny meadow streams full of brook trout to raging canyon rivers home to solid cut-throats. It also features Yellowstone's second-best brown trout run. In short, this part of the park offers something for just about everybody.

Good base areas for this part of the park include the town of Gardiner, Mammoth Hot Springs, Tower-Roosevelt, and Canyon Village. Additional campgrounds at Tower Fall, Indian Creek, and Slough Creek are also good choices, while the towns of Cooke City and West Yellowstone, plus several other campgrounds, also make sense if you're up for a bit of a drive.

Both the Yellowstone and Gardner have many excellent tributary streams that offer great small-stream fishing. The species composition of these creeks varies, as does the difficulty in accessing them. If you're interested in small streams, ask area fly shops for details. These creeks typically fish best from early July through early September, and you usually don't need anything but attractor dries, small hoppers, and a few beadhead nymphs. There are also several good small lakes in this part of the park. These lakes hold everything from grayling to some of the park's largest brook trout. Most lakes in this area require a hike of 45 minutes to an hour, though there are also several lakes near the road and several others that require more strenuous hikes.

You should bring at least two fly rods if you plan to fish this part of the park. A 9-foot 6-weight is ideal for the rivers. Rig these rods with floating lines and leaders tapered to 2-4X, but also have a short sink-tip available in case the trout want streamers. A much lighter rod, say an 8-foot, 3- or 4-weight rod rigged with a floating line and a leader tapered to 4X, is great for smaller streams. You should also bring your backpack and boots since a lot of the best water in this part of the park is ideal for anglers who like to walk. Just be sure to have a good map, plenty of water, and bear spray.

➤ **Yellowstone River—Grand and Black Canyon Sections:**

From Chittenden Bridge to the town of Gardiner where it leaves the park, the Yellowstone River cuts the park's two largest canyons. The first and deeper of these is the Grand Canyon, which is about 15 miles long. The upper Grand Canyon, in the vicinity of the famous Upper and Lower Falls of the Yellowstone, is permanently (and sensibly) closed to angling to protect visitors.

Black Canyon of the Yellowstone. Walter Wiese

The river reopens at Silver Cord Cascade roughly two miles downstream, where the canyon widens slightly and the walls aren't quite as steep. This central portion of the Grand Canyon, from Silver Cord Cascade down to within two miles of the mouth of Tower Creek, is an athlete's dream. This water is accessible only by strenuous hikes of 5-6 miles each way

Large Black Canyon hybrid. Walter Wiese

involving huge amounts of climbing. In the lower canyon, from two miles above Tower Creek down to the Lamar River confluence, access is much easier, with hikes of a half-mile to two miles to put you on the water. Small portions of the lower Grand Canyon can even be accessed right off the Northeast Entrance Road Bridge, though of course the water under the bridge sees heavy pressure.

The Grand Canyon occasionally fishes well right from the park opener in late May, but more often it drops out of runoff between June 15 and June 25. It fishes well from this point until late September or early October. The Grand Canyon is home primarily to cutthroat trout averaging 10 to 13 inches, with reasonable numbers of fish to 18 inches. There are also small numbers of rainbow and cuttbow hybrids in the same size range and a handful of dink brook trout.

The Black Canyon begins at the Lamar confluence and extends to the mouth of the Gardner River just upstream of Gardiner, where the river leaves the park. This chunk of water is about 20 miles long. The Black Canyon is not as extreme as the Grand Canyon. Short sections of sheer canyon walls divide long stretches where the river flows between benches covered in grass and sagebrush, places where only a short, steep climb down through boulders and scree is necessary to reach the river. Virtually the entire Black Canyon is paralleled by hiking trails, and two foot bridges make it possible to access both banks. This is still a very rugged, physically demanding stretch of river. Accessing them requires hikes and some climbing. Some hikes are only a bit over a mile in length, though many are much longer.

The Black Canyon only becomes fishable before July 4 during drought years due to the influence of snowmelt out of the Lamar system. It can fish well from this point through the close of the park season, with late-season fishing particularly good in the bottom couple miles of the canyon near Gardiner. After thunderstorms muddy the Lamar, the Black Canyon can get too dirty to fish for a couple days at a time. This typically happens three or four times each season. While cutthroats predominate throughout the Black Canyon, there are also plenty of rainbows and hybrids. At Knowles Falls—seven miles upstream of Gardiner—brown trout join the mix. You'll also find some whitefish from a short distance above the falls down. Most trout range from 10 to 18 inches, but there are a few fish in the 22- to 24-inch class.

The canyons fish similarly, save for slightly different peak seasons and the greater potential for mud in the Black Canyon. The Yellowstone in the canyons is deep, fast, and often quite narrow and rough. Wading deeper than your knees is usually a poor idea, and you can often fish right from the shore. Early in the season, the structure is limited to eddies and pockets along the bank. As the season progresses, boulder fields off the banks and occasional riffles and runs also produce fish, but the bank-side structure continues to fish well all year wherever the current runs tight to the bank. Plan to cover the water quickly. The fish here are not picky, except during hatches; either they'll eat or they won't. If they're not eating in one spot, move on to the next. The fish in the canyons tend to pod up, so once you find the fish, you'll find a lot of them.

Streamers work well all season, particularly combos of a large Woolly Bugger trailing a small one.

Salmonflies and Golden stoneflies begin hatching between the middle of June and the first week of July, and can last until the first week of August near cold tributary streams, especially following winters with heavy snowfall. Accompanying these large bugs are Yellow Sallies, several species of caddisflies, and occasionally some Pale Morning Duns or Green Drakes. These insects hatch through July and into early August. Because of the wide variety of natural insects and the fast water, attractor dry flies are typically more effective than hatch-matching flies. Coachman Trudes and Chubby Chernobyls are probably the best bets overall. Drop a beadhead attractor nymph behind your dry.

In August and September, attractors continue to work, but terrestrials are usually better. Large grasshoppers and crickets are the most popular choices, but don't neglect small hoppers and ants, as well.

In September, mayfly hatches intensify and continue until cold weather shuts down the fishing. Blue-winged Olives predominate, but Tan Drakes (T. hecuba) and Mahoganies are also common. Don't hesitate to fish a Purple Haze Cripple or similar attractor dry instead of a precise mayfly imitation during fall hatches. The trout here love purple.

➤ **Gardner River:** In its upper reaches, the Gardner River is a small stream that's an easy, pretty hike off the Mammoth-Norris Road. This stretch runs from the river's headwaters in the deep backcountry near the crest of the Gallatin Range to Indian Creek Campground, where the river comes into sight of the road for one-half mile. The river typically runs 20 feet wide here. It occasionally breaks into pocket water where it cuts between hills, but more often it's a gentle riffle-pool stream. It's chock full of 6- to 9-inch brook trout, which makes this ideal water for beginners. The Gardner's tributaries in this reach all offer similar fishing to the main stem, but several are even easier to access.

Large Black Canyon cutthroat. Walter Wiese

The middle portion of the Gardner, from the vicinity of Sheepeater Cascade to a mile upstream of the Mammoth-Tower Road, flows through Sheepeater Canyon, a narrow, rugged canyon that is challenging to access and holds brook and rainbow trout no larger than those upstream. Unless you're a sucker for punishment, ignore this stretch.

The lower Gardner, from the mouth of tiny Glen Creek at the bottom of Sheepeater Canyon to the Gardner's confluence with the Yellowstone near Gardiner, Montana (yes, town and river are spelled differently), could not be more different than the upper river. It's much larger, much faster, much steeper, much rockier, and home to a mixed bag of trout. Rainbows predominate, but there are also some cutthroats and cuttbows, brook trout, brown trout, and whitefish. While the average trout in this stretch run from 8 to 13 inches, some can get quite large. This is particularly true in the fall, when a great run of browns enters the Gardner from the Yellowstone. The fall-run browns average 14 to 18 inches, but every year several of my shop's clients catch one between 22 and 25 inches.

The lower Gardner is primarily a fast-flowing, turbulent river flowing as endless pocket water in a shallow, steep-walled trench with banks covered in sagebrush and meadow grasses, with occasional patches of willows, cottonwoods, evergreens, and aspens to catch your backcast. Portions of the riverbanks are canyon-like, making access impossible for 50 or a 100 yards at a time. There are also several short meadows.

Access to the lower Gardner is very good. Upstream of the Mammoth-Tower Road Bridge, game trails and angler tracks from the bridge lead down to the water. Downstream of this bridge, the river is either beside the North Entrance Road or a hike of no more than a mile away from it for the river's remaining five-mile run to Gardiner. That's not to say access is easy. This is primarily a rough, fast, boulder-strewn body of water that requires anglers to do a bit of climbing or scrambling to reach the river, and then be steady on their feet once there.

The lower Gardner can fish well right from the beginning of the park season. Any time there's a foot of visibility or more, it's worth pounding large stonefly and attractor nymphs tight to the banks. The early-season fishing can be particularly effective below Boiling River, a major hot spring that enters about three miles upstream of the Yellowstone. The fishing gets much more consistent in late June, when runoff recedes and the Salmonfly and Golden Stonefly hatches begin. The lower Gardner is an ideal habitat for these insects, and hatches are heavy. Nymphs are usually more productive than dries, but dries can also draw good action. Don't hesitate to fish these drowned, just under the surface.

In July and August, fishing attractor dries or grasshoppers with beadhead droppers is the most effective technique. There are also occasional evening caddis hatches. The water below Boiling River can get quite warm in August, so it's usually best to fish the extreme lower Gardner only in the morning in late summer unless the weather has been cool.

In September, hopper/dropper rigs continue to work well, but the first pushes of fall browns begin. The fishing for these brutes gets better and better until the middle of October, when it reaches a crescendo that lasts almost until the close of the

Above. Lower Gardner River fall-run brown trout pool. Walter Wiese

Inset. Typical upper Gardner River brook trout— just prettier than most. Walter Wiese

park season. Look for these big browns in the deeper pools on sunny days, but they might also be in the larger, turbulent pockets on gray, cold days. These fish attack large stonefly and attractor nymphs, and in October egg patterns can also produce. The fish move into shallow water to spawn beginning around October 20. Please leave the shallow spawners to do their business in peace. There's still plenty of fish in deep water. October also brings occasional Blue-winged Olive hatches. The big browns seldom eat these, but every resident trout in the river will.

➤ **Tackle and Gear**

Rods and Line: A 9-foot 6-weight (rigged with floating lines and leaders tapered to 2-4X) is ideal for the rivers. A short sink-tip is good for streamers. An 8-foot, 3- or 4-weight rod rigged with a floating line and a leader tapered to 4X, is great for smaller streams.

Terminal Tackle and Flies: In the tributary streams to the Yellowstone and Gardner Rivers, attractor dries, small hoppers, and a few beadhead nymphs are key. In the canyons, streamers work well all season, particularly combos of a large Woolly Bugger trailing a small one. Salmonflies and Golden Stoneflies begin hatching between the middle of June and the first week of July. Yellow Sallies, several caddis imitations, Pale Morning Duns, and Green Drakes are good to have on hand. Because of the wide variety of natural insects and the fast water, attractor dry flies are typically more effective than hatch-matching flies. Coachman Trudes and Chubby Chernobyls are probably the best bets overall. The trout in these waters love purple, so be sure to have some Purple Haze Cripples on hand. In the lower Gardner, fishing attractor dries or grasshoppers with beadhead droppers is the most effective technique. There are also occasional evening caddis hatches. In September, hopper/dropper rigs continue to work well. Large stonefly and attractor nymphs and October egg patterns will entice big browns to strike.

Both the Yellowstone and Gardner Rivers hold excellent populations of Salmonflies. Walter Wiese

Cascade Lake in the Yellowstone drainage holds Arctic grayling. Walter Wiese

Below. Angler working an ideal pool on the Gardner for fall-run browns. Walter Wiese

Inset. Beautiful Grand Canyon of the Yellowstone cuttbow hybrid. Walter Wiese

AROUND THE PARK

Note that opening and closing dates, regulations, and fees are discussed in the Introduction section of this chapter. Specific guides, outfitters, restaurants, and other services listed here apply generally to the area we've labeled Yellowstone National Park, North.

Gardiner, Montana is the entry point and base of operations for this part of the park as well as fishing on the famous Paradise Valley section of the Yellowstone River and other waters in southwest Montana. Gardiner serves as the north entrance to Yellowstone Park and is where the famous "Roosevelt Arch" stands.

CLOSEST AIRPORT

Bozeman Yellowstone International Airport (BZN), just west of Bozeman, Montana—Direct flights are seasonally available from many major cities in the continental United States, while year-round connecting flights are available through Las Vegas, Seattle, Salt Lake City, Minneapolis, and Denver. This airport is less than 90 miles from Gardiner and the park's north entrance via Interstate 90 and U.S. Route 89, both excellent and scenic highways. Bozeman and Livingston (78 miles northwest and 53 miles north of Gardiner by road, respectively) provide abundant shopping and dining opportunities and nightlife, as well as medical services.

OPENING/CLOSING PARK DATES OR FISHING DATES

All major waters in this part of the park follow the general regulations found in the Introduction section of this chapter. However, several minor waters, including one pond and a couple short sections of creek, open later (precise opening dates vary). Additional short-term closures may apply due to bear activity, wildfires, or drought conditions. Check current regulations or ask in local fly shops for specifics on these non-standard regulations.

CLOSEST FLY SHOPS

One dedicated fly shop serves Gardiner. There are also many fly shops in Bozeman, Livingston, and Paradise Valley as well as several whitewater raft companies and other businesses in Gardiner that offer

some fly tackle, and in some cases, guided fishing trips. The following shops are located within about 30 miles of Gardiner and focus their summer business exclusively on fly fishing. Note that fly tackle selection at stores within the park is very limited.

Parks' Fly Shop
202 Second St. South (US-89)
Gardiner, MT 59030
406-848-7314
http //www.parksflyshop.com
richard@parksflyshop.com or
ycflyfishing@gmail.com

Angler's West
Emigrant, MT 59207
406-333-4401
http //www.montanaflyfishers.com

CLOSEST GUIDE/OUTFITTER SERVICE

Yellowstone Country Fly Fishing
(serving YNP via Parks' Fly Shop, and the author's business)
P.O. Box 182
Gardiner, MT 59030
406-223-8204
http //www.montanafishing.guide,
http //www.ycflyfishing.com or
ycflyfishing@gmail.com

Hubbard's Yellowstone Lodge
287 Tom Miner Creek Rd.
Emigrant, MT 59027
406-848-7755
http //www.hubbardslodge.com/
info@hubbardslodge.com

Dome Mountain Ranch
2017 U.S. Route 89 South
Emigrant, MT 59027
800-313-4868
http //www.domemountainranch.com/
jim@domemountainranch.com

BEST PLACES TO STAY IN THE PARK

All Yellowstone National Park lodgings besides campgrounds are reserved by contacting Yellowstone National Park Lodges at 866-439-7375 or http //www.yellowstonenationalparklodges.com.

Mammoth Hot Springs Hotel & Cabins
Grand Loop Rd.
Yellowstone National Park, WY 82190
307-344-7311

Roosevelt Lodge Cabins
1 Grand Loop Rd.
Yellowstone National Park, WY 82190
307-344-7311

BEST PLACES TO STAY NEAR THE PARK

Yellowstone River Motel
14 Park St.
Gardiner, MT 59030
406-848-7303
http //www.yellowstonerivermotel.com
sleep@yellowstonerivermotel.com
(budget motel)

Yellowstone Basin Inn
4 Maiden Basin Dr.
Gardiner, MT 59030
406-848-7080
http //www.yellowstonebasininn.com
innkeeper@yellowstonebasininn.com
(high-end hotel)

Gardiner Guesthouse
P.O. Box 173
112 Main St. East
Gardiner, MT 59030
406-848-9414
http //www.gardinerguesthouse.com
innkeeper@gardinerguesthouse.com
(bed & breakfast)

Riverside Cottages
P.O. Box 677
521 Scott St. West
Gardiner, MT 59030
http //www.riversidecottages.com
info@riversidecottages.com
(rental cabins)

CAMPGROUNDS

Canyon Campground (outside YNP in the Gallatin National Forest)
· Located 16 miles north of Gardiner on U.S. Route 89
· First-come, first-served

Tower Fall Campground (in YNP)
· Located two miles south of Tower Junction on the Grand Loop Rd.
· First-come, first-served

BEST PLACES TO EAT IN THE PARK

Make all dining reservations inside Yellowstone Park by contacting Yellowstone National Park Lodges at 866-439-7375 or http //www.yellowstonenationalparklodges.com.

Roosevelt Lodge Old West Dinner Cookout
1 Grand Loop Rd.
Yellowstone National Park, WY 82190
307-344-7311

WALTER WIESE (pronounced wee-zee) is owner/outfitter of Yellowstone Country Fly Fishing and head guide at Parks' Fly Shop, in Gardiner, Montana. He has been fly fishing since age six, tying since age 11, and guiding since 2001. He became a USCG-licensed Captain in 2012, is a contract fly designer for Montana Fly Company and is a commercial fly tyer. His writing has appeared in *Fly Rod & Reel, American Angler, Fly Fishing & Tying Journal, Flyfisher*, and many smaller publications, and he is the author of three books and e-books about fly fishing. His most-recent e-book is *Fly Fishing Yellowstone Country—A Basic Guide to Fly Fishing Yellowstone Park and Southern Montana*. Contact Walter at ycflyfishing@gmail.com, http //www.montanafishing.guide and http //www.ycfly-fishing.com or catch him snowboarding or skiing at Bridger Bowl near Bozeman.

PLACES TO EAT NEAR GARDINER

Yellowstone Pizza Company
210 Park St.
Gardiner, MT 59030
406-848-9991

Lighthouse Restaurant
752 Montana 89 South
Corwin Springs, MT 59030
406-848-2138
(ethnic and eclectic)

The Raven Grill
220 West Park St.
Gardiner, MT 59030
406-848-7600
(high-end but casual)

BEST PLACE TO GET A DRINK INSIDE THE PARK

Roosevelt Lodge Dining Room
866-439-7375
http //www.yellowstonenational
parklodges.com.

BEST PLACE TO GET A DRINK OUTSIDE THE PARK

Iron Horse Bar & Grill
212 Spring St.
Gardiner, MT 59030
406-848-7888

MUST SEE

Tower Fall, a 132-foot fall on Tower Creek, a major Yellowstone River tributary. It doesn't hurt that the fishing in the Yellowstone just down the hill is excellent.

NEAREST HOSPITAL/URGENT CARE TREATMENT CENTER

Mammoth Clinic
1 Lower Mammoth
Yellowstone National Park, WY
82190
307-344-7965

CELL PHONE SERVICE

Cell phone service varies wildly depending on location. Generally, locations near developments within Yellowstone Park or communities at park entrances enjoy reasonable service while other locations see spotty service at best. The town of Gardiner itself has excellent service, particularly for Verizon customers.

FOR ALL ELSE, VISIT:
http //www.nps.gov/yell/index.htm

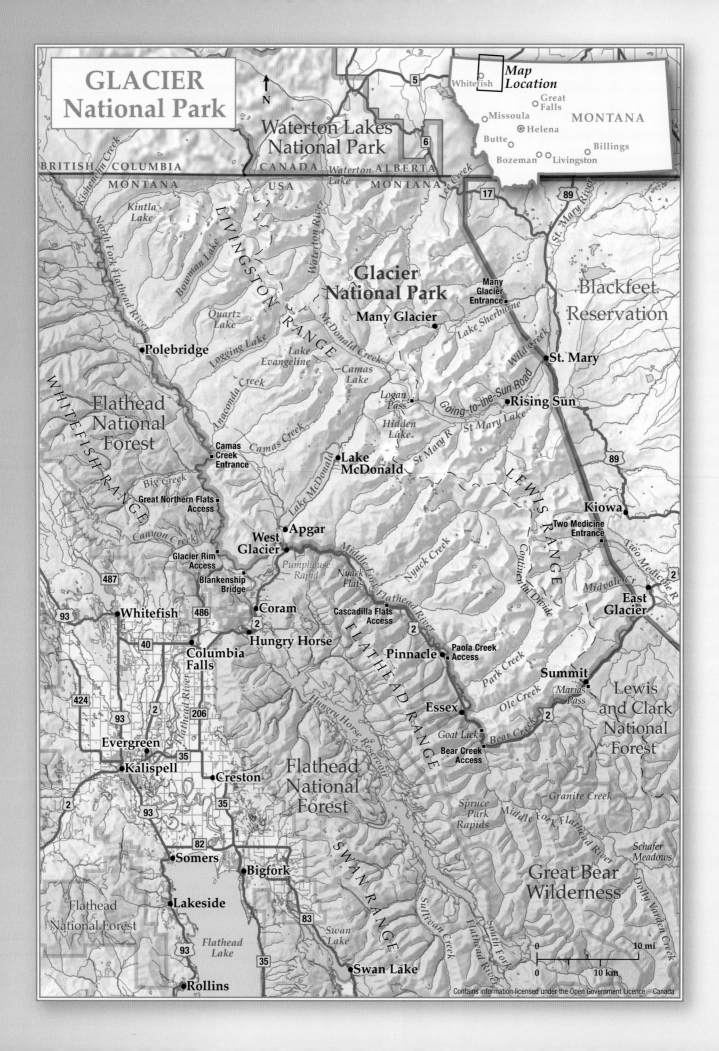

GLACIER
National Park

N

Map Location
Whitefish

Great Falls

Missoula ⊛ Helena   MONTANA

Butte

Bozeman   Livingston   Billings

Waterton Lakes National Park

BRITISH COLUMBIA   CANADA   Waterton ALBERTA
MONTANA   USA   Lake   MONTANA

5

6

17   89

Kishenehn Creek

North Fork Flathead River

Kintla Lake

LIVINGSTON RANGE

Bowman Lake

Quartz Lake

Logging Lake

Lake Evangeline

Anaconda Creek

Lee Creek

Glacier National Park

Many Glacier Entrance

Many Glacier

Lake Sherburne

Wild Creek

Blackfeet Reservation

St. Mary River

St. Mary

McDonald Creek

Camas Lake

Camas Creek

Logan Pass

Hidden Lake

Going-to-the-Sun Road

St Mary Lake

St Mary R

Rising Sun

89

WHITEFISH RANGE

Polebridge

Flathead National Forest

Camas Creek Entrance

Big Creek

Canyon Creek

Great Northern Flats Access

Lake McDonald

Lake McDonald

LEWIS RANGE

Continental Divide

Kiowa

Two Medicine Entrance

Two Medicine R

487

93

Glacier Rim Access

Blankenship Bridge

West Glacier

Apgar

Pumphouse Rapid

Middle Fork Flathead River

Nyack Creek

Nyack Flats

Midvale Cr

East Glacier

2

Whitefish

486

Coram

2

Cascadilla Flats Access

FLATHEAD RANGE

Paola Creek Access

Park Creek

2

40

Hungry Horse

Pinnacle

Summit

Marias Pass

Lewis and Clark National Forest

424

Columbia Falls

206

Flathead River

Hungry Horse Reservoir

Essex

Ole Creek

2

93

2

Evergreen

35

Goat Lick

Bear Creek

Bear Creek Access

Kalispell

Creston

35

Flathead National Forest

Spruce Park Rapids

Middle Fork Flathead River

Granite Creek

Schafer Meadows

93

82

SWAN RANGE

Somers

Bigfork

83

Sultrain Creek

South Fork Flathead River

Great Bear Wilderness

Dolly Varden Creek

Lakeside

Flathead National Forest

Swan Lake

35

Flathead Lake

Swan Lake

93

Rollins

0   10 mi

0   10 km

Contains information licensed under the Open Government Licence – Canada

Glacier National Park

A beautiful day on the North Fork of the Flathead bordering Glacier National Park. Freddie Terranova

➤ **Location:** Glacier National Park is located in the northwest corner of Montana along the spine of the Rocky Mountains.

The park is accessible via auto and air by these routes:

Via auto:

West Entrance—Near the communities of Kalispell, Whitefish, and Columbia Falls, the West Entrance provides access to the Lake McDonald area, Park Headquarters, the Apgar Visitor Center and is the west entry point to the Going-to-the-Sun Road. From Kalispell, take U.S. Route 2 north to West Glacier, approximately 33 miles.

St. Mary, Two Medicine, and Many Glacier Entrances— Closest to the town of Browning, all three entrances can be reached by taking U.S. Route 89 north from Great Falls to the town of Browning (about 125 miles) and then following signage to the respective entrance. The St. Mary Entrance is the east entry point of the Going-to-the-Sun Road and provides access to the St. Mary Visitor Center and services at Rising Sun. The Many Glacier Entrance provides access to the Many Glacier Valley and visitor services.

Via air:

Several commercial service airports are located within driving distance of Glacier National Park.

West Entrance—Glacier Park International Airport is located near Kalispell and is about 30 miles west of the West Entrance. Missoula International Airport is located about 150 miles south of the West Entrance.

St. Mary, Two Medicine, and Many Glacier Entrances— Great Falls International Airport is located between 130 miles to 165 miles east of East Glacier Park, St. Mary, Two Medicines and Many Glacier Entrances.

Car rentals are available at both airports. Shuttles are available at Glacier Park International Airport.

Clear water and a beautiful place in the Great Bear Wilderness. Freddie Terranova

The region in and around Glacier National Park has been inhabited for more than 10,000 years by the Blackfeet peoples on the prairies east of the mountains, and the Salish and Kootenai tribes of the western valleys. In the late 1800s, Europeans journeyed west to the mountains of Glacier seeking their chance to take part in the fur trapping and trading business. Following the fur trappers were miners, and after the discovery of Marias Pass, the Great Northern Railway reached completion in 1891. With the railroad offering easier accessibility to Northwestern Montana, the area grew in popularity. George Bird Grinnell, an avid explorer and conservationist, pushed to create a national park area and was rewarded by President William Howard Taft signing the bill to establish Glacier as the country's tenth national park in 1910.

"Far away in northwestern Montana, hidden from view by clustering mountain peaks, lies an unmapped corner—the Crown of the Continent."

—George Bird Grinnell (1901)

There is a reason that a select few avid fly fishers give up the comforts of electricity and indoor plumbing to spend their summers living in tents and trailers just minutes from the heart of West Glacier, Montana. Glacier National Park presents the opportunity to witness geology from 1.6 billion years ago, two mountain ranges along with the Continental Divide, and pure native westslope cutthroat trout all from its beautiful North and Middle Forks of the Flathead River.

Both the North and Middle Forks of the Flathead River offer the opportunity to chase westslope cutthroat trout, a species that has been an integral part of the local watershed for 14,000 or more years. The result of this extended history of habitation is a population of fish that are programmed to frantically feast on local hatches, providing exceptional dry-fly fishing to anglers who are quick on the hook-set and anxious to net beautifully colored and healthy trout.

Local organizations have been fighting vigorously to return the Flathead fishery to its original state, consisting of only native westslope cutthroat trout, bull trout, whitefish, and the occasional grayling. After the introduction of non-native rainbow trout (together with habitat loss and overharvest) local organizations and fisherman have spent the last decade promoting the protection and restoration of native species. Guides and local anglers stress the importance of minimal time out of the water to protect fragile, native trout. It is imperative to the health and survival of these fish that anglers use barbless hooks, which will decrease handling time. Using a net to corral fish for hook removal, wetting hands before touching the fish, and a proper release with the fish facing upstream and swimming out of a gentle grip will ensure maximum survival rates, ultimately leading to a larger and healthier trout population.

Westslope cutthroat live in beautiful places next to Glacier National Park. Freddie Terranova

While the rivers are the main destination for anglers visiting the park, there are several high mountain lakes within hiking distance. Small Parachute Adams patterns, Caddis, and small Spruce Moths are good choices. A slowly stripped peacock or brightly colored Prince Nymph along with a small Woolly Bugger will also attract fish hiding near structures. Still waters require sneakier presentation; a 9-foot 5X or smaller leader will do the trick. Depending on the lake, anglers can expect to see Arctic grayling, lake trout, whitefish, cutthroat, and the occasional rainbow.

Hopeful fly fishers will be best equipped with a 9-foot, 5-weight fly rod. This set up is appropriate for dry-fly fishing and nymphing the North, Middle, and Upper Middle Forks of the Flathead. Those planning to fish the North Fork might consider bringing along a 4-weight rod to add more thrill to smaller cutthroat. Although bear sightings are rare, we suggest you bring a can of bear spray along if you plan to be tromping around the river. Making plenty of noise and being aware of your surroundings is typically enough to deter bears. Although mountain lions exist in the Columbia Falls area, it is very rare to see any while fishing. Checking in with your fly shop for recent sightings typically offers more peace of mind.

➤ **North Fork:** Anglers seeking milder rafting conditions and views of an expansive landscape, including the Livingston Mountain Range, will find their haven on the North Fork. With 59 miles to fish from the Canadian Border access to Blankenship Bridge, there are countless riffles and deep pools to drift through. Large log jams and river splits char-

acterize the North Fork, making up-to-date information of year-to-year river changes crucial knowledge for boaters. As the western boundary for the park, multi-day boaters are not permitted to camp on river-formed beaches. However, there are a few beautiful camp sites dotted along river right between the gaps of private land, which is yet another reason a river map and up-to-date knowledge is crucial when planning a trip on the North Fork.

There are both half- and full-day floats available that are close to the town of West Glacier. Putting in at the Glacier Rim access offers anglers four miles of deep underwater cliffs, rock gardens, and large eddies to throw a fly into.

The North Fork offers a few options for wade anglers; however, those looking to escape crowds will need to have a few hours on their hands. The Great Northern Flats River Access offers large eddies that consistently hold trout mid-July through September. From the established parking lot, walk downriver from the boat ramp. A massive eddy that makes up the first bend of this stretch is easy wading and offers a great foam seam that extends roughly 50 yards. Later in the summer as the river level drops, wading fishermen will have better access to fish in the far bend of this run that is characterized by a steep drop-off along a rock wall.

For wade fishing closer to West Glacier, anglers willing to walk a little less than a mile and battle potential crowds have the opportunity to fish an eddy that lies upriver from the Blankenship Bridge river access which is located roughly 10 minutes from the Glacier Outdoor Center. Because of the

Darwon Stoneman (left), one of the founders of Glacier Raft Company/ Glacier Anglers, still having fun after 40 years. Freddie Terranova

inconsistent presence of road signs and the "back roads" feel of the drive, it is recommended that directions and maybe a hand-drawn map be obtained from the fly shop. Once you reach the bridge, cross the river to the small parking lot on the right. Walk upriver from the confluence (you will be walking on the river right shoreline) until you reach a bend characterized by a small section of rapids and boulders. Anglers have plenty of room to backcast into this eddy, and once late summer water levels arrive, fly fishers can fish this eddy further into the seam along the rapids as well as the pools underneath the bridge. Late August and early fall water levels typically allow wader fishermen access to fish the seam formed by the confluence of the Middle and North Fork, which can be seen from Blankenship Bridge.

Fishing the North Fork in the morning will generally produce more opportunities for cutthroats, while rainbows become more active closer to the evening. Once the yearly runoff sediment has settled (typically mid-July), fly fishers will find luck throwing large foam terrestrials and hoppers accompanied by a Prince Nymph.

➤ **Middle Fork:** The Middle Fork of the Flathead River caters to those looking to not only feed their addiction of fighting native cutthroat whose characteristic head-shake fights pack more punch on average than those of the North Fork, but also those who are seeking an adrenaline rush. Launching at the Moccasin Creek river access sends rafters on a nine-mile float that includes white water with rapids ranging from Class I to Class III. Above the Moccasin Creek put-in, boaters have the option to begin their journey at Bear

Creek, Essex, Paola, or Cascadilla Flats river accesses. Each access requires technical rowing, whether through the rocky passages from Bear Creek through Cascadilla, or the log-jammed Nyack Flats from Cascadilla to Moccasin Creek.

Serving as the boundary between Glacier National Park and the Great Bear Wilderness, the Middle Fork of the Flathead River flows between roughly two million acres of protected land. The aesthetic result of the strict protective laws has allowed the Middle Fork to maintain clear waters, offering 30 feet of crystal-clear, aqua visibility from mid-July on through the rest of the summer.

Proterozoic granulated argelite can be seen along the river, characterized by fossilized patterns from prehistoric Glacial Lake Missoula. Just down river from the Bear Creek river access, floaters pass directly beneath a geological formation known as the "Goat Lick." The salty mineral deposits consistently attract mountain goats; however, dropping anchor or stepping out of your boat is illegal throughout this section of river.

Those looking to wade the Middle Fork can do so easily right from the town of West Glacier. Before crossing the bridge to the west entrance of Glacier National Park, take a right onto Old River Bridge Road and follow it to the river. This approach offers an easily accessible opportunity to spend from a half-hour to a whole day wade fishing without leaving West Glacier. Anglers have the option to hike up river not even a half-mile to fish the bottom of Pumphouse rapid, or down river all the way to the new bridge. The shoreline offers a few braids depending on the time of year, along with large boulders and riffles that are sure to hold trout.

Alternatively, wading fly fishers can take a left onto River Bend Drive, which is located at the same intersection as Old River Bridge Road. Following this road past the golf course will lead to the West Glacier River Access. Drive past the turn for this access until the river is visible from the road—about 100 yards. There are two eddies fishable from river left located next to each other. Both of these are easily accessible after a little crawling down the boulder-lined river. Later in the summer, the bend river left from the confluence of McDonald Creek is also a great option for wade fishermen. Follow River Bend Drive past the golf course and West Glacier River Access just as if you were going to fish the earlier mentioned eddies until the river makes a massive bend to the left. The later in the summer you wait to fish this run, the more options you will have. Mid-July typically allows for one fishable run, while mid-late access reveals a gravel bar mid-river, and the lower water levels allow anglers to wade across to fish the run along the mouth of McDonald Creek.

Although clarity and runoff vary from year to year depending on the severity of the preceding winter, the Middle Fork is typically fishable by late June. While varying colors of Parachute Adams and caddis entice hungry cutthroat, the largest hatch of the year explodes during late spring and into early summer: the beloved and wildly-anticipated stonefly hatch. After the river levels drop and the stonefly hatch concludes, anglers will strike luck tossing brightly colored lime green and orange Humpies, Wilcox Specials, and Chubbies through riffles next to creeks and the rejoining of braids.

➤ **Upper Middle Fork:** While the North and Middle Forks of the Flathead River are the most accessible, the trip of a lifetime begins with either a half-hour flight in a Cessna or a seven-mile mule pack along Granite Creek. (Note: After July 1, rafts will probably have difficulty getting down the river to Granite Creek.) The Upper Middle Fork of the Flathead River's headwaters lie deep in the Great Bear Wilderness in an area called Schaefer Meadows. Because of the inaccessibility of this river and the dangerous waters that present themselves to floaters, the native West Slope cutthroat of this river are given the chance to grow much larger. The limited numbers of people who seek these fish every year leave them practically fearless of flies, and completely unknowing that something they attack may be artificial.

It is highly recommended that individuals seeking to immerse themselves in the seclusion and way of life of the wilderness use a professional and local guiding company. Pack mules are a necessity to carry rafts along the trail to the river. Rafts, food, and supplies for four to five days will need to be packed. An expert rower with advanced rescue skills is a crucial element to those looking to embark on this trip. The wild and beautiful waters of the Upper Middle Fork offer multiple series of Class IV rapids, the most intense being Spruce Park, which is the last series of the trip. Massive boulders, small canyons, and downed trees present not only exciting whitewater opportunities, but also emphasize the imperative need for an expert rower.

Fighting the crowds on the Upper Middle Fork of the Flathead. Freddie Terranova

Rafts arriving at the Upper Middle Fork in the Great Bear Wilderness via mule express. Freddie Terranova

For those hungry to fight primarily native and aggressive cutthroat trout, the best conditions are generally in mid-July through early to mid-August. The conditions of this river are highly dependent on yearly snowpack and precipitation; therefore, it is highly recommended that prospective fishermen contact local guiding services to seek the most recent river forecasts and conditions. Dry-fly fishermen will find success using a size 12 Chubby, Purple Parachute patterns, along with your favorite classic Royal Wulff or Coachman. Within the Great Bear Wilderness, anglers are permitted to have a combined three fish daily in possession, none of which may be over 12 inches.

While native bull trout have been making their comeback within the Flathead fishery, the targeting of these fish is illegal on the North, Middle, and Upper Middle Forks of the Flathead. Year to year, there is a specific season on the South Fork of the Flathead when anglers can obtain a special permit to fish for these trout. Incidental catches do occasionally happen due to the predatory nature of these fish. Guides report incidents each summer of bull trout chasing and eating smaller fish being fought by clients, and in this case, it is crucial to handle these fish as quickly and carefully as possible to allow them to return to the river.

All waters west of the Continental Divide (as well as Midvale Creek in the Two Medicine River drainage and Wild Creek in the St. Mary River drainage) are subject to catch-and-release fishing only for cutthroat trout. However, two cutthroat trout may be harvested from Hidden, Evangeline, and Camas Lakes in accordance with park fishing regulations. Daily catch and possession limits will not exceed five fish, including no more than

· Two cutthroat trout
· Two burbot (ling)
· One northern pike
· Two mountain whitefish
· Five lake whitefish
· Five kokanee salmon
· Five grayling
· Five rainbow trout
· Five lake trout

There is more than one way to get down the river. Freddie Terranova

There is no limit on lake trout in park waters west of the Continental Divide, no limit on lake whitefish in Lake McDonald, and the park-wide brook trout daily catch and possession limit is 20 fish. Due to the constantly changing regulations for waters in and around the park, it is highly advised that anglers request an up-to-date copy of fishing regulations from park rangers located at park entrances.

Any angler seeking a transcendental communion with wild trout and untouched wilderness will find themselves at home in Glacier's waters. Whether you are an adrenaline junky or if you are looking for a quiet, peaceful, solitary opportunity to cross waters with spectacular native trout, Glacier National Park will always be there as the ultimate sought-out haven for fly fishers from all walks of life.

➤ Tackle and Gear

Rods and Line: A 9-foot, 5-weight fly rod with 9-foot 5X or smaller leader is recommended. When fishing the North Fork, consider packing a 4-weight rod.

Terminal Tackle and Flies: Small Parachute Adams patterns, Caddis, and small Spruce Moths are good choices. A slowly stripped peacock or brightly colored Prince Nymph along with a small Wooly Bugger is highly effective. Brightly colored lime green and orange Humpies, Wilcox Specials, and Chubbies are Middle Fork favorites in early summer. In the Upper Middle Fork, try a size 12 Chubby, Purple Parachute patterns, or the classic Royal Wulff or Coachman.

A beautiful day on the North Fork of the Flathead. Glacier Anglers

CLOSEST CITY OR POINT OF ENTRANCE
· The northwest corner of Montana along the spine of the Rocky Mountains adjacent to the town of West Glacier, Montana
· Near Kalispell, Whitefish
· Columbia Falls, Montana

AIRPORTS AND CAR RENTAL
· Glacier Park International Airport, Kalispell, Montana: 45-minute drive
· Missoula International Airport: Three-hour drive

FEES
Park entrance and user fees change periodically. For up-to-date fees, free days and other exceptions, visit http://www.nps.gov/glac/index.htm.

CLOSEST FLY SHOP
Glacier Outdoor Center
12400 U.S. Route 2
West Glacier, MT 59936
406-888-5456
glacierraftco.com
www.info@glacierraftco.com

CLOSEST LODGING
Glacier Raft Company
12400 U.S. Route 2
West Glacier, MT 59936
800-235-6781
glacierraftco.com
www.info@glacierraftco.com

Belton Chalet
12575 U.S. Route 2
West Glacier, MT 59936
406-888-5000
www.beltonchalet.com

Vista Motel
12340 U.S. Route 2
West Glacier, MT 59936
406-888-5311
www.glaciervistamotel.com

Village Inn at Apgar
Lake View Dr.
West Glacier, MT 59936
855-733-4522

Glacier Park Incorporated
1 Midvale St.
East Glacier, MT 59434
Lodging around Glacier National Park
844-868-7474
www.glacierparkinc.com

Xanterra Parks and Resorts
Lodges in Glacier National park
303-600-3400
www.xanterra.com

KELSEY CARLSON HOSKINS grew up fishing the Touchet River of Dayton, Washington with her grandpa. She fell in love with the rivers of Montana while attending the University of Montana and playing soccer for the Griz. Kelsey guides fishing trips for Glacier Anglers/Glacier Raft Company in the summer months, and heads south for the winter, fishing the waters around Missoula, Montana, and teaches high school English.

CLOSEST CAMPGROUND

Glacier Campground
12070 U.S. Route 2
West Glacier, MT 59936
888-387-5689
www.glaciercampround.com

West Glacier KOA
355 Halfmoon Flats
West Glacier, MT 59936
800-562-3313
www.koa.com

CLOSEST RESTAURANTS

Belton Chalet
12575 U.S. Route 2
West Glacier, MT 59936
406-888-5000
www.beltonchalet.com

The Back Room Restaurant
522 Ninth St. West
Columbia Falls, MT 59912
406-892-3131
www.niteowlbackroom.com

Craggy Range Bar & Grill
10 Central Ave.
Whitefish, MT 59937
406-862-7550
www.thecraggyrange.com

MUST SEE

Going-to-the-Sun Road: A construction marvel that spans 50 miles through the park's wild interior, winding around mountainsides and treating visitors to some of the best sights in northwest Montana

MEDICAL SERVICES

West Glacier Clinic
100 Rea Rd.
West Glacier, MT 59936
406-888-9924
(Open Memorial Day through Labor Day)

Kalispell Regional Medical Center
310 Sunny View Ln.
Kalispell, MT 59901
406-752-5111

North Valley Hospital
1600 Hospital Way
Whitefish, MT 59937
406-863-3500

CELL PHONE SERVICE

Cell service is limited or unavailable within the park. Verizon Wireless service is available throughout West Glacier and roughly one mile past Belton Chalet on U.S. Route 2.

FOR ALL ELSE, VISIT
http://www.nps.gov/glac/index.htm

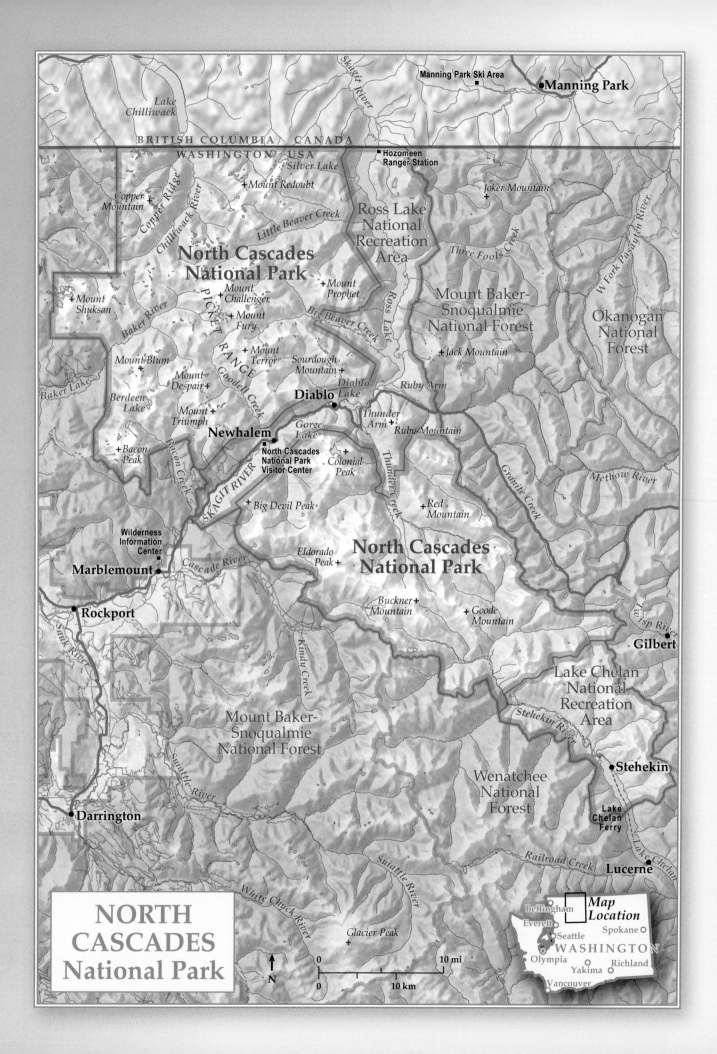

Lake Chilliwack

Manning Park Ski Area

● **Manning Park**

Skagit River

BRITISH COLUMBIA / CANADA
WASHINGTON / USA

Silver Lake

■ Hozomeen
Ranger Station

+ Mount Redoubt

Joker Mountain

Copper
+ Mountain

Copper Ridge

Chilliwack River

Little Beaver Creek

**North Cascades
National Park**

Ross Lake
National
Recreation
Area

Three Fools Creek

+ Mount
Shuksan

PICKET RANGE

Baker River

+ Mount
Challenger

+ Mount Prophet

Big Beaver Creek

Ross Lake

Mount Baker-
Snoqualmie
National Forest

Okanogan
National
Forest

+ Mount
Fury

Mount Blum

+ Mount
Terror

+ Jack Mountain

Baker Lake

Goodell Creek

+ Mount
Despair

Berdeen
Lake

+ Mount
Triumph

Sourdough
Mountain

Diablo
Lake

Diablo ●

Ruby Arm

Thunder
Arm

Ruby Mountain

Methow River

+ Bacon
Peak

Bacon Creek

Newhalem

Gorge
Lake

■ North Cascades
National Park
Visitor Center

+ Colonial
Peak

Thunder Creek

Granite Creek

SKAGIT RIVER

+ Big Devil Peak

+ Red
Mountain

**North Cascades
National Park**

Wilderness
Information
Center

Cascade River

Eldorado
Peak

Marblemount ●

Buckner +
Mountain

+ Goode
Mountain

Twisp River

● **Gilbert**

● **Rockport**

Sauk River

Kindy Creek

Lake Chelan
National
Recreation
Area

Stehekin River

Mount Baker-
Snoqualmie
National Forest

Suiattle River

Sulphur Creek

Wenatchee
National
Forest

● **Stehekin**

Lake
Chelan
Ferry

Lake Chelan

● **Darrington**

Suiattle River

Railroad Creek

● **Lucerne**

White Chuck River

Glacier Peak

**NORTH
CASCADES
National Park**

↑
N

0 _____ 10 mi

0 _____ 10 km

Mount Skuksan in the northwestern corner of the park as viewed from Artist Point. Numerous fish-filled backcountry lakes surround this 9,131-foot peak. Scott Willison

➤ **Location:** The snow-capped spires of the North Cascades rise up like a wall just a stone's throw from the fjord lands of Puget Sound—jagged, vast and wild. Within its glacial crags and valleys, North Cascades National Park (NCNP) offers a diversity of picturesque streams, lakes and rivers. The park complex—located in Washington State, northeast of Seattle—was established in 1968. The park consists of three main units:

· North Cascades National Park
· Ross Lake National Recreation Area
· Lake Chelan National Recreation Area, adjoined by several wilderness areas and two provincial parks on the Canadian side

Primary access to both North Cascades and Ross Lake National Recreation Area is from the Washington 20 corridor. The Silver-Skagit Road and Washington 542 are jumping off points for many northern regions of the park including Hozomeen, Mount Shuksan, and Copper Ridge.

· From the west, Washington 20 (North Cascades Highway) connects with Interstate 5 (Exit 230) at Burlington.
· From the east, the Washington 20 intersects with U.S. Route 97 at Okanogan and with Washington 153 at Twisp.
· The Washington State Department of Transportation typically closes the roadway between Ross Dam Trailhead and Lone Fir Campground from November to April due to avalanche danger.

A large male upper Skagit River bull trout donning spawning colors. Scott Willison

Campgrounds, roads and visitor centers are open from late May through October. Gas and other amenities are largely unavailable east of Marblemount around mile marker 10 for another 75 miles across the Cascade Divide, so check your gas gauge prior to going eastward.

Beyond its many angling opportunities, NCNP attracts boaters, campers, hikers, horseback riders and climbers to enjoy its extensive wilderness water routes, trail systems and technical ascents of ominously named peaks such as Mount Fury and Mount Terror. All wilderness camping within the park complex requires a backcountry permit and is allowed only in established sites along trail corridors. Permits are free at the Wilderness Information Center in Marblemount and several ranger stations; they are issued on a first-come, first-served basis.

The North Cascades Highway veers east from Interstate 5, an hour north of Seattle, and serves as the main thoroughfare through the park, following the nearly 60-mile course of the Skagit River toward the western park entrance near Newhalem. The Skagit is the third largest river on the West Coast. Also, the Skagit is an historical epicenter for Pacific Northwest steelheading on the fly from noted pioneering angler Ralph Wahl, who chronicled his early experiences in *One Man's Steelhead Shangri-La.* The river is also central to the development of modern Spey casting techniques and Skagit lines.

All five species of Pacific salmon, native bull trout, rainbow, cutthroat and whitefish reside in the Skagit's cold, clean waters. Bald eagles, Roosevelt elk, black-tailed deer, black bears and cougars occupy the valley's lush evergreen forests along with less frequent grizzlies, wolverines, moose and gray wolves as you approach the northern border of the park. The Skagit, with its tributaries and impoundments, make up a significant portion of the fisheries one can readily explore. Though much of the river flows just outside the park boundary before emptying into northern Puget Sound, it would

Above. Larry Carton surveys the water on a broad Skagit run. The North Cascades' Pickett Range is a welcome backdrop visible throughout the Skagit Valley corridor. Scott Willison

Inset. A Skagit River pink salmon showing off its characteristic penchant for pink flies. Scott Willison

require an angler's steely resolve to ignore the succession of smooth, cobbled runs that beckon for a swung fly.

The river opens to fishing on the first Saturday in June and closes January 31. A short section remains open through February 15 from the Washington 530 bridge in Rockport to the Rockport-Cascade bridge in Marblemount. Much of the winter season is restricted around threatened Puget Sound wild steelhead. Seasons and restrictions might change in future years. Be sure to consult the Washington State Sport Fishing Rules Pamphlet prior to a trip. Note that salmon angling is closed above Marblemount at all times. Camping on the Skagit is available at the National Park's Goodell Creek and Newhalem Creek Campgrounds, both situated near milepost 120.

Three Seattle City Light hydroelectric projects—Ross, Diablo and Gorge Dams—regulate much of the Skagit's flow. Early summer water conditions might be high and cold from dam releases. However, the river will typically run very clear

above its principal tributary, the Sauk River, which enters near Rockport.

Bull Trout are present throughout the season and can grow to 10 pounds and larger, though the average fish is around 20 inches. Bulls will take a variety of large streamers such as the Willy Whitefish, Dali Llama, White Zonker and Double Bunny. In the fall and early winter, egg patterns become effective in the wake of prolific spawning salmon runs. Later, flesh flies gain prominence as the salmon dissolve into drifting, bony carcasses. Anglers encounter wild rainbows less regularly than the abundant char, but do find the occasional large fish employing the same tactics and flies used for bull trout.

In odd-numbered years, the Skagit receives upwards of 1,000,000 pink salmon filling its banks from August through early October, and fly fishing for these 3- to 6-pound "humpies" can be nothing short of amazing. Small pink Comet flies cast and retrieved on a light sink tip or clear intermediate line through the many sloughs and slower inside bends produces

223

multi-fish days and sore arms. When fishing for trout, char and pink salmon a 5- or 6-weight single-hand switch or Spey rod with a variety of sink tips is appropriate.

Coho (silver salmon) run from August through the end of the year, accompanied by chum salmon in November and December just as the first vanguard of winter steelhead filters into the river. Coho are readily found in slower, off-channel sloughs or "frog water" and will take a variety of small, sparse flies. Rolled Muddlers in chartreuse, blue, or black, Egg-sucking Leeches in purple or olive, California Neils (sometimes misspelled as Neals) in green, along with Flash Flies in blue/silver and green/copper are effective Coho catchers. Fish a floating line and weighted fly or clear intermediate line on a 7- or 8-weight rod using a variable retrieve through the slow water. The first winter steelhead appear as early as late November, building in numbers throughout the winter and early spring. The Skagit and Sauk historically supported a fabulous spring catch-and-release fishery, but it has closed at the end of January for the last several years. Consult the Washington Sport Fishing Pamphlet for current seasons before planning a trip. Spey rods offer a distinct advantage in covering the expansive Skagit runs, fishing efficiently and effectively for winter steelhead, which can be taken on Intruders, leeches and other colorful marabou Spey patterns.

➤ **Gorge Lake:** Completed in 1924, Gorge Dam backs up the Skagit another six miles beyond Newhalem, creating the 210-acre Gorge Lake. Gorge is narrow and steep-walled in its lower end and more closely resembles a river below the powerhouse near the highway exit to the town of Diablo. Fly anglers will find both smaller rainbow trout and some larger char throughout the relatively shallow, stump-filled lake. Gorge can be notoriously windy as it snakes through the tight canyon of the former river. On calm days, slow-trolling Carey Specials, Doc Spratleys and Woolly Buggers from a float tube, pontoon or small watercraft will locate willing trout. Limited primitive camping is available at Gorge Campground on the northern shore of the lake, along with a car-accessible boat launch.

➤ **Diablo Lake:** Seattle City Light finished construction on the Diablo Dam in 1936, forming the larger impoundment of Diablo Lake. At milepost 130, nestled in old-growth forest beneath the shadow of Colonial Peak, Colonial Creek Campground offers lakeside camping and a developed boat ramp, providing easy access to the water. Thunder Creek tumbles into the eastern end of Diablo, often spilling glacial melt in the heat of summer, which can make the water murky. A canoe, kayak or small boat equipped with an outboard motor offers much greater range on this 910-acre body of water. Those who venture west will generally escape the turbidity of Thunder Arm to discover a richly emerald green lake filled with rising rainbow trout and the occasional large char. Diablo may be effectively fished with the same flies and presentation as Gorge. Three boat-in campsites exist on Diablo for those seeking to further distance themselves from the creature comforts of a developed campground.

➤ **Ross Lake:** The last in the series of Skagit Hydroelectric projects was completed in 1952. Ruby Dam, later renamed for Seattle City Light engineer J.D. Ross, rises above Diablo, and marks the southern end of the sprawling 24-mile long

Spectacular fall colors accompany late-season fishing in the Stehekin Valley. John Wilsey, Stehekin Fishing Adventures

Ross Lake. Ross arguably offers some of the best fly fishing in the park for several reasons. The only vehicle access to the lake is reached internationally beginning at Hope, British Columbia and then heading south for a rough 30 miles along the washboard-riveted Skagit-Silverhope Road, which deadends at Hozomeen Campground just inside the U.S. border and National Park Boundary.

Anglers can access Ross from the south by launching a kayak or canoe at Colonial Creek, paddling five miles to the end of Diablo, and portaging around Ross Dam over a mile-long, switch-backed gravel road. Ross Lake Resort, a series of well-maintained cabins built on a floating log boom along the lake, offers perhaps the most accommodating gateway to this scenic paradise. Visitors can reach the resort either by ferry from Diablo Dam off Diablo Dam Road or by hiking in from the dam. The resort offers electricity, boat rentals, some fly-fishing tackle and flies, a water taxi service to the lake's

Another healthy westslope cutthroat comes to net on the Stehekin River. John Wilsey, Stehekin Fishing Adventures.

remote wilderness campsites and trailheads, portage services around the Ross Dam, and some of the most tranquil and visually stunning vacation quarters anywhere in the Pacific Northwest—provided you're not rattled by the distant cries of lonely loons in the lingering twilight.

With the grunt work of simply getting there behind them, fly fishers will find themselves primed for a multi-day fly-fishing adventure. A decade ago, Ross produced average pan-sized rainbow, typical of many deep, nutrient-poor mountain lakes. Following a mysterious introduction of redside shiners, the trout population boomed in response to an ever-expanding food supply. Anglers catch trophy rainbows up to 26 inches each season along with some stocky bull trout. Ross produces the occasional cutthroat and Eastern brook as well.

Ferocious grabs from the lake's monstrous trout and char can be had by fishing with 5- to 7-weight rods and fast-sinking lines, with white or olive Zonkers and Clouser Minnows, white beadhead Dude Friendly's, Dali Llamas, large olive Bunny Leeches or Woolly Buggers. Locate these fish by trolling the lake's edge or by sighting the scattering bait balls of shiners that are being corralled to the surface by trout, much like Coho salmon attacking herring in the open ocean. Nineteen boat-in wilderness campgrounds of varying sizes pro-

vide multiple jumping-off points from which to experience the many bays, points and islands staggered throughout the lake. Take note of special regulations within the Ross Lake watershed. Some of the areas around tributary mouths are closed to protect spawning fish, as is the first mile of most feeder streams. The lake and its tributaries open and begin fishing well in July, continuing through the end of October. Because all three Skagit impoundments are flooded forest and river valley, they are filled with stumps and woody debris. That means you should bring plenty of flies because you can expect to lose a few.

The Upper Skagit River, entering Ross Lake just north of the Hozomeen boat launch (just beyond the park and international boundaries) also offers exceptional fly fishing for rainbow and bull trout. This area is regulated under the same fishing season as the lake. Anglers will encounter a strong Green Drake mayfly hatch early in the season, little yellow stoneflies, caddis and some terrestrials throughout the summer with a batch of smaller drakes appearing in the fall. Large bull trout can be caught using Dali Llamas, Zonkers, Double Bunnies and Egg-sucking Leeches. The upper Skagit Valley has a unique micro-climate with both western red cedar and lodge pole pine growing adjacent to one another, along with the easternmost population of native rhododendron. You'll also encounter plenty of hungry mosquitoes, making bug spray and repellent clothing a must.

➤ **Lake Chelan National Recreation Area:** The Lake Chelan National Recreation Area, as with much of NCNP, is somewhat off the beaten path and requires some additional planning to reach. With no roads into the recreation area at the upper end of Lake Chelan, it is most easily accessed via the passenger ferry, "Lady of the Lake," or by airplane operated by Chelan Seaplanes. Both navigate the 50-plus-mile glacial basin of Lake Chelan to Stehekin, a small community at the far end of the lake. More intrepid anglers can reach Stehekin on foot via several backpacking routes, ranging from 18 to nearly 100 miles in length, many accompanied by small trout-filled streams along the way.

Regardless of how one chooses to get there, the Stehekin Valley is well worth a visit for those willing to put forth the effort. Carving its way through the valley, the glacially influenced Stehekin River and tributaries offer pocket water and classic runs along with some very respectable fish in its 23 miles. The river hosts rainbow trout, westslope cutthroat, cuttbows, a few char, as well as providing the spawning grounds for Lake Chelan's landlocked Chinook and Kokanee salmon population.

The key word for this location is "planning." Visiting anglers will need to prepare for a multi-day trip and will find a variety of lodging options in the community of Stehekin. Anglers can choose free wilderness camping by permit at several park campsites along the lower valley and into the upper valley beyond the reach of vehicles. Anglers who don't want to camp can rent cabins, stay in a park concession–operated lodge, or enjoy a full-service experience with gourmet meals at the Stehekin Valley Ranch. Food service is limited, so plan ahead and bring what you need.

Transportation options for exploring the Stehekin include bike rentals, a shuttle that makes several daily trips in the lower nine miles of the valley, and exploring on foot. Renting a cabin that comes with a vehicle provides ultimate flexibility. Stehekin Fishing Adventures, the local guide service that operates a small fly shop at the head of the lake, will share the beauty of the valley and the fishery with you, with walk-and-wade trips or a float of the lower river.

A variety of rod sizes can be used here. Lightweight 2- to 3-weights are perfect higher in the river and its tributaries, while 4- to 6-weight, 9-foot rods are appropriate in the lower river. Attractor dries from Humpies, Coachmen and small caddis to huge Sofa Pillows and Stimulators, with or without Prince or stonefly nymph droppers, catch plenty of fish. Later in the season, when the Kokanee appear, egg patterns produce strikingly golden-hued and hook-jawed west slopes and thick-sided silver 'bows that reach 14 to 20 inches and larger. Small Adams and Drake patterns in blue-gray and green can work on cool and early season days. The larger fish reside in the lower river, while scores of smaller fish are caught higher in the watershed. Caddis, Yellow Sallies, Golden Stones and mayflies hatch throughout the summer months on the Stehekin, with larger stones and terrestrial patterns gaining importance by August and into the Stehekin fall season. Medium-sized Bunny Leeches and streamers imitating Sculpin and juvenile parr can entice the river's larger fish.

The North Cascades are painted with watery treasures, varied and colorful salmonids, waiting to be tempted with a fly. Beat the oppressive summer heat, cinch up your bootlaces and get ready to explore. Like most tough things in life, the reward can be well worth the effort.

➤ **Tackle and Gear**

Rods and Line: For trout rivers and streams, rods in the 3- to 6-weight range matched with floating lines and 9-foot 4 or 5X leaders; 10-foot sinking poly leaders work well for streamer fishing. When fishing trout lakes, 5- or 6-weight rods matched with floating, intermediate and full-sinking lines and 7.5- to 9-foot 3 to 5X leaders are best. When fishing for steelhead, salmon and river char, we recommend a 6- to 8-weight Spey rod or switch rods matched with Skagit or switch lines, along with a variety of sink tips from Type 3 through Type 8. We recommend short leaders of 10-pound Maxima.

Terminal Tackle and Flies: If you're fishing for bull trout, large streamers such as the Willy Whitefish, Dali Llama, White Zonker and Double Bunny are effective. In the fall and early winter, egg patterns are the ticket, and later flesh flies are a good choice. Pink salmon are susceptible to Small pink Comet flies on a light sink tip or clear intermediate line. Rolled Muddlers in chartreuse or blue, black, purple or olive Egg-sucking Leeches, green California Neils (sometimes misspelled as Neals) along with blue/silver and green/copper Flash Flies are effective Coho catchers. Rainbow trout and Artic char can be taken by slow-trolling Carey Specials, Doc Spratleys and Woolly Buggers. When fishing in Ross Lake, white or olive Zonkers and Clouser Minnows, white bead-head Dude Friendly's, Dali Llamas and large olive Bunny Leeches or Woolly Buggers are recommended.

CLOSEST TOWN OR ACCESS TO THE PARK

· Marblemount, Washington (West Entrance)
· Winthrop, Washington (East Entrance)
· Hope, British Columbia (Hozomeen Access)
· Chelan, Washington (Chelan NRA)

CLOSEST AIRPORT, AUTO RENTAL AND OTHER TRANSPORTATION SERVICES

Bellingham International Airport or Sea-Tac (Seattle/Tacoma) International Airport, both of which offer hotel/motel and car rental services.

ENTRY FEE TO THE PARK

· No entry fee is required.
· Some trailheads require a Northwest Trail Pass for parking—$30 annual or $5 per day.
· There are several fee-free days for the Northwest Forest Pass.
· A complete listing is available at www.fs.usda.gov/.

PARK FISHING LICENSE

License options are

· Valid Washington State Freshwater. Fishing license within the National Park Complex in Washington.
· British Columbia Non-Tidal Freshwater Fishing License (if you plan to fish within the adjoining provincial parks in British Columbia, Canada).

OPEN/CLOSING PARK DATES OR FISHING DATES

· Most streams/rivers open the first Saturday in June through October 31.
· The Skagit River from Newhalem downstream is generally open from the first Saturday in June through January 31.
· Ross Lake and tributaries are open from July 1 through October 31.
· Gorge, Diablo and most lakes are open year-round.
· The Stehekin River is open from March 1 through October 31.

FISHING REGULATIONS

· Limits vary greatly by stream and species.
· Consult the Washington Fishing Rules Booklet for more information.

· Catch-and-release angling is encouraged on all native fish in and around the park complex.

CLOSEST FLY SHOPS

The Confluence Fly Shop
2620 N. Harbor Loop Dr. #9
Bellingham, WA 98225
360-312-7978
www.theconfluenceflyshop.com

Stehekin Fishing Adventures
P.O. Box 5
Stehekin, WA 98852
johnwilsey@hughes.net

Pacific Fly Fishers
1018 164th St. SE #A-22
Mill Creek, WA 98012
425-742-2402
www.pacficflyfishers.com

Avid Angler
17171 Bothell Way NE #A272
Lake Forest Park, WA 98155
206-362-4030
www.avidangler.com

Ross Lake Resort
503 Diablo St.
Rockport, WA 98283
206-386-4437
www.rosslakeresort.com
(Flies and limited rods, reels, lines and leader for Ross Lake and surrounding area)

CLOSEST GUIDE SERVICES

Dickson Fly Fishing
P.O. Box 295
Arlington, WA 98223
425-330-9506
streamsideflyshop@yahoo.com

Stehekin River Fishing Adventures
P.O. Box 5
Stehekin, WA 98852
johnwilsey@hughes.net

Methow Fishing Adventures
509-429-7298
www.flyfishersproshop.com

North Cascades Fly Fishing
509-996-3731
www.fishandfloat.com

Cascades Fly Fishing Expeditions
360-510-0483
www.cascadesfly.com

CLOSEST OUTFITTERS

Ross Lake Resort
503 Diablo St.
Rockport, WA 98283
206-386-4437
www.rosslakeresort.com

Stehekin Outfitters
P.O. Box 36
Stehekin, WA 98852
509-682-4677
www.stehekinoutfitters.com

CLOSEST LODGES

Ross Lake Resort
503 Diablo St.
Rockport, WA 98283
206-386-4437
www.rosslakeresort.com

Stehekin Valley Ranch
P.O. Box 36
Stehekin, WA 98852
509-682-4677
www.stehekinvalleyranch.com

Sun Mountain Lodge
604 Patterson Lake Rd.
Winthrop, WA 98662
800-572-0493
www.sunmountainlodge.com

CLOSEST HOTEL

Buffalo Run Inn
60117 State Route 20
Marblemount, WA 98267
360-873-2103
www.buffaloruninn.com

BEST HOTEL

Sun Mountain Lodge
604 Patterson Lake Rd.
Winthrop, WA 98662
800-572-0493
www.sunmountainlodge.com

CLOSEST, BEST CAMPGROUND

Colonial Creek Campground
Washington 20
Rockport, WA 98283
877-444-6777
Colonial Creek Campground is about 25 miles east of Marblemount. With 142 sites, it is the largest campground within the park. Water, flush toilets, garbage and recycling services are available, however showers and RV hookups are not available. Colonial

SCOTT WILLISON is the owner of the Confluence Fly Shop in Bellingham, Washington. He's been fly fishing for more than 30 years throughout his home state of Washington, as well as the Bahamas, France, Colorado, Montana, Wyoming, Oregon, Wisconsin, British Columbia, Costa Rica and Mexico. Scott has an English writing and teaching degree from Western Washington University. He serves as a Native Fish Society River Steward for the North Fork Stilliguamish River and is an active member of the Fourth Corner Fly Club.

Creek is scenically stretched along the shores of Diablo Lake and offers a boat launch, pier and access to numerous hiking trails.

CLOSEST RESTAURANT
Que Car BBQ
60076 Washington 20
360-873-4227
Marblemount, WA 98267

BEST RESTAURANT
The Old Schoolhouse Brewery
155 Riverside
Winthrop, WA 98862
509-996-3183
www.oldschoolhousebrewery.com

CLOSEST PLACE TO GET A DRINK
Buffalo Run Restaurant
60117 Washington 20
Marblemount, WA 98267
360-873-2461
www.buffaloruninn.com

BEST PLACE TO GET A DRINK
The Old Schoolhouse Brewery
155 Riverside
Winthrop, WA 98862
509-996-3183
www.oldschoolhousebrewery.com

MUST SEE
· North Cascades Highway—Stunning and majestic mountain views and some surprise appearances by wildlife on the side or even in the middle of the road. (Available only during summer months.)

NEAREST HOSPITAL/URGENT TREATMENT CENTER
West Entrance
Peacehealth United General Medical Center
2000 Hospital Drive
Sedro-Woolley, WA 98284
360-856-6021
https://www.peacehealth.org/united-general/Pages/default.aspx

East Entrance
Wenatchee Valley Hospital
820 North Chelan Ave.
Wenatchee, WA 98807
509-663-8711
http://www.wvmedical.com/Locations/WenatcheeValleyMedicalCenter.ashx?p=1115

CELL PHONE SERVICE:
Cell service is extremely limited to non-existent within most of the park complex.

FOR ALL ELSE, VISIT:
http://www.nps.gov/olym/index.htm

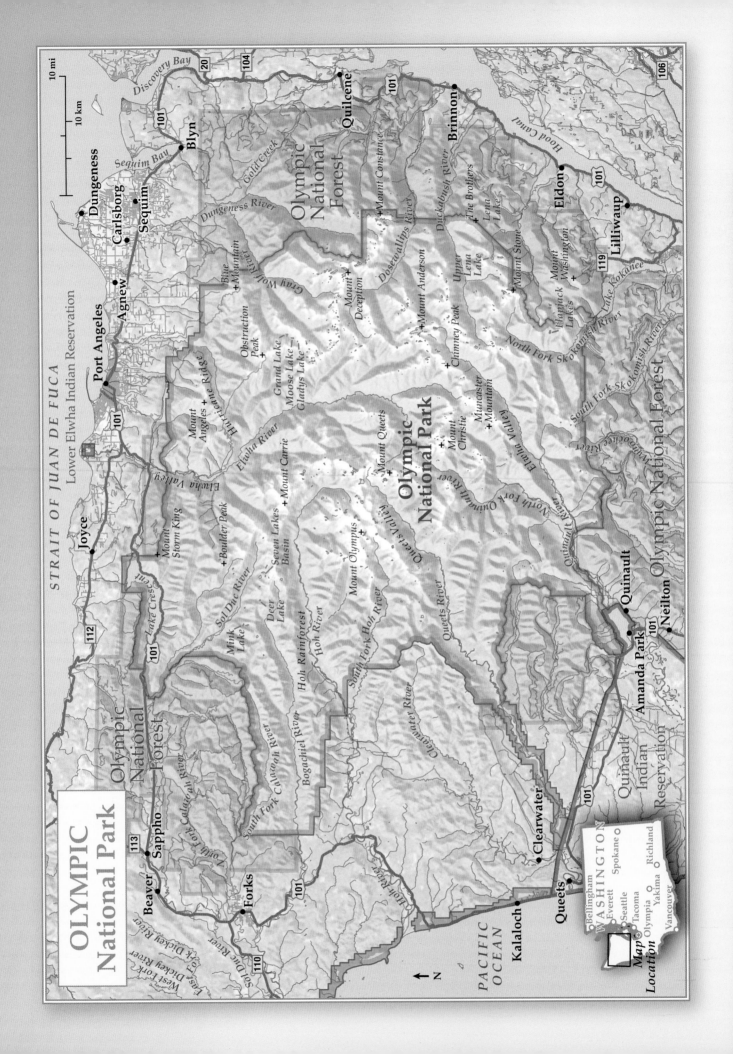

The ever-changing floodplain on the upper Hoh River in late winter. John R McMillan

➤ **Location:** Olympic National Park is on the Olympic Peninsula in the northwest corner of Washington State, about a three-hour drive from Seattle. You can reach Olympic National Park via the Interstate 5 corridor or by any one of the quieter state roadways. Once you arrive on the Olympic Peninsula, connect to U.S. Route 101 to reach any destinations in and around Olympic National Park. The Greater Puget Sound area is served by Sea-Tac International Airport and Victoria International Airport, Victoria, British Columbia, Canada.

President Grover Cleveland designated the forests of the Olympic Peninsula as the Olympic Forest Reserve in 1897. Ultimately, in 1938, President Franklin Roosevelt signed the act establishing Olympic National Park. It is an unusual national park because it's also been designated as a World Heritage Site and Biosphere Reserve. This rather remote corner of the state is surrounded on three sides by saltwater: Hood Canal to the east, the Strait of Juan de Fuca to the north and the Pacific Ocean to the west. U.S. Route 101 is the main road that also surrounds the peninsula and the national park. The city of Port Angeles, on the northern border of the park, is the largest town on the Olympic Peninsula with the

most amenities. It is also where the ferry leaves for Vancouver Island and the city of Victoria in British Columbia, Canada.

Access to ONP, where not snowed in, is open year-round. The entire area is a Mecca for the outdoor enthusiast and adventure seekers are scrambling around the peninsula every month of the year. Olympic National Park maintains 800 miles of trails with hundreds of miles more outside the park. Hiking and backpacking are the most popular non-fishing activity. There are also a large number of kayakers plying the rivers, lakes and saltwater year-round and the area is well-known as a mountain biking destination with world championships held just outside of Port Angeles every year.

Olympic does not have an extensive road system that bisects the park like Yellowstone. Most roads only enter a short distance, which means most of the park is only accessible by non-motorized means. Except for a couple of peak months in the summer and the couple of steelhead spots in the winter, most of the trails are uncrowded, and it is still easy to get away from people.

Olympic National Park offers fly fishers some of the most diverse, year-round opportunities in the country and is an ideal place for the adventurous angler. The general attitude

*Above. Chasing sea-run cutthroat trout
on a Quillayute tributary. John R. McMillan.*

*Inset. Protected bull trout are present in all the glacially
influenced rivers on the peninsula. John R. McMillan*

for the fly fisher inside the national park is one of quality, not quantity. Sometimes the fishing can be difficult, but while fishing in one of the most incredible places on earth, catching fish is a bonus. The majority of anglers who travel to ONP and the surrounding waters are there to catch steelhead and salmon. However, there is a relatively dynamic trout fishery throughout the park and surrounding state waters. While there might not be the same consistent epic trout fishing encountered in places such as Montana, the OP has a lot to offer even the well-traveled angler.

Olympic National Park is actually three parks in one, as the park's own literature correctly states. The majority of its approximately 900,000 acres encompass a core of gla-cier-studded mountains, out of which drain a dozen major watersheds and thousands of miles of rivers and streams, all originating in the park and draining into marine waters. ONP is home to all five salmon species—king or Chinook, silver or

Coho, sockeye or red, pink or humpy and chum or dog—and also supports relatively healthy runs of wild trout and char. There are thousands of miles of trails leading to hundreds of high alpine lakes, some quite easy to reach and some that require a major effort. Plus, there are 60-70 miles of pristine coastline along the Pacific with unique intertidal habitats.

Diverse populations of fish are supported in each of these ecosystems.

➤ **The Rivers:** On the east side of the park, most of the rivers flowing into Hood Canal are closed to steelhead and salmon fishing. There are no runs of native fish healthy enough to allow harvest or even the risk of harm that would warrant an open fishery. There is fishing for a short period in the fall at the mouths of a couple of the rivers for hatchery fish, but about the only fishing on these smaller rivers and creeks is on the upper Skokomish for rainbows.

Traveling west toward the towns of Sequim (pronounced Squim) and Port Angeles, you will first encounter the Dungeness. This beautiful gem of a river is just a shadow of its former self. Not too long ago, it was still full of king salmon and steelhead. For such a small, steep drainage, it produced an amazing number of fish. The pink salmon have come back in big numbers during the last couple of cycles, but the prized steelhead and king salmon continue to struggle. The upper Dungeness River, above the tributary Gold Creek, and the Gray Wolf River, are open for trout fishing in the summer months.

To the west, just outside of Port Angeles, is the mighty Elwha River, now free of both of the dams that have kept steelhead and salmon confined to five miles of river for about 100 years. Closed to all fishing until at least 2017, the Elwha was our best and most productive trout fishery. Great evening dry-fly fishing was the standard pastime of many local and travelling anglers. Hiking into the upper river for 5, 10 or 15 miles, the prepared angler could experience some of the best wilderness trout fishing in the northwest. Those fish are still there. The river at one time produced king salmon up to 100 pounds, and whether we will ever see them that big again is

Right. Bright fall coho from the Bogachiel River. John R. McMillan

Below. Mature male coho with the prominent hooked nose. John R. McMillan

233

Summer trout water in the Quillayute headwaters. John R. McMillan

hard to imagine, but also very hard to predict. Salmon and steelhead are returning to the river and are going up above the former dam sites in pretty good numbers. They know what to do, and the potential for recovery is huge. The river is already showing real promise and the future is bright for the Elwha Valley.

Further west toward the coast you will eventually enter the town of Forks, and the beginning of the rain forest. Forks is the hub for salmon and steelhead fishing on the coastal rivers. Rivers such as the Sol Duc, Bogachiel, Hoh and Queets have been famous for decades for their productive salmon and steelhead fishing and draw hundreds of anglers from around the globe to pursue a fish of a lifetime and/or a fish for the cooler. The Quillayute system, which includes the Sol Duc, Bogachiel, Calawah, Dickey and Quillayute Rivers are productive trout fisheries from spring through fall. This holds true from the salt water to the headwaters in the national park.

- Sol Duc Hot Springs Road will take you up into the park water, which is open in the summer only.
- The Calawah in the park (summer only) is a tiny stream that requires a good bushwhacking to get to and is not worth the effort.

- The Bogachiel requires at least a one-mile hike to get into the park, and it can be some of the best hiking and fishing for trout since anglers lost the Elwha. The bulk of these rivers are in Washington State and most of the fishing for steelhead and salmon is done outside the park.
- The Bogachiel is the only Quillayute tributary that is open in the national park in the winter for steelhead. It's best to fish it earlier in the season (January-February) and leave it to the spawning fish in late March and April.

Hoh River: Heading south from Forks, anglers will enter the Hoh Rain Forest and the Hoh River, perhaps the most famous of the Olympic Peninsula rivers. With the headwaters on Mount Olympus in the national park, the Hoh is heavily influenced by glaciers and snow melt, and it most often has at least a tinge of gray color to the water. The vast majority of fishing pressure on the Hoh is in the state water. There is a small piece of national park water at the mouth of the river at tidewater. This can be a magical spot to swing a fly for steelhead and salmon. Chrome-bright fish just minutes from salt water, with the surf pounding in the background, makes this one area an incredibly precious place. About 25 miles upstream from the mouth is the normal park boundary where anglers travel toward the trailheads and the headwaters. It is open to steelhead fishing in the winter months, but has been closed for the last couple of summers. From the park boundary up to the Hoh Campground is fly fishing only. This is nice to have, but it is not the best fly water on the river. A lot of it is in braided channels with shallow, fast water with few places for fish to hold. Some years, the upper park water is pretty good; some years it is poor. Most of the good water for swinging flies is downstream in the state water. This coastal area gets more than 100 inches of rain per year, with most of it from November through March and some storms produce huge floods that completely reform and/or destroy productive runs. So, all anglers on the Hoh have to relearn their spots after every high water.

Queets River: The next river south is the Queets, and it is entirely in the national park, except for the lower few miles where the Queets Indians have their village and fishing rights. Two access roads take you into the Queets Valley: one for the lower half of the river valley and one other for the upper half, site of the Queets campground. After wading across the river near the campground, hardcore backpacking steelheaders trudge up the trail each winter and summer for the chance to experience native steelhead fishing in pristine wilderness conditions. The two roads will also lead to good river access. They parallel the river in a few places, making it easy to get to the water. Steelhead, salmon and cutthroat are the target species here, too. There are bull trout (char) in all of the glacial rivers, but they are protected and cannot be targeted by fishermen. They are unavoidable while fishing for steelhead and salmon, and must be released unharmed.

Quinault River: The Quinault River is next to the south and is very lightly fished in the national park. The Quinault Valley is a stunningly beautiful place to fish. Only open in the summer months, the Quinault in the park does have some decent fishing for rainbow trout, with most fish being on the

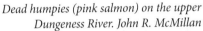

Dead humpies (pink salmon) on the upper Dungeness River. John R. McMillan

Rainforest river during summer—a time to fish for cutthroat trout. John R. McMillan

small side. There is still a small population of native summer steelhead that head up into the park. Often hard to find, these chrome bullets make the hike and the search well worth it.

All of the coastal rivers face some real management issues for the future. The fish have to swim through a gauntlet of predators—both human and non-human—before they can get to river mouths and then the upper water in the park. Both commercial and sport fishing have major impacts. All of these rivers are co-managed by the Washington Department of Fish and Wildlife, the native tribes at the mouths of the rivers and the national park. Politics can play a big role, and the fish generally suffer because of it. The Hoh has actually been closed in recent summers in an attempt to protect depleted stocks of spring and summer Chinook salmon. Most rivers will remain open for catch-and-release fishing, but regulations can change from season to season and year to year. Because of the complexity of the dozens of unique populations of salmon, trout and char in the many different river systems, the fishing regulations are also complex and often confusing. It is catch-and-release for all wild steelhead (those unmarked and identified by an intact adipose fin) and all other unmarked, native fish species. Bait is prohibited in all park rivers. Fishing for bull trout and Dolly Varden is not allowed in any park waters. Hatchery steelhead may be retained, but it is essentially catch-and-release for all other species in the rivers of the park. It is best to check the current year's regulation booklet or the local fly shop for the most up-to-date information.

Most of the Peninsula Rivers, both inside and outside of the park, have aquatic insect species that are similar to those found in most Rocky Mountain streams. Golden stones and yellow sallies are the most prevalent stoneflies and are around from June through August. There are Green Drakes, PMDs,

March Browns and Baetis. Besides the normal smaller tan and olive caddis, we also have the luxury of great numbers of October Caddis. This nearly inch-long bomber draws a lot of attention from trout, summer steelhead and occasionally fall salmon. Hoppers are not too important, but ants and termites are relished by OP trout.

So, even though there are quite a few local patterns that are used here, the Olympic National Park and Olympic Peninsula angler can keep it pretty simple and use some of the patterns they probably already have in their boxes. Standard beadheads such as Pheasant Tails, Princes and Copper Johns in sizes 8-14 work well, and a size 8 Pat's Rubber Leg is a killer stone pattern; they eat it for the October Caddis, too. All trout love the Royal Wulff, and so do Olympic trout. It's a great fly in the lakes and the rivers, whether targeting sea-run or resident fish. Stimulators, Sofa Pillows and other caddis/stonefly patterns in yellows and oranges, sizes 6-16 will work consistently. We also fish a lot of streamers and wet flies for our trout in the rivers. Cutthroats love Sculpin, so various Muddler variations are always productive. Streamers in the 1- to 2-inch range work more consistently for trout than larger flies most of the time. A 4- to 6-weight rod will work for any of the trout fishing in the rivers. While most fishing is with a floating line, a sink-tip or sinking leader can help at times.

For summer steelhead, anything from a 6-weight single-handed rod to a 7-weight switch or Spey rod is used, depending on the river and conditions. Traditional wets like the Fall Favorite or Silver Hilton in sizes 4- through 8 will work, but we also fish small leeches and will skate dries like the Grease Liner, especially when the October Caddis are around. Floating lines are the norm on the Quillayute rivers in the summer, but a light sink-tip can be required on the Hoh and Queets.

For winter steelhead or salmon, an 8- or 9-weight single-handed rod or a 7- to 9-weight switch or Spey is ideal. A line with interchangeable sink-tips is the most effective and efficient system. The various winter conditions mean various sizes of flies are also needed, and we sometimes fish flies that are 4 to 6 inches long in very high, dirty water. The Intruder has been a very popular and productive pattern, as have bunny leeches in pink, orange, purple, blue and black. The ubiquitous Egg-sucking Leech in all of its many variations is always a safe bet. Don't forget the old patterns like the Polar Shrimp or Skykomish Sunrise in sizes 1 and 2. Many anglers fish with an indicator and an egg pattern, and this does certainly produce its share of fish.

➤ **The Lakes:** Season: Last Saturday in April until October 31. Lake Crescent is June 1-October 31.

Even though it might not have the great rivers, the Hood Canal area is a very popular launching point for anglers hiking into the high lakes, both inside and outside the park. Lakes such as Lena Lake (outside the park) and Upper Lena and Flapjack Lakes (inside the park) have been well-known and popular destinations for decades.

There are trailheads leading from numerous spots around the park, and they all have potential fishing value. A popular must-see for the park visitor is the drive up to Hurricane Ridge, which heads straight up the mountain south from Port Angeles. Here you will find perhaps the most spectacular view from anywhere in the park. At an elevation of about 5,200 feet, surrounded by more mountain peaks and alpine meadows, one is treated to an amazing view of Puget Sound, Vancouver Island and the Strait of Juan de Fuca. On the way up the hill, there are a few lakes to consider hiking into. Look for Obstruction Point Road. This takes you to the trailhead for Grand Valley and the trio of Grand, Moose and Gladys

Lakes. The trip covers about eight miles, making it a comfortable day trip, though there's also a very nice place to camp. Heading toward the Sol Duc River headwaters and the end of the Hot Springs Road, there are great options for the lake enthusiast. Mink and Deer Lakes are shorter hikes and quite doable in a day. One of the best areas in the entire park is Seven Lakes Basin. It's about a 20-mile round trip, ideal for a couple of nights of camping and fishing. Brook trout are the most numerous trout in the lakes, and the park service considers them an invasive species, so there are no restrictions on keeping these. In fact, bait, treble and barbed hooks are allowed, and rainbow and cutthroat trout can also be retained in the lakes.

Keep your fly selection simple for the high lakes. A few dries such as Elk Hair Caddis, Parachute Adams and ants work well. Subsurface patterns like Carey Specials, Zug Bugs,

Average-sized, fresh, male winter steelhead with just a hint of blush. John R. McMillan

The Elwha River with a fresh dusting. John R. McMillan

soft hackles and leeches are good producers. A 9-foot, 4- or 5-weight rod with a floating line will cover most of your needs. A sink tip line or a sinking leader would be a good add-on to take with you.

Lake Crescent, the crown jewel of the park, is about 20 miles west of Port Angeles and the park's best known still-water fishery. Beardslee rainbows and Crescenti cutthroats (a.k.a. Lake Crescent Cutthroat Trout) are the two unique trout found only in this lake; they have been documented up to 20 pounds. A huge one now is 12 or 13 pounds. There are lots of smaller fish around the edges of the lakes that can be caught on all kinds of trout flies. Attractor dry flies, large carpenter ants and moths work on the surface. Sculpin, black leeches and minnow imitations work subsurface. Small kokanee are the main food source for the larger fish, so larger saltwater baitfish is useful here. Fish early in the mornings with deep sunk lines for the large fish. Regulations call for barbless, artificial flies and lures and strict catch-and-release here. A 6- or 7-weight rod may be more appropriate on this large lake.

➤ **The Salt Water:** The saltwater fishery off the Washington coast is a big opportunity for many; however, unless you're on a boat, off the coast the fly-fishing is limited and challenging. The many miles of secluded beaches will offer some fishing for red tail surfperch when surf conditions calm down in the spring and summer. Fish sink-tip lines with pink and orange shrimp patterns. The beaches around Kalaloch are ideal for this. The nearly 40-mile coastal strip north and south of the Quileute Indian Reservation is a road-less wilderness area. This area offers one of the more unique hiking experiences anywhere on the peninsula. Be careful that you monitor the tides to safely negotiate the headlands and creek mouths. Perch fishing is excellent, as is fishing for sea-run cutts in the creek estuaries, such as Mosquito or Goodman, in the fall. A Washington State Recreational Fishing License is required to fish the Pacific Ocean from shore.

There is a robust fishery for sea-run cutthroats, and in some areas resident Coho salmon, all along the beaches of Puget Sound outside of the national park. These fish are around most all of the year in these more protected water-

238

ways. The Pacific is a much rougher place, and the cutthroat won't be available here until they get near the protection of their natal streams.

➤ Tackle and Gear

Rods and Line:

Trout: A 9-foot, 5-weight is hard to beat for an all-around trout rod most anywhere, and it holds true for the Olympic Peninsula and Olympic National Park as well. One could fish 2- or 3-weights for the brookies in the high country, or even Tenkara, but the classic 9-5 will be the best match. Some of the larger rivers in the fall or massive Lake Crescent are better suited to a 6-weight, especially in the wind or with air-resistant October Caddis dries or skated Muddlers. Floating lines are usually all one needs. At times, a sinking leader or sink-tip line will be helpful. The same holds true for the high lakes. Deeper lakes such as Crescent—when not searching for risers with a floater—are most effectively covered with a full-sinking line. Standard 9- to 12-foot leaders tapered to 3X or 4X will work most of the time. Tippet from 2X to 5X will cover all of your bases. Fluorocarbon might be helpful in Lake Crescent, but not in many others.

Steelhead: For summer steelhead, whether fishing a floating, light sink-tip or heavy sink-tip line depends on many factors—one of those being personal preference. Throughout the summer and fall, there are ample opportunities to do all three, especially if the angler jumps around between the diverse river systems. The Quillayute system can quickly become a dry line show. It gets low and clear quite quickly in the summer. Leaders from 12 to 18 feet tapered to a 0X or 2x tippet are standard. The glacially influenced rivers such as the Hoh, Queets, and Quinault can oftentimes require some sort of sink tip for most, if not all, of the summer depending on the year. Use 1X or 2X leaders from 3 to 7 feet. Traditional anglers who swing flies for winter steelhead use a sink-tip line almost exclusively—often quite heavy ones. At times, the water is very low and a floating line can be used, but it is fairly rare. However, every year a few dedicated steelheaders will get winter fish to respond to surface patterns. It just depends on how one wants to catch them. Most of the anglers using floating lines are dead drifting egg patterns, fuzzy yarn balls or beads, where they employ leaders tapered down to 1X or 0X. Leaders for winter steelhead are usually much shorter and stouter; 2- to 6-feet in length with a tippet of 12-pound Maxima (about 03X).

Salmon: This is almost identical to the above steelhead info. Most of the time, sink tips and short, heavy leaders are the norm, but at times with low, clear water, long leaders fished with a floating line are required.

Terminal Tackle and Flies: Standard bead heads such as Pheasant Tails, Princes and Copper Johns in sizes 8-14 work well and a size 8 Pat's Rubber Leg is a killer stone pattern. The Royal Wulff is a solid producer. Stimulators, Sofa Pillows and other caddis/stonefly patterns in yellows and oranges, sizes 6-16, will work consistently. Streamers and wet flies are recommended for our trout in the rivers. Cutthroats love Sculpin, so various Muddler variations are always productive. Streamers in the 1- to 2-inch range work more consistently for trout than larger flies most of the time. For summer steelhead, traditional wets such as the Fall Favorite or Silver Hilton in sizes 4-8 will work, as will small leeches and skate dries, such as the Grease Liner. When fishing for winter steelhead or salmon, reach for the Intruder, as well as bunny leeches in pink, orange, purple, blue and black. The Egg-sucking Leech in all of its many variations is always a safe bet. Polar Shrimp or Skykomish Sunrise in sizes 1 and 2 also will work. In the lakes, dries such as Elk Hair Caddis, Parachute Adams and ants work well. Subsurface patterns such as Carey Specials, Zug Bugs, soft hackles and leeches are good producers.

The lower Elwha River with a tinge of spring snow melt. John R. McMillan

Sol Duc River spey fishing on a clear, crisp winter day. John R. McMillan

Adult bull trout, common in the glacial rivers, in its underwater world. John R. McMillan

CLOSEST CITY OR POINT OF ENTRANCE
The main entrance, the park headquarters and what is considered the gateway to the park is Port Angeles, Washington.

CLOSEST AIRPORT
Seattle/Tacoma (Sea-Tac) International—Full hotel/motel, auto rental and all other services are available.

OPENING/CLOSING DATES OR FISHING DATES:
· The park is open to visitors and hikers year-round, but the fishing seasons are different.
· The lowland lakes open the last Saturday in April and close October 31.
· The exception is Lake Crescent which does not open until June 1, but still closes October 31.
· The general season for the rivers in the park is June 1–October 31.
· However, there can be closures so check current regulations.
· Some rivers in the park remain open through the winter months and some do not.

CLOSEST FLY SHOP
Waters West
140 W. Front St.
Port Angeles, WA 98362
360-417-0937

CLOSEST GUIDE/OUTFITTERS SERVICE
Olympic National Park has separate guide license requirements than the State of Washington. Names of licensed guides change frequently, so check with the park headquarters to obtain the most recent roster of licensed guides: 360-565-3130.

Jim Kerr Rain Coast Guides
291 Three Rivers Rd.
Forks, WA 98331
360-301 4559
jimkerrguides@me.com
(Guiding inside and outside the park)

Waters West
140 W. Front St.
Port Angeles, WA 98362
369-417-0937
www.waterswest.com
info@waterswest.com
(Guiding outside the park and Lake Crescent)

CLOSEST FULL-SERVICE LODGES
None

BEST PLACES TO STAY IN THE PARK
Visit http://www.olympicnationalparks .com/accommodations.
Lodging accommodations are available seasonally inside the park at the following:

Lake Crescent Lodge
416 Lake Crescent Rd.
Port Angeles, WA 98363
360-928-3211

Log Cabin Resort
3183 E. Beach Rd.
Port Angeles, WA 98363
360-928-3325

Sol Duc Hot Springs Resort
12076 Sol Duc Hot Springs Rd.
Port Angeles, WA 98363
360-327-3583

Kalaloch Lodge
157151 U.S. Route 101
Forks, WA 98331
360-962-2271
(Year-round, on the coast)

BEST PLACES TO STAY NEAR THE PARK
Red Lion Hotel
221 N. Lincoln
Port Angeles, WA 98362
360-452-9215
portangelessales@redlion.com

DAVE STEINBAUGH grew up in the Finger Lakes region of upstate New York fishing the local streams for the migratory rainbows, browns, bass and landlocked salmon that flourished there. In 1982, he followed a childhood dream and moved to Montana to live in what was trout Mecca at the time. The guiding and commercial fly tying began very soon after. The fishing-bum lifestyle led to winters fishing for steelhead on the Olympic Peninsula beginning around 1988. Basing out of West Yellowstone, Dave guided all over the southern half of Montana, throughout Yellowstone Park, and some in Idaho and Alaska until 1998.

That year, Waters West, which began in 1994 as a mail-order catalog, transformed from a nomadic guiding and fly-tying operation into a brick-and-mortar store in downtown Port Angeles, Washington, where it is still going strong today.

Olympic Lodge
140 Del Guzzi Dr.
Port Angeles, WA 98362
360-452-2993

Quillayute River Resort
473 Mora Rd.
Forks, WA 98331-9432
360-374-7447

BEST CAMPGROUND IN THE PARK
Kalaloch Campground next to Kalaloch Lodge
157151 Washington 101
Forks, WA 98331
360-962-2271 or 866-662 9928

Hoh River Campground
(at the end of Upper Hoh River Rd.)

Mora Campground
(on the Quillayute River near Rialto Beach)

BEST CAMPGROUND NEAR THE PARK
Elwha Dam RV Park
47 Lower Dam Rd.
Port Angeles, WA 98363
360-452-7054
paradise@elwhadamrvpark.com

Salt Creek Recreation Area
3506 Camp Hayden Rd
Port Angeles, WA 98363
360-928-3441

BEST PLACE TO EAT IN THE PARK
Lake Crescent Lodge
416 Lake Crescent Rd.
Port Angeles, WA 98363
360-928-3211

Kalaloch Lodge
157151 U.S. Route 101
Forks, WA 98331
360-962-2271

BEST PLACE TO EAT NEAR THE PARK
Next Door Gastropub
113 W. First St.
Port Angeles, WA 98362
360-504-2613

Michael's Seafood & Steakhouse
117B E. First St.
Port Angeles, WA 98362
360-417-6929

Toga's Soup House Deli & Gourmet
122 West Lauridsen Boulevard
Port Angeles, WA 98362
360-452-1952
info@togassouphouse.com

CLOSEST AND BEST PLACE TO GET A DRINK
Barhop Brewing & Pizza
124 W. Railroad Ave.
Port Angeles, WA **98362**
360-797-1818

Next Door Gastropub
113 W. First St.
Port Angeles, WA 98362
360-504-2613

MUST SEE
Hurricane Ridge. In clear weather, fantastic views can be enjoyed throughout the year. Hurricane Ridge is 17 miles south of Port Angeles on Hurricane Ridge Road, off Mount Angeles Road

NEAREST HOSPITAL / URGENT CARE CENTER
Olympic Medical Center
939 Caroline St.
Port Angeles, WA 98362
360-417-7000

Forks Community Hospital
530 Bogachiel Way
Forks, WA 98331
360-374-6271

CELL PHONE SERVICE
Cell service works pretty well in a lot of the park with dead spots here and there. Verizon works the best.

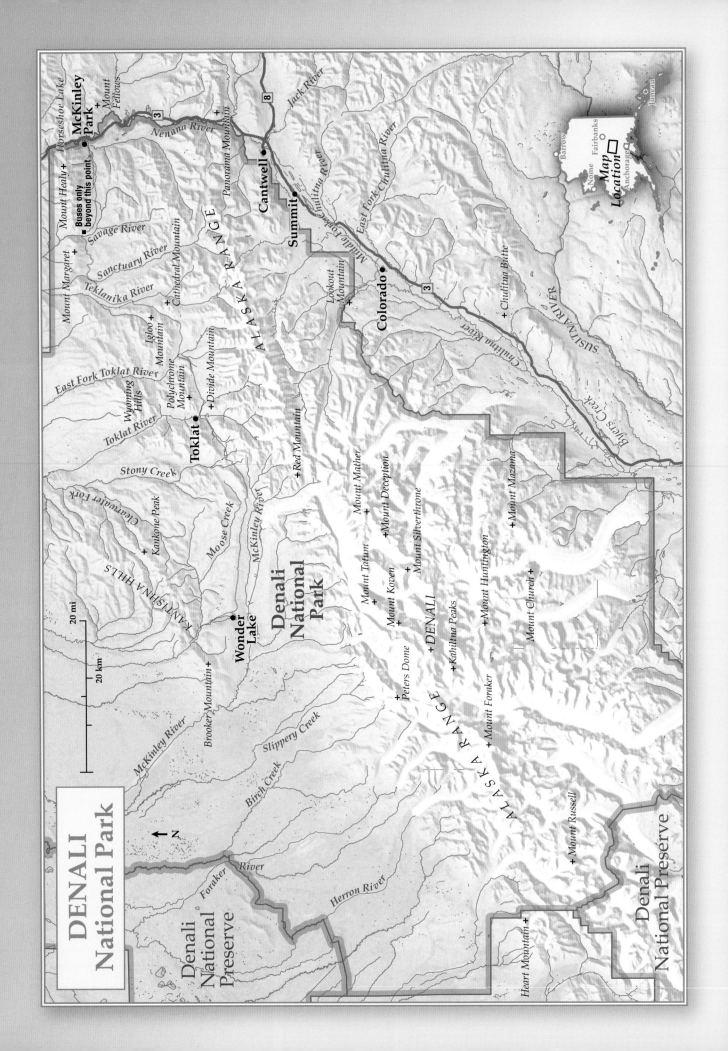

Denali National Park and Preserve

Alpine lakes and forest of Denali National Park. Carol M. Highsmith

➤ **Location:** The park is most easily accessed in the following ways:
- There is one road entrance into Denali National Park and Preserve on the George Parks Highway (also called Alaska Highway 3) about 240 miles north of Anchorage, 120 miles south of Fairbanks, and 12 miles south of Healy, the nearest year-round community.
- Alaska's state-owned railroad connects Anchorage to Fairbanks and runs directly through the entrance of Denali.
- Air travel to either Anchorage (ANC) or Fairbanks (FAI) is the easiest entry to Alaska.

- Personal transportation with a rental car, bus or train is the best ways to reach Denali, or if you plan on covering a lot of ground.

Denali National Park and Preserve encompasses more than six million acres and is about five times larger than the state of Rhode Island! The park features amazing wildlife and Denali (formerly Mt. McKinley)—the tallest peak in North America. It is also home to thriving wild rainbow trout, salmon, and Arctic grayling populations.

The divide that sends water north to the Yukon River or south to the Mat-Su River runs down the spine of the park east to west. To the south, opportunities for rainbow trout and

243

all the salmon species abound with a few opportunities for grayling and lake trout at higher elevations. To the north, grayling make up most of the sport fish due to a lack of salmon runs near the north side of the park.

Road access to the park itself is limited. The Parks Highway from Anchorage to Fairbanks runs down its east side. Most access for rainbow trout is on the Parks Highway south of Cantwell on the Chulitna River drainage. Byer's Creek, mile marker 144, is a popular rainbow trout and salmon fishery with several camp-grounds north of the creek on the Parks Highway. Byers Creek is at the edge of Denali National Park and falls in Denali State Park.

Sockeye salmon return to spawn on the southern edge of the park. Terry Gunn

There is a very dense brown bear population in this area so always be aware of your surroundings.

The Denali Highway heads east out of Cantwell, about 20 miles south of the Park Road. Excellent fishing and camping opportunities for grayling and lake trout exist on this 135-mile dirt road. Brushkana Creek offers excellent fishing opportunities and a campground. The Denali Highway isn't maintained in the winter and has very little in the way of services along the way to Paxson. The drive can be done in a long day in good conditions, but a solid spare tire kit is recommended.

Around the Cantwell area, the Ahtna Native Corporation has its land marked by orange signs. This is private proper-ty requiring a permit to cross. There are clearly designated points where trails allow access through Ahtna Land to the State Land on the other side. Always check rights of way and access before crossing.

The Park Road runs 92 miles into Denali National Park and is the park's only road. It crosses numerous small streams known to have grayling. After the first 15 miles, scheduled buses become the only access, making exploration of fishing opportunities farther into the park more difficult. Horseshoe Lake is one of the easiest places in the area to access for a chance to catch some grayling just inside the park entrance.

Inside Denali National Park, it is recommended that all users go to the visitors' center to observe rules and guidelines for using the park and to arrange access by bus.

A word of caution in the backcountry:

- People experiencing this area for the first time are overwhelmed by its vastness and beauty, but the remote landscape presents challenges and dangers that warrant constant awareness.

- Never travel alone.
- Always tell someone where you are going and when you will be back.
- Prepare for inclement weather.
- Wear layers and remember it's better to be cool with layers to add than sweaty and cold.
- Also, never wear cotton. The saying in Alaska is "cotton kills." Hypothermia, especially after being immersed in water, is the leading killer of outdoorsmen in Alaska
- Big game in Alaska doesn't need to be feared, but a healthy respect for potential danger is important for anyone outdoors. Pepper spray is a good idea, but many Alaskans go their whole lives never needing to defend themselves simply by being aware.
- Make plenty of noise when line of sight or cover noise (such as running water) might allow fisher-men to accidentally spook big game.
- Never run from a bear—any bear!

If a moose charges, run and take cover; a tree larger than a few inches around its base makes an effective obstacle to keep a charging moose at a distance. Cow moose with calves are a great photo opportunity, but keep in mind a cow moose with a calf is the most dangerous animal you will find in North America.

Three simple rules:

1. Always keep a clean camp.
2. Never feed wildlife.
3. Give wildlife plenty of room.

Down the valley towards Denali on a beautiful day, with the one park road wending its way. Nic McPhee

➤ **Fishing for Grayling:** Grayling start moving before green-up, from mid-May to early June. After the snowmelt is gone, insect life increases to take advantage of the short summer season. Grayling can be caught using many of the same tactics used for other small trout species, such as brook trout or smaller rainbows. Fly rods 4-weight and lighter are recommended for wild grayling ranging from 6 to 18 inches. A standard assortment of small nymphs and dry flies sizes 12 to 18 will cover most grayling fishing situations. Cloudy, rainy days are tough days to fish for grayling, making unorthodox attractors such as the Salcha Pink essential to any dry-fly box.

If catch-and-release is the intent, then it is recommended that anglers always crimp their barbs for grayling or rainbows to reduce the stress and harm to the fish. With grayling, barbless should be stressed because of their very soft mouths and catch-and-release should be emphasized because of their slow growth of about one inch per year. If fly fishers want to keep a grayling to eat, it should be consumed within an hour because they become inedibly soft if left longer.

➤ **Fishing for Trout and Salmon:** Rainbow fishing is slow at the southern edge of the park in June, but a few resident fish that go up the small streams to lakes for the winter can be found chasing salmon smolt and early insects. King salmon start to run in June, but until there are salmon eggs in the river, most of the rainbows stay farther south towards Talkeetna. Fly rods from 5- to 7-weight are recommended for wild rainbows ranging from 12 to 24 inches. King salmon are only legal to pursue in certain waters, but where they can be caught, large bright flies work well on rods 10- to 12-weight with sink-tip lines.

In July, the insect life is at full capacity and grayling settle into large pools by the dozen. Tourist season peaks with nearly 24 hours of daylight and temperatures as warm as the 80s. And yet, snow in July isn't unheard of, reminding locals and tourists to prepare for a wide range of conditions. Streams become more stable and clear because of less runoff from snow melt. Look for insect activity and rising fish anywhere there is a body of clear water. Grayling can boil into a feeding

Arctic grayling will readily take a dry fly. Terry Gunn

frenzy if a big enough hatch starts. Anglers will find grayling are quick at spitting the hook, requiring a no-delay hook-set while not setting too hard because of their soft mouths.

Rainbow fishing picks up considerably in July as kings die off and leave their nests undefended. Rainbows will be opportunistic, looking for big meals as they ambush salmon smolt while they pour downstream. Egg and smolt patterns must match seamlessly with the food sources present, making an assortment key. If your assortment doesn't have a perfect match, the rule that big fish eat big food is true anywhere in Alaska. Dali-Llamas, Egg-sucking Leeches, and Sculpin are go-to rainbow patterns and should be kept in tan, olive, purple, and black. Large, articulated patterns do very well in sizes 2 and 4. Mouse patterns such as the Moorish Mouse make excellent attractors, and rainbow fishers should always carry a few. Small fish and saltwater shrimp patterns work well for the sockeye (red) salmon that show up in greater numbers toward the end of July with the fishing improving into mid-August. 7- to 9-weight rods are recommended for all salmon other than kings.

August is the beginning of the end of the season in the higher elevations. Grayling are packing on the ounces for the long winter and as the temperatures drop, as do insect numbers. Early in the month, weather can be very warm, but leaves start to change quickly and the weather follows closely. Caddis and mayflies start to come out in larger numbers and nymphing becomes more important as rainy fall weather occurs more frequently, making breaks of sunshine a rare opportunity for both insect and angler.

As the month progresses, the salmon begin to die off, bringing rainbow season to its climax from mid-August to early September until it stops, abruptly, one section at a time as trout turn and head downstream for the winter. Light-colored salmon flesh patterns, large streamers, large dry flies, mice, and washed beads all work well along cut banks, logs, and large holes. Clear water is the key, so fall rains and flooding can make the fish leave early.

September is the last push for life in the region. Moose and caribou start sparring for the mating season and tracks are everywhere. Bears look for late salmon. Wolves follow moose and caribou up and down the drainages. Early snow covers mountaintops, and as the tundra freezes the rivers start to drop. The first week of September is the most picturesque time of the year to be in the Denali area and the best time of year to see wildlife.

Grayling come down from the higher elevations toward the deeper water. As they move downstream, other fish turn and follow, making large schools. Seams where cloudy, silted rivers and clear streams come together are good places to find fish. Heavily weighted nymphs dead-drifted near the bottom do very well this time of year.

Muddy, flooded waters make chasing rainbows difficult on the south side of the park in September. Large streamers and flesh patterns fished deep along places where rainbows can rest and hide can still produce sizeable fish, but depending on the season many move back towards Talkeetna as soon as the salmon have spawned.

➤ **Local Services:** Denali Fly Fishing Guides is the area's only service offering fully guided and outfitted fly-fishing trips. Primarily guiding the Denali Highway, DFFG also maintains an Ahtna permit allowing them access to many of the area's best grayling streams within view of Denali. Full-day trips are also available for rainbows south of Cantwell. Not an expert fly caster? A full casting lesson is part of the trip. Heading north from Cantwell, DFFG is located on the boat launch immediately south of the Nenana River Bridge and west of the Park's Highway at mile marker 214.5.

For non-fishing travel companions, Terry Boyd Photography Tours offers a personalized tour of the area seeking wildlife and landscape photo opportunities. The tour offers an excellent chance to learn about getting more from your camera and has very good access for visitors with limited mobility.

Independent travelers with transportation seeking local hospitality find it at the Backwoods Lodge. The Backwoods Lodge is in Cantwell at the start of the Denali Highway, making it a great starting point for adventures on area streams. It is also walking distance from a view of Mt. McKinley. Note: Only 20 percent of visitors see Mt. McKinley every-year because it is not visible from park-area lodging north of Cantwell and frequent cloud cover often obscures the peak.

Denali Mountain Morning Hostel, mile marker 224, offers accommodation for the traveler on a budget, including a shuttle service to and from the park entrance. After a long day traveling or fishing, the hostel is conveniently located across from several favorite eateries including Panorama

Grizzly bears are common through the park. Terry Gunn

Pizza Pub. Up the road at mile marker 229, on the west side of the Parks Highway, is 229 Parks, without doubt the best fine dining in the area and a favorite for locals on special occasions while remaining true to Alaska, where blue jeans are common.

Past the Park Road heading north on the Park's Highway is Glitter Gulch, numerous hotels and gift shops blanket both sides of the road. At the north end on the east side of the road is Denali Mountain Works, mile marker 240 the closest place to buy fishing tackle, locally tied flies, maps, and fishing licenses. They also carry a wide variety of camping and outdoor gear.

The Alaska Department of Fish and Game sets regulations annually. Due to changes, it is recommended you carefully read all regulations for the area you will be fishing—especially in salmon waters.

Be aware that
· Felt-soled waders are illegal.
· Droppers (using more than one fly) are illegal.
· Certain waters might regulate gear types such as treble hooks and bait. When it is not legal to catch a certain salmon species, it is also illegal to "molest," or catch them intentionally or unintentionally.
· It is important to understand that lifting a fish from the water, even for a picture, even if hooked accidentally, can result in a ticket.
· Only one rod at a time is legal in Alaska.

➤ Tackle and Gear

Rods and Line: Fly rods 4-weight and lighter are recommended for wild grayling ranging from 6-18 inches. Fly rods from 5- to 7-weight are recommended for wild rainbows ranging from 12 to 24 inches. King salmon are only legal to pursue in certain waters, but where they can be caught, rods 10- to 12-weight with sink-tip lines are recommended. 7- to 9-weight rods are recommended for all salmon other than kings.

Terminal Tackle and Flies: A standard assortment of small nymphs and dry flies in sizes 12 to 18 will cover most grayling fishing situations. Cloudy, rainy days are tough days to fish for grayling, making unorthodox attractors such as the Salcha Pink essential to any dry-fly box. Crimping the barbs of your hooks is recommended for the health of the fish you plan to return to the water. When fishing for king salmon, large, bright-colored flies are recommended. When fishing for 'bows, egg and smolt patterns must match seamlessly with the food sources present, so have an assortment handy. Dali Llamas, Egg-sucking Leeches, and Sculpin are go-to rainbow patterns and should be kept in tan, olive, purple and black. Large, articulated patterns do very well in sizes 2 and 4. Mouse patterns such as the Moorish Mouse make excellent attractors. Small fish and saltwater shrimp patterns work well for sockeye (red) salmon. Good late-season choices include light-colored salmon flesh patterns, large streamers, large dry flies, mice, and washed beads.

Grizzly Bears come in both blonde and dark phases. Always give a sow with cubs a very wide berth. Terry Gunn

CLOSEST CITY OR POINT OF ENTRANCE TO THE PARK
· The entrance into Denali is along Alaska Highway 3 (also called the George Parks Highway) about 240 miles north of Anchorage, 120 miles south of Fairbanks, and 12 miles south of Healy, the nearest year-round community.
· Talkeetna, about 100 miles north of Anchorage and 140 miles south of the park entrance, is Denali's mountaineering headquarters, although park access is only by airplane for people climbing Denali.

CLOSEST AIRPORT
· Fairbanks International in Fairbanks to the north
· Anchorage International in Anchorage to the south
· Merrill Field in Anchorage for charter and bush flights

FEES
· $20 per vehicle.
· $10 per person for seven days.
· Park entrance and user fees change periodically.
· For up-to-date fees, free days and other exceptions, visit http://www.nps.gov/dena/index.htm.

CLOSEST FLY SHOPS
Denali Mountain Works
Mile Marker 238.5 Parks Hwy.
Denali National Park, AK 99755
907-683-1542

Big Ray's Fly Shop
507 Second Ave.
Fairbanks, AK 99701
907-452-3458

Mountain View Sports
11124 Old Seward Hwy.
Anchorage, AK 99515
907-563-8600

LODGING
Backwoods Lodge
133.7 Denali Hwy.
Cantwell, AK 99729
907-987-0960

Denali Mountain Morning Hostel
Carlo Creek
Mile Marker 224 Parks Hwy.
907-683-7503
www.denalihostel.com

Above. Silver Salmon are eager to eat a fly and are
the most aerobatic of all salmon. Terry Gunn

Below. Rainbow trout in this area can reach
more than two feet long. Terry Gunn

Born in Juneau and raised on the Kenai Peninsula,
Alex Hundertmark is a longtime Fairbanks resident,
and has been chasing trout and salmon since childhood. Alex started fly fishing for grayling in college
and continued his passion as a guide and manager
at Denali Fly Fishing Guides. While fishing all over
the Denali Highway and Chulitna River drainage,
he has fished grayling, salmon, and rainbow trout in
the shadow of Denali for years, enjoying the peace
and quiet of the remote waterways.

BEST PLACES TO EAT

Panorama Pizza
Carlo Creek
Mile Marker 224 Parks Hwy.
Denali National Park and Preserve,
AK 99755
907-683-2623

229 Parks Restaurant and Tavern
Mile Marker 229 Parks Hwy.
Denali National Park and Preserve,
AK 99755
907-683-2567

Denali Salmon Bake
Mile 238.5 George Parks Hwy.
Denali National Park and Preserve,
AK 99755
907-683-2733

OTHER SITES, TOURS AND ACTIVITIES

Terry Boyd Photography Tours
479-747-7407
www.terryboydphotography.com

Denali Outdoor Center
Bike rentals, cabins and
campground north of the park
907-683-1925
www.denalioutdoorcenter.com

MUST SEE
North America's tallest peak: 20,310-foot
Denali (Mt. McKinley)

NEAREST HOSPITAL/URGENT CARE
CENTER
Canyon Health Clinic Urgent Care Center
(At the Park Entrance; seasonal facility)
907-683-4433

Tri-Valley Community Center
Usibelli Spur Rd.
P.O. Box 246
Healy, AK 99743
907-683-2615
www.myhealthclinic.org/

Fairbanks Memorial Hospital
1650 Cowles St.
Fairbanks, AK 99701
907-452-8181

CELL PHONE SERVICE:
Cell service is not available, or is
sporadic at best except near town
and the park entrance.

FOR ALL ELSE, VISIT:
http://www.nps.gov/dena/index.htm

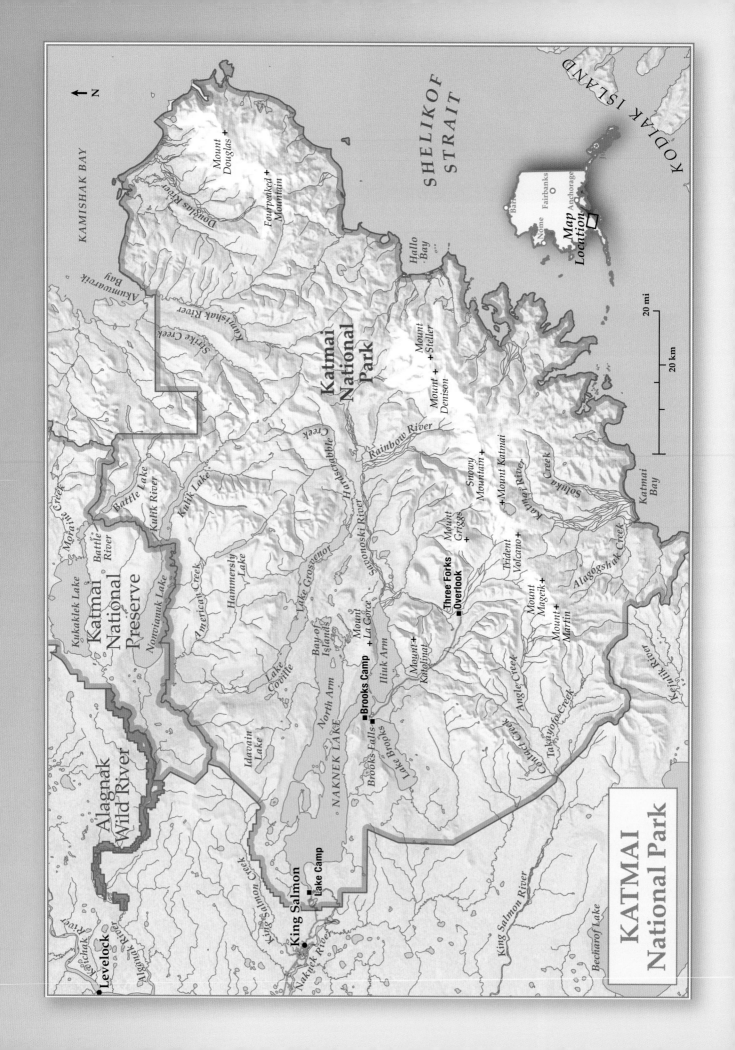

N

KAMISHAK BAY

Douglas River

Mount Douglas +

Fourpeaked + Mountain

Alumiarrok Bay

Strike Creek

Kamishak River

SHELIKOF STRAIT

Hallo Bay

Mount + Steller

Mount + Denison

Katmai National Park

KODIAK ISLAND

Nome
Barrow
Fairbanks
Anchorage
Map Location

20 mi

20 km

Rainbow River

Mount Katmai +

Soluka Creek

Katmai River

Katmai Bay

Morraine Creek

Battle Lake

Battle River

Kukaklek Lake

Kulik Lake

Kulik River

Hardscrabble Creek

Snowy Mountain +

Mount Griggs +

Trident Volcano +

Alagogshak Creek

Katmai National Preserve

Norrianuk Lake

American Creek

Hammersly Lake

Lake Grosvenor

Swikshak River

Three Forks Overlook ■

Mount Mageik +

Mount + Martin

Alagnak Wild River

Idavoin Lake

Lake Coville

Bay of Islands

North Arm

Mount + La Gorce

Iliuk Arm

Mount + Katolinat

Angle Creek

Contact Creek

Takayofo Creek

Brooks Camp ■
■

Kvichak River

Moraklek River

Alagnak River

King Salmon Creek

NAKNEK LAKE

Brooks Falls
Lake Brooks

Lake Camp ■

King Salmon ●

Naknek River

Levelock ●

King Salmon River

Bechorof Lake

Ketlik River

KATMAI National Park

Katmai National Park and Preserve

➤ **Location:** Katmai National Park and Preserve is located on the northern Alaska Peninsula, northwest of Kodiak Island and southwest of Homer, Alaska. The park's headquarters is in King Salmon, about 290 air miles southwest of Anchorage.

Unlike most national parks, Katmai is almost exclusively accessed by plane or boat. Many companies provide a variety of commercial visitor services including transportation, guided day trips, guided multi-day trips, overnight accommodations and food services. Commercial partners are authorized by permit to operate in the park.

Katmai National Park and Preserve spans more than four million acres of remote Alaskan wilderness on the northeast portion of the Alaskan Peninsula. In 1918, Katmai National Monument was established to study and preserve the area's volcanic activity. The eruption of Novarupta on June 6, 1912 was the most powerful volcanic blast of the 20th century, spreading ash as far as Africa. Heavy ash deposits were left nearest to the volcano, punctuated by many fumerals that sent steam into the air.

Robert Griggs led four expeditions to the area and named it "The Valley of Ten Thousand Smokes," an area appearing as an abstract moonscape cut through by rivers. It is still a geological attraction even though the steam has ceased. The park and preserve expanded its boundaries in 1980 to where they are today.

Because it is so remote, most anglers visit Katmai by staying at one of the many lodges in the area. There are three lodge operators in the park and preserve itself; others are on nearby rivers or in King Salmon. Typically, the day on the river starts early and concludes in mid- to late afternoon. Guides from lodges accompany their clients throughout the day and

Katmai offers some of the best fishing in Alaska along with spectacular scenery. Terry Gunn

The "Workhorse of Alaska," the DeHavilland Beaver, is the best mode of travel for this remote area. Terry Gunn

are there to assist with fly/bead selection, catch-and-release, grip 'n' grin photography, fish cleaning and processing (where allowed) as well as everything else expected from a guide. In addition to "normal" duties, guides must also be constantly aware of the bears in Katmai.

Katmai is home to one of the world's largest concentrations of brown bears. If fishing any water during salmon spawn, expect to see bears. Often, there are many of them in sight, and guides are very helpful at negotiating the terrain while limiting interaction, and they act as a second set of eyes for clients who are focused on fishing. If fishing on your own, being constantly aware of your surrounding is absolutely necessary. Although bears aren't as prevalent on the rivers when salmon aren't spawning, always be aware of the possibility of seeing one or having an encounter. Anyone visiting Katmai should be familiar with bear safety. The best weapon during an encounter is your brain. Most guides carry bear deterrents in one form or another but rarely use them. The bears in Katmai are often indifferent to anglers, and this can lead to complacency. It is important to observe the rules the park and operators have established in regard to bear safety distances.

While there are exceptions, such as being directed by a park official, the enforced distance is at least 50 yards.

Katmai offers access to all five species of Pacific salmon as well as an abundance of freshwater fish. Many anglers come to Katmai seeking the opportunity to catch a very large rainbow trout. Arctic grayling, Dolly Varden, Arctic char, lake trout and northern pike can also be targeted on many of the rivers and lakes.

Katmai is open year-round. However, few visit during months before June and after October. Services at Brooks Camp open June 1 and end September 17. Most lodges operate after the first week of June until the end of September, which loosely coincides with the availability of fish and relative cooperation of weather. Some lodges do stay open longer, meaning opening and closing dates can fluctuate yearly.

It is not uncommon for fish to retreat out of rivers and into ice-covered lakes for the winter. Most flowing waters or lakes, within 1/2 mile of inlet or outlet, cannot be fished between April 10 and June 7. June 8 brings the new fishing season to Katmai. Since the fishing is heavily dependent on the salmon life cycle, it is easy to divide the season into three segments:

- Early season fishing offers opportunities at surfacing fish on patterns imitating the migrating salmon fry or smolt.
- The middle of the season—after the fry and smolt migration and before the salmon spawn—offers dry-fly fishing and nymphing and
- Late season fishing is productive with egg imitations and flesh patterns.

Fishing streamers such as Woolly Buggers, Articulated Leeches or Sculpin patterns can be productive through the season. These segments in the season can overlap and intertwine with one another, which can be extremely productive and fun or—on occasion—stupefying.

Fishing in Katmai can change drastically in a matter of minutes. Weather changes very quickly and can impact the approach to fishing. It is important to be ready to adapt. Often, winds can make casting difficult, and a streamer buzzing by your head is barely tolerable. Learning to cast in wind is important, and most guides offer a few techniques to make things easier. Rain, cold, the odd thunderstorm and snow can impact your fishing day, although the latter is usually only present early and late in the season. It is important to dress properly, wearing appropriate base layers, good waders, and a quality rain jacket. Felt wading boots are illegal throughout the state of Alaska. Any day of any month can be miserable if not dressed properly. As nasty as the weather can be, it can also be very pleasant and often changes back and forth in the same day. As winds die down, insects come out and trout will feed on mayflies, caddis, stoneflies and other insects only an hour after ducking your streamer in the wind.

Above. Millions of sockeye salmon return to spawn in the park each year. Terry Gunn

Below. Brown bears will often be fishing the same waters as anglers. Terry Gunn

The giant rainbows lay behind the spawning salmon to feed on the abundant eggs. Terry Gunn

The insects anglers don't care for also pop up when the winds are down. Mosquitoes, no-see-ums, white socks and others will take a nibble on an angler and often seem to ignore the strongest repellents. Although chemical repellents, head nets, and other insect deterrents or protection do seem to help, in the end, some tolerance will be required.

Depending on the type of salmon that is being sought, time of year is important. When fishing for salmon species, they are targeted during the run and before they are on their redds or in active spawn. They are sought before their body begins its physiological changes. Most notably, the crimson red in sockeye, Chinook and Coho salmon and a change in shape signify a metamorphosis where the salmon begins to deteriorate. Chinook, Coho and sockeye salmon are the three most targeted for consumption. Pink and chum salmon are fun to catch on a fly but are seldom retained. Chinooks begin their run in the middle of June and will last roughly a month. Chinook salmon are often targeted using techniques besides

fly fishing. There is opportunity for the fly angler to catch a Chinook, but it often requires patience and determination to hook and land a nickel bright specimen. Sockeye are available through July; Coho run August through the first week of September. All time frames are estimates and subject to differ due to environmental or regulatory changes.

Brooks Camp is the heart of Katmai National Park and the point of public access. It is the primary destination for people who want to photograph bears and other wildlife. It's also the starting point for the tour in the Valley of Ten Thousand Smokes and offers other activities such as hiking, kayaking, camping, archaeological cultural sites and, of course, fishing.

Brooks River is a dynamic and productive fishery throughout the season, offering rainbow trout, grayling, lake trout, Dolly Varden, silver salmon and sockeye salmon. Also, northern pike are nearby. The world-famous Brooks Falls provides an ideal area for bears to display their fishing skills when the salmon are running and serves as a marker between two distinct stretches of river. There is no fishing or access 100 yards above or below the falls (it's marked with signs). Trails are marked with flagging that lead you around the falls and to the falls/riffles bear-viewing platform. It is worth stopping and seeing the falls and the bears fishing. Above the falls is water that typically holds fish in the 14- to 22-inch range holding in pocket water and sweeping corners. The stretch below the falls is much calmer and easier to wade. Typically, fish are a bit more selective, but the opportunity to catch a rainbow pushing the magical 30-inch mark is ever-present. Special consideration must be observed to abide by the rules at Brooks Camp. In many cases they are different from the rest of the park regarding personal property, food and drink on the river and more. If staying at a lodge that is part of the Brooks River Guide Program, these rules will be communicated to you before you arrive at Brooks; otherwise you must attend a mandatory bear orientation upon arriving.

Stretching more than 35 miles, American Creek offers an assortment of fishing opportunities. Flowing out of Hammersely Lake and into Lake Coville, it is possible to float the entire river, but it does require camping on the water and lasts around a week. This is the only way to access the entire river. If visiting for a day, the Upper American offers rainbow trout and Dolly Varden, typically between 16 and 22 inches. The upper section is generally accessed by walking in after a float-plane trip to a nearby lake. It offers deep runs, pocket water, and fast slots that can all hold fish.

The lower portion of American Creek is only accessible by jet boats belonging to various lodges, or you can see it on the latter part of a week's float trip. Nearest lodge access would be out of Grosvenor Lodge on the opposite end of Lake Coville. If fishing this stretch of the river is something on your list, inquire with the lodge or outfitter. While traveling up river, the first couple of miles meander casually, and the water offers few surface features with the exception of rising fish along the grass banks. As you continue upstream, the riverbank becomes lined with spruce trees— many of which fall into the water and provide cover for the rainbow and Dolly Varden. A few more miles upstream, the river braids out and the jet boat can no longer be used to access the narrow veins of water leading in different directions. At this point, you can continue to walk and fish water that often presents itself as untouched. Due to the limited number of operators, the Lower American can often offer the sense and peace of fishing alone in Alaska, and occasionally it is the reality.

The Kulik River is a short stretch of water between Kulik and Nonvianuk Lakes. It can be accessed by jet boat, inflatable raft or by walking up or down. As it is less than two miles long, the river provides ample opportunity for wildlife viewing and photography, especially during the fall months when both bear and angler seek fish on the river. The wading in most stretches is easy and— depending on water level— can generally be waded top to bottom. The Kulik offers an

These sockeye salmon eggs will hatch, and three to five years later the adults will return to spawn in the same stream from which they hatched. Terry Gunn

A big "dime bright" rainbow. These amazing fish are abundant throughout Katmai. Terry Gunn

Alutiiq people have called the Katmai region home for thousands of years. Terry Gunn

Below. Katmai is home to Alaska's largest population of brown bears. Terry Gunn

enjoyable day for both novice and experienced angler, providing opportunities to fish different patterns and experiment with many flies. Rainbow trout are prevalent throughout the river with lake trout and occasionally other species. You can also explore the lakes around the river by boat, weather permitting, and can often find a few fish eager to eat.

Fishing the rivers and lakes in and around Katmai offers a variety of techniques and abundance of species that can be found in few other places. There are many different bodies of water, including those on the Nushagak drainage, Kvichak drainage, Naknek drainage, Alagnak drainage and other rivers and streams in and around Katmai National Park and Preserve. The Kamishak, Moraine, Funnel, and Battle are all worth looking into. Lodges are familiar with what rivers they want to fish and when they want to be there. If a certain species, water or time is on your agenda, contacting the lodges in the area is your best bet.

Note: Lodges and camps with access to these waters fill quickly; make your reservations early.

➤ **Tackle and Gear**

Rods and Lines: Seven-weight rods and reels with both floating and sink-tip lines accommodate most species. Inquire with the lodge or outfitter for recommendations for specific species.

Terminal Tackle and Flies: Recommended fly patterns are contained within the body text above and most lodges/outfitters will have appropriate tackle.

Few places on earth produce the size of rainbows that you will find in this remote region of Alaska. Terry Gunn

CLOSEST CITY OR POINT OF ENTRANCE TO THE PARK
King Salmon, Alaska

CLOSEST AIRPORT
King Salmon with service from Anchorage, Fairbanks and others. Air taxi, lodge flights and charter services from King Salmon into the park.

OPEN/CLOSING PARK DATES OR FISHING DATES
· The park is open year-round, however, there are the obvious severe weather hazards.
· Fishing season is generally June 8 through early October.
· Brooks Camp is open June 1-September 17.

· An Alaska sport fishing license is required of all nonresidents 16 and over and most residents 16 to 59.
· You might also need a harvest record card and/or king salmon stamp before you fish.
· Special federal regulations, in addition to state regulations, exist for the Brooks River.
· For more information and to buy your licenses, stamps, and tags online, visit the Alaska Department of Fish & Game License and Permits web site at http://www.adfg.alaska.gov/index.cfm?adfg=home.main.

CLOSEST FLY SHOPS
Mountain View Sports
11124 Old Seward Hwy.
Anchorage, AK 99515
907-563-8600

Mossy's Fly Shop
750 W. Dimond Blvd #114
Anchorage, AK 99515
907-770-2666

Cabela's
155 W. 104th Ave.
Anchorage, AK
907-341-3400

Sportsman's Warehouse
8681 Old Seward Highway
Anchorage, AK 99515
907-644-1400

CLOSEST GUIDE/OUTFITTER SERVICES
See lodges in and near the park and air taxi services below.

CLOSEST FULL-SERVICE LODGES
Lodges and fishing guides, photography, bear-watching, hiking and kayaking services contract with the National Park Service, referred to as Commercial Use Authorizations. These change periodically. For an up-to-date list, write or phone
Katmai National Park and Preserve
P.O. Box 7
King Salmon, AK 99613
907-246-2113
http://www.nps.gov/akso/management/concession_docs/CSD/CSD-KATM-2015.pdf

FULL-SERVICE LODGES IN THE PARK
Katmailand, Inc.
Angler's Paradise Lodges
(Kulik, Brooks and Grosvenor lodges)
4125 Aircraft Dr.
Anchorage, AK 99502
800-544-0551 or 907-243-5448
info@katmailand.com

Enchanted Lake Lodge
(Overlooks Nonvianuk Lake)
June 1-October 1
P.O. Box 97
King Salmon, AK 99613
907-246-6878 907-273-0044
info@enchantedlakelodge.com

Royal Wolf Lodge
P.O. Box 190207
Anchorage, AK 99519
907-248-3256
http://www.royalwolf.com/

FULL-SERVICE LODGES NEAR THE PARK
Crystal Creek Lodge
Box 872729
Wasilla, AK 99687-2729
907-357-3153
http://crystalcreeklodge.com/

Alaska Sportsman's Lodges
(Alaska Sportsman's Lodge, Bear Trail Lodge, Bristol Bay Lodge)
October-May
P.O. Box 231985
Anchorage, AK 99523
June-October
P.O. Box 4068
Igiugig, AK 99613
888-826-7376
http://www.fishasl.com

Rapids Camp Lodge
200 W. 34th Ave.
PMB 1170
800-344-3628
Anchorage, AK 99503
www.deneki.com/rapidscamp/

No See Um Lodge
6218 Beechcraft Cir.
Wasilla AK 99654
907-232-0729
www.noseeumlodge.com/

RIVER-BASED FISHING CAMPS NEAR THE PARK
Anglers Alibi
1 River Front Rd.
King Salmon, AK 99613
561-222-9416
www.anglersalibi.com/
john@anglersalibi.com

Alagnak Lodge
800-877-9903
www.alagnaklodge.com/

Katmai Lodge
4125 Aircraft Dr.
Anchorage, AK 99502
Phone: 800-544-0551 Fax: 907-243-0649
www.katmai.com/

EPIC Angling and Adventure
2319 Westoak Dr.
Austin, TX 78704
512-656-2736
www.epicaaa.com/
info@epicanglingadventure.com

AIR TAXI SERVICES WITH FLY-IN FISHING PACKAGES
Katmai Air
4125 Aircraft Dr.
Anchorage, AK 99502
Phone: 800-544-0551 Fax: 907-243-0649
Email: info@katmailand.com
www.katmaiair.com/

Branch River Air
October-May
4540 Edinburgh Dr.
Anchorage, AK 99515
Phone: 907-248-3539
or
June - September
P.O. Box 545
King Salmon, AK 99613
Phone: 907-246-3437
www.branchriverair.com/

C-Air
C-Air/Sky Trekking Alaska
P.O. Box 871370
Wasilla, AK 99687
907-315-6098
skytrekkingalaska.com/day-trips-charters/c-air/
info@skytrekkingalaska.com

FLOAT TRIPS
Ouzel Expeditions
P.O. Box 935
Girdwood, AK 99587
800-825-8196
www.ouzel.com/alaska/alagnak-river
paul@ouzelexpeditions.com

BEST PLACES TO STAY NEAR THE PARK
King Salmon Lodge
165 West Housing Rd.
King Salmon, AK 99613
907-246-8643

Antlers Inn
P.O. Box 471
King Salmon, AK 99613
907-246-8525

King Ko Inn
Mile 15 Alaska Peninsula Hwy.
King Salmon, AK 99613
907-562-0648 (mid-October to mid-April)
907-246-3377 (mid-April to mid-October)
866-234-FISH (234-3474).
kingkoinn@gmail.com (preferred)

BEST CAMPGROUND IN THE PARK
Brooks Camp Campgrounds
P.O. Box 7
Katmai National Park and Preserve
King Salmon, AK 99613
Reservations: 877-444-6777
www.recreation.gov
· Adjacent to Naknek Lake
· Surrounded by electric bear-deterrent fences
· $12 per person per night
· June 1 through September 17

BEST PLACE TO EAT IN THE PARK
Brooks Lodge
P.O. Box 7
Katmai National Park and Preserve
King Salmon, AK 99613
Reservations: 877-444-6777
www.recreation.gov
Brooks Lodge is the only public place to eat that is not provided by a lodge or outfitter.

Growing up in Lakewood, Colorado, **Chaad McBride** initially began wandering the streams of the Rocky Mountain West. Having found his passion for fly fishing in his early twenties, he knew he had some catching up to do. As a result, he spent every available minute on the water; and if there were no water handy, Chaad would spend time spinning up "bugs" at a vise. Never willing to pass up a chance at wetting a line in an alpine lake, small creek or many of the numerous rivers, curiosity led him to wander further from the streams he called home. He moved to Alaska. Starting as a dishwasher and camp assistant, he honed his skills and knowledge of the rivers in southwest Alaska. Then, for the next decade, he became a guide—five of those years as head guide. Early in 2016, he was named manager of the prestigious Kulik Lodge.

BEST PLACES TO EAT NEAR THE PARK

King Salmon Lodge
165 West Housing Rd.
King Salmon, AK
907-246-8643

Eddie's Fireplace Inn
1 Main St.
King Salmon, AK 99613
907-246-3435

CLOSEST PLACE TO GET A DRINK IN THE PARK

Brooks Lodge
P.O. Box 7
Katmai National Park and Preserve
King Salmon, AK 99613
Reservations: 877-444-6777
www.recreation.gov
Brooks Lodge offers a bar with beer, wine and liquor; otherwise, fishing lodges are the best place to share your stories over a drink.

CLOSEST PLACE TO GET A DRINK OUTSIDE THE PARK

Antlers Inn
P.O. Box 471
King Salmon, AK 99613
907-246-8525

King Salmon Lodge
King Salmon, AK 99613
907-246-8643

Eddie's Fireplace Inn
1 Main St.
King Salmon, AK 99613
907-246-3435

MUST SEE
Bear watching at Brooks Falls and the "Valley of Ten Thousand Smokes"

NEAREST HOSPITAL/URGENT TREATMENT CENTER

Camai Community Health Center
P.O. Box 211
Naknek, AK 99633
907-246-6155

King Salmon Health Clinic
King Salmon, AK 99613
907-246-3322

Park Service
King Salmon
24-hour Emergency
907-439-7275

CELL PHONE SERVICE
Cell service is limited to say the least. Depending upon your carrier, service might be available in King Salmon.

FOR ALL ELSE, VISIT
http://www.nps.gov/katm/index.htm

Philanthropy

We at Stonefly Press feel that it's important to view ourselves as a small part of a greater system of balance. We give back to that which nourishes us because it feels natural and right.

Stonefly Press will be donating a portion of our annual profits to conservation groups active in environmental stewardship. We encourage all our readers to learn more about them here, and encourage you to go a step further and get involved.

American Rivers
(americanrivers.org)

Bonefish & Tarpon Trust
(bonefishtarpontrust.org)

California Trout
(caltrout.org)

Coastal Conservation Association
(joincca.org)

Friends of the White River
(friendsofwhiteriver.org)

Riverkeeper
(riverkeeper.org)

Trout Unlimited
(tu.org)

Western Rivers Conservancy
(westernrivers.org)

Fishing the Merced River in the western end of Yosemite Valley with Bridal Veil Falls in the background. Andrew Maurer

Index

Photo by Terry Gunn